CAMBRIDGE STUDIES
IN ENGLISH LEGAL HISTORY

Edited by
D. E. C. YALE
*Fellow of Christ's College and
Reader in English Legal History in the
University of Cambridge*

CAMBRIDGE STUDIES
IN ENGLISH LEGAL HISTORY

THE ANCIENT STATE AUTHORITIE, AND PROCEEDINGS OF THE COURT OF REQUESTS BY SIR JULIUS CAESAR

EDITED AND WITH AN INTRODUCTION BY

L. M. HILL

Associate Professor
University of California, Irvine

CAMBRIDGE UNIVERSITY PRESS

Published by the Syndics of the Cambridge University Press
Bentley House, 200 Euston Road, London NW1 2DB
American Branch: 32 East 57th Street, New York, N.Y. 10022

Library of Congress Catalogue Card Number: 73–93399

ISBN: 0 521 20386 4

First published 1975

Printed in Great Britain by
Alden & Mowbray Ltd
at the Alden Press, Oxford

To Professor Joel Hurstfield

CONTENTS

ACKNOWLEDGMENTS

It has been my good fortune to have had the opportunity to discuss the text and introduction of this book with scholars whose judgment I respect and whose capacities for patient criticism are nigh limitless. I hope that an appreciable element of their good advice has found its way on to the pages of this edition of *The Ancient State*. While I cannot thank all of those to whom I owe a debt of gratitude, there are several individuals to whom I must make particular reference. Professor Joel Hurstfield had the prudent foresight to suggest that I edit *The Ancient State* before going on to a full-scale study of Caesar's public career. As was so much of the advice that he gave me when I was his student in London, this advice was timely, thoughtful and well-taken. I wish to dedicate this work to him with great respect. Professor Elizabeth Foster, who is surely the dean of scholarly editors, assisted me in conceptualising the problem and in establishing a working scheme for undertaking the task. Professor T. G. Barnes was unstinting in his assistance as I was threading my way through the labyrinth of Caesar's legal notations. When finally I felt that I had a key to making sense of Caesar's arguments it was Professor Barnes, Professor G. R. Elton and Mr D. E. C. Yale who aided me in refining my ideas. In like manner I also thank Professor W. J. Jones for his exhaustive commentaries and criticisms. It was of the greatest use to me to have J. Beardesly, Esq. read and comment upon the introduction from the point of view of the practising lawyer. He modestly insisted that his advice was nothing; I can only demur. Notwithstanding all of this assistance, for which I am grateful, I am solely responsible for the text and its interpretation.

In preparing this edition I was greatly aided by Miss Mary Beemer who undertook the translations from Latin into English. The painstaking reading and correcting of Mr Iain White, the sub-editor, was surely beyond that which any author is entitled to expect.

The University of California at Irvine has been bountiful in its support of my work. With greater numbers of scholars calling upon diminishing resources, I have found it most gratifying to have received support from the School of Humanities as well as from the Humanities Institute of the University of California. Without the support of the University I would have been unable to accomplish this task. I also appreciate the careful assistance of Mr David Heifetz who assisted me in preparing the index.

The text of this edition is published with the kind permission of the Trustees of the British Museum. The supporting data was derived from the collections of the Public Record Office whose staff was unfailingly patient in fetching scores of little used manuscripts for which I often had need for little more than a few minutes' use. In particular I should like to thank Mr D. Lea of the P.R.O. staff whose knowledge of the vast collections exceeds that of most scholars of my acquaintance.

IRVINE, CALIFORNIA   L. M. H.
Michaelmas, 1973

INTRODUCTION

(i)

In 1591, in the case of *Locke* v. *Parsons*, a complaint was lodged in the Court of Requests concerning the lease of a house in London. The Court found for the plaintiff. The defendant in turn lodged an information in Common Pleas alleging that the Requests had lacked jurisdiction to hear and determine the case and asking that Common Pleas issue a prohibition forbidding any further action in the Requests. Privy Council, acting for the Court of Requests, ordered Common Pleas to stay execution of the prohibition pending the results of an enquiry by the Solicitor General and the Attorney General. The law officers, after consulting the parties and their counsel, found that the Court of Requests had exercised proper jurisdiction and the prohibition was subsequently rescinded. Although the prohibition did not succeed the attempt itself was important: it was the first time that the jurisdictional sufficiency of the Court of Requests had been challenged in this manner by one of the common-law benches. This frontal attack upon the court coincided with the installation of a new Master of Requests, Dr Julius Caesar, an experienced civilian who foresaw the difficulties which lay ahead because of the precedent which had been set. The case of *Locke* v. *Parsons* did indeed begin a long series a prohibitions against the court and the new Master became its principal apologist when, several years later, he published *The Ancient State, Authoritie, and Proceedings of the Court of Requests*.

In the matter of *Locke* v. *Parsons* the law officers had found that the Court of Requests had 'declared as was convenient and stoode with all equitie and conscience seeking to establish that which was affirmed at the Common lawe'.[1] But the first attempted prohibition led to many more; enough to cause an anonymous commentator to draw up what has been called a 'melancholy list' of prohibitions issuing from Common Pleas from 1591 until about 1600.[2] The

---

[1] H. L. Huntington Library, Ellesmere MS 2924.
[2] W. B. J. Allsebrook, 'The Court of Requests in the reign of Elizabeth' (unpublished M.A. thesis, University of London, 1936), 152. [Hereafter cited as Allsebrook.]

THE ANCIENT STATE

litigants who sought prohibitions displayed their contempt for the authority of the Court of Requests. The Council was not willing to countenance such contempt but at the same time the Council did not have the time to involve itself in the Court's affairs. But concern for public order forced the Council into a mediating and occasionally into a penalising role. If the parties could not be ordered back to the Court of Requests or if both the Court and Common Pleas could not concur in the matter of jurisdiction then the Council would order the party seeking the prohibition to desist on pain of contempt. This intervention was a nuisance for the Council whose impatience was apparent when they were diverted by these jurisdictional squabbles.

Conciliar concern for the Requests was to prove inadequate protection against the next major blow which befell the Court: the decision in the case of *Stepneth* v. *Flood* which was finally determined in 1598.[1] While the controversy surrounding *Locke* v. *Parsons* had impelled Caesar to begin his researches into the origins and jurisdictions of the Court, the *Stepneth* v. *Flood* case, even before it was decided, brought his closet scholarship into the light of day.

The case itself had begun in the Court of Requests several years before when Flood was sued by his wife for separate maintenance. She alleged that he had treated her miserably and she obtained her decree from the court but Flood refused to pay the maintenance that had been ordered. Finally a writ of attachment was issued out of Requests against Flood. Alban Stepneth, the sheriff of Carmarthenshire, received the attachment and proceeded to arrest Flood who made bond to appear before Requests and was subsequently released from Stepneth's custody. Once free of the sheriff, Flood did not appear before the Requests and Stepneth eventually put the obligation in suit in the Common Pleas. Anderson, C. J. and Glanville, J. heard the case and found for the defendant. They found that Flood had indeed entered into the bond with the sheriff and would normally have been liable for its satisfaction, but in this instance, the overriding consideration was that the Court of Requests was *coram non judice* and that the attachment issuing from it had no force at law. For this reason the court determined, the plaintiff had suffered false imprisonment at the hands of the defendant. By way of *obiter dictum* the court went

[1] P.R.O. CP 40/1610.

on to point out to the sheriff that in future he should not serve any process of the Court of Requests although he was obliged to act for the Court of Wards and the Duchy Court which were deemed courts of judicature because they enjoyed statutory sanction.[1] As we shall see, this case was of the greatest importance to Sir Edward Coke when he came to argue against the Court of Requests. At the same time the decision appears to have stimulated Caesar to publish *The Ancient State*.

As we mentioned above, when Caesar came to the Court of Requests in 1591, *Locke* v. *Parsons* was a current issue. In his epistle dedicatory to Burghley, dated January 1598, Caesar recalled the 'great contention on foote betwene the Judges of the Comon Pleas and the Masters of Requests then being, touching the jurisdiction of her Majesties court at Whitehall'.[2] The Masters averted 'bitter inconveniences' to the poor suitors in the court by their 'suffering, yet necessary patience and forbearance'. In his letter Caesar told Burghley that he held it an important and necessary task to collect in one volume the records of the Court at White Hall then dispersed in seventeen volumes and to make them known 'that in this Court (as in the Chancery, Kings Benche, Comon Pleas and Exchequer) Actes past might be presidentes of things to come'. This then was Caesar's stated purpose: to present the record of his Court in order that it might take its place beside the other central courts 'of record' in Westminster. In the beginning he had intended only to 'satisfie [his] owne conscience, and to understand what aperteined to the place where [he sat] as Judge'. However, the pressure of the prohibitions against his Court eventually led him to prepare a limited publication.[3]

It would be folly to inflate the importance of Caesar's little book but it is far too easy to make less of it than it deserves. Caesar's work cannot be compared with the work of Coke, Egerton or Lambarde but within the rubric of the *apologia* Caesar wrote an important tract. W. B. J. Allsebrook has styled *The Ancient State* a 'controversial and pseudo-antiquarian' work.[4] It was indeed controversial, but then the Court was engaged in a heated controversy and at the least Caesar did not intend preemptive sub-

[1] Croke, *Reports*, i, 646.
[2] Caesar used the spellings 'Whitehall' and 'White Hall' interchangeably to refer to the chamber in Westminster Palace known as the White Hall.
[3] *Infra*, fos. 26r–26v. [i.e. BM Lansd. MS 125].   [4] Allsebrook, i.

mission to the Common Pleas. As for the 'pseudo-antiquarian' character of the work, one wonders what the term was meant to convey. Parts of the work are frankly antiquarian and lose much because they appear to be *receuils inédits* but there is also a strong argument running throughout which cannot easily be set aside. Allsebrook summarised his objections to Caesar's work in a few sentences.

> Dr. Caesar's object was not to give a clear account of the history and procedure of the Court where he sat as judge, but to provide an army of weapons against its assailants among the ranks of the Common Lawyers. As a result, his book is little more than collections of precedents as to the jurisdiction and powers of the Court, many of which depended for their value and relevance upon the soundness of his theory that the Court is merely an aspect of the Privy Council. His avoidance of major issues and his continued reference to medieval precedents betray more anxiety to observe than to settle fairly a controversy which was threatening the very existence of the Court as a judicial body.[1]

Allsebrook's comments provide us with useful material on the basis of which to attempt an assessment of Caesar's argument. While we might agree that Caesar was writing no history of the Requests, what was he doing and how well?

The book consists of two parts which are dated 2 October 1596[2] and 13 February 1593[3] respectively. In the epistle dedicatory to Burghley, Caesar spoke of having undertaken two tasks; the collecting of what he regarded as the principal records of the court and the creation of a 'brieff table of [the] colleccions themselves':

> ... not to the end to make them common but of purpose to deliver some of them to suche, either Counsellors of Estate or counsellors at Lawe, or such students of antiquities and of histories, as from whose wisdomes and good observacions either in lawe, or storie or antiquities there might be drawne such amendment of things amisse or addition of things obscured or reducing into course, things wrested out of course as might breed hereafter a continewall peace betwene the Judges of the Common Lawe and her Majesties Counsell and

---

[1] Allsebrook, ii.   [2] *Infra*, fo. 9r.   [3] *Infra*, fo. 43r.

might without offence of the subjects, establishe her Highnese prerogative for ever.[1]

The two dates, 1593 and 1596, represent the two phases of this work. The collection was started shortly after Caesar became a Master of Requests when the great contention was afoot between the Common Pleas and the Requests. It would appear that this venture was finished by February 1593. The 'brieff table', completed in October 1596, which served as a topical guide to the contents of the collection contained the kernel of Caesar's argument. Without this topical guide the collection of cases would have been uselessly antiquarian. When one consults the topics in the table and then follows the references to the collection of Caesar's cases, his argument emerges from the mass of citations.

The burden of Caesar's argument was carried by his elaborate explication of the jurisdiction of the Court of Requests, and by his proofs of its long-standing association with the Council. Caesar's first proposition in the printed edition set the tone for the rest of the work: 'The Court of (Whitehall or) Requests now so called was and is parcell of the Kings most honourable Counsell.'[2] As with all of the propositions in the first part of *The Ancient State*, Caesar followed the statement with a bracketed list of references to the extracts from the order and decree books of the Court which were reproduced in the second part of the book. Prepared in haste, the printed topical table was not sufficiently explicit. But this failing was well compensated in the interleaved folios of Caesar's copy of *The Ancient State* because in these manuscript folios one can clearly detect the grain of Caesar's argument. 'That the king of England is the fountain of all English justice in all causes, from whence all judges . . . derive their . . . authority no man can deny . . . upon . . . pain' and further, that the king 'never did nor doth grant any jurisdiction to any court . . . but so as he still retaineth in himself and [in] his Council attendant upon his person a supereminent authority and jurisdiction over them all'. To support this last statement Caesar referred the reader to Britton. If these propositions were true, then it followed 'that the jurisdiction of the King and his Council extendeth to the hearing and determining of causes publick, mixt and private . . .'.[3] Upon this plenitude of power Caesar based his determined assertions of the peculiar authority of the Requests. He

---

[1] *Infra*, fos. 26r–26v.   [2] *Infra*, fo. 9r.   [3] *Infra*, fo. 8r.

declared that no Court, save the High Court of Parliament and the Privy Council, could reexamine a cause already decreed in Chancery nor discharge a prisoner committed from Chancery, 'but this court hath done it'.[1] Likewise, no Court, other than Parliament and the Council, 'hath accustomed to cause noblemen to attend on it *de die in diem* and not to depart without licence as namely Dukes, Earls, Barons and the like . . . but this court hath alwaies accustomed the same . . .'. This functional analysis contrasted sharply with Coke's analysis as we shall see below but there was a similarity between Caesar's rhetoric in *The Ancient State* and Coke's in the *Fourth Institute*.

Notwithstanding his rhetoric the matter of greatest importance to Caesar was the close connection which he observed between the Requests and the Council. The Privy Seal could only be moved by the hand of a Privy Councillor as was assured by the oath of the clerk of the Privy Seal, 'but every of the Judges of this court, his hand commaundeth the said Privy Seal'.[2] If the common lawyers wished to level their biggest guns at the Requests, Caesar was determined that they should be seen to be laying siege to the authority of Council at the same time, thus entering the forbidden realm of prerogative affairs; that realm which James I described in 1616 as 'the absolute Prerogative of the Crowne, that is no Subject for the tongue of a lawyer, nor is lawful to be disputed'.[3] Caesar's list began with broad principles but it terminated in a wandering file of specific examples of the sundry activities of the Court of Requests. Yet the complete list is valuable because it provides us with an overall view of the scope of the Court's jurisdiction. This pragmatic treatment of the Court and its authority is in marked contrast with Coke's more theoretical analysis.

Sir Edward Coke was the common lawyers' most outstanding spokesman in the attack made on the conciliar or prerogative, courts, most particularly the Court of Requests. This attack was as much a function of the common lawyers' efforts to define their own jurisdictions as it was a function of internecine competitiveness. He readily admitted that the Masters of Requests were officers of ancient origin enjoying places close to the King, but they were not judges; they were the King's agents charged with the

---

[1] *Infra*, fo. 11r.   [2] *Infra*, fo. 11v.
[3] C. H. McIlwain, *The political works of James I* (1918), 333.

responsibility for referring petitions of redress from both subjects and strangers to the courts best suited to adjudicate the questions at hand and to provide satisfaction. Simply because the joint meeting of these Masters was commonly referred to as a court did not convey judicial authority any more than in the case of the Court of Audience and Faculties. It was Coke's opinion that during the reign of Henry VIII the Masters had managed to usurp power by securing commissions authorising them to hear and determine causes in equity. But 'those commissions being not warranted by Law (for no Court of Equity can be raised by Commission) soon vanished; for that it had neither Act of Parliament nor prescription time out of mind of man to establish it'.[1] Evidence of this seemingly arbitrary expansion of power is not quite as clear as Coke indicated. While it is true that in 1529 the term 'Court of Requests' was first used in the Order Books, during the 1530s the Court was still identified with the Council as it had been throughout Henry VIII's reign. There were quiet changes taking place over a period of time but there does not appear to have been the dramatic change that Coke intimated in his account of the period.

Coke asserted, quite correctly, that neither the Year Books, Saint German, Fortescue nor other principal legal authorities mentioned the Court of Requests; men had, nonetheless, been deceived by the Court's apparent respectability and it was against this appearance that he was struggling. He wrote that,

> as Gold or Silver may as current money pass even with the proper Artificer, though it hath too much Allay, until he hath tried it with the Touchstone, even so this nominative Court may pass with the Learned as justifiable in respect of the outside by vulgar allowance until he advisedly looketh into the roots of it, and try it by the rule of Law, as (to say the truth) I my self did: but *errores ad sua principia referre, est refellere*, to bring errors to their first is to see their last.

The *Stepneth* v. *Flood* decision was Coke's touchstone as well as his proof positive that the Court of Requests had no standing in law. But he could not ignore the troublesome fact that, properly or improperly, the Court flourished with overt royal sanction. He was thus forced to acknowledge the court *de facto* which he believed to

---

[1] Coke, *Fourth Institute*, 97.

have no rightful existence *de jure*. In the last paragraph of his discussion of the Requests, Coke said that,

> although the Law be such as we have set down, yet in respect
> of the continuance that it [Requests] hath had by permission,
> and of the number of decrees therein had, it were worthy of
> the wisdom of a Parliament, both for the establishment of
> things for the time past, and for some certain provision with
> reasonable limitations (if so it shall be thought convenient to
> that High Court) for the time to come: *et sic liberavi animam
> meam*.[1]

Coke's distinctly theoretical and constitutional approach to the problem met its antithesis in Caesar's commitment to both a *de facto* and a *de jure* defence of his Court. The *de facto* defence was self-evident, being spread out across virtually every page of *The Ancient State*. The *de jure* defence turned upon the meaning of 'right'. Was it 'right' as understood by the common lawyers with their insular myopia or was it the 'right' of the King to administer the law and provide for justice in any way that he saw fit? To deal with this question we must consider the intellectual and jurisprudential fabric of Caesar's argument. As an antiquarian Caesar attempted to give credence and acceptability to his Court in the best way that he knew: citing vast numbers of ancient references to the Court, either as an independent body or as an adjunct of the Privy Council. But there was, as we shall see, more to this work than simple antiquarianism.

Returning to *The Ancient State* we might recall that Caesar's case for his Court was quite straightforward. He had alleged that the Court of Requests was and always had been a part of the King's Council, that the judges were of the Council and that their places of meeting had once been determined by the itinerary of the King on progress. In addition, he alleged, his Court was a court of record, its procedure was the summary procedure of the civil law and its jurisdiction extended to officers of the King's Household, to paupers and to causes 'specially recommended from the King, to the examination of his Counsell: or causes concerning Universities, Colledges, Schooles, Hospitales and the like'.[2] These

---

[1] *Ibid.*, 98.

[2] *Infra*, fo. 12r. 'Summary' procedure was Caesar's reference to the occasional practice of the Requests by which oral responses were received and quick decisions reached.

last were of particular interest because, being corporations, they were the King's creatures and enjoyed their corporate life at his pleasure.

The type of cause over which the Requests exercised its jurisdiction was spelled out in detail in *The Ancient State*, but the precarious *modus vivendi* which was reached with the Common Pleas after the spate of prohibitions was evident in the following holographic note added to one of the printed pages.

> But it is to bee understood that causes ecclesiasticall, maritime, ultramarine, and causes triable by the common lawe are not determinable in this Court, unles ther bee some matter of equitie in them not remediable in theire proper Courts, videt., to remedie fraudes, breach of trust, extremity of common lawe or undue practices.[1]

There then followed folios both of printed and manuscript references to the multitude of causes over which the Court had assumed jurisdiction, presumably because of 'some matter of equitie in them' not susceptible to the common law.

At some point after he had published his little volume Caesar added an almost equal number of folios containing holographic and other manuscript evidence to support his contentions. Among these are the medieval precedents to which Allsebrook made reference when he assessed the value of Caesar's work. These precedents served but one purpose: to establish the nigh timeless authority of the Council and to prove 'that the Court of Whitehall or Requests is a member and parcell of the Kings most honorable Counsell attendant on his person'.[2] As tendentious as this last allegation may have been, it was a matter of faith for Caesar who required the dignity of this connection to enhance the dignity of his own Court.

Caesar was a civilian by training as well as by disposition but he was really a legal hybrid. As we shall observe below, he rose to great dignity within the Inns of Court although he never practised as a common lawyer nor was he trained to be one. While not a common lawyer he was of their society, he knew how they thought, and he was prepared to use the arguments of the common law to defeat them. Thus, Caesar was no ordinary LL.D. for he regarded the civil law in which he was trained as an integral part of the

[1] *Infra*, fo. 12v. [2] *Infra*, fo. 10v.

English Law, indeed, of the 'common law', if one used that term to describe all laws common to all Englishmen and not as a generic definition of judge-made law augmented by statute. Here we find Caesar's unique place: he was a civilian through-and-through who thought and acted with great facility as a common lawyer. He demonstrated this legal ambidexterity in the methodology that he employed in the pages of *The Ancient State*. Caesar used the techniques of his adversaries as he sought from among the precedents of the Court of Requests and of the Council as well as from among the statutes and the commentaries upon the English law, the evidence that he required to prove the antiquity of his Court. The pursuit of the immemorial which marked the *Fourth Institute* was not absent from Caesar's work. Medieval precedents were crucial to Caesar's allegation that the Court of Requests rested upon as firm a customary foundation as that of the Common Pleas.

We have seen that Coke alleged in the *Fourth Institute* that the King could establish no Court of Equity by commission and that such a Court could be justified only by an Act of Parliament or by proof of its existence time out of mind of man. Caesar agreed and proceeded to prove that his Court, as an extension of the Council, had indeed existed time out of mind of man. Agreeing with Coke's assertion Caesar made his case in Coke's own terms. The methodology that he used was the careful collection of precedents, a method dear to his common-law colleagues. Beginning with ordinances and statutes, adding the commentaries of Bracton, Britton and Fortescue, and finally turning to the records of Council and to the Year Books, Caesar built a case which was contained entirely within the framework of the English law. While there had not been a Court of Requests immemorially there had been a King's Council and Caesar rested his case on the identity of the one with the other. How little his technique, both in respect of the citation of precedent and the use of analogy, differed from the common lawyers'!

But what of the other material contained in Lansdowne MS 125, material which, in some cases does not appear to bear directly upon the Court of Requests at all. Some of the manuscript additions are lists of judges and dignitaries who had sat in the Court or who had been parties to actions there. These lists were gathered out of the records of the Court and simply emphasised Caesar's contention that the Court had long been recognised both by the Crown and by the legal community. Then there are letters from justices of the Common Pleas and other prominent officials asking the Requests to take over a case from the common law because of some need for equity which they could not provide.

In Caesar's addenda there was a letter from Lord Keeper Puckering, dated 2 February 1593, asking for Caesar's help in sorting out a problem which arose when the defendant in a particularly long litigation had died before he could satisfy the execution of the common-law sentence against him. If the plaintiff wished to enforce the execution he would have to institute an entirely new action against the defendant's estate and such an action promised to be as protracted as the first had been. Recognising the expedient means available in the Requests, Puckering wished to utilise its good offices.[1] In another case, Anderson, C. J. and Periam, J. wrote to the Masters of Requests in 1592 asking them to make final order in disposing of an action already determined in Common Pleas. The matter was *res judicata* but enforcement was impossible. The judges having explained their problem, concluded the letter:

> Thus leaving the said cause to bee further ordered by your good discretions in her Majesties said Court of Requests, which wee in the said Court of the Common Pleas, being a Court of Common Lawe tied to the strict and precise course thereof, could not so well helpe as wee wished.[2]

Yet again in 1599, the Common Pleas sent a note to Caesar and his colleagues which informed them that leave had been given to a defendant to go into the Requests for an injunction. The licence had been granted because the Common Pleas believed that proper jurisdiction lay with the Requests since the cause concerned intestacy and involved a crown servant. Walmsley, J., who wrote the note appealing to the Requests, justified his action by explaining the faults in the Common Pleas' jurisdiction in that particular case.[3] Thus we have several instances of the Common Pleas finding that, even after the advent of the prohibitions, it was necessary, and indeed expedient, to turn to the Requests for such relief as the common law could not provide.

Perhaps the most interesting ancillary documents in the volume are those various orders which were given from time to time to

---

[1] *Infra*, fo. 153r.   [2] *Infra*, fos. 153r–153v.   [3] *Infra*, fo. 155r.

organise better the business of the Court. But there are also orders, issued much later in Caesar's life, which concern attendance in the King's Chapel and the protocol for meetings of the Council, both of which date from the seventeenth century. Why were these orders, which seem to be totally irrelevant, interleaved with Caesar's personal copy of *The Ancient State*? If we recall Caesar's contention that the Court and the Council were nigh indistinguishable, we can perhaps better understand these documents.

The first document, 'for civility in sittinges ether in Cappell or elsewhere in court', was dated 1 January 1623.[1] Caesar's apparent motive for including this otherwise incongruous statement of precedence seems pathetic but is fully in keeping with his fundamental belief in the intimate relationship of the Requests to the Council and of the dignity of members of the Council. The order required decorous conduct and the observance of a rigid protocol at Court. It restricted approach to the royal person to those of the rank of baron or above with the exception of members of Privy Council. As far-fetched as this connexion was, it provided Caesar with a useful bit of evidence to indicate that the Council enjoyed peculiar supremacy and so also, by association, did the Court of Requests. The other obscure document in Caesar's collection also bears upon his notions of the importance of the Council. This document contains orders made 7 November 1630.[2] They required that members of the Council attend its meetings regularly and they spoke of members making a more impressive public appearance by passing through public chambers to meetings rather than through back-passages. It is interesting that these Orders for the Council were made shortly before the issuance of the Book of Orders. The King in Council was about to re-emerge as the effective administrative head of the kingdom without the impediment of Parliament. Caesar, by then in his seventies, quite possibly felt that this development was the fulfilment of his desire to see the King in Council firmly in control. Both of these documents then, although they gave the appearance of irrelevance, were quite in keeping with Caesar's theories, idiosyncratic though they may have been.

In conclusion we might assess the importance of BM Lansd. MS 125. As a document complementary to the records of the Court

[1] *Infra*, fos. 33r–35r.   [2] *Infra*, fos. 40v–42v, 167v–168r.

of Requests, Caesar's collection has greater value for us now than it had for his contemporaries when it was written. Caesar used records which lay in the Tower and in the custody of the Court. He intended these records to be used in conjunction with his work, why else did he so carefully insert the folio reference to the original documents after each entry. Furthermore, these records had never been foliated prior to Caesar's use of them. The folio numbers are in his hand written in the brownish ink with which he did so much of his work. In the intervening centuries since Caesar wrote *The Ancient State* much of the original material has been lost or severely damaged. Thus Caesar's book constitutes the only extant substitute for a series of gaps in the Order and Decree Books. *The Ancient State* is also a singular instance of the attempt of an uncommon civilian, who was well acquainted with the techniques and methods of the Common Lawyers, to use his opponents' own best weapons in defence of his own interests.

As one considers Caesar's book, with its manuscript addenda, one is struck by the sense that the author had an idea which he only partially realised. He felt threatened by his rivals in other courts and he attempted to answer their allegations but the answers were incomplete. Perhaps lack of skill or lack of time accounted for Caesar's publication of a skeleton that wanted further study to add flesh. The great number of interleaved folios suggests that the initial publication was a premature reaction to *Stepneth* v. *Flood*. Had there been more time (or less urgency) perhaps all of the material would have been published. The skeletal treatment of the Court of Requests, however, was not so much a matter of lacking time or talent but rather a matter of the brief that Caesar gave himself. He wanted to associate his Court with the Council and the King. In this respect he succeeded admirably. There is also in the work a systematic statement of the Court's jurisdiction and dignity, as well as a statement of medieval origins and precedents to support his contentions. But there is no analysis of the cases themselves; indeed, given the frame of reference that Caesar established for himself, there was no place for such an analysis. For the modern scholar a detailed study of the Court of Requests, its jurisdiction, its procedure and its decisions will be most welcome. One hopes that when such a study is undertaken, *The Ancient State* will provide useful evidence both as to the institution itself and its most important member, Dr Julius Caesar.

(ii)

Dr Julius Caesar was born in London in 1558, six months before Queen Mary's death.[1] His father, Cesare Adelmare, was a court physician who had emigrated to England from his native Padua in 1550 and subsequently married Margery Periant whose father was an official in Dublin. During Mary's reign Adelmare prospered and by the time his first son, Julius, was born, he was well enough connected at court to provide a notable set of god-parents for the boy including a *locum tenens* for the Queen. Adelmare died in 1568 and his wife was soon remarried to an adventurous merchant, Michael Locke. The family into which Julius and his brother and sisters moved as a result of this marriage gravitated towards the redoubtable puritan lady, Anne Locke. It was perhaps Anne Locke's circle that encouraged Caesar to go up to Oxford to join the puritan enclave in Magdalen Hall. He took his B.A. in 1575, proceeded to his M.A. in 1578 and upon coming down went to Paris to continue his legal studies. While in Paris he studied the Civil and Canon Law as well as foreign languages, returning to London for a year in 1580.

During this year Caesar, who already belonged to Clement's Inn, was admitted to Inner Temple. This proved a useful connexion for him although there is no reason to believe that he studied the common law. Caesar was a most unusual civilian in the light of his intimate association with Inner Temple. Simply being a member of the Inn would not have been so remarkable but he rose to preside over the house in the 1590s. From January 1592 through November 1593 he and Coke, a fellow bencher, presided over most of the parliaments of the Inn and from 23 November 1595 until 30 January 1597 Caesar presided over every parliament. On 11 November 1593 his fellow benchers elected him Treasurer of the Inn, in which capacity he served until 3 November 1595 when Coke succeeded him. In the year following his Treasurership Caesar gave £300 towards the construction of a new block of chambers for which the society thanked him profusely and styled the block, Caesar's Chambers. All of this activity in the Inn was

---

[1] For a detailed study of Caesar's origins see my thesis 'The public career of Sir Julius Caesar: 1584–1614' (unpublished Ph.D. thesis, University of London, 1968).

exactly coterminous with Caesar's work on *The Ancient State*
and his running skirmish with the great common lawyers over
the jurisdiction of his Court; but we have gotten ahead of the
story.

When Caesar returned to Paris after his year in London he
began to receive the degrees in law for which he had been studying.
In April 1581 he received his LL.B., his licentiate in both laws,
and his LL.D. On 10 May of the same year the young Dr Caesar
was accorded the unusual honour of being admitted as an advocate
in the *parlement de Paris*. This was a gesture usually accorded to
great foreign jurists and political figures when they visited Paris
and Caesar was neither of these. In a letter that he wrote to his
patron, Lord Burghley, Caesar told of how the King of France had
offered him a place in Paris. Upon declining the offer in favour of
returning to England, Caesar allegedly received a second offer from
the French King which was an offer of a pension for the young
civilian.[1] While this claim may have been hyperbolic, there seems
little doubt that Caesar was very well received during his stay in
Paris.

Back in England in late 1581 Caesar was assisted by Dr David
Lewes, the Judge of the High Court of Admiralty and a very senior
civilian, as well as by Sir Francis Walsingham. He was admitted to
practice in the court of Arches, a necessary antecedent for admission to Doctors' Commons, and was made a commissioner for
piracy causes. In addition, Lewes commissioned Caesar his commissary in the Hospital of St Katharine next to the Tower where
the old judge was the Master. Lewes also sponsored Caesar when
he supplicated for the D.C.L. from Oxford shortly before the
judge's death. During these early years Caesar also managed to
acquire a mastership in Chancery and a place as commissary to the
Bishop of London with responsibility for parts of Essex, Hertfordshire and Middlesex.

Shortly before his death in 1584 Lewes made arrangements with
the Lord Admiral, Lincoln, for Caesar to be favoured when the
time came to select a new judge for the Admiralty Court. Caesar
had often sat as a deputy for Lewes and he had been virtually a
full-time judge during the last months of Lewes' life. The problem
inherent in Lewes' arrangements was that the office was held in

---

[1] British Museum, Lansdowne MS 157, fo. 212v (23 January 1585). [This series
is hereafter cited as BM Lansd. MS.]

reversion by John Herbert, a diplomat on the Queen's service in Poland when Lewes died. Before Herbert could return to England to claim his place or before Caesar could mount an attack upon the reversion and attempt thereby to secure a place for himself, Lord Admiral Lincoln died and Charles, Lord Howard of Effingham became the new Lord Admiral. Thus it was not until the early part of 1586 that Caesar and Howard, with assistance from Burghley, could arrange for an elaborate swap that satisfied Herbert. In return for giving up his reversion, Herbert became a Master of Requests, which Burghley procured for him at Caesar's behest, and received a large sum of money from Caesar. Caesar alleged that this sum had cost him £1,300 in interest by 1592 but it had secured the office even though he was unable to secure a life patent to the judgeship until 1589.

During the time that Caesar was working with some notable skill and diplomacy as judge of the High Court of Admiralty, he was also spending a great deal of time and energy trying to secure a mastership of Requests for himself. He reckoned that he was spending more money than he was earning each year simply to perform the duties expected of the judge of the Admiralty but he knew very well that Elizabeth would not compensate him for his services or for any extraordinary expenses. The only hope of compensation lay in receiving some additional office which would provide increased revenue and influence. A mastership of Requests would have had the incalculable advantage of placing Caesar in the Queen's Household close to the monarch's person, thus there was much to be gained if his suit were successful. After much delay, Caesar was finally able to secure the mastership by linking his petition for a new job to his present work in the Admiralty Court in a way that would directly benefit the Queen.

From the moment that Caesar began to administer the affairs of the Admiralty Court on his own in 1585, he had been keen on establishing a circuit during the long summer vacation. Dr Lewes had proposed a similar idea several years before and Caesar believed that it had merit as it would hopefully make some order out of the chaos which prevailed in the provinces because of the privateering war with Spain. Caesar calculated that such a circuit would dramatically demonstrate the power of the High Court of Admiralty in remote regions along the coast while the judge's presence there might help to stem the flow of lost revenue due to

the number of cases which managed to escape the Court's jurisdiction.[1]

At first Caesar was not able to move his patron, Lord Burghley,
with his ideas about a circuit and neither Walsingham nor Howard
was much interested in the project. Thus Caesar let the matter lie
fallow while he concentrated his efforts upon gaining security of
tenure in the Admiralty Court and upon the quest for a mastership. By 1589 he had secured a life patent in the Admiralty and
now he began once more to agitate for the circuit, however, this
time he linked his suit for the circuit to his older plea for a mastership of Requests. Caesar suggested to the Queen that if she would
grant him the mastership, which would cost her nothing, he would
then have sufficient funds with which to carry out the admiralty
circuit. If the circuit were successful, Caesar argued, he would
increase the Queen's revenue and strengthen central authority
along the troubled coast.

The suit for the mastership had moved in fits and starts for
several years. From no success at all in his first attempts Caesar
had by 1588 received word that the Queen intended to make him
a Master. But the Queen had not given Caesar a specific date for
fulfilling her promise. The Queen's initial agreement was due
largely to Walsingham's pleadings in Caesar's behalf, but Walsingham had to notify Caesar that the promise would remain vacant
until the Queen was ready to act upon it although he agreed to
have a word with the monarch at the most advantageous moment.

Caesar was anxious to press forward with his suit and thus he
turned to Burghley for assistance because he felt that the time for
the appointment seemed right; Herbert was ailing and another
Master, Ralph Rookesby, was lame. Surely the Queen was prepared to place a vigorous younger man among the Masters of
Requests? Caesar went on to explain to Burghley that he was keen
on the appointment not only for himself and his own fortunes but
also for the advantages that it would provide him in executing his
duties in the High Court of Admiralty. There had been difficult
relations among the many Courts in Westminster and Caesar
believed that such a mark of royal esteem as a Master's place would
enhance his own standing as judge of the Admiralty and thus the

---

[1] For the results of this circuit see my article 'The admiralty circuit of 1591:
some comments on the relations between central government and local
interests', *The Historical Journal*, XIV, 1 (1971), 3–14.

authority of his Court. Furthermore, if he were within the Household and enjoyed access to the Queen's presence, he could more quickly settle the petitions of foreign merchants who were clogging his Court during the privateering war. These merchants, impatient with the progress of their various actions in the Admiralty Court, would frequently petition the Queen or the Privy Council for relief. If Caesar were a Master of Requests he would be the officer who received these petitions and he would be able to give expert advice based upon his experience in the Admiralty Court.

One might well ask why a man with Caesar's qualifications had so difficult a time getting satisfaction in his suit. His hard work in the Admiralty Court was both well known to and appreciated by the Queen and her Council but Elizabeth was notoriously mean and her reluctance to pay for the services of her officers was legend. Rather than pay cash, Elizabeth would always seek some other form of remuneration which would cost her Exchequer nothing. If Caesar had only to bear the burdens of the Admiralty Court with its attendant fees, he would have had little reason to complain. However, in addition to his ordinary responsibilities, the judge was constantly called upon to deal with foreign merchants and ambassadors who were seeking justice from the Crown because of the privateering war. Caesar was constantly called upon to intercede, to negotiate or to placate, often at his own expense, in order to make the impossible diplomatic tight-rope walking of the war with Spain into a possibility. All that Caesar had received from the Queen was a fairly routine grant which allowed him to receive fees in the Admiralty Court.[1]

Among the other factors which militated against Caesar's rise were his relative youth and the fact that he had a foreign father. Although he rarely used his patronym, Adelmare, and his adopted surname seemed quite unexceptional to his colleagues there were those who were prejudiced against him. In addition there was a matter which is not easily subjected to proof; an allegation that he was corrupt. Indeed he accepted gifts and favours on a scale which was within the acceptable limits of the day. Dr K. R. Andrews has neatly summarised Caesar's position and, for that matter, that of scores of officials like him.

[1] See E. Nys, 'Les manuscrits de Sir Julius Caesar', *Revue de droit international et de legislation comparée*, t. xix (1887), 461–71.

The patronage of the great was something no man in Caesar's position could reject or scorn without grave danger to himself, and it required stronger character than his to rise above the prevailing sychophancy of the official world. He cultivated his noble friends, preserved their correspondence with loving care and by judicious use of influential contacts manoeuvered himself into a well earned niche in the Jacobean establishment.[1]

But it is more than likely that the reasons for Caesar's difficulties in gaining preferment had little to do with his ancestry, his youth or his public morality. These allegations were the symptoms of an aversion to Caesar's civilian training. A few years later we find Cecil's aunt, the Dowager Lady Russell, writing to her nephew in order to frustrate Caesar's attempt to rise within the ranks of the masters. She was supporting a man trained in the common law when she wrote, 'Let not Dr Caesar, a civilian, deprive him [the common lawyer] of the fee due to a temporal lawyer and not to a civilian' especially since she thought that Caesar was too wealthy anyway.[2]

Caesar was fortunate in that he had highly placed supporters. Although Walsingham died in 1590 before his protegé was sworn, the unlikely combination of Burghley and Essex continued to assist Caesar. On 10 January 1591 he was summoned to Richmond and there, before the Privy Council, was sworn a Master of Requests. The records of the Council show that following the administration of the oath the new Master was 'greatly commended for his diligence, wisdome and great discrecion in executing the office of the Judge of the Admiralty'.[3] Caesar would serve both in the Admiralty and in the Requests until he was named Chancellor of the Exchequer in 1606.

(iii)

Upon first encounter the cases which Caesar noted in *The Ancient State* seem a chaotic jumble but they are none the less the evidence upon which he based his several assertions. Principally he was

K. R. Andrews, *Elizabethan privateering* (1964), 26.

[2] *Historical Manuscript Commission Reports*, Hatfield MSS, vi, 215 (15 June 1596).

[3] *Acts of Privy Council, 1590–91*, 207.

showing the working relationship of his Court to others in the
judicial establishment and he was demonstrating the various forms
of relief available in the Requests which were not available in the
common-law courts. In addition Caesar demonstrated the particular devices which allowed the Requests to accomplish its tasks.
Our examination of these points will help us to understand better
Caesar's argument and also to see the Court of Requests at work.
From the start it is important to remember that Chancery could
do eveɪything that the Requests could do and thus Caesar could
make no claim to singularity except regarding the relationship of
the Court of Requests to the Council. Also, one should remember
that Caesar at no time turned his argument into a civilian attack
upon the common law for although he was very much a civilian,
he believed that the law of England was informed by civilian principles and, thus, there was no conflict. No 'reception' question
beclouded Caesar's argument.

In the pages which follow there are many cases cited by Caesar
in *The Ancient State* which are relevant to his argument. The cases
are, however, deceptive without a word of warning. While we
know that the Court of Requests, along with the other Courts and
agencies of sixteenth-century England, was undergoing great
change, we are dealing here with an observer of the Court who
viewed its history in a static fashion. For Caesar a precedent drawn
from the reign of Henry VII was as relevant as one drawn from the
reign of Elizabeth. We might even venture to suggest that he
found the earlier precedents more relevant when we consider the
relative scarcity of Elizabethan citations in his book. There is
therefore no sense of development of the Court over time. But this
was a failing which Caesar shared with his common-law brothers.
Had this study been expanded to include more references from the
years in which Caesar was writing it would have presented a better
picture of the Elizabethan Requests but it would have, at the same
time, thrown Caesar's argument out of the particular context in
which he chose to place it. Should we not be mindful of the way in
which Caesar weighted his own evidence with earlier rather than
more contemporary citations we should run the risk of inviting a
serious distortion of the Elizabethan Requests and its history.

The Court of Requests was intended to be a forum for the rapid
and inexpensive resolution of poor men's causes as Caesar noted in
describing the style which was first used in 20 Henry VIII: the

Court of poor men's causes in the Court of Requests.[1] But the Court tried when it could to avoid abuses of its availability to the poor. There were many cases of the remission of causes to other Courts because the parties were 'able to proceed' at law,[2] or because the parties were not poor.[3] We cannot assume that the remainder of the parties qualified as paupers as they clearly did not. There was one reference, however, to a cause in the Requests by reason of poverty but also 'for want of Justice in the law courts'.[4]

The Court's other major jurisdiction was over the Household. The Court was open to members of the Household so that they could be both a party to civil litigation and available to serve the Crown. Thus, a cause which was admittedly within the jurisdiction of the Court of the Council of the Marches was taken up by the Court of Requests because the plaintiff was an officer of Her Majesty's pantry.[5] Although Caesar did not spell out the jurisdiction over the Household it becomes apparent from the list of dignitaries at Court whose actions were heard in the Requests that the Court was their tribunal.

The Court of Requests as an equity bench could mitigate the rigours of the common law but this did not mean that the Requests was intended to be a means to avoid the jurisdiction of the common lawyers. In fact, mitigation more often than not provided a complementary equitable remedy which the common law in the sixteenth century could not provide. In one case, allegations of failure to perform an indenture having been tested in the Requests, the matter was returned to the law for its determination of the possessory questions involved.[6] In another case cross-actions for debt had been introduced at common law. The Requests stepped in to assist the law, as Caesar noted in a margin gloss. The defendant's action was stayed until he made bond to answer the plaintiff's action at law and also until the defendant answered the plaintiff's bill in the Requests.[7] But this same power to force cooperation with the common law could be used to suspend any further action at law until either the Requests or another court was satisfied. An action in the King's Bench was suspended until the plaintiff in that court (who was the defendant in the Requests) had

[1] *Infra*, 28 June, 30 H. 8.
[2] *Infra*, 11 December, 11 H. 7.
[3] *Infra*, 26 May, 6 E. 6.
[4] *Infra*, 5 May, 3&4 P. & M.
[5] *Infra*, 9 November, 3&4 P. & M.
[6] *Infra*, 16 February, 3 H. 8.
[7] *Infra*, 15 May, 21 Eliz. 1.

answered a complaint in the Requests.[1] The Court ordered another common-law action to be stayed until the defendant in that action had proved his title in the Court of the Lord President of the Council of the North.[2]

The rigours of the law were not limited to the common law; the Requests was equally concerned with local courts such as manorial courts which were of particular interest in the sixteenth century.[3] The lord of the manor both in law and according to custom was the chancellor of his manor in matters pertaining to the equity of the customary law of the individual manor.[4] The customary tenant had therefore to appeal in the first instance to the same lord from whose decision he sought relief. If the appeal failed the customary tenant could proceed by petition in Chancery or in the Court of Requests but this was not a matter of right but of royal favour. The petition sought a subpoena against the lord requiring him to appear with the manorial rolls or other appropriate evidence. Fitzherbert reported a Chancery decree in the midfifteenth century which went so far as to suggest that even an ousted tenant at will had recourse to subpoena against his lord. But this was not a singular instance of such intervention. Littleton and Coke each report subpoenas of a like nature, the former in 1467 and the latter in 1390. None the less these were exceptional cases and one cannot ascribe typicality to this use of the subpoena.

Of course, some lords contemptuously tried to ignore interference in their manors by the central courts, and they were successful as long as their tenants did not press the matter further.

Because the common law had come to recognise that a copyholder by custom enjoyed an estate, it was necessary for a customary tenant who wished to proceed in Chancery or in the Requests to allege his requirement for equitable relief in terms which went beyond simple customary tenancy. One of the most frequently encountered of these requirements concerned allegations of the hostility or partiality of the lord of the manor. The lord

---

[1] *Infra*, 13 October, 10 Eliz. 1.   [2] *Infra*, 17 October, 2&3 P. & M.

[3] Another customary institution which was breaking down in the sixteenth century was the marketing system. Under several categories one can adduce cases which go directly to troubles in the market place occasioned by the rapid growth of private marketing. See A. Everitt, 'The marketing of agricultural produce' in *The Agrarian History of England and Wales*, IV (1967), 563.

[4] The following material regarding the manor is derived largely from E. Kerridge, *Agrarian problems in the sixteenth century and after* (1969), 69 *passim*.

or his agent could and often would apply pressure to manorial juries, while a lord who was also a justice of the peace might use his magisterial authority to intimidate litigants and witnesses. This situation alone necessitated resort to the Requests and to similar courts. The fact that some causes were dismissed when allegations of partiality on the part of the lord (or the lady) of the manor or on the part of the steward or bailiff were not substantiated in no way detracts from the importance of this aspect of jurisdiction.[1] It was important nevertheless that a successful allegation of partiality could traverse manorial jurisdiction. Caesar included one case which gives us the burden of the allegation of partiality although it did not concern a manor. The entry merits repeating as it reflects the way in which the court came to see its own role.

> A cause heard and decreed in Court of Requests for that the defendants were men of great wealth and greatly alied and friended in the saide Countie and greatly borne by the Jurors and ring-leaders of the same shire, etc.[2]

Notwithstanding its intervention in the business of other courts (including the arrest of a defendant in the Requests for laying a Bill of Middlesex against the plaintiff),[3] the Court during most of the sixteenth century cooperated with other jurisdictions. Remissions of causes had been made to Common Pleas,[4] to Chancery,[5] to the Court of the Council in the Marches of Wales,[6] to the Court of General Surveyors,[7] to the Council Learned,[8] and to the 'common law' in general.[9] In this atmosphere of cooperation which continued past the advent of the prohibitions from the Common Pleas, Caesar was both annoyed and offended to find that the courts with which the Requests was cooperating were turning against it.

The equitable remedies which were used in the Court of Requests were distinguished by the use of the subpoena, the injunction and the ordering of specific relief. The injunction was intended to require a party not to do that which the Court forbade (or not to fail to do that which the court ordered) while specific

---

[1] *Infra*, 1 July, 1&2 P. & M., 10 February, 4&5 P. & M.
[2] *Infra*, 9 May, 4&5 P. & M. [3] *Infra*, 23 January, 4 Eliz. 1.
[4] *Infra*, 15 March, 11 H. 7. [5] *Infra*, 6 February, 14 H. 7.
[6] *Infra*, 28 April, 7 H. 8. [7] *Infra*, 14 October, 34 H. 8.
[8] *Infra*, 3 November, 21 H. 7.
[9] *Infra*, 4 July, 24 H. 8; 6 June, 38 H. 8; 7 July, 6 E. 6.

relief was intended to force compliance with a positive (and pre-existing) undertaking. This distinction can best be illustrated in the context of the procedure used in the Court of Requests. The plaintiff filed a bill of complaint in the Court which caused a writ of Privy Seal to issue to the defendant requiring his appearance and his answer under pain of a penalty of £100. The parties could appear in the Requests accompanied by counsel and there were many causes in which the Court allowed the defendant to appear by attorney with his answer, a practice which grew more common as the Court became more popular and thus more crowded.

Both the plaintiff and the defendant had to agree to remain in the Court until their litigation was settled and to pay whatever costs were awarded. This agreement was enforced also by a writ of subpoena. After the cause had been heard and determined the decree might be secured by an undertaking on the part of one or both parties to abide by its terms under penalty of a stated amount. Thus, the subpoena was used both at the beginning and at the end of the action to assure appearance, attendance and obedience. It was this subpoena power which was particularly offensive to the common-law courts. When one considers speculation concerning the 'reception' question in sixteenth-century England and the attempts that have been made to pit the common law against equity (as a proto-civilian threat) in order to explain the controversies between the Courts, it is instructive to consider the far more important problem of the subpoena. It gave the courts that used it a measure of control over their litigants which the common lawyers could only maintain occasionally and with the greatest of difficulties. Caesar was quite well aware of his Court's use of the subpoena and its importance judging from the fact that there was an example of the subpoena on almost every page of his collection of cases.

The subpoena under the initial Privy Seal was not as interesting as was the subpoena which was used to enforce injunctions and other forms of specific relief. Injunctions were generally of a temporary nature pending the final determination of the action. A common use of injunctive relief occurred in those cases where there was a parallel suit pending at law. The injunction would be employed to stay the action at law (or, in some instances, to prevent the execution of a judgment) while the issue was before the Requests. While this was of particular importance as the competition between the Requests and the Common Pleas intensified, the injunction had been used from Henry VII's reign when a matter was pending in both courts.[1] In 8 Henry VII a party was enjoined, under penalty of £300, not to proceed to judgment and execution at law even though he had a verdict until the matter was discussed in Council and further order was made.[2] Even when a cause was remitted to another court the Requests would enjoin the parties to avoid dilatory pleas.[3] Likewise, the Court supported the authority of the Prerogative Court of Canterbury by enjoining against appeal from its ruling in a testamentary matter to 'any forraine Courte out of this land'.[4] In the event of contempt of an injunction the Court was not reluctant to arrest the contumacious party and to commit him to the Fleet.[5]

The injunction was most frequently used in real property actions. In the sixteenth century there was a marked increase in real property actions, particularly those which would provide the plaintiff with peaceful possession. The need for this remedy was occasioned especially by the decay of traditional common-law real actions and the concomitant emergence of the action of ejectment. Since ejectment did not conclusively settle possession, litigants commonly went to Chancery for an injunction which would provide quiet possession and enjoin further action at law. Similarly the tenant might procure an injunction securing his possession while his suit against his landlord was being heard at law.[6] The process used in Chancery was mirrored in the Court of Requests. A defendant was enjoined to preserve unaltered the manor in question pending further order in the plaintiff's cause.[7] The injunction in another case stated that the defendant in the Requests was not to call for judgment in an action of *ejectione firmae* pending at law. Although the entry ends abruptly with an 'etc.' we can assume that the injunction was made pending the outcome of the cause in the Requests.[8] Injunctive relief in real property litigation was not the product of the jurisdictional disputes of Elizabeth's reign. There had been similar injunctions in the reigns of Henry VII and Henry VIII. One forbade recourse to the law while the Court

---

[1] *Infra*, 7 July, 16 H. 7.   [2] *Infra*, 10 June, 8 H. 8.
[3] *Infra*, 18 May, 26 H. 8.   [4] *Infra*, 4 November, 6 E. 6.
[5] *Infra*, 3 May, 20 Eliz. 1.
[6] W. Holdsworth, *A history of English law*, v, 323. [Hereafter cited as Holdsworth.]
[7] *Infra*, 4 February, 25 H. 8.   [8] *Infra*, 2 May, 20 Eliz. 1.

established whether an alleged feoffment was made to the use of Robert Parker and whether he had received a money payment in conjunction with the feoffment.[1] The second of these early injunctions ordered a party to refrain from recourse to the King's justices while the matter at issue was before the Requests under a penalty of £300.[2]

Specific relief took a variety of forms and was available in a multitude of circumstances. It was the positive counterpart of the injunction. Specific relief was most often encountered in matters of debt but it was also to be found in the wide range of actions growing out of the insufficiency of the common law. Holdsworth styled this last category 'relief against the rigidity of the law'.[3] One means of relieving this rigidity was by way of the injunction to stop further proceeding at the common law but there were several types of situation in which a positive order to restore or to perform was more appropriate. There were those cases which dealt with error, fraud and duress; those which concerned undue advantage taken within the strict letter of the law, and those which dealt with subjects which the law was unable to handle. In many of these cases the law was anxious to solicit the assistance of an equity court.

The plaintiff in one case had formerly assured the defendant of the honesty of two chapmen but he was now suing the defendant for the recovery of goods valued at £60 which the defendant had bought from the chapmen upon the plaintiff's advice. Because of the fraud practised, both by the plaintiff and the chapmen, the cause was dismissed.[4] A litigant was enjoined to appear before the Council to answer for his having forged a deed.[5] A decree was made which cancelled a deed of gift of chattels alleged to have been made to the donor's use. This contention was accepted: the donee was a servant of the donor, a countess, and the gift was to her use and not to his. But the Requests did order a new gift to be made amounting to £100 of which £80 was for the donee's children.[6] In a case in which a plaintiff had made a gift of goods and chattels to the defendant in trust for the plaintiff's use, the Court found that the defendant had 'entered uppon the plaintiffs goods and chattels' contrary to the terms of the trust. The decree was for the plaintiff

---

[1] Infra, 15 November, 19 H. 7.
[2] Infra, 10 June, 8 H. 8.
[3] Holdsworth, v, 325.
[4] Infra, 22 March, 24 H. 8.
[5] Infra, 15 May, 14 H. 8.
[6] Infra, 28 November, 1 M.

ordering the defendant to restore all the goods and chattels and to pay the costs.[1] In these two latter cases the Court was specifically enforcing the execution of a trust.

Similar relief was used in cases of debt where we find the greatest incidence of specific relief. A debt without specialty was enforced by the Requests,[2] although in another instance a secured debt which was made under a bond of statute merchant was likewise enforced in the Court even though it was equally enforceable at the common law.[3] In like fashion the Court took up the matter of a debt secured by a debenture.[4]

The application of specific relief extended into areas of litigation in which the law was simply inadequate. There was a challenge made to the assessment of the fifteenth by the subsidy collectors. The collectors brought the challenger in the Court of Requests to require his payment of their assessment although the Barons of the Exchequer could just as well have heard the action. The Court agreed with the defendant's claim that his land was customarily assessed at 31*s*. 2*d*. and that there was no justification for raising the assessment. Since the customary amount had been offered to the collectors and had been turned down by them, the defendant was excused from appearance in the Requests and the suit was dismissed.[5] Likewise, there was an action upon a breach of marriage contract. The defendant brought the cause to Requests for relief because he claimed that his having been an apprentice had prevented his entering into a marriage contract. The Court decreed that since the young man was now out of his apprenticeship, and because a consideration had passed by virtue of the promise to marry when the contract had been made, he should either marry his fiancé or pay her 20 marks 'for her advauncement'.[6] While the common law could provide the same choice of performance on the payment of damages, the cause had been brought to the Requests, perhaps in the light of the apprentice's straitened circumstances.

In addition to the various procedures used within the court there was also an important extra-mural procedure, the commission, upon which the Requests came to depend. The need for commissions arose out of the requirement of personal appearance and the

[1] *Infra*, 1 February, 1&2 P. & M.
[2] *Infra*, 3 March, 12 H. 7.
[3] *Infra*, 14 November, 14 H. 7.
[4] *Infra*, 3 June, 15 H. 7.
[5] *Infra*, 5 February, 30 H. 8.
[6] *Infra*, 4 June, 38 H. 8.

necessity in equity to take testimony of witnesses regarding the parties' allegations. Because litigants came from throughout the kingdom the commission provided a means of extending the presence of the court into distant parts. Faced with the same problem, the Chancery had adopted the commission in the mid-fifteenth century; it was not surprising, therefore, that the junior equity bench should have adopted the same procedure.[1]

Depending upon its charge the commission could take answers, examine witnesses by administering interrogatories, take depositions, hear and wherever possible determine causes (i.e. serve as arbitrators) and inquire into local custom. The composition of the commissions varied according to the nature of the tasks they were assigned. Some were made up of lawyers, officials and local gentry while others, those which were empowered to examine witnesses and to administer interrogatories, were constituted of an equal number of nominees of the respective parties. Commissions to take the defendant's answer (known as commissions *dedimus potestatem*) were only infrequently mentioned by Caesar.[2] Presumably he regarded the process as unremarkable and did not think that the argument that he was advancing would be materially assisted by expanding upon it.

The commission to hear and determine was a different matter. Although its name was similar to the common-law commission of oyer and terminer, the similarity was only superficial. The common-law commissions referred to the trial of an indicted crime by a special commission, the commissions in the Court of Requests had nothing to do with indictments. They were a means by which the Court in White Hall could extend itself to the provinces by calling together the parties and their witnesses before the nominees of the Court who were to hear and attempt to determine the cause. If such a determination or 'final end to the matter' were not possible, the commissioners were to certify their proceedings to the Court and further action could be taken. These were, in fact, commissions to arbitrate which had evolved from the more narrowly defined commission to ask certain prescribed questions. It is not surprising that as time passed these commissions of lay-

---

[1] J. P. Dawson, *A history of lay judges* (Cambridge, Mass., 1960), 150–2; and C. J. Bayne, *Select cases in the Council of Henry VII*, Selden Society, 75 (1956), cv–cvi.

[2] *Infra*, 23 January, 34 H. 8; 7 November, 5&6 P. & M.; 10 October, 1 Eliz. 1; 13 May, 17 Eliz. 1.

men began to make spontaneous suggestions for compromise solutions to the litigation which would permit settlement then and there at reduced cost to all concerned.[1] This *ad hoc* practice had arisen in Chancery where it was institutionalised by the express commissioning of men of standing in the litigants' community to try to reach an accord between the parties out of court. The same practice was employed in the Court of Requests. Arbitration could be undertaken with minimal formality: the parties and their witnesses told their stories before the commissioners and then bargaining began. Hopefully the commissioners could direct the litigants to a compromise, a 'determination', to which they could subscribe. Failing successful arbitration the matter would be returned to the Court. But the Court in certain cases would use pressure to force the parties to submit to binding arbitration. The pressure usually took the form of a requirement that the parties make recognizances which committed them to accept and abide by the award of the arbitrators. Dawson has suggested that the need for arbitration in the sixteenth century was a direct function of the insularity of English law which had become so ossified that a channel was needed 'to restore sense and decency in private law'.[2]

Because of the high incidence of land tenure cases which came before the Court in the sixteenth century, particularly those regarding copyhold tenure, the Court needed to employ commissions of inquiry to determine the customs of a manor prior to making a decree. These cases were often an early form of class action: the tenants of a manor *versus* their landlord regarding conflicting claims as to the common rights. Whenever it was possible the extant manorial rolls were produced to substantiate the plaintiff's claim. Thus we encounter orders to the stewards of manors requiring them to bring before the court all of the relevant manorial documents concerning the action.[3] But when the manorial rolls were either missing or inconveniently remote, the Court would name commissioners to make enquiries of the tenants of the manor or to examine the records where they lay. In the case of copyholders with no copy or of contradictory statements of manorial custom, the commissioners were to ascertain whether

[1] The following comments regarding arbitration rely upon Dawson, *Lay Judges*, 163 *et seq.*
[2] Dawson, 169f.
[3] *Infra*, 8 February, 18 H. 7; 7 November, 2&3 P. & M.

common memory could establish the copyholder's title or determine the elusive custom of the manor.

(iv)

Caesar tells us that he collected the material for *The Ancient State*
from seventeen 'great volumes in folio' which contained the records
of the orders and decrees of the Queen's Court at Whitehall [*sic*].
Although that Court had come, even in Caesar's day, to be known
as the Court of Requests, it is apparent that its identity prior to the
middle of Henry VIII's reign had been unclear. While there had
been members of the King's Council who had met frequently to
dispatch business in a manner nearly identical with the later
practices of the Court of Requests, there had not been an institution of that name until the 1520s. What then had been the nature
of the pre-existing body of councillors and how did it relate to the
Court in which Caesar sat?

From as early as 1483 there had been a second clerk of Council
described by Pollard as the clerk charged with the keeping,
registering and expediting of poor peoples' 'bills, requests and
supplications'.[1] In a later article Pollard recalled that during
Henry VII's first Parliament a bill was introduced in Commons
which proposed that the Court of Requests be annulled and
'occupied no more'. The bill appears to have passed through
Parliament only to be ignored by the King. Eight years later when
Henry felt more secure upon his throne, he set about 'ignoring the
Commons bill of 1485 and [began] silently reviving the court of
requests'.[2] The series of Order and Decree Books which Caesar
used began at this time, a fact that supports Pollard's allegation.
But the initial entry in the series, which was also the first entry in
the cases in *The Ancient State*, was not a judicial matter but rather
a bit of conciliar housekeeping: the assignment of members of
Council to accompany the King on progress.[3] The subsequent
entries however were judicial as well as administrative, thus con-
firming Professor Elton's suggestion that these registers were one
of at least two records series which related to different aspects of
one body: the King's Council. The other series of records which

[1] A. F. Pollard, 'Council, starchamber and privy council under the Tudors',
English Historical Review [EHR], 37 (1922), 344.
[2] A. F. Pollard, 'The growth of the Court of Requests', *EHR*, 56 (1941), 300–3.
[3] Public Record Office, Req. 1/1/1r.

we know today as the Acts of Privy Council had their origin later in the reign of Henry VIII. The first series of records would eventually come to be the records of the Court of Requests, fully independent and with its own process. The institutionalisation of the Requests was due to the reorganisation of the Council by Wolsey; there was no such institution prior to the great Cardinal's rule.[1] I. S. Leadam, on the other hand, has treated these records as the records of the Court of Requests from first entry in 1493, rather than make the distinction between the committee of Council which handled poor men's causes and the subsequent institutionalised Court with its own establishment.[2] It is this confusion in perception that has made it most difficult to establish the origins of the Court of Requests.

If we return to Pollard's argument regarding Henry VII's surreptitious revivification of the Court, we must concede that he was partially correct. Functionally the King's Council, when it was determining civil causes brought to the King by petition, was acting in the same way that the Court of Requests would come to act. To this extent Pollard was quite right but in the institutional sense he missed the mark. As an institution with its own identity, personnel, registers and locus, the Court of Requests was, in the last decade of the fifteenth century, nearly a quarter century away. Another problem with Pollard's argument lies in the absence of evidence of a Court prior to 1493 and the always dangerous business of making positive historical statements upon a foundation of negative evidence. As we have noted above, there was a group of the King's Council assigned to the disposition of civil causes after 1493; the Order and Decree Books show us that. What is not evident is that the Council had not been acting in a similar fashion before 1493 but without the confirmation of extant registers.

Professor Elton has defined a body of advisors, ministers and officers known as the King's Council which in its protean form assumed many identities without any necessary consistency. There was only one King's Council, notwithstanding the efforts of generations of historians to divide it and to give it different names. Citing Baldwin's work, Elton has said that 'all the King's council-

---

[1] G. R. Elton, 'Why the history of the early-Tudor Council remains unwritten', *Annali della Fondazione Italiana per la storia Amministrativa*, I (1964), 287ff.

[2] I. S. Leadam, *Select cases in the court of Requests, 1497–1569*, Selden Society, 12 (1898), xiv.

lors were of one kind, even if they did different work; no organic division on the lines of their work was carried out or even contemplated'.[1] Evidence of this undifferentiated and highly fluid Council can be found in the Public Record Office class known as the proceedings of the Court of Requests (Req. 2). These proceedings contain bills, answers and other working papers of the councillors sitting in the White Hall or travelling with the King on progress. Among them are papers relating to Star Chamber which Elton suggests indicates that the designation 'star chamber' or 'White Hall' was unimportant as the councillors were all members of the King's Council and not of separate courts.

New economic and social realities in the sixteenth century had created problems with which the unreformed common law was unable to cope. Although the common lawyers were attempting to manipulate the existing law to meet the demands of the moment, the existing law was not sufficiently flexible. In time equitable practices, which had once had a place in the common law, would find their way back into the mainstream of the law. In the meantime the development of legal fictions and new forms of action were symptomatic of the problems of the common lawyers. Common-law actions were grounded for the most part in the relationships which arose out of the possession of property; as long as the community revolved about a feudal economy in which land tenure was the linch pin of wealth and status, the old law was suitable. The social, economic and political transformations which were taking place in sixteenth-century England, however, were producing a nation in which wealth was no longer derived principally from land but also from commerce, the professions and the law. The law of a landed society was manifestly unsuited to commercial affairs. The courts of the common law, for example, were able to deal with ordinary freeholds, leaseholds, and some copyholds but trusts were beyond their ken. Chancery provided one alternative tribunal which was better able to cope with the changes which faced the law. The Court of Requests, a conciliar court, was another alternative.

The conciliar courts operated by the authority of the undelegated (or residual) royal prerogative. They were not dependent upon precedent and were the principal repositories of equity in

---

[1] G. R. Elton, *The Tudor revolution in government* (1953), 317.

England. This situation permitted them to fill the gaps left by the rules of the Common Law. But as constitutional questions came to occupy men's minds and the superiority of the Common Law came to be identified with constitutional propriety, the courts of equity in turn came to be associated with arbitrary assertions of the royal prerogative. Few contemporaries, however, recognised that the increasing complexity of English life was at the centre of the seeming assertiveness; of the Prerogative Courts; in brief, equity was filling a vacuum.

In its purest form, equity was an expression of justice which was subjective in nature and which was founded solely on the facts of the particular situation. The King had a feudal obligation confirmed in the coronation oath to provide justice (i.e. both equity and law) to his subjects, an obligation which was satisfied first by Chancery and then by the addition of the Conciliar Courts. But Chancery had begun to ossify, although not as seriously as had the Common Law. Chancery equity had come to decide cases not purely upon general notions of equity and conscience but also with reference to the previous practices of the Court in like cases. The inception of formal records of the Court's decrees both enabled and encouraged a greater recourse to Chancery precedents and the Court was beginning not only to settle cases but more consciously to create a body of legal doctrine, especially in relation to the law of trusts and uses.[1] Although equity to some degree influenced all of England's legal systems, there was only one Court with national jurisdiction in the sixteenth century in which traditional equity was practised. This Court was the Court of Requests, a court of conscience and, occasionally, of speedy justice.

The Common Lawyers, especially in the Court of Common Pleas, at a time when they were engaged in defining their own authority could not abide the rather inocuous inroads which were being made into their ordinary jurisdiction by the Court of Requests. Had the Requests strictly limited itself to its avowed jurisdiction there would have been less difficulty. Members of the Royal Household, their servants and those persons engaged in the Crown's service were allowed the privilege of the King's own justice as were the poor and the various corporations such as colleges, hospitals and towns which owed their corporate lives to

---

[1] My thanks to Mr D. E. C. Yale for his assistance on this matter of Chancery precedent.

the King's charter. The common lawyers did not argue that the King did not have the responsibility to provide the means of justice to these and to all of his subjects. They realised that their courts were so expensive and their procedures so protracted that the poor especially were frequently unable to bring actions in them. Thus a genuine pauper, who would not generate fees in any event, was welcome to take his pleadings before the Requests but there was no systematic procedure for declaring one's poverty and having that declaration verified. In Elizabeth's reign license to proceed as a pauper was granted without much inquiry but it would appear that when another party made sufficient commotion about fraudulent allegations of poverty the Court would investigate and dismiss an action if the circumstances required.[1] But it was not the matter of paupers or of the abuse of jurisdiction that most upset the common lawyers.

At root the common lawyers were disturbed by the use of the injunction and of the subpoena, devices which made the Court of Requests popular and, in turn, detracted from the business of the central law courts. The common lawyers were not selfless defenders of judicial and jurisdictional propriety; they were practical men who wished to preserve the flow of litigants through their courts which provided them with the fees upon which they depended for their livings. It was the great misfortune of the Requests that it was not a part of one of the major judicial establishments, an association which could have provided it with protection from attack. Dr Jones tells us that there were several courts in 'the governmental heart of England' which were not capable of being classified as either Chancery or common-law and which did not utilise a procedure which was in the main stream of English legal tradition. They were not regarded by local authorities as being strong enough to enforce their writs from the centre. These courts (the High Court of Admiralty, the Court of Requests and some of the ecclesiastical Courts) were 'central but specialised in jurisdiction, recognised and yet distinctive, [and] lived increasingly in the no-man's-land between metropolitan advantage and a near provincial disregard. Prohibitions and other process were to make most of these Courts feel threatened.'[2] It was a case of small fragments being ground up by the abrasive power

----

[1] Allsebrook, 126.

[2] W. J. Jones, *The Elizabethan Court of Chancery* (1967), 21.

of increasingly more monolithic national judicial systems. Perhaps no one has so well summarised the crisis in the courts at the end of the sixteenth century as has Dr Jones. There was no judicial institution which did not require review and reform. Tinkering was done in bits and snatches but there was no systematic attempt to rationalise an irrational procedure. 'When the use of the injunction, first by the court of Requests and subsequently by Chancery, was called in question, this should have been envisaged as a reasonable criticism of an increasingly absurd situation. The need for the injunction and the frequency of its application were becoming intolerable.' Having set up the problem Dr Jones then turned to his major point which was the absurdity of the contemporary answers.

> The judges of the Common Pleas, later reinforced by Coke, asked the wrong question and came up with the wrong answer. It was not the injunction which was absurd, but the situation necessitating its use, and in the creation of this situation all the courts concerned were at fault. Even down the centuries, we can still feel the warmth of Caesar's incredulous indignation at the sheer effrontery of the attack on the court of Requests' application of this writ. The available records and the short memory of active men were sufficient, Caesar realised, to destroy this criticism, yet the offensive went on.[1]

Caesar, while not able to move much sympathy for his position, was among the few (such as Burghley, Egerton and Cecil) who saw the problems faced by the courts and attempted to attack them straightforwardly.

(v)

There are less than twenty extant copies of *The Ancient State*. The revised *Short Title Catalogue* will show that copies are located in the British Museum, Lambeth Palace Library and Doctor Williams' Library in London; the Bodleian Library and in Exeter College, Oxford; the Cambridge University Library and in Trinity Hall, Cambridge; King's Inn, Dublin; the Folger Library in Washington, D.C.; the Huntington Library, San Marino,

[1] Jones, *Chancery*, 490f.

California; the Houghton Library, Harvard University, Cambridge, Massachusetts; and the John Carter Brown Library, Brown University, Providence, Rhode Island.[1] In addition there is an excellent copy in the Keeper's library of the Public Record Office.

Unfortunately there are not many clues in the extant copies nor amongst Caesar's papers to tell us how and to whom he distributed the book. We know from the epistle dedicatory that Caesar sent a copy to Burghley but there is no inscription to identify the copy that he received. We must assume that Burghley's copy no longer exists or that it was passed on to someone else without any mark being made. Otherwise, we know from the inscriptions that Caesar gave copies to John Davies of Inner Temple,[2] Dr Daniel Dunn,[3] Robert Bowyer,[4] William Lambarde,[5] and Francis Harewell.[6] We may conjecture that the Bridgewater Library copy, now in the Huntington Library collection, was presented to Egerton but there is no inscription to substantiate such an assumption. There is also evidence that copies of The Ancient State found their way into important ecclesiastical hands but we have no inscriptions to indicate whether they were direct gifts made by Caesar. This is particularly apparent in the two copies of the book which lie in the Lambeth Palace Library. One of the copies is bound together with Martin Fotherby's Four Sermons and bears the initials 'R.B.' on the front cover. These were the initials of Richard Bancroft who, as Archbishop of Canterbury, had begun the library in Lambeth Palace in 1610. These initials may mean nothing, being present on the covers of hundreds of volumes which lay in the library during Bancroft's reign. But there is no reason to suspect that Caesar might not have sent along a copy of The Ancient State to the Archbishop as a mark of respect,[7] a particularly appropriate gift in the light of Bancroft's ill will towards common lawyers. Likewise, the second Lambeth copy bears the arms of Archbishop Abbott on its binding.[8] In this instance The Ancient State is not bound with any other writings.

It is of some interest to note in those cases where there are

[1] My thanks to Miss Katherine Pantzer of the Houghton Library, Harvard University for this information.
[2] Public Record Office, Keeper's Library, L. 98.
[3] Bodleian Library: 4° Rawl. 552.   [4] Bodleian Library: Tanner 264.
[5] British Museum: 1380 g. 21.   [6] British Museum: C. 122, bb 28 (3).
[7] Lambeth Palace Library: 1608. 14.   [8] Lambeth Palace Library: 1597. 14.

dated inscriptions that Caesar was making gifts of *The Ancient State* a number of years after it was printed. The copy which was given to Robert Bowyer was dated 22 December 1606 while Dr Daniel Dunn was given his copy in 1614. It would appear that Caesar continued to take pride in the work, wished to give it to his friends and considered its case to be germane even after the events of the 1590s which had caused him to prepare *The Ancient State.*

The Ancient State, Authoritie and Proceedings of the Court of Requests was printed in London by George Bishop in 1597. It was a small quarto bound originally in limp vellum with ties. The work actually was in two parts. The first part bore the title assigned to the whole while the second had no title as such but was known by the opening words of the first page: '*In nomine Domini nostri Jesu Christi, 13 Februarii 1592.* Actes, Orders and Decrees made by the King and his Counsell, 9.H.7, remaining amongst the Records of the Court of Requests.' The first part of the printed book comprised five printed leaves without pagination, while the second comprised pages numbered 1 through 162. There was also a page of errata and corrigenda which has not been reproduced in this edition because the various items have been incorporated into the text.

Landsdowne MS 125, upon which this edition is based, contains the 87 leaves which are to be found in the printed edition plus an additional 99 interleaved folios upon which Caesar entered his vast collection of additional data. There are several other manuscript copies of *The Ancient State*: Additional MSS 36,111 and 36,112 were prepared by Caesar, the former being as close to a preliminary draft as one can find. Both of these are holographic copies but there is also a rather formal copy of the printed book without any of Caesar's additions which is headed by a page marked: No. 9, Henrye Fielde, 1642.

We do have evidence of Caesar's having discussed the matter of his work with another legal writer of his day, Edward Hake. It would not be surprising to find that Caesar had given a copy of *The Ancient State* to Hake in the course of their discussions. Hake, whose work *Epieikeia* was in progress when Caesar had finished his own writing, was preparing a general treatise on the status of equity in the law at the end of the sixteenth century.[1] In letters

---

[1] E. Hake, *EPIEIKEIA: a dialogue on equity in three parts*, ed. D. E. C. Yale, Yale Law Library Publication No. 13 (New Haven, 1953).

written in the winter of 1597–8, he told Caesar of the scheme he was using, of the premises upon which he was basing his argument, and of the large areas of similarity between their works.[1]

As we have mentioned there is virtually no evidence in Caesar's papers regarding the way he went about distributing his little book, indeed we have very little to go on from the extant copies. But it is interesting to observe that the printer had a quantity of sheets left in stock long after Caesar's death. One of the Bodleian Library copies of *The Ancient State* is a part of the Rawlinson collection of miscellaneous tracts and pamphlets.[2] The collection in which it was bound was entitled *Orders of Bartholomew Hospital* which was item one of the collection. *The Ancient State* was item thirteen. Rawlinson apparently frequented the tallow chandlers and wastepaper-mongers of early eighteenth-century London. From them he would acquire leaves from the bundles of sheets that they purchased in bulk from printers' lofts. The tallow chandlers used the leaves as liners in pouring candles and as wrappers for the finished product. Rawlinson salvaged what he could and bound up his discoveries in miscellaneous collections.[3] Thus, there were some of the sheets from *The Ancient State* remaining with the printers as late as the early eighteenth century long after the Court of Requests could have had anything more than antiquarian interest and long before its historical importance came to be recognised.

The editor wishes to thank the Trustees of the British Museum for their kind permission to publish the contents of Landsdowne MS 125.

EDITORIAL SYMBOLS AND PRACTICES

. . . or * indicates a holographic insertion by Caesar

[ ] indicates a deletion by Caesar

All references to BM Lansdowne MS 125 contain only the folio number without the volume or collection designation (e.g. fo. 25r

[1] BM Lansd. MS 161, fos. 233r–233v (7 December 1597) and fos. 43r–43v (15 February 1598).

[2] Bodleian Library: Gough Lond. J. 203.

[3] B. J. Enright, 'Rawlinson and the chandlers', *Bodleian Library Record*, IV (1952–3), 216–27.

rather than BM Lansd. MS, fo. 25r). All other manuscript references are given with full apparatus.

When there is a printed page reference from BM Lansd. MS 125 as well as a folio reference, the two references are placed together within square brackets (e.g. [fo. 56v (p. 24)]).

The references to entries from the Order and Decree Books and from the proceedings in the Court of Requests have been placed after the individual entries within square brackets but without the designation 'P.R.O.'. (e.g. [Req. 1/1/2r]). Caesar drew his information from the Order and Decree Books but as there are several which are no longer extant or which have been badly damaged the editor has turned to the proceedings to cite the reference.

When there is no extant record to confirm Caesar's entries the letters NR have been placed in square brackets to indicate 'no record'.

Because the order of the material in Lansd. MS 125 is disjointed due to Caesar's extensive interleaving, the editor has rearranged the contents in an order that conforms as closely to the original as possible while still making sense.

All Latin and French passages have been translated into English. In those passages which have been translated the spelling and punctuation is modern. In the passages which were in English in BM Lansd. MS 125, the original spelling has been preserved. There are the following exceptions: *j* has been substituted for *i* and *v* has been substituted for *u*. While the dipthong *y* (the thorn) has been rendered *th*, 'ye' used as a pronoun has been retained. Abbreviations have been expanded in most instances.

Caesar printed an errata sheet at the end of *The Ancient State* (BM Lansd. MS 125, fo. 162r) which has not been included in this edition because the individual corrections have been incorporated into the text.

The dating through the work is old style, although the year changes 1 January rather than 25 March.

The Ancient State
Authoritie and Proceedings of
the Court of Requests

1

THE EPISTLE DEDICATORY FROM
CAESAR TO LORD BURGHLEY

[fo. 25r]

Myne humble dutie done to your Lordship. About vii yeares since, shortlie after I was made Maister of Requests, I found a great contention on foote betwene the Judges of the Comon Pleas and the Masters of Requests then being, touching the jurisdiction of her Majesties court at Whitehall; whereby would have growne manie bitter inconveiences to to [*sic*] her Majesties poore subjects, if the Masters of Requests had not quenched the same in tyme, by their owne suffering, yet necessary patience and forbearance. To meet with theise mischeiffs, I held it a necessary worke, and a labor worthie of some thanks, to gather into one volume, the principall records of that court from the begining of the Registrie, nowe dispersed in xvii great volumes in folio, and to make them knowne, that in this Court (as in the Chancery, Kings Benche, Comon Pleas and Exchecquer) acts past [fo. 25v] might be precedents of things to come. In the perusall and gathering whereof I have observed: First, the severall names names [*sic*] wherewith that Court hath bene termed; Secondly, what the Judges have bene whoe have satt in that Court; Thirdly, in what places that Court hath bene kept; Fowerthly, what forme of proceeding that Court hath observed; Fiftly, whoe the persons were which have bene plaintiffs and defendants in that Court; Sixtly, what causes said Court hath embraced and decreed. And lastly howe the said Court hath bene accustimed to execute her orders and decrees, with manie other things worthy of note not unpropperly to be referred to some of the seaven heads. Wherein as myne intent was, first to satisfie myne owne conscience and to understand what aperteined to the place wherein I sitt as a judge, thereby onely intending the glorie of God, [fo. 26r] the good of my contrie, and the dischardge of a good conscience and not anie private vaine glorie or affected singularity, so I have desired that some others (no doubt as well affected as my self) might veiwe my labors, that uppon this ground, they might frame some

3

further building not unworthie the perusall. And to that purpose, finding it overchargeable to write manie copies, I caused: First, a brieff table of my collections themselves to be imprinted, not to the end to make them common but of purpose to deliver some of them to suche, either Counsellors of Estate or Counsellors at Lawe, or such students of antiquities and of histories, as from whose wisdomes and good observacions either in lawe, or storie, or antiquities there might be drawne suche admendment of things amisse or addition of things wanting or justification of things misconstrued, or explaining of things obscured [fo. 26v] or reducing into course, things wrested out of course as might breed hereafter a continewall peace betwene the Judges of the Common Lawe and her Majesties Counsell and might without offence of the subjects, establishe her Highnes prerogative for ever. To the mainetenance wherof every one sworne of her Majesties counsell is directly tyed by his oathe. And for that your Lordship hathe most justly deserved the most honorable and highe tytle of *Pater patriae* and have for manie yeres (especially theise xvii yeres of my knowledge since I came to be judge) bene the Father of Englishe Justice and my good lord and onely maister, whome ever I served, and from whome (next to her most excellent Majestie) I acknowledge my self to have resived that poore advancement in this common wealth which I nowe enjoye, I have [fo. 27r] made choice of your good Lordship to be the disposer of theise my labors that either under your allowance, after your perusall of them, they maie receive some comfort of further proceeding, or else uppon your mislyke, they maie be committed to the fire, as things unprofitable for the common good.

But if your Lordship, being continewally imployed in the great affaires of this state, shall finde no leisure to read over matters of this nature then it maie please your Lordship that Master William Lamberd, whoe is a gentleman of great learning and sincerity, or some other one or more of like sufficiency might be intreated to peruse such collections as I have gathered, bothe of precedents of the said court and of expresse Acts of Parliament, auncyent records, histories, and Common Lawe touching this cause. And thereuppon to make report of so muche as he or they shall finde proved, that her Majesties Court of Whitehall maie enjoye suche [fo. 24v] authoritie as to the same of right belongeth.

And so humbly craving pardon for this my tedious letter and the continewance alsoe of your Lordships most honorable favor towards me I beseech the Almighty to voutchsafe your Lordship a long life, encreas of honor and of healthe, and a full accomplishment of all your godly desires.

St. Catherins, this xvi th of January, 1598.

Your good Lordships most bounden,
*Jul. Caesar

Copie
To the right honorable my singular good Lord, the Lord Burghley, Lord Highe Tresorer of England.

THE COURT'S AUTHORITY AS
DEMONSTRATED IN THE RECORDS OF
THE COURT OF REQUESTS

[fo. 9r] # The Ancient state, authoritie, and proceedingss of the Court *of Whitehall or* of Requests

2 October 1596

The Court *of whitehall or* Requests now so called, was, and is parcell of the Kings most honourable Councell, and so always called, and esteemed.

29 April and 1 July, 17.H.7; 27 May, 21.H.7; and 18 September, 6.H.8; [28 November, 12.H.8; 18 July, 14.H.8]; 30 November, 27.H.8; 6 November, 30.H.8; [21 April, 31.H.8]; 3 July, 32.H.8; 8 July, the same; 14 March, 33.H.8; 15 November, 35.H.8; [11 November 36.H.8]; 1 February, 37.H.8; 1 June, 38.H.8; 29 July, the same; 25 September, the same; and 5 July, 6.Edw.6; 1 February, 7.Edw.6; 8 May, the same; and 7 May, 1 Mary; 25 October, 1&2.P&M; 21 November, the same; [28 November][1] 2&3.P&M; 12 June, [the same; 19 June, 3&4.P&M and 29 June, the same; and 12 February, 19.H.7]]

[fo. 9v]

The Judges of that Court were alwaies of the Kings most honorable Councell appointed by the King to keepe his Councell[2] [board]

---

[1] There is no corresponding entry in the text.
[2] These are generally lists of names of the various judges and other councillors who sat in the Court particularly in the early part of the sixteenth century when the Court was more clearly associated with Council. The numbers of councillors became much smaller as Henry VIII's reign progressed. Caesar's notations were eventually reduced to two or three of the Council who took order and such-like.

12 February, 9.H.7; 21 March, 12.H.7; 28 May, 13.H.7; 29 June, 14.H.7; 11 March, 15.H.7; 9 March, 17.H.7; 22 November, 21.H.7 and 28 January, 20.H.8; ⟦10 July, 24.H.8; and⟧ 23 May, 25.H.8; 24 November, 26.H.8; 23 January, 29.H.8; 28 June, 33.H.8; 6 November, the same; 10 February, the same; and 27 November, 1.E.6; 29 January, 6.E.6; ⟦12 June,[1] 7.Edw.6; and 19 November,[1] 1 Mary; 26 January, the same; 1 June the same; 20 January⟧[1] 1&2.P&M; 6 May, ⟦the same; 24 November, 2&3.P&M⟧; 25 November, 3&4.P&M; 3 November, 4&5.P&M.

[fo. 183v]

*4.H.4, cap. 23. That neither by the king himself, ⟦the⟧ nor the kings counsell nor the Parliament any judgement given in the kings court shalbee reversed but by attaint or errour.

[fo. 186r]

*34.H.8, cap. 4, the kings most Honorable Privy Council

*Abridgement of Statutes, *titulum* champertie, sect. 3. Gilbert Rowbery, Clerk of the Kings Counsell, 20&21.E.1.

*13.Ric.3, cap. 2, in a question betwene two jurisdictions, the kings Counsell the judge.

[fo. 9v]

The keeping of this Court was never heretofore tied to any place certeine; but onely where the Councell sate, the suitors were to attend: But ⟦now of late⟧ *a. in 11.H.7.* for the ease of suitors, it ⟦hath bene⟧*b. began to bee* kept in the White-hall in Westminster, ⟦and onely⟧ in the terme time. ⟦viz.⟧* and so hath continued ever since, saving onely at such times as the common lawe terme hath bene kept elsewhere, and then this Court hath followed the same course,[2] *videt* at Hartford, 3 February, 6.Eliz. and 6 November, 24.Eliz. and at St Albans 15 November, 35.H.8.

At Sheene: 3 March, 9.H.7

At Canterbury: 12 April, the same

At Windsor: 20 July, the same

At Langley: 6 September, 10.H.7

At Woodstock: 7 October, the same

At Worcester: 9 July, the same

At Nottingham: 24 August, 11.H.7

At Leicester: 29 August, the same, etc.

---

[1] There are 'Masters of Requests' mentioned in these entries rather than members of the Council.

[2] These locations have only one date following them but there were in fact several meetings at each location on many days.

The Court of Requests is a Court of Record. 5 July, 3&4.P&M.[1]
Recognizaunces taken by the Kings Councell (in his Court
of *c. Whitehall or* Requestes) at Westminster.

13 June and 18 June, 13.H.8; 15 October, the same; 26 April,
21.H.8, 11 June, the same; 8 July, 25.H.8.

[fo. 12r]

The forme of the proceeding in this Court was altogether according to the processe of summary causes in the Civill Law.

5 February, 13.H.7; [[14 November]];[2] 14.H.7; 3 December, [[the
same]]; 20 March, the same; [[18 March, 15.H.7]];[3] 17 December,
10.H.8; and 18 November, 22.H.8; 18 November, 31.H.8; and
21 May, 3&4.P&M; and 5 June, 1 Elizabeth.

The persons plaintifs, and defendants, betweene whom they
judged, were alwayes either privileged as officers of the Court, or
their servants, or as the Kings servants, or necessarie attendants on
them; or els where the Plaintifs povertie, or mean estate was not
matchable with the wealth, or greatnes of the Defendant; or where
the cause meerely conteined matter of equity, and had no proper
remedy at the Common Law: or where the cause was specially
recommended from the King, to the examination of his Councell:
or causes concerning Universities, Colledges, Schooles, Hospitalles,
and the like. As

18 November, 11.H.7; 27 November, the same; 11 December,
the same; 26 November, 14.H.7; 1 May, the same; 6 July,
17.H.7; 13 March, 18.H.7; 31 July, the same; 28 May, 21.H.7;
14 February, 23.H.7 and 27 October, 3.H.8; 13 July, 11.H.8;
4 February, 12.H.8; 21 February, the same; 6 June, 13.H.8;
18 October, 22.H.8; 4 July, 24.H.8; 17 November, 25.H.8;
6 June, 29.H.8; 2 and 4 November, 30.H.8; 6 February, 31.H.8;
8 June, 32.H.8; 12 February, the same; 17 October. 38.H.8;
20 November, the same; 26 November, the same; and 4 February,
1.E.6; and 6 February, the same; 22 May, the same; 28 June, the
same; 5 July, the same;[4] 18 October, the same; 30 January, 2.E.6;
9 February, the same; 9 June, the same; 26 November, 4.E.6; and

---

[1] This entry states simply that there was 'a complaint remaining of records in
[the] Court'.
[2] There is no apparent reason for Caesar's having stricken this entry. These
cases reveal the use of the summary process as much as do the cases which
remain.
[3] This entry notes that the Council was held in Baynard Castle.
[4] This should read 5 July, 1.E.6.

24 January and 24 April, 5.E.6; 26 May, 6.E.6; 26 April, 1 Mary;
28 May, the same; *7 May, 1 Mary; 1 May, 2&3.P&M; 24
October, 3&4.P&M;¹ ⟦5 May, the same⟧; 10 February, 4&5.P&M;²
9 May, the same; 24 June, the same;³ *19 May, 3.Eliz.
[fo. 11r]
The causes wherewith they deale, and whereof they judge, are
of all sorts: as Maritime, Ecclesiasticall, Temporall, but properly
of Temporall causes, and onely of the other sort as they are mixt
with Temporall. *But it is to bee understood that causes ecclesiasticall, maritime and ultramarine and causes triable by the common
lawe are not to bee determined in this Court, unles there bee some
matter of equitie in them not remediable in theire proper Courts,
videt, to remedie fraudes, breach of trust, extremity of common
lawe, or undue practises.*
Ecclesiasticall.
2 March, 17.H.7; 15 July, 20.H.7; and 25 November, 8.H.8;
12 February, 21.H.8; 25 May, 33.H.8; 25 November, 34.H.8;
20 November and 21 February, 35.H.8; ⟦and 22 June⟧;⁴ 2.E.6;
28 November, ⟦the same; 20 May, 3.E.6;⁵ 28 November, the
same⟧;⁶ 23 November, 5.E.6; 22 June, 7.E.6; and 7 May, 1 Mary;
18 November, 4&5.P&M; *and 1 May, 25.Eliz.; and 8 February,
6.E.6.⁷
Maritime.
3 March, 9.H.7; 24 March, 10.H.7; 21 April, the same; 25 April,
the same; and 30 March, 11.H.7, *27 E.3, c. 13; and 2.Rich.3,
fol. 2.*
Ultramarine.
21 May, 15.H.7; 13 July, 17.H.7; and 16 February, 10.H.8;

---

¹ This cause was dismissed out of the Court of Requests and sent to the common
  law as title to an annuity was properly determined at common law.
² This cause was sent to the manor court for trial because plaintiff alleged no
  partiality in the Lady of the manor or in her steward.
³ This cause dismissed because the parties were rich and could appear in the
  City court or elsewhere.
⁴ There is no clear reason for Caesar having stricken this entry. Many of his
  prior citations have been to marital and testementary causes heard in the Court
  of Requests. This cause was sent to 'the Kings Delegates' on appeal of a
  testementary cause from the Prerogative Court. The council would not hear
  the cause any further until the appeal was settled.
⁵ A cause of tithes remitted to ecclesiastical judges because the appropriate
  statue required that it be tried by those judges.
⁶ A legacy decreed.
⁷ 6.E.6 may be 7.E.6 but the cause was for an annuity.

stet[1] [[and 27 February, the same; and]] 4 November, 6.E.6;
25 October, 3&4.P&M; *and 16 November, 37.H.8.[2]
Temporall: as temporall offices, etc.*
25 February, 14.H.7; and 22 October, 31.H.8; 4 July,[3] 38.H.8;
and 4 June, 3.E.6; 30 April, 5.E.6; 19 February, 7.E.6; *13.Rich.2,
cap. 2; and 11 May, 5.E.6; and 20 October, 1&2.P&M;[4] and
5 July, the same.*
[fo. 15r]
Temporall: as matters of title, and possessions of lands.
17 February, 11.H.7; [[15 February]][5] 12.H.7; 17 February, [[the
same]]; 30 November, 14.H.7, 2 May, the same; and 9 May, the
same; and 17 August, the same; [[and]] *9* November, 18.H.7;
15 November, 19.H.7; and 16 December, 2.H.8; 15 May, 7.H.8;
1 July, 8.H.8; 27 May, 9.H.8; 9 November, 15.H.8; 6 July,
31.H.8; *37.E.3, cap. 18.*
Matters of title onely.
28 November, 3.H.8; 10 and 13 November, 8.H.8; [[23 May,
11.H.8]];[6] 13 November, 13.H.8; 9 December, 17.H.8; [[18 May,
26.H.8]];[7] 2 June, 30.H.8; 15 May and 16 November, 37.H.8;
14 July, 38.H.8;[8] [[and 28 October, 4.E.6;[9] *7* July, 6.E.6]]; 10
May, 7.E.6;[10] *Assisarum librarum* 20, *assisa.* 14, and 20.E.3,
Fitzherbert, *tit.* verdict, 32.*
Matters of possession onely.
18 October, 11.H.8;[11] 5 February, the same; 15 February, 12.H.8;
8 November, 13.H.8; 25 May, 28.H.8; 25 October, 31.H.8;
22 December, 37.H.8; and 20 April, 2.E.6; 18 May, 4.E.6;
31 May, 2.Eliz.
Matters of annuities, estents, debt with specialities and without
[[deteining of evidences, rent, assurance of lands, etc.]]

[1] In those cases where Caesar has reconsidered a deletion he has entered the notation *stet* in the margin. I have placed the notation before the deletion which should be read as an integral part of the text.
[2] There is no corresponding entry in the text.   [3] 4 July should read 4 June.
[4] There is no corresponding entry in the text.
[5] This entry concerns itself with title and possession but it is also concerned with enclosures.
[6] Caesar has noted in the margin of the text that this cause was in fact for a lease.
[7] This cause was for title to a messuage. There seems to be no reason for this deletion.
[8] This cause was not for title but for the value of the land.
[9] 28 October should read 24 October. No apparent reason for its deletion.
[10] The cause concerns titles to certain tenements.
[11] There is no corresponding entry in the text.

[24 October, 13.H.8];¹ *3 March, 12.H.7; 14 November, 15.H.7;²
and 3 June, the same*; 18 May, 22.H.8; 30 November, 27.H.8;
29 May, 33.H.8; 6 May, 34.H.8; 30 April, 37.H.8; and 8 July,
3.E.6; 30 May, 6.E.6; 8 February, 7.E.6; 13 May, 2.Eliz.; *21
June, 16.H.7.*

[fo. 15v]

Matters of contracts, villainage, water courses, and covenants,
and high wayes. 10 February, 8.H.8; 24 November, 10.H.8;
[13 February, 11.H.8];³ 6 November, 26.H.8; 25 June, 36.H.8;
25 November, the same; 27 November, 37.H.8; *stet* [6 June,⁴
38.H.8 and]; 31 January, 2.E.6; 11 February, 4.E.6. *17.R.2,
cap. 6. and 13.E.4, fol. 9.*

Matters of dower, joynture; [and contracts for marriages.]
[15 March, 11.H.7;⁵ 14 November],⁶ 14.H.7; 24 February, [the
same]; 16 February, 24.H.8 *and 26 November, 4.Eliz.*

Matters of wilfull escape.

23 May, 4&5.P&M; 20 October, 5&6.P&M.

Forfeitures to the King by recognizance, or otherwise. 9 November,
11.H.7; 5 March, 13.H.7; 26 February, 19.H.7; 14 October,
22.H.7; and 4 *June* 38.H.8; and 4 February, 2.E.6; and 12 May,
the same;⁷ *Fitzherbert *Natura Brevium*, 233 A, in brief *de
ideota inquirendo* and 46.E.3, forfeiture, 18 Fitzherbert *abridgement.*

Riots, and routs, forgerie, and perjurie.

9 February, 13.H.7; 23 February, 14.H.7;⁸ 16 November, 16.H.7;
6 December, 18.H.7; and 15 May, 14.H.8; 10 November, 33.H.8;
*32.H.8, cap. 9 in the abridgement of statute title maintenance,
membrane 7, Whitehall there called one of the Kings Courts,
likewise 5.Eliz. c. 9.*

Causes tried heere, whereas the defendant dwelt in the Marches
of Wales, or in the North.

[27 April]* 1May *2&3.P&M; [and] *9* November, 3&4.P&M.

---

¹ A matter of enforcing the payment of rent. Caesar struck out this category.
² 14 November should read 24 November.
³ A cause for delapidations. See fo. 13r *infra*, 'causes of delapidations'.
⁴ A cause to recover goods and chattels seized by the Lord of the manor.
⁵ A cause which was returned to common law as it was first raised there, concerning 'certain title and right of dowry'.
⁶ A cause concerning joynture but the issue turned on disseisin from the
joynture.
⁷ This cause concerns the restitution of goods improperly seized.
⁸ There is an action for riot on 6 February of this year.

Sometimes causes referred to the Judges of the law, and their advise required. 10 June, 7.H.8, 14 March, 10.H.8; 11 November, 13.H.8;[1] 4 February, 17.H.8;[1] and 27 October; 6.E.6 and 10 February, 2&3.P&M; *and 28 [[Octob]] November 16 Elizabeth.*

[fo. 13r]

*Causes of dilapidations

*22 May, 3.E.6, fol. 85; and 15 February, 12.H.8, fol. 93; and 13 February, 11.H.8, fol. 18; and 8 July, 38.H.8.

*Rents issueing out of landes due to private men or places as annuities

*21 May, 2.Eliz.; and 9 May, 18.Eliz.; and 28 October, 22.Eliz.; and 3 November, 15.H.7,[2] fol. 64; and 21 June, 16.H.7; and 18 August, 18.H.7; and 12 October, 2.H.8; and 10 June, 8.H.8; and 27 May, 9.H.8; and 20 June, 13.H.8; and ii[3] July; and and [*sic*] 28 October, the same; and 28 November, 26.H.8.

*Touching chatels or goods delivered in trust and the trust broken or denied

*10 December, 10.H.7; and 27 January, 18.H.7; and 13 December, 20.H.7; and 20 July, 9.H.8; and 26 May, 11.H.8; and 21 November, 34.H.8; and 6 February, 4.E.6; and 10 February, 6.E.6; and 6 February, 7.E.6; and 1 February, 1&2.P&M.

*Touching landes assigned in trust and the trust broken, etc.

*25 May, 1&2.P&M; and 4 February, 25.H.8; and 28 November, 1 Mary.

*Copyholds, fines and common

*24 April, 13.H.8; and 29 July, 23.H.8; and 5 July, 31.H.8; and 13 February, 31.H.8; and 4 February, 32.H.8; and 6 May, 34.H.8; and 13 May, 34.H.8; and 12 May, 37.H.8; and 1 June, 38.H.8; and 8 February, 1.E.6; and 27 January, 2.E.6; and 8 February, 4.E.6; and 13 February, 5.E.6;[4] and 27 November, 4.E.6; and 16 February, 5.E.6; and 20 November, 21.H.8.

[fo. 13v]

*Decrees executed against the executors or administrators of the parties condemned

---

[1] Advice here is given by the King's Counsel learned in the law.
[2] This entry does not appear in Caesar's collection.
[3] Caesar copied this entry from his holographic text notes. In the text the date is
[4] 11 July not ii July.
This entry is simply a citation without any indication of the matter under consideration.

*2 February, 33.Eliz.[1]

*Damages and costes of sutes given to the defendant before sentence

*5 February, 13.H.7; and 5 June, 1.Eliz.

*Damages and costs of sute given to the plaintiff before sentence

*10 December, 18.H.7; and 24 November, 4&5.P&M; and 11 November, 1.Eliz.; and 22 November, 2.Eliz.

*Contempts punnished by imprisonment

*4 April, 13.H.7; and 16 May, 2&3.P&M; and 27 April, 1.Eliz.; and 19 May; 3.Eliz.; and 18 November, 4.Eliz.; and 24 January, 4.Eliz.; and 30 January, the same; and 1 June, the same; and 4 July, 13.Eliz.; and 9 October, 14.Eliz.; and 22 May, 16.Eliz.; and 18 November, 17.Eliz.; and 23 April, the same; and 3 May, 20.Eliz.; and 20 October, 22.Eliz.; and 27 April, 25.Eliz.; and 11 November, 26.Eliz; and 19 November, 27.Eliz; and 12 May, 13.H.8; and 23 November, 1&2.P&M.

[fo. 14r]

*An executor or administrator sued for money, chatels or goods delivered in trust to the testator or defunct

30 June, 21.H.8; and 20 May, 23.H.8.

*An executor of an executor-plaintiff for a debt due to the first testator

*12 February, 9.H.8.

*An executor sued for the debt of the first testator

*15 May, 30.H.8; and 1 December, 6.E.6; and 9 December, the same.

*To save the plaintiff harmeles from a bond or debt or ware bought, for which hee standeth bound as suretie or hath paid for the defendant or standeth in daunger

*5 July, 16.H.7; and 10 February, 11.H.8; and 18 May, 26.H.8; and 6 May, 34.H.8; and 15 June, 2.E.6; and 23 February, 7.E.6.

[fo. 14v]

*For rentes reserved uppon leases, or otherwise due out of land or tenements

*23 November, 24.H.7; and 20 October, 26.H.8; and 1 July, 33.H.8; and 20 November, the same; and 29 June, 38.H.8; and 28 June, 1.E.6;[2] and 9 May, 18.Eliz.; and 31 May, 20.Eliz.; and 28 October, 22.Eliz.

---

[1] The record kept by Caesar did not advance beyond 27 Elizabeth. There is no explanation other than error for this entry.

[2] This is a cause by the executor of an estate to recover a part of a debt which had

*For the tithes or glebe landes belonging to a parsonage or vicar-edge or prebend
*30 June, 7.H.8; and 27 June, 17.H.8; and 4 December, 20.H.8; and 28 November, 31.H.8; and 20 November, 38.H.8;[1] and 26 November, 1.E.6; and 1 June, 3.E.6, and 2 June, the same; and 30 November, 5.E.6; and 14 November, 6.E.6; and 22 November, the same; and 27 October, the same; and 24 June, 7.E.6; and 22 November, 1&2.P&M.

*For evidences, estrights, charters, patents or other wrightings concerning the plaintiffs right to landes or offices
*27 June, 9.H.8; and 3 July, 33.H.8; and 27 November, 11.H.7; and 31 January, 13.Eliz.; and 24 June, 14.Eliz.

[fo. 16r]

*For goods seized by the Lord of any manour or any officer as forfeited, etc.
*20 July, 9.H.8; and 18 November, 10.H.8; and 29 May, 33.H.8; and 6 June, 38.H.8.

*For goods violently carried away and deteyned
*20 July, 9.H.8; and 13 July, 11.H.8; and 29 July, 1.E.6.

*Causes of the Isles of Gernsey and Jersey heard and decreed in this Court
*16 February, 10.H.8; and 16 November, 37.H.8; and 25 October, 3&4.P&M.

*Matters of forgery and cosenage
*27 February, 10.H.8; and 28 June, 23.H.8; and 22 March, 24.H.8.

[fo. 16v]

*An executor sued for delivery of certain bonds of the plaintiff left by the testator uncancelled and yet discharged in his life time
*25 November, 31.H.8.[2]

*For a lease
*23 May, 11.H.8; and 28 November, 11.H.8; and 15 February, 12.H.8; and 1 May, 13.H.8; and 23 June, 17.H.8; and 15 February, 20.H.8; and 15 November, 30.H.8; and 4 February, the same; and 26 October, 31.H.8; and 6 November, the same; and 20 June, 32.H.8; and 10 February, the same; and 5 July, 33.H.8; and 30 June

---

previously been decreed for him. It does not appear to fit the category within which Caesar placed it.
[1] 20 November should be 26 November.
[2] There is no corresponding entry in the text.

36.H.8; and 1 June, 3.E.6; and 8 July, the same; and 23 November, 4.E.6.

*For the performance of an arbitrament
*25 May, 11.H.8; and 20 May, 3.E.6; and 6 February, 4.E.6; and 23 May, 5.E.6; and 6 November, 1.Mary; and 23 November, 4.E.6.

*For the perfourmance of covenants and promises specified in writing or without
*10 November, 22.H.8; and 5 July, 30.H.8; and 23 November, 31.H.8; and 11 February, 33.H.8; and 29 November, 1&2.P&M;[1] and 28 November, the same; and 31 October, 1.Mary; and 27 May, 2.Eliz.

[fo. 17r]
*For a mill, a mildam and a way
*12 February, 24.H.8; and 4 November; 25.H.8; and 23 November, 31.H.8; and 25 May, 33.H.8; and 28 June, 36.H.8; and 21 November, 1&2.P&M.

*For landes or goods or money graunted in mariage
*26 June, 25.H.8; and 4 June, 38.H.8; and 8 February, 6.E.6.

*For payment of the kings tenthes, fifteenths or subsidies
*5 February, 30.H.8.

*For money of debt due uppon accoumpt, or received by the defendant to the plaintiffs use
*1 May, 13.H.8; and 1 May, the same; and 4 May, 2.E.6; and 4 June, 25.Eliz.

*For a petition of landes or devision of money
*5 November, 36.H.8; and 14 May, 2.E.6.

[fo. 17v]
*For recompence of injuries and blowes given or done by the defendant to the plaintiff
*4 May, 13.H.8; and 10 May, 14.H.8; and 20 June, 2.E.6;[2] and 24 November, 1&2.P&M;[3] and 7 November, 1.Eliz.[4]

*Attachments graunted for wants of apparance
*12 February, 12.H.7;[5] and 17 November, 14.H.7; and 6 July, 15.H.7; and 30 May, 14.H.8; and 18 November, 11.Eliz.; and 9 May, the same.

[1] Caesar changed this date to 30 November in the text.
[2] An action for false and wrongful imprisonment.   [3] An action for slander.
[4] An action for injuries done to plaintiff in execution of a Yeoman Cutter's place.
[5] There is no entry under this date.

*That the judges of this court may take bondes and recognizances for apparances to bee made, performance of orders, not to sue at common lawe, good behaviour and the like

*26 April, 12.H.7; and 22 November, 21.H.7; and 17 December, 10.H.8; and 16 May, 13.H.8; and 13 June, the same; and 18 June, the same; and 15 October, the same; and 26 April, 21.H.8; and 11 June, the same; and 18 November, 22.H.8; and 8 February, the same; and 27 June, 24.H.8; and 19 November, the same; and 8 July, 25.H.8; and 24 November, 26.H.8; and 1 April, 7.E.6; and 20 October, 21.Eliz.; and 30 January, 22.Eliz.

*Sometimes fines imposed by the Judges of this Court

*9 February, 13.H.7; and 13 May, 2.Eliz.

[fo. 18r]

The maner of proceeding in the sayd Court:

1. First by Privyseale, letter missive, or injunction, or messenger or bond.
2. Second by attachment.
3. Third by proclamation of Rebellion.
4. Fourth by commission of Rebellion.
5. Fift by Sergeant at armes.

11 November, 11.H.7; 14 December, the same; 10 February, 12.H.7; 21 February, the same; 14 April, the same; 4 February, 17.H.7; and 30 May, 14.H.8; and 6 April, 7.E.6; *and 6 July, 15.H.7.

Apparances by vertue of the Privie Seale. *vide bundellum brevium Regis de Anno 35 Henry 6 in the Tower, where bee divers returnes of Privy Seal to appeare before the king and his Councel in private causes betwene partie and partie.* [6 July, 15.H.7];[1] 5 July, 16.H.7; 16 November, 18.H.7; 15 July, 19.H.7; 21 June, 20.H.7; 29 March, 21.H.7; 2 June, the same; 15 October, 22.H.7; 27 January, the same 21 April, the same; 23 October, 23.H.7; [27 November, 23.H.7]; 19 May, the same; and 4 November, 3.H.8; 6 November, the same; 20 January, the same; and 4 March, 6.H.8; 20 October, 7.H.8; 15 June, 9.H.8; 16 October, 12.H.8; 22 April, 14.H.8; 4 July, 24.H.8; 23 January, 25.H.8; 22 June, 33.H.8.

Apparances by bond, or letter missive [in the Starre chamber or elsewhere], or the Kings signet.

---

[1] This action concerns itself with an appearance by writ of Privy Seal and there seems to be no reason for Caesar's having stricken it.

15 August, 9.H.7; 26 April, 12.H.7; 6 March, 16.H.7; 3 November,
21.H.7; and 30 October, 2.H.8; 8 July, 10.H.8; 18 November,
the same; 13 October, 11.H.8; 17 October, the same; 12 November
12.H.8; ⟦28 January, the same;¹ and 10 May, 16.H.8⟧.²
[fo. 18v]
Apparances by messenger, either pursuivant, or Sergeant at
Armes
1 June, 14.H.7; 20 May, 18.H.7; 7 June, 19.H.7; 12 June, the
same; and 1 May, 13.H.8; 28 June, 31.H.8; and 28 April, 1.Mary;
18 June, 2&3.P&M.
Apparances being so enjoined by Commissioners.
3 June, 12.H.7; 18 October, 18.H.7; ⟦24 October, 23.H.7; 18
February, the same⟧; and 16 October, 3.H.8; 4 November,
7.H.8; 11 May, 11.H.8; 5 July, the same; 4 November, the same;
23 January, 12.H.8; 26 October, 14.H.8; 5 February, the same;
and 10 October, 34.H.8; and 26 January, 1.Mary; 27 April,
1.Mary.³
Possession of landes given for contempt in not appearance: as
17 February, 12.H.7; 16 January, 4.E.6; ⟦8 June, 2&3.P&M⟧;⁴
27 January, 4&5.P&M; and 19 October, 1.Eliz.; and 5 February,
2.Eliz.; and 2 May;⁵ 10 May; and 16 November, the same.
That the party defendant attend *de die in diem* on the Councell,
till he have made his aunswere to the Plaintifs bill, and be licenced
to depart upon caution *de judicio sisti et iudicato solvendo*, and
constitution of his Atturney and Counsell by name.
3 March, 12.H.7; 23 February, 14.H.7; 9 May, 14.H.7; and
7 December, 17.H.7; 13 April; 29 June; and 2 July, 17.H.7;
31 October; and 4 November, 18.H.7; 29 November, 21.H.7;
and 9 May, 4.H.8; 20; and 22 June, 9.H.8; 9 February, 9.H.8;
24 June, 10.H.8; 31 January, the same; and 10 May, 11.H.8;
28 January, the same; ⟦H.8, 21 May, 14.H.8⟧; 2 July, the same;
12 June, 17.H.8; 21 June, 22.H.8; and 7 November, 6.E.6; and
9 February, 3&4.P&M; *and 17 November, 25.H.8.
[fo. 21r]
Sometimes answeres put into the Court by the Gardian of an

---

¹ This is an appearance by a letter missive and there is no apparent reason for
Caesar's having stricken it.
² This is a recognizance.
³ 27 April, 1 Mary should read 25 April, 1 Mary.
⁴ An affidavit for contempt.
⁵ There is no entry for this date.

Infant: *which gardians have bene usually appointed by this Court and allowed theire disbursements.*

24 November, 4&5.P&M; *17 April, 15.Eliz.; and 22 June, 16.Eliz.

Sometimes answeres taken by Commission, upon othe made, that the party for olde age or infirmity can not appeare: as ⟦13 November, 11.H.7;[1] and 19 October, 1.H.8;[2] 29 January, 11.H.8;[3] 25 June, 14.H.8⟧; 26 June, 30.H.8; and 7 November, 5&6.P&M; and 10 October, 1.Eliz.

Sometimes answeres of the Defendant respited, till the plaintife have payde charges given against him by a former decree: as 8 November, 2&3.P&M.

That both parties, or the one of them sometimes commaunded to bring into the Court, all their Evidences, writings, miniments, Bindes, etc. concerning the cause.

6 September, 11.H.7; 15 December, the same; 12 April, 14.H.7; 14 February, 17.H.7; 30 May, the same; 10 December, 18.H.7; and 10 February, 29.H.8.

Sometimes both the plaintife and defendant; sometimes but one of them bound to the peace for himselfe, and his men ⟦as⟧ *and committed to prison till they find sureties or put in bond to that purpose.*

*10 February, 12.H.7; 19 April, 12.H.7; *stet* ⟦and 26 April, 21.H.8⟧[4] *and 4 April, 13.H.7;[5] and 5 June, 8.Eliz.[6]

[fo. 21v]

Injunctions granted to bar the defendant from suing the plaintife at the common law, and to stay the sute at the common law, before commenced, and not to arrest the body of the plaintife till further order be taken by the Kings Councell: as

*13 November, 11.H.7; 5 May, 12.H.7; 7 July, 16.H.7; 27 March; and 21 June, 18.H.7; and 24 May, 19.H.7; 6; and 7 May, 22.H.7; 28 October; and 18 November, 23.H.7; and 10 June, 8.H.8; 4 July, the same; 12 May, 13.H.8; 18 July, 14.H.8; 8 February, 22.H.8; 19 November, 24.H.8; and 13 February; 2.E.6; 28

---

[1] This was taken before Council rather than by a Commission.

[2] This was a proxy appearing because of the litigant's infirmity.

[3] Council in this action allowed another to appear for an infirm man.

[4] Contained within the recognizance was the party's promise that neither he nor his servants would kill the King's deer.

[5] This entry refers only to finding personal sureties and does not concern itself with the conduct of others.

[6] A ship's master bound herein not to molest the plaintiff's friends at sea.

November, 6.E.6; and 17 October, 2&3.P&M; 17 November, the same; 10 February; and 6 May, the same; and 27 November, 3&4.P&M; 19 May, the same; 19 November, 4&5.P&M; and 24 November, the same; and 15 February, the same.
Injunctions not to fell wood, etc.
7; 23; and 25 November, 2&3.P&M; and 5 June, 1.Eliz.
That the execution of [a] *an order or* decree may be done either by imprisonment of the person disobeying, being partie, or claiming under the party, or by levie of the sum adjudged upon his lands: as
stet [4 April, 13.H.7];[1] 10 June, 17.H.7; 12 November, 4.E.6; 1 April, 7.E.6; and 18 June, 1&2.P&M; and 16 May, 2&3.P&M; and 27 April, 1.Eliz.; 19 May, 3.Eliz.; 18 November, 4.Eliz.; and *5.E.6 in the booke of presidents and 11 Eliz., *ibid.*; and 27 January, 10.Eliz. and 4 June, 22.Eliz. and 1&2.P&M in the olde book of'presidents and 10 Eliz. *ibidem.*
[fo. 19r]
*Possession etc. sometimes directed for the plaintiff in execution of a judgement at common lawe
*9 November, 18.H.7; and 26 June, 16.Eliz.
*Sometimes letters sent to Stewards of Courts to send up theire rolles of Court
*8 February, *8.H.7; and 7 November, 2&3.P&M.
*Commissions awarded to the Shriefe or Justices of the Peace next adjoyning to put the plaintiff in possession of the thing demaunded
*1 July, 8.H.8; and 5 February, 11.H.8; and 17 February, 12.H.7; and 8 November, 13.H.8; and 5.E.6, p. 150 in my booke[2] and fol. 71 in the olde booke of presidents.
*The wife plaintiff against her husband for maintenance
*25 November, 34.H.8; and 21 February, 35.H.8; and 22 June, 7.E.6.
[fo. 19v]
*Triall in a county indifferent
*County Palatine causes heard here or marches of Wales, or councel in the North or Cinque Portes
*9 November, 3&4.P&M; and 10 November, the same year; and 25 January, the same year.

---

[1] A decree concerning an imprisonment pending making good sureties.
[2] The page cited is in fact that folio number from the Order and Decree book.

*County Palatine causes remitted thether or marches of Wales or Councel in the North, or Cinque Portes
*13 November, 11.H.7; and 28 April, 7.H.8; and 7 May, 1.Mary; and 28 May, 1.Mary; and 17; and 18 June, 2.Eliz.; and 12 November, the same year.
[fo. 20r]
*Sometimes Judges of the common lawe required by the Judges of this Court to assist them with theire advise
*14 March, 10.H.8; and 28 November, 16.Eliz.
*Judges of this Court plaintiff or defendant in the same
*17 October, 38.H.8.
*The husband forced to pay costs and damages wherein the wife is condemned
[fo. 22r]
*Damages and costes given to the defendant after sentence
*18 November, 31.H.8; and 23.H.8, c. 15; and 17.R.2, c. 6; and 1 February, 7.E.6; and 10 May, 7.E.6; and 15 May, the same; and 16 October, 1&2.P&M; and 18 April, 9.Eliz.; and 9 February, 2.E.6.
*Damages and costes given to the plaintiff after sentence
*10 February, 1&2.P&M; and 27 May, 9.H.8; and 3 March, 34.H.8; and 25 June, 36.H.8; and 20 April, 2.E.6; and 23 November, the same; and 3 March, 12.H.7; and 26 October, 31.H.8; and 20 June, 2.E.6; and 8 February, 4.E.6; and 11 February, 6.E.6; and 14 November, the same; and 27 October, the same; and 27 February, 7.E.6;[1] and 1 February, 1&2.P&M.
*Injunctions graunted to stay the sutes at common lawe uppon boindes or specialities for debt
*4 July, 8.H.8; and 18 July, 14.H.8; and 13 February, 2.E.6; and 8 May, 5.Eliz.; and 15 May, 21.Eliz.
*Injunctions graunted to stay the sutes at common lawe uppon bondes for performance of covenants
*28 November, 6.E.6.
[fo. 22v]
*Injunctions to stay the sutes at common lawe uppon assumpsits for leases or the like
*25 November, 8.H.8.
* Injunctions to stay the sutes at common lawe uppon title of land

---

[1] This date is incorrect although on 23 February of the same year there is a case that would apply.

*15 November, 19.H.7; and 10 June, 8.H.8; and 14 October, 3.Eliz.; and 2 May, 20.Eliz.

*Injunctions to stay the sutes at common lawe uppon actions of the case, of trespass, debt, or the like

*⟦10 February, 1&2.P&M;[1] and 13 November⟧; 19 November, 4&5.P&M;[2] and 13 October, 10.Eliz.; and 1 May, 14.Eliz.

[fo. 23r]

*Universities causes and schollers called to the Kings Counsell and Proceedings in the universities stayed

*18 November, 11.H.7; and 27 October, 3.H.8; and 13 July, 24.H.8;[3] and 22 June, 33.H.6; and 9 June, 2.E.6.

*Injunctions to the defendant not to arrest sue or impleade the plaintiff in any other court during the dependency of his sute here

*24 May, 19.H.7; and 6 May, 22.H.7; and 27 May, 9.H.8; and 15 February, 4&5.P&M; and 20 October, 1.Eliz.; and 25 October, the same; and 16 October, 2.Eliz.

*Matters of wardship

*15 December, 11.H.7; and 10 November, 1.Mary.

[fo. 23v]

*Injunctions to stay the sutes at the common lawe after judgement there obteined

*23 November, 1&2.P&M; ⟦and 4 July, 8.H.8⟧; and 19 November, 4&5.P&M; and 20 October; and 23 October, 3.Eliz.; and 30 January, 4.Eliz.; and 26 November, 16.Eliz.; and 9 May, 21.Eliz.; and 17 June, 25.Eliz.; and 14 May, 28.Eliz.[4]

*Injunctions to stay the sute at the common lawe till answere to the bill in this Court made, etc.

*27 March, 18.H.7; and 12 May, 13.H.8; and 13 October, 10.Eliz.; and 23 June, 11.Eliz.; and 15 May, 21 May; and 25 October, 25.Eliz.

*Injunctions graunted or causes held for avoyding multiplicity of sutes

*Causes of reconvention

---

[1] This is properly a decree rather than an injunction.

[2] The reference in the text under this date is to a stayed execution of a common law judgment rather than a stayed action.

[3] There are two entries under the date 13 July, 24.H.8 and neither of them deal with University causes nor scholars.

[4] There are no entries after 27 Eliz., but there is an entry 14 May, 26.Eliz. which is appropriate to this heading.

*Injunctions to stay the sutes at the common lawe against such as are imployed in the Kings service at home or abroad

*Injunctions to stay [sureties] sutes against the sureties of the imployed in publick service

[fo. 10r]

*That Counsell, which since 33.H.8 hath bene called commonly the Kings Privy Counsell, in former times hath bene 1. sometimes called the Kings Counsell without anie other title, as: 25.E.3 [Stat. 5] cap. 4; and 42.E.3, cap. 3; and 17.Ric.2, cap. 6;[1] and 28.H.8, cap. 16; and 11.H.6, cap. 11; Westminster 2, cap. 49 namely 13.E.1; and abridgement of statutes, titulus Champetrie, sect 3; Gilbert Rowbey, Clerk of the Kings Counsell, 20.&21.E.1; and 13.Ric.2, [Stat. 1] cap. 2[2] in question betwene other Jurisdictions the kings Counsell the Judge; and 4.H.6, cap. 5; and the Statute of Exeter, 14.E.1; and 10.H.6, cap. 3; and 37.E.3, cap. 15; and 9.E.3 [Stat. 2] cap. 7; and 1.H.7, cap. 7; and 31.E.3, stat. 2, cap. 2; and *articuli super chartas*, 28.E.1, cap. 20; and 2.&3. P&M, cap. 2; and 20.E.3, cap. 1; and 3; and 12.Ric.2, cap. 10; and 2.H.5, cap. 1, stat. 2; and 1.H.6, cap. 1; and 12.Ric.2, cap. 11; and 8.H.6, cap. 27; and 31.H.8, cap. 8; and 38.E.3, cap. 1,2, and 4, stat 2; and 3.Ric.2, cap. 3; and 13.Ric.2, stat 2, cap. 3; and 16.Ric.2, cap. 5;[3] and 28.E.1, *articuli super chartas* 2; and 13.E.1, statute of merchants; and 8.Ric.2, cap. 4; and 21.H.8, cap. 13;[4] and 13.H.4, cap. 7;[5] and 2.H.5, [Stat. 1] cap. 8; and 32.H.8, cap. 14; and statute *de finibus Levatis*, 27.E.1; and the *Abridgement of the Statutes*, *titulus* Sherifs, sect. 5; and 33.H.8, cap. 20; and 5[&6]E.6, cap. 11; and 13.H.8,[6] cap. 12, the Kings Graces Counsell; and cap. 23; and 4.H.4, cap. 30; and 11.E.3, cap. 1; and 31.E.3, [Stat. 1] cap. 9; and 4&5.P&M, [cap. 8] the Kings and Queens Council in the Starchamber.

*2. Sometimes called the kings Honorable Counsell, as 25.H.8, cap. 21; and 19.H.7, cap. 18, the Lords of the kings Honorable Counsell in the Starchamber at Westminster. Adde 23.Eliz., cap. 6, the Queens Honorable Privy Council.

[fo. 10v]

*3. Sometimes called the kings most honorable Counsell, as 22.H.8, cap. 14; and 24.H.8, cap. 13; and 33.H.8, cap. 1; and 3.H.7, cap.

---

[1] See *infra*, fo. 174v. [2] See *infra*, fo. 174v.
[3] See *infra*, fo. 174v. [4] See *supra*, fo. 8v and accompanying note.
[5] See *infra*, fo. 178r. [6] There was no parliament in 13.H.8.

1;[1] and 21.H.8, cap. 20;[2] and 2.[&3].E.6, cap. 6; and 33.H.8, cap. 9; and 27.H.8, cap. 20; and 21; and 25.H.8, cap. 2; and 27.H.8, cap. 26; and 31.H.8, cap. 10, the kings most honorable Council. *4. Sometimes called the kings Counsell Attendant on his person, as 33.H.8, cap. 21; and 33.H.8, cap. 39. The kings most honorable Counsell daily attendant on his person; and 33.H.8, cap. 10, the kings Privy Counsell Attendant on his person. Adde 5.Eliz., cap. 4, the Queens Privy Counsell attendant on her person.[3] I find likewise a Counsell, called the Kings great Counsell, as 37.E.3, cap. 18;[4] and 28.E.3, cap. 13, the Great Counsell; and Westminster 2, cap. 22, namely 13.E.1, the king and all his Counsell.[5]

*Reasons to prove that the Court of Whitehall or Requests is a member and parcell of the kings most honorable Counsell attendant on his person.

1. The Masters of Requests, Judges of this Court, are sworne of the Kings Privy or Small Council, as appeareth by the oath following in this booke, which my selfe and my predecessors in this place have taken.

2. The billes here bee directed to the king himselfe.

3. The apparances here are before the king and his Counsell.

4. The proces here is sealed with the Seal proper [for] to the Kings Counsell.

5. The Judges here alwaies called in the actes of this Court, the kings Counsell, or the kings honorable Counsell, or the kings most honorable Counsell; sometimes with this addition, in his Court of Requests or Whitehall.

6. The Register or Clerk here hath alwaies bene a Clerk of the Privy Seal and of the Counsell.

7. The Yere Bookes of 13.E.4, fol. 9[6] and 2.Ric.3, fol. 2 [fo. 11r] touching relieving of strangers robbed and all the statutes giving jurisdiction to the kings most honorable Counsell in private causes, executed by the Judges of this Court, as appeareth by the actes thereof.

8. No court (under the highest court of Parliament) can re-examine a cause decreed in Chauncery, or discharge a prisoner committed from thence, saving onely the Kings Counsell: but

---

[1] See *infra*, fo. 178r.   [2] See *infra*, fo. 178v.
[3] There is no such reference to Privy Council within this statute.
[4] See *infra*, fo. 174v.
[5] There is no mention of Council within this statute.   [6] See *infra*, fo. 175r.

this Court hath done it, as appeareth 1.Edw.6, in the record thereof;[1] therefore namely 42 *Liber Assisarum, placitum* 5.[2]

9. No Court (under the highest Court of Parliament) hath accustomed to cause noblemen to attend on it *de die in diem* and not to depart without licence, as namely Dukes, Erles, Barons and the like, saving onely the kings Counsell: but this Court hath alwaies accustomed the same. 1 May, 14.H.7; and 28 May, 21.H.7; and 17 November, 25.H.8; and 24 January, 5.E.6; and 13 April, 17.H.7; and 9 February, 9.H.8; and 10 May, 11.H.8; and 21 June, 20.H.7: The Earl of Essex appeared and had to appear from day to day until, etc.

10. This Court is one of the kings Courts, 32.H.8, cap. 9; and 5.Eliz., cap. 9, and standeth onely by prescription of the kings Counsell, as appeareth by the actes of this Court and the common lawe, it having neither commission under the Greate Seale, or act of Parliament to establish it otherwise: but the kings Council prescribeth onely for it selfe, thus.

11. King Edw. 1 in his booke of lawes (commonly called Britton) reserveth a jurisdiction to himselfe and his Counsell above all the Jurisdictions in his realme, Britton, fol. 1; and Bracton, *de rei divisio*, cap. 2, mem 7; and in *tractatus de actionibus*, cap. 9 and 10. But every supreme Jurisdiction conteineth in it power for decision of causes publick, mixt and private and the Kings Counsell hath not elswhere then in this Court dealt judicially in private causes; thus this court the kings [court] Counsell.

[fo. 11v]

12. Some Judges of this Court have from time to time till 1 Eliz. sat, *alternis vicibus*, as Judges in the Starchamber, wher none may sit as Judges but such as bee of the kings most Honorable Counsell, saving onely the 2 Justices named in the statute of 3.H.7, cap. 1 and 21.H.8, cap. 20. The former is proved by the recordes of both Courts, the Starchamber and Requests.

13. The Judges of this Court (nowe commonly since 4.E.6 called Masters of Requests) were alwaies numbered and provided for in the bookes of the kings howshold as the kings Counsell, without anie distinction [of] or difference or more Counsels then one, as may appeare by the Black Booke of the said howshold and by the titles given unto them, who then had the care to take and answere the requests and supplications

[1] See *infra*, fo. 122r *sub dat*. 27 November, 1.E.6.   [2] See *infra*, fo. 177v.

made unto the king; 31 January, 27.H.8; and 28 June, 33.H.8; and 6 November, the same.

14. Robert Dacres, Esquire, in the year 1543, 35.H.8 used this title ensueng, as appeareth under his owne hand (which I have seene) in the beginning of a booke: Sum Roberti Dacres armigeri, Serenissimo H.8. dei gratia Anglie, Franciae et Hiberniae Regi á Secretioribus Consiliis, necnon à tabellis suplicatoriis. Mr. Dacres of Cheston in Hartfordshire hath that booke.

15. No mans hand but a Counselors can commaund the kings Privy Seal as appeareth by the auncient othe of the Clerks of the Privy Seal. But every of the Judges of this Court his hand commaundeth the said Privy Seal, thus.

16. That Counsell, which since 33.H.8 hath bene called commonly the kings Privy Council, was alwaies heretofore called the kings Council without any other title, or els entitled the kings Honorable or most Honorable Council with this further title sometimes, daily attendant on his person, as appeareth by the statute imprinted: but the kings Council in Whitehall hath all those titles, as appeareth by the recordes of that Court, in the times of H.7, H.8, E.6, M.1 and Eliz., thus.

17. The ancient presidents and recordes of every court are the common lawe of the land for the warranting of like proceadings in that Court as appeareth at large by the case of the mines in Plowdens Commentaries, Michaelmas Term, 9&10. Eliz. but the recordes of Whitehall prove the Judges there the kings most Honorable Counsell, thus.

[fo. 3r]

*The names of such as have sat in the starchamber since the 9 yere of King Henry the 7 untill the 4 and 5 of Phillip and Mary.[1]

*9.H.7

Bishop of Exeter, Keeper of the Privy Seal[2]

Bishop of Rochester[3]

---

[1] One finds a number of such lists in Caesar's and Burghley's papers. See Leadam, 'Appendix to Introduction', in *Select Pleas*. The following notes are intended to be supplementary or corrective to Leadam's fuller notes to which the reader should also refer.

[2] The former Bishop of Exeter, Richard Fox, was translated to Bath and Wells 1492 and in July 1494 (9.H.7) he was translated to Durham. He was Keeper from 1487 until 1516.

[3] John Kendal.

Lord Prior of St. John's[1]
Lord Brook, Lord Steward of the Household[2]
William Hussey, Lord Chief Justice[3]
Sir Reginald Bray, Chancellor of the Duchy of Lancaster
Sir Richard Guilford[4]
Sir Thomas Lovel,[5] Treasurer of the Household
David Williams, Master of the Rolls[6]
Dr. Aynsworth[7]
Dean of the King's Chapel[8]
*10.H.7
Dr. Mayo[9]
Dr. Hatton[10]
John Morgan, gentleman[11]
Richard FitzJames, gentleman[12]
*11.H.7
Dr. Hoton[13]
*12.H.7
Lord President of the King's Council[14]
[fo. 3v]
*13.H.7
Bishop of London[15]
Dean of the King's Chapel[16]

---

[1] Thomas Savage.
[2] Robert, Lord Willoughby de Broke.
[3] L.C.J. of King's Bench.
[4] Personal advisor and friend to Henry VII.
[5] Lovell.
[6] David Williams became Master of the Rolls 26 February 1487 but was replaced by John Blyth in 1492. Blyth was in turn replaced by William Warham, 13 February 1494 (9.H.7).
[7] Henry Aynsworth, LL.D., the King's Clerk.   [8] Thomas Jane.
[9] King's Chaplain and an ambassador.
[10] Richard Hatton, King's Chaplain and an LL.D.
[11] There was a John Morgan, LL.D. It is peculiar, however, that his academic distinction was not used instead of his social distinction. There appears to have been another John Morgan about who we know nothing.
[12] Fellow of Merton College, Oxford and sometime Vice-Chancellor of the University prior to gaining a place in the household as Almoner and ecclesiastical dignity.
[13] This does not appear to be the same Hatton as above but it may be and there is no other LL.D. at the same time.
[14] See Walter Richardson, *Tudor Chamber Administration* (Baton Rouge, La., 1952) 19 n. 20 for a terse account of the ambiguity of this title and its earliest uses.
[15] Thomas Savage.   [16] Geoffrey Simeon.

Dr. Christopher Middleton, Judge of the High Court of the Admiralty of England[1]
Lord Prior of St. John's
*14.H.7
Bishop of London[2]
Bishop of Rochester[3]
*15.H.7
Bishop of Rochester, [Lord] President of the King's Council
G. Bergavenny, gentleman[4]
*21.H.7
Sir Robert Drury[5]
*20.H.8
Bishop of London[6]
Dr. Wolman[7]
Sir Thomas Nevil[8]
Abbot of Westminster[9]
Sir John Hussey[10]
Sir William Fitzwilliams[11]
Sir Roger Townesend[12]
[fo. 4r]
*29.H.8
Bishop of Chichester[13]
*33.H.8
John Tregonwell, gentleman, Judge of the High Court of the Admiralty of England

---

[1] Leadam provides an elaborate argument regarding the identification of the various Middletons. See *Select Cases in Requests*, cx, n. 6 and cxviii, n. 113.

[2] Thomas Savage.   [3] Richard FitzJames.

[4] George Neville, 3d. Baron Bergavenny. There is no apparent reason for Caesar's attaching the designation 'gentleman' to this name.

[5] Speaker of the House of Commons and a prominent barrister of Lincoln's Inn.

[6] Cuthbert Tunstall.

[7] Richard Wolman, Master of Requests, ordinary and *ex officio* member of Council, Dean of Wells.

[8] Brother to Abergavenny, Speaker of the House of Commons, councillor and member of the Household.

[9] John Islip.

[10] Eldest son of Sir William Hussey, became Baron Hussey of Sleaford, prominent in Household.

[11] This is probably FitzWilliams, Junior, later Earl of Southampton. It could have been FitzWilliams, Senior, as both sat in Council, held important Household posts and were often confused in contemporary records.

[12] Master of Requests appointed in 1529.   [13] Richard Sampson.

*6.E.6

Sir Nicholas Hare, Master of the Rolls[1]

Sir John Tregonwell

William Cooke, LL.D., Judge of the High Court of the Admiralty of England

*1.Mary

Sir Thomas White[2]

*3&4.P&M

John Boxal, Principal Secretary

*I find uppon serch that the persons above names have sat in the said court and so of record it appeareth.

William Mill

A copy of his certificate to mee. 3 March, 37.Eliz.

All and every of the aforenamed Judges in the Starchamber sat also *alternis vicibus* in the said yeres respectively in the kings Court at Whitehall or wheresoever the King helde his Counsell for the hearing of private causes betuene partie and partie as appeareth by the actes of the said Court.

[fo. 4v]

*Over and beesides the aforenamed theise following sat as Judges in the kings Court of Whitehall, as Counselors to the king.

Tempore H.7

The Bishop of Bath[3]

The Lord Dawbeney

Sir Andreue Dimock, knight[4]

Dr Warham[5]

Dr. Martyn[6]

William Grevile[7]

Robert Sherborne, gentleman[8]

---

[1] The entry is out of place as Hare did not become Master of the Rolls until 18 September, 1 Mary.

[2] Lord Mayor of London in 1553 and prominent supporter of the Queen. Defended the City against the rebellion in that year.

[3] While probably referring to Richard Fox it could also refer to Oliver King and Adriano de Castello.

[4] Solicitor-General, puisne Baron of Exchequer.

[5] Master of the Rolls, Bishop of London, Archbishop of Canterbury, Lord Chancellor.

[6] Diplomat, Household officer, Master in Chancery. Confused by Leadem with Richard Martin who was out of favour during Henry VII's reign.

[7] Serjeant and (in 1509) Justice of Common Pleas.

[8] Dean of St Paul's and later Bishop of St David's and then of Chichester.

Dr. Benbrike[1]
Charles Somerset, gentleman[2]
Dr. Nicks, Dean of Norwich[3]
Dean of York[4]
George Simeon, gentleman[5]
Edward Vaughan, gentleman[6]
Sir Robert Reade, knight, Chief Justice of Common Pleas
Viscount Wells[7]
Sir Richard Pole, knight[8]
John Wats, clerk[9]
The Erle of Kent[10]
Tempore H.8
Thomas Benbrike, Archbishop of York
John Veisie, Dean of the Chapel
John Gilbert, gentleman[11]
Dr. Rowland, Vicar of Croydon[12]
Dr. Lupton, Roger, Provost of Eaton[13]
Dr. Cromer[14]

[1] Dr Christopher Bainbridge ended his career under Henry VII as Archbishop of York and became a cardinal in 1511.
[2] Actually Sir Charles Somerset. He was a diplomat and naval officer who was to become the Earl of Worcester in 1514.
[3] Served as Dean of the Chapel Royal, before becoming Bishop of Norwich.
[4] There were several Deans of York during Henry VII's reign. Since we are dealing with the period after 1493, and because Bainbridge, who was one of the Deans, has already been mentioned by name, it would appear that either William Sheffield or Geoffrey Blythe was the Dean in question.
[5] This could be Geoffrey Simeon, Dean of the Chapel Royal.
[6] Treasurer of St Paul's and subsequently Bishop of St David's.
[7] One of the King's comrades from Bosworth. Married a Plantagenet but was principally a country figure and a soldier.
[8] A quite unimportant figure who was married to Margaret Plantagenet by Henry VII. His greatest significance was his being the father of Reginald Pole.
[9] No such clerk can be identified.   [10] Edmond Grey.
[11] An important Devonshire man if Leadam's identification is correct. If not there is no record of Gilbert.
[12] Dr. Rowland was Rowland Philips who became Vicar of Croydon in 1522.
[13] The 'Dr' is unexplained as he had but an LL.B. of Cambridge. He was the King's Chaplain in addition to the provostship and the clerkship of the Hanaper.
[14] While I am no more certain than is Leadam which of the several 'Cromers' this Dr Cromer was, I am amused by his exhaustive circumlocution which simply reveals his having missed the point regarding the nature of the relationship of Requests and Council. To exclude possible 'Cromers' because they were not of Privy Council makes no sense at all. And furthermore there are many who appear elsewhere in the list who are not to be found in Privy Council

Dr. St. Jermine[1]
The Bishop of St. Assaph[2]
The Bishop of Chichester[3]
Thomas Thirleby, gentleman[4]
Dr. Edmond Bonner[5]
Edward Carne[6]
Robert Southwell, gentleman[7]
Lord Prior of St. John's[8]
Dr. John Stokesley, the kings Almoner
Robert Dacres, gentleman, Privy Councillor
*Tempore E.6
The Bishop of Norwich[9]
Dr. William Mayo, Deane of Paules[10]
John Cocks, gentleman[11]
John Lucas, gentleman[12]
*Tempore Mariae
John Throgmorton, gentleman[13]
*Tempore Eliz.
Walter Haddon, LL.D.[14]
Thomas Seckford, gentleman[15]
The Bishop of Rochester, Lord Almoner[16]

(a term of difficult usage this early on) although no mention was made. In this particular instance perhaps George Cromer, Archbishop of Armagh, was the right man.

[1] Dr Christopher Saint-German.
[2] Either Dafydd ap Owain, Edmund Birkhead, Henry Standish or Robert Warton. Leadam confidently identifies the Bishop as Henry Standish but I do not know why.
[3] Either Robert Sherburne or Richard Sampson, although his prior service to the kind before consecration would favour Sampson.
[4] The future Bishop of Westminster.
[5] Bishop of London.
[6] Sir Edward Carne, D.C.L.
[7] Member of Middle Temple and a Master of Requests.
[8] Sir William Weston.
[9] Thomas Thirlbey, translated from Westminster.
[10] Dr William May.
[11] Leadam exhaustively explains why he believes this is Dr John Cockes, a prominent cleric.
[12] Member of Middle Temple and a Privy Councillor.
[13] Master of Requests and Justice of Chester.
[14] Regius Professor of Civil Law, Master of Requests and judge of the Prerogative Court.
[15] Barrister of Grey's Inn and commissioner for causes ecclesiastical.
[16] Either Edmond Gest, Edmond Freake or John Pierse. They were all the King's Almoner as well.

Thomas Wilson, LL.D.[1]
Valentine Dale, LL.D.[2]
Sir William Gerrard, knight[3]
David Leues, LL.D., Judge of the High Court of the Admiralty of England[4]
Rafe Rokeby, gentleman[5]
John Herbert, gentleman[6]
William Awbrey, LL.D.[7]
Julius Cesar, LL.D., Judge of the High Court of the Admiralty of England and knight
Roger Wilbraham, knight[8]
Daniel Dun, Doctor of Lawe and knight[9]
Christopher Perkins, Doctor of Lawe and knight[10]
[fo. 5r]
*It appeareth likewise by the signing of the billes for Privy Seal that theise following were Judges in this Court in the yeres ensueng respectively, over and beesides the abovenamed.
George Simeon in 21, 22, and 23.H.7 and 16 and 17.H.8.
William Atwater[11] and John Denton[12] and John Dalby[13] and Richard Sutton[14] and Edward Higgons[15] in 1, 2, 3, 4, and 5.H.8 [and 17 and 16.H.8]
Sir Thomas Lovel, Tresorer of the Howsehold, in 7.H.8.
Richard Rawlins, the Kings Almoner, in 8.H.8
Thomas Cheiney,[16] in 11.H.8
John Clerk, Dean of the Chapel, in 12.H.8 and 14.H.8
Thomas,[17] Bishop of London, 13.H.8
Richard,[18] Bishop of Rochester, Robert Sampson[19] and Thomas Hobby,[20] 18.H.8

[1] A Marian exile whom Elizabeth made a Master of Requests and eventually a secretary.
[2] A civilian and diplomat.   [3] Master of Requests.   [4] Master of Requests.
[5] Master of Requests.   [6] Master of Requests.
[7] Master of Requests.   [8] Master of Requests.
[9] Leadam gets completely befuddled by Dun's name. He believes it should be David although he contradicts his own idea elsewhere.
[10] Master of Requests.   [11] Bishop of London.   [12] Dean of Lichfield.
[13] Leadam thinks that this is Thomas Dalby, Archdeacon of Richmond, Yorks.
[14] Member of Council.   [15] LL.D.
[16] Treasurer of the Household to Henry VIII, Edward VI and Elizabeth.
[17] Thomas Savage was translated to York in 1501. Cuthbert Tunstall was, however, translated to London in 13.H.8 and may be the bishop that Caesar had in mind.   [18] The Bishop of Rochester in 18.H.8 was John Fisher.
[19] Richard Sampson, Bishop of Coventry and Lichfield.
[20] A diplomat and lawyer.

William Atwater,[1] 16 and 17.H.8

Sir William Suliard, knight[2]

[fo. 6v]

*1. Judges of other high Courtes plaintiff in this Court, as namely,

Sir Ambrose Cave, knight, Privy Councillor, and Chancellor of the Duchy, 19 May, 3.Eliz.

The Lord Robert Dudley, Privy Councillor, 13 [Eliz] November, 3.Eliz.

Sir John Bourne, knight, Privy Councillor and Principal Secretary, 24 November 2&[3].P&M

Sir James Croftes, knight, Privy Councillor and Controller of the Household, 31 January, 13.Eliz.

The Erle of Leicester, Privy Councillor, 13 May, 14.Eliz.

The Erle of Warwick, Privy Councillor, 24 June, 14.Eliz.

Roger Manhood, esquier, Judge of the Common Pleas, 1 May, 16.Eliz.

Thomas Wilson, LL.D., Privy Councillor and Principal Secretary, 31 May, 20.Eliz.

Sir Nicholas Hare, knight, Privy Councillor [17] and Master of the Requests, 17 October, 38.H.8.

King H. the 8, 6 June, 13.H.8

King H. the 8, 6 February, 31.H.8

King H. the 7, 5 March, 13.H.7

and in my time since the year 1590 the Archbishop of Canterbury, Privy Councillor and Justice Fenner, Justice of the Kings Bench and likewise the Lord Keaper and Master of the Rowles.

*2. Judges of other high Courtes defendant in this Court, as namely,

John Russell, knight, Lord Russell, Lord Privy Seal, 4 February, 1.E.6

The Erle of Shreusbury, Privy Councillor, 19 November, 20.Eliz.

Sir Humfrey Browne, knight, Justice of the Common Pleas, 26 November, 4.E.6

Sir Edward Marvyn, knight, Justice of the Kings Bench, 24 January, 5.E.6

Sir Ambrose Cave, knight, Privy Councillor and Chancellor of the Duchy, 9 May, 6.Eliz.

---

[1] Bishop of Lincoln who died in 1521. The dates quoted here are from four years later.

[2] A barrister of Lincoln's Inn.

Sir Richard Sackvile, knight, Privy Councillor and under-tresorer of the Exchequeur, 6 November, the same.

*3. That Noblemen, *videt*. Barons and of equall or higher degree have bene plaintiff in this Court, as namely,

The Lord Zouch, 4 July, fol. 186, 24.H.8

The Bishop of Chichester, 6 June, 29.H.8, fol. 102

The Lord Windsor, 30 January, 2.E.6, fol. 27

Sir William Huet, knight, Lord Mayor of the City of London, 4 May, fol. 185, 2.Eliz.

Edmond Gest, Bishop of Rochester, 26 November, 3.Eliz., fol. 232.

The Bishop of Norwich, 6 February, 4.Eliz., fol. 8.

The Lord Straunge, 19 November,[1] 9.Eliz., fol. 98.[2]

The Lord Grey, 25 October, 9.Eliz., fol. 263.

The Lord Wentworth, 26 January, 10.Eliz., fol. 311.

[fo. 7r]

Lord Viscount Bindon, 23 June, 11.Eliz. fol.[3]

Anne, Countesse of Sussex, 12 February, 14.Eliz., fol.

Gregory, Lord Dacres of the South, 1 May, 16.Eliz., fol. 499.

Philip, Erle of Surrey and Dame Anne his wife, 15 June, 16.Eliz., fol. 572.

Giles, Lord Poulet, 1 November, 18.Eliz., fol. 329.

Thomas, Lord Buckhurst, 9 May, 21.Eliz., fol. 225.

Henry, Erle of Huntington, 15 May, 21.Eliz., fol. 230.

*4. That noblemen, videt. Barons and of equall or higher degree have bene defendant in this Court, as namely,

Henry, Lord Clifford, 27 November, 11.H.7, fol.

The Lord Dalaware, 26 November, 14.H.7, fol.

The Lord Dacres of the South, 1 May, 14.H.7, fol.

The Duke of Buckingham, 28 May, 21.H.7, fol.

Silvester, Bishop of Worcester, 14 February, 23.H.7, fol.

William, Lord Sturton, 13 July, 11.H.8, fol.

The Bishop of Landaf, 17 November, 25.H.8, fol. 245.

The Lord of Rutland, 4 November, 30.H.8, fol. 5.

The Lady Margaret, Marques Dorcet, 12 February, 32.H.8, fol. 46.

The Archbishop of York, 26 November, 38.H.8, fol. 292.

Robert, Bishop of Carlisle, 6 February, 1.E.6, fol. 298.

Thomas, Lord Wentworth, 28 June, 1.E.6, fol. 9.

---

[1] 19 November should read 28 November.   [2] fol. 98 should read fol. 105.

[3] This and the following seven folio numbers were left blank in the MS.

The Lord Scroupe, 18 October, 1.E.6, fol. 9.

Thomas, Lord Wharton, 15 February, 1.Eliz., fol. 73.

The Lord Zouche, 10 October, 1.Eliz., fol. 128.

Henry, Lord Barkley, 18 October, 1.Eliz., fol. 130.

The Earle of Cumberland, 13 November, 3.Eliz., fol. 355.

Henry, Lord Aburgavenny, 14 October, 6.Eliz., fol. 284; and 28 November, 16.Eliz.

The Lord Willowghby, 22 October, 8.Eliz.,[1] fol. 108.

The Lord Hastings of Loughborough, 20 November, 9.Eliz., fol. 121.

[fo. 7v]

The Lord Latimer, 13 October, 10.Eliz., fol. 450.

William, Lord Willowghby, 8 May, 12.Eliz., fol. 111.

The Erle of Southampton, 14 November, 12.Eliz., fol. 161.

The Lord St. John, 6 February, 14.Eliz., fol. 13.

The Lord Marques of Winchester, 28 April, 14.Eliz., fol. 46.

Henry, Lord Aburgavenny, 12 November, 15.Eliz., fol. 366.

William West, Lord Delaware, 26 June, 16.Eliz., fol. 580.

Richard, Bishop of Chichester, 13 May, 17.Eliz., fol. 92.

Thomas, Lord Howard, Viscount Bindon, 12 February, 18.Eliz., fol. 194.

The Lord Cromwell, 9 February, 22.Eliz., fol. 362.

The Erle of Essex, 21 June, 20.H.7.

*5. This Court of Whitehall (so called 32.H.8, cap. 9 and 5.Eliz., cap. 9) was called Court of Requests,

28 November, 12.H.8, fol. 68; and 14 July, fol. 289, 14.H.8 and similarly in 20, 23 and 24.H.8 and in Michaelmas Term held at the town of St. Albans; a Court held by the kings Council called White Hall, 15 November, 35.H.8, and the Judges of the Starchamber, and of the Whitehall called the kings Honorable Counsell, 1 February, 37.H.8, fol. 260; and 1 June, 38.H.8, fol. 269; and the kings Honorable Counsell attendant uppon his person and commonly sitting in the kinges Majesties Court of Whitehall at Westminster, 29 July, 38.H.8, fol. 285. The kings most Honorable Court of Requests, 5 July, 6.E.6, fol. 44. The Queens most Honorable Counsell in her Court of Requests, or, in the Whitehall at Westminster, 7 May, 1.Mary, fol. 219, and 21 November, 1&2.P&M, fol. 265 and sometimes the superlative article, most, left out as 29 June, 3&4.P&M, fol. 204.

[1] 8. Eliz. should read 9. Eliz.

[fo. 8r]

*6. That the king of England is the Fountaine of all English justice in all causes, from whence all judges (bee they ordinary or delegates) derive theire ordinary or extraordinary authority, no man can denie, uppon the paine expressed in 1.Eliz., cap. 1 and 35.H.8, cap. 1 and it appeareth by Bracton *de re diviso*, cap. 2, number 7 and in *tractatus de actionibus*, cap. 9 and 10.

*7. That the king of England never did nor doth graunt any Jurisdiction to any Court in his dominions, but so, as hee still reteineth in himselfe and his Counsell attendant uppon his person, a supereminent authority and jurisdiction over them all, appeareth by king Edward the 1, his booke of lawes (commonly called Britton) fol. 1.

*8. That the Jurisdiction of the king and his Counsell extendeth to the hearing and determining of causes publick, mixt, and private, appeareth as followeth:

1. To prove the Jurisdiction of the king and his Counsell in publick causes, vide 16.Ric.2, cap. 5; and 40.E.3, 34 D. Amendment 15 Trinity Term;[1] and 31 March, 1552 in the Privy Council booke of 6.E.6[2] and throughout that booke, and all the Privy Council bookes since that time, and 22.H.8, cap. 14; and Westminster 2, cap. 22;[3] 13.E.1; and 13.Ric.2, [Stat. 1] cap. 2; and 4.H.6, cap. 5; and 33.H.8, cap. 39;[4] and 10.H.6, cap. 3; and 37.E.3, cap. 15; and 9.E.3. [Stat. 2] cap. 7; and 1.H.7, cap. 7; and 31.E.3, stat. 2, cap. 2;[5] and 20.E.3, cap. 1; and 3; and 12.Ric.2, cap. 10; and 2.H.5, cap. 1, stat. 2 [*sic*]; and 1.H.6, cap. 1; and 12.Ric.2, cap. 11;[6] and 1&2.P&M, cap. 3; [and 19.H.7, cap.] and 33.H.8, cap. 9; and 27.E.3, [Stat. 1] cap. 1; and 28.E.1 *articuli super chartas* 2; and 7.E.6, cap. 1; and 25.H.8, cap. 21; and 33.H.8, cap. 20; and 33.H.8, cap. 23; and 4.H.4, cap. 30; and 11.E.3, cap. 1.

2. To prove the Jurisdiction of the king and his Counsell in mixt

---

[1] *Year Book*, 40.E.3, p. 34.

[2] *A.P.C.*, *1552–1554*, p. 9.

[3] This statute governs the determination of waste between joint-tenants in common. It sets out the writ of waste but this does not appear to be a germane citation. This may be an error. Cap. 42 of the same statute would be a more suitable citation.

[4] The Act established to Court of Surveyors. This is not so much a reference to the King and Council as it is evidence of the King's powers to create new courts, lay down its procedures, etc. But this is not a power of the King alone but of the King in Parliament.

[5] Cap. 2 should read cap. 3.   [6] See *infra*, fo. 177r.

causes, *ubi vertitur tam intereim partis lese intereim reip. vide. liber* 43 *assisarum* 38;[1] and 5.E.3, cap. 10;[2] and 12.Ric.2, [Stat. 1] cap. 11; and 13.H.4, cap. 7; cap. 8; and [fo. 8v] and 3.H.7, cap. 1; and 21.H.8, cap. 20; [Mich. Term] 7. and 8.Eliz. in Diers Reports,[3] fol. 245; and 2.Ric.2 [Stat. 1]; 33.H.8, cap. 1; and 2&3.P&M, cap. 2; and 19.H.7, cap. 18; and 38.E.3, stat. 2, cap. 1; 2; and 4; and 13.Ric.2, stat. 2, cap. 3; and 16.Ric.2, cap. 5; and 8.Ric.2, cap. 4; and 13.H.4, cap. 7; and 2.H.5, [Stat. 1] cap. 8; and 4&5. P&M cap. 8.

3. To prove the Jurisdiction of the King and his Counsell in private causes betwene partie and partie, vide., 37.E.3, cap. 18, and 13.Ric.2, [Stat. 1] cap. 2;[4] and 17.Ric.2, cap. 6; and 20 *liber assisarum* 14;[5] and 13.E.4, fol. 9; and Fitzharbart, *Natura Brevium*, 233 A in the writ *de ideota inquirendo*;[6] and 46.E.3, *titulus* forfeiture, in Fitzharbart *abridgement* 18;[7] and 22 *liber assisarum, placitum* 75;[8] and 27.E.3, cap. 13;[9] and 39.E.3, fol. 14;[10] and 42 *liber assisarum, placitum* 5; and 4.H.4, Recordes in the Tower;[11] and 8.H.4, Recordes in the Tower; and 8.H.6, Recordes in the Tower; and 21.H.8, cap. 13.[12] A notable decree made by the King and his said Counsell, 10 May, 1552,[13] in the Privy Council booke of 6.E.6 touching a debt without specialty, it being lost, recovered by a private man against the Duke of Somerset; and 26 June, 1551. George Sidenham appeared before the Lords of the kings Privy

---

[1] See *infra*, fo. 175r.   [2] See *infra*, fo. 176r.

[3] A debtor in London secured a *corpus cum causa* against himself and thus was removed from the Fleet to the Marshalsea. He then confessed to the alleged felony and then took his clergy in order to remove himself from the jurisdiction of the temporal law. The Crown, in the light of this fraud, 'per Privie Seale directe a lest Justices de son Benche, commaund eux de surcesser de proceeder al arraignement, tan que ils ussent commaundement de luy et son Counsaile al contrarie'. See *infra*, fo. 178v.

[4] See *supra*, n. 4, p. 35.

[5] See *infra*, fo. 175r.   [6] See *infra*, fo. 175v.   [7] See *infra*, fo. 175v.

[8] See *infra*, fo. 176v.   [9] See *infra*, fo. 176r.   [10] See *infra*, fo. 177r.

[11] This and the two following references to the 'recordes in the Tower' are uncertain references but they may well refer to the records which were published from the Cotton collection. (Sir Robert Cotton, *Abridgement of the Records in the Tower of London* (1657).) In the three regnal years which Caesar cites there are lists of the Petitions of the Commons with their answers and in each case Council is being used to settle a private cause which has been brought before the King on petition.

[12] This stature only applies if it is meant to show how the King can interfere with land use, in this instance the possession of farms and other properties held by 'spirituall persons'. There is no mention of Council.

[13] *A.P.C., 1552–1554*, p. 42.

Council in a cause touching a Lordship betwene him and his tenants, *sedentibus tunc in Consilio*, the Lord Tresorer, the Lord Greate Master, the Lord Privy Seal, etc. as appeareth by the Privy Counsell booke of that yere;[1] and 11.H.7, cap. 25.

[fo. 153r]

*A letter written to the Masters of Requests from the Lord Keeper, as followeth: After my verie hartie commendacions whereas (as I ame given to understand) a cause hath depended before you theise 4 yeres, in which Laurence Sill was plaintiff against John Mason, defendant, and a decree therein graunted, after which and before the same could bee executed the said Mason died so that the plaintiff was enforced to revive the sute against Thomas Gibson and Isabell, his wife, the widoe and executrix of the deceased Mason, uppon which neue bill (as I ame enformed) order hath bene delivered by you that the defendant should come in and sheue cause whie the decree should not bee in force. And bycause that further daies bee still given and the plaintiff feare [*sic*] infinite delaies, hee hath so greatly importuned mee, as that I coulde not but satisfie his earnestnes. Wherefor I pray you to have that consideration of the cause, that the man may have no cause to complaine for want of undelayed Justice and that after the maner of your court you will speedily dispatch him, with that favour also (Justice regarded) as the cause requires. And so I bid you most hartely fareuell. From Russell howse, this 2 of February, 1593.

Subscribed, your very loving frend, John Puckering, C.S.

*7 February, 25 April, 18 June and 11 October, 36.Eliz. decreed against an executor, Gibson, to pay that which was formerly decreed against Mason, the testator, 28 November, 33.Eliz.

*A letter written to her Majesties Counsell of her Court of Requests from the Justices of the Common Plees, to relieve a cause after judgement and execution in the Common Plees, as followeth: The matter depending in the Common Plees betwene Walter Hele, plaintiff and Hugh Wilsdon and Hugh Culume, defendants, in an action of debt of 200 libri for payment of 100 libri was the last Hillary terme by the consent and, as we take it, at the

---

[1] *A.P.C., 1550–1552*, p. 310. Sidenham made a recognizance for 500 marks to appear (before Council ?) on the first day of the next term and in the mean time to refrain from disturbing the tenants in his manor of Brent and from disturbing their tenancies.

[fo. 153v]

request of the said Heles counsell, by order of the said Court referred to the determination and ending of Mr. Justice Periam. Whereuppon, at the last assisses at Exeter, both the parties being called before the said Mr. Justice Periam, hee thought good that Culme should pay to Hele, 120 libri in full recompence of the said debt and penalty of the said bond, costes and damages, which Culme was content presently to have payed accordingly. But Hele though hee were earnestly requested by the said Mr. Justice Periam to accept thereof, utterly refused the same and this Easter terme the said Court of Common Plees being verie importunately called on by Hele for execution, could not any longer stay the same, but awarded execution, the rather, for that the said Court thought her Majesties Court of Requests, being a Court of Equity, would as is meete, take such order in the said cause as to conscience should apperteine. Uppon which execution so awarded out of the said Court, the said Culme brought into the said Court the whole condemnation being in all with the costes [£]206. 13[s.] 4[d.] which was presently delivered to Heles Atturney. Thus leaving the said cause to bee further ordered by your good discretions in her Majesties said Court of Requests, which wee in the said Court of Common Plees, being a court of the common lawe tied to the strict and precise course thereof, could not so well helpe as wee wisshed. So take leave of you. From Serjeants Inne in Fletestreete, this 14 of May 1585.

Your loving frendes
Edmond Anderson
William Peryam

3

EXCERPTS FROM THE ORDER AND DECREE BOOKS AND OTHER RECORDS OF THE COURT OF REQUESTS

[fo. 43r (p. 1)] In the name of Our Lord Jesus Christ 13 February 1592

Actes, Orders, and Decrees made by the King and his Counsell, 9.H.7 remaining amongst the Records of the Court, now commonly called the Court of Requests.

On the 12th day of February 9.H.7. By His Royal Highness the lords and other Councillors written below are chosen to attend to his Council from the aforesaid 12th day, through the whole circuit to be made by the same lord King after Easter, in the following manner.

The Bishop of Bath, after Easter continuously.

The Bishop of Exeter.

The Bishop of Rochester continuously. *president of the King's Council. It is evident from the acts of the Star Chamber Court from the year 15.H.7.

The Lord Prior of St. John's, after 15 days after Easter continuously until the next month of August.

The Lord of Daubeney for the months of August, September and October.

The Lord of Broke for the same months as the lord Prior.

[fo. 43v (p. 2)]

The Lord William Hussie for the months of July, August, and September. [Req. 1/1/1r]

Robert Reede from the aforesaid 12th day until July.

Andrew Dymocke, Reginald Bray, Richard Gilford, and Thomas Lovell, knights continuously.

The Keeper of the Rolls.

Janne, ⟦Winsworth⟧ *Ainsworth*, and Warrham doctors continuously. [Req. 1/1/2r]

3 March 9.H.7.[1] With the bishops of Sarum and Rochester, the dean of the chapel, the lord Seneschal, Reginald Bray and Thomas Lovell knights, and Robert Reede sitting. To the petition of Richard Close and of other merchants of the city of London is granted a letter of summons to be directed to the Officer of Arms, under the Privy Seal, by which the said Officer should make a requisition to the Archduke of Austria for restitution to be made to the aforesaid Richard and other plaintiffs for the above-mentioned complaints, according to the power, form and effect of the same letters, done at Shene. [Req. 1/1/81r]

12 April 9.H.7. In court held at Canterbury, the Bishop of Bath, keeper of the Privy Seal were seated together with Thomas Lovell, and Richard Gilford knights.

20 July 9.H.7. Court held at Windsor. [Req. 1/1/85v]

9 August 9.H.7. In court held at Shene the Bishops of Bath and Rochester, doctor Middleton, and Andrew Dymocke, knight, were seated. [Req. 1/1/85v]

15 August 9.H.7 at Windsor. Note that on the same day in the Chamber assigned thereto, Thomas Cresset gentleman appeared in accordance with a certain judgment, as Thomas declared in the same place, done before the lord Chancellor in the Star Chamber, to appear personally before the lord king in his Council wheresoever on the said 15th day of August; And he has to personally appear from day to day, until it shall be otherwise decreed etc. in this matter by the said lord king and his Council, and under that incumbent peril. [Req. 1/1/87r]

[fo. 45r (p. 3)]

Actes, Orders and Decrees made by the King and his Counsell, 10.H.7 remaining amongst the Records of the Court, now commonly called the Court of Requests.

6 September 10.H.7 at Langley. The President of Magdalen College, Oxford and Reginald Bray, King's Councillors. [Req. 1/1/89v]

7 October, 10.H.7 at Woodstocke, Doctor Mayo, King's Councillor. [Req. 1/1/91r]

[fo. 44v]

*10 December 10.H.7, fol. 106.[2] John Harding, plaintiff, against

---

[1] The list of councillors was taken from the margin by J.C.

[2] The printed foliation corresponds with the original foliation in Req. 1/1.

John Zouche, defendant, for certain goods and chattels unjustly withheld. Restitution decreed. [Req. 1/1/106r]

[fo. 45r (p. 3)]

5 March 10.H.7 at Shene. The Keeper of the Rolls, D. Daubne, etc. King's Councillors. [Req. 1/1/94r]

23 March 10.H.7 at Shene. Doctor Martin and Turbervile, knight, King's Councillors. [Req. 1/1/94v]

24 March 10.H.7 at Shene. Letters issued under privy seal, directed to the customs collectors and bailiffs of the port of Weymouth, to administer justice to Jacques de Maiore for the restitution of a ship with the provisions of the same immediately upon sight, otherwise to appear before the Lord King and his Council wheresoever within 12 days of receiving said letters, to show cause why, etc. [Req. 1/1/95r]

8 April 10.H.7. Doctor Hatton, Andrew Dymocke etc. King's Councillors at Shene. [Req. 1/1/97v]

21 April 10.H.7 at Shene. Ruthmercat of Denmark appeared personally before the Councillors of our Lord King, and while he touched the holy gospels of God, freely promised that he did not henceforth intend to harm, disturb or molest any of the subjects of our lord the King, by cause of his imprisonment, (for he was at the time imprisoned on suspicion of the crime of piracy)[1] and then by the command of the said Lord King was excused. [Req. 1/1/99v]

On the same day.[2] It was decreed by the command of the Lord King, that John Whale of Winchelsea, whenever

[fo. 45v (p. 4)]

he shall conveniently be able, be allowed to capture a ship or ships of Penmarke in any part of the sea, and to bring them with him into any port of England, and keep them in the same place, until satisfaction shall have been duly made to the same John, of the just value of a certain ship and merchandises on the same pertaining to the said John, and unjustly taken and withheld by the inhabitants King, of Penmarke. [Req. 1/1/39v]

25 April 10.H.7. By the decree of the Lord King and the other lords of his Council at Shene in the chamber assigned thereto, it is decreed that John Whale of Winchelsea should peaceably enjoy the

---

[1] The parenthetical note was added by J.C. presumably from Admiralty Court records.

[2] This is bound out of sequence in Req. 1/1. It was perhaps from another volume of orders and decrees and was inserted in its proper chronological place by the P.R.O.

possession of a certain ship taken by him, which ship came from the regions of Penmarke. Provided always that the said John, after the said ship shall have been appraised by four impartial men, shall give sufficient security and shall provide to Master Robert Ridon Judge of the Admiralty to produce the said ship, or its value after its appraisal, whenever he shall have been lawfully summoned and interrogated, and at that time to answer the charges and things to be charged by the inhabitants of Penmarke. Signed by Thomas Rochester, Thomas Jon, Robert Middleton and Richard Hatton King's Councillors. [Req. 1/1/39v]

25 June H.7.10. John Morgan, King's Councillor at Woodstocke. [Req. 1/1/111v]

27 June 10.H.7. Richard Mayo, King's Councillor at Woodstocke. [Req. 1/1/112v]

Richard Fitz-James and Williame Grevile, King's Councillors at Worcester, 9 July 10.H.7. [Req. 1/1/114r]

Acts, Orders and Decrees made by the king and his counsell, 11.H.7 remaining amongst the Recordes of the Court commonly called the Court of Requests.

24 August, 11.H.7 at Nottingham. In the suit of John Northall of Browood, against Thomas Cowper.

[fo. 46r (p. 5)]

of Blexwich, of and concerning certain lands and tenements lying in the aforesaid Blexwich, the evidence of the aforesaid parties having been seen and understood by the lord King's Council, it was decreed that the aforesaid Cowper should enjoy the possession of the aforesaid lands and tenements without disturbance, interference or harm by agency of the aforementioned John Northall or any other, and this under penalty of 40 pounds to be raised from the goods and chattels of the said John Northall for the use of the said lord King; in case anything shall have attempted or shall have caused to be attempted in opposition to this judgment for the part of the said John Northall as far as other effectual circumstances, let them be told before the said Council and tried in the same place, by reason of which the same Council may settle and decide otherwise in the same case. [Req. 1/1/121r]

29 August 11.H.7. King's Councillors were seated at Leicester. And there on the same day in the case of John Powtrell against John Babington knight, of and concerning the title and lawful claim to certain lands and tenements, it was enjoined by the Lord

King's Council to both the aforesaid John Powtrell and John Babington to appear before the said King's Council at Westminster the day after the next coming All Souls' Day, to see further process in the same case. [Req. 1/1/121r]

6 September[1] 11.H.7 at Coliweston. It was decreed and enjoined by the lord King's Council to Bartholomew Holcrofte under penalty of 100 pounds to personally appear before the said Council wheresoever, fifteen days after next Michaelmas, bringing forward with him all writings, evidences and remembrances concerning certain lands and tenements then in dispute between the said Bartholomew and Henry Holcroft, and to see further process in the same case. And meanwhile the said Bartholomew took it upon himself, under the same penalty, to keep peace with the said Henry. And the same Henry took it upon himself in like manner to keep peace with the said

[fo. 46v (p. 6)]

Bartholomew under penalty of 100 pounds. [Req. 1/1/123v]

27 October 11.H.7.[2] John Patten, Attorney, before the Lord King's Council held at Westminster. [Req. 1/1/137r]

2 November 11.H.7 at Westminster. Thomas Hoton sworn Doctor of canon law[3] is admitted into the king's council, and promises that he will keep the content of the oath taken from him in this matter as far as his discretion and knowledge in the matter permit him. [Req. 1/1/137r]

9 November 11.H.7 at Westminster. It was decreed by the lord king's Council that a writ should be directed under Privy Seal to John Poole of Hertingdon, to permit Nicholas Buckstones to use and enjoy possession of certain tenements with a garden lying in Longenor, according to the decree and presentment of the Court recently held there. If otherwise, however, to appear before the said Council within 15 days after seeing these letters, to state cause why he should not be compelled to act in this manner, and also to answer to the lord king for the forfeiture of a certain recognizance, according as it appears more fully in the same. [Req. 1/1/142v]

On the same day. William Tunstall king's Councillor. [Req. 1/1/143r]

11 November 11.H.7 at Westminster. It was decreed by the lord

---

[1] 6 September should read 5 September.

[2] An action for a poor widow by the name of Agnes to recover a debt which was owed to her.

[3] *decretorum Doctor.*

king's Council that a privy seal be directed to the Mayor and Bailiffs of the town of Bristol and the sheriff of the county of Wiltshire to publicly proclaim Thomas Hawley a rebel because he scorned two privy seals directed and delivered to him, according as it is more fully contained in the certification made on that account. [Req. 1/1/144v]

13 November 11.H.7 at Westminster. Thomas Punt sworn says within the power of his oath that Thomas Dilworthe is so detained by old age and infirmity that he cannot conveniently ride nor appear before the lord king's Council except with grave bodily danger, and also on the same day, certifying the same, he showed a certain certification sealed with the seals of separate men

[fo. 47r (p. 7)]

affirming that the said certification was true. It was enjoined to the same Thomas Punt to personally appear before the lord king's Council from day to day, until he shall have provided security to the lord Surrey to settle with the same in all cases raised between the said lord Surrey and the certain Thomas Dilworthe, and this under penalty of 100 pounds. [Req. 1/1/145v]

On the same day. It was enjoined by the Lord King's Council to Humphrey Beysels that he should permit the Abbot of Netley to use and enjoy the possession of a certain bull, unjustly taken and withheld against the form of law, by the said Humphrey, and this under penalty of 40 pounds: and also enjoined to the said Humphrey under this penalty that he not implead, harass, disturb or otherwise vex the said Abbot for the title, right or claim of three bulls, more fully specified in the bill of the said Abbot, or anyone else claiming the said bulls in the name of the said Abbot in whatsoever courts or elsewhere, until he shall have had otherwise in decrees by the said Council. [Req. 1/1/146r]

On the same day. Randolph Citley and Randolph Wade were excused from personal appearance because they remained within the county of Chester, and they were remitted to the Council of the lord Bishop. *A cause remitted to the County Palatine.* [Req. 1/1/146r]

On the same day. It was enjoined to Philop Lokier to deliver or cause to be delivered to John Wood of Calicia, a certain allodial tenure[1] unjustly seized by him, and this under penalty of 40

---

[1] J.C. has the word *allium* in the text. As this is surely incorrect (there was doubtless no action for parcel of a garlic) the reasonable alternative is *allodium*.

pounds, before next Monday, because by the certification of Richard Nantfant, knight, it has reached our notice that the same John had and has legitimate and just title to possessing it, according as it is more fully contained in the same. And as far as the moneys of the said John spent in the same case, it is remitted to the judgment of the aforesaid Richard. [Req. 1/1/146v]

18 November 11.H.7 at Westminster. Scholars of Cambridge University were remitted, against whom

[fo. 47v (p. 8)]

it was complained by the Mayor in the same place, before the Lord King and the lords of the Council and the Chancellor in the same place. And it was enjoined to the Vice-Chancellor, then personally present, that according to the statutes and laudable customs and laws of the said University, malefactors should henceforth be punished by him whether Scholars or servants of Scholars should be doing wrong or committing riots or disturbance of the peace in any way, thus and in such a way that from hence just cause of complaint should not appear with occasion of punishment appropriate to them not inflicted. And it was also enjoined to the said Vice-Chancellor that he should hastily and without delay go to the aforesaid university, and when the chiefs and governors of the students of the separate places have been called together, he shall enjoin the same that they should provide that peace and good order be kept with regard to the Mayor and community of the said town by the Scholars and Students living and henceforth being obliged to live in their places. And the parties (to wit) the Vice-Chancellor for the University and the Mayor for his party have to appear in the next Octave of Hilary in person or by a subordinate person sufficiently authorized for both of them, and at that time they will show their charters, and by inspection of the same let that which each party justly claims be granted to them by the lord King and the Council. Beyond these premises the Vice-Chancellor has to call together before him those by whom the house, about which complaint is being brought, was knocked down, and that he should impose upon them a fine sufficient that this house can be repaired and restored to its former condition, around next Christmas until it is otherwise decided by the lords of the Council in this matter by hereupon showing and exhibiting evidence. The Vice-Chancellor also has to suspend single actions, judgments and executions of judgment attempted against John Bell and others of

the community of the said town brought into judgment before him [fo. 48r (p. 9)]
until they shall have had authorization in this matter for proceeding further against the same from the lord King and Council. And if and insofar as a prohibition of any content shall have gone forth at any time through Wood the jurist in the aforesaid shown Council, let it be revoked and stand void, so that the scholars may be at their liberty to make amends and sell by whomsoever within the said town, for their pleasure of will, as if such a prohibition had never gone forth. [Req. 1/1/147v]

27 November 11.H.7 at Westminster. In the case of Thomas Lacy against Henry, Lord Clifford, day was given to lord Clifford to appear on the next 15th day of Hilary, in person or by his Attorney sufficiently instructed in this case, and on the same day to show releases and other writings and remembrances for the right and title of the said Lord Clifford to lands and tenements in dispute between the aforesaid parties. And it was also enjoined to the same lord Clifford, that meanwhile he should not involve himself with the said lands and tenements, until he shall have had otherwise in decrees by the lord King's Council. [Req. 1/1/50r]

Adrian Nause, 10 December 11.H.7 at Westminster appointed John Patten his Attorney, in all cases, and principally to seek his justice against John Sommerset with a clause to abide in judgment and to pay charges. [Req. 1/1/154r]

11 December 11.H.7. Thomas Herbert, party plaintiff, and William Morgan, party defendant of and concerning right, title and possession of certain lands and tenements in dispute between them, are remitted to Common Law, because the aforesaid parties may be able enough to prosecute to have remedy in this matter at Westminster. [Req. 1/1/154v]

14 December at Westminster. Margaret Hall and William Heiluse appear, by sergeant-at-arms, and have to appear next Friday to answer to the bill of complaint of Richard Friday. [Req. 1/1/155r] [fo. 48v (p. 10)]

Vavasor and Pennocke, 15. December 11.H.7. at Westminster, King's Councillors: on which day, day was given to John Seyvell, knight, to wit, to show on the next 15th day of Hilary writings, evidences, witnesses and remembrances to prove title and claim by which he keeps the ward and marriage-portion of George Robert,

son and heir of John Robert, recently deceased, and this under penalty of 100 pounds. [Req. 1/1/155v]
The Councillors were seated at the Tower of London 23 January. 11.H.7. [Req. 1/1/155v]
4 February 11.H.7 at the Tower of London.[1] Master Sherbourne, King's Councillor. [Req. 1/1/160v]
10 February 11.H.7 at Shene. William Durrant was excused from personal appearance before the lord King's Council, and is remitted to Common Law, because the case concerns lands and tenements. [Req. 1/1/162v]
17 February 11.H.7 at Shene. John Matthew was excused from personal appearance before the lord King's Council in the suit of Elizabeth Greene, and this case is remitted to common law because it concerns lands and tenements. [Req. 1/1/164r]
On the same day. In the case of William Balon against the Warden of Winton College of and concerning the right, title and possession of certain lands and tenements in dispute between the aforesaid parties, moved before the lord King's Council, and all circumstances of this case being seen and understood, it was decreed by the said Council, that the same William Balon should permit the aforesaid Warden and his tenants to peaceably use and enjoy six closed areas of pasture or arable land called Mynschet, lying in Welde, in satisfaction of 15 pounds paid beforehand by the aforesaid Warden to the aforesaid William without any disturbance by the aforesaid William or another whosoever of his agency, and this under incumbent peril. Moreover all other lands and tenements shall belong to the aforesaid
[fo. 49r (p. 11)]
William, without any disturbance by the said Warden against due form of law, and this under incumbent peril. [Req. 1/1/164r]
2 March 11.H.7 at Shene. Thomas Jon, King's Councillor. [Req. 1/1/165v]

[1] It would appear from Req. 1/1 that Council met in the Tower from 20 January until 24 February (which was the next entry in which a new location was specified). Fo. 156v notes the first meeting in the Tower while fo. 157r notes the 23 January meeting. There is no location specified again until fo. 166r when the Court met at Shene on 2 March. J.C. entered the word 'Shene' in Req. 1/1 on fo. 163r, the entry for 12 February. The Court may have been in progress passing by Westminster along the way. Thus when they met in Westminster no mention was made, as that was the seat of the Court to the extent that it had one. Throughout the Order and Decree volumes there were few indications of meetings at Westminster.

15 March 11.H.7 at Shene. The case of Alice Mascall against Eleanor Howtinge, of and concerning certain title and right of a dowry, is committed by the lord King's Council to common law, because this case had first been raised in the King's common bench by the same Alice and not discussed. [Req. 1/1/168v]

17 March 11.H.7. Thomas Robins and John Patten Attorneys before the King and his council at Shene. [Req. 1/1/169r]

30 March 11.H.7 at Shene. In the case of Martin Gavilene, merchant of Spain and captain of a certain ship called La Mary de la Retho in Spain, against Thomas Barrowe of Dover, James Justice, Henry Heyward of the same town, John Shepley, John Langot of Kingesdowne, William Tayler of Sandwitch, John Priser of Deale, Gregory Foster of Walmer, and inhabitants of St. Margaret's parish next to Dover, of and concerning the plundering of the said ship with merchandises and equipment being in peril upon the Goodwine sands in the sea: it was decreed by the Lord King's Council, having seen and understood the danger of the said ship and the merchandises in the same, that the previously written things shall be recovered by the aforesaid Thomas Barrowe and others and not plundered, but in this regard an Inventory of the recovered merchandises shall be made by the same men.* Halfe the goods saved given for salvage.* That the aforesaid Martin Gaviline concerning the said merchandises and other things pertaining to the said ship recovered by the aforenamed Thomas Barrowe and his helpers, after they are appraised by separate men, half its value should pertain to the aforesaid Martin and the other half should pertain to the aforesaid Thomas and his helpers for their labors

[fo. 49v (p. 12)]

to be sustained in this matter and rendered to the said Martin, on next May 1. Always with the provision that as often as a legitimate claim shall have been made[1] by the party of the said Martin concerning other merchandises or other things pertaining to the said ship, further admitted by them to be in the hands of the aforesaid Thomas or others, that then by the power of this decree he shall enjoy half of the same. [Req. 1/1/169r]

Actes, Orders, and Decrees made by the King and his Counsell, anno 12.H.7 remaining amongst the Records of the Court, now commonly called the Court of Requests.

---

[1] The word in the original was not *facta* but *approbatic*.

10 February 12.H.7 at Westminster. Richard Bowet appeared by virtue of a decree of the lord King's Council, and has to appear before the said Council next Monday, and to answer to a complaint bill of William Colson, and also to provide security for keeping the peace with regard to the said William Colson, and meanwhile to keep the peace under penalty of 100 pounds. [Req. 1/1/12r][1]

13 February 12.H.7. William Gascoyne, knight, has to appear next Wednesday to answer to a bill of complaint proposed against him by George Stanley, and this under penalty of 100 pounds. [Req. 1/1/12v]

On the same day. The investigation of the case between the inhabitants of the town of Offley against John Shepherd was committed to Master Fisher and Doctor Hatton, and to report to the Lord King's Council according to their findings next Wednesday, and the parties have to appear on the same day, to see further process in the same, and this under penalty of 100 pounds. [Req. 1/1/12v]

15 February 12.H.7. The investigation of the case between the inhabitants of the town of Offley against John Shepheard of and concerning the right, title and possession of certain

[fo. 50r (p. 13)]

fields[2] enclosed by the said John Shepheard, was committed to the investigation of John Fisher Sergeant at Law and William Poulton, to be finally decided before next Easter. [Req. 1/1/12v]

On the same day. Henry Vernon, knight, was excused from personal appearance before the Lord King's Council in the suit of Thomas Leighton, knight, because the same Thomas would not prosecute his case against the said Henry Vernon. [Req. 1/1/13v]

17 February 12.H.7. In the case of William Smith against Thomas Hawley, gentleman, of and concerning right, title and possession of the manor of Dansey with appurtenances, in the county of Wiltshire, moved before the Lord King's Council, it was decreed, because the aforesaid Thomas did not appear before the said Council on the days lawfully fixed for him, but contumaciously refused, in contempt of the said Council, to such an extent that a solemn proclamation was issued against the same Thomas Hawley

---

[1] The foliation is apparently from a different Order and Decree book which came to be bound in the volume now known as Req. 1/1.

[2] The word 'fields' (*agrorum*) was inserted by J.C. The original was 'commons' (*communium*).

as more fully contained therein; and whereas the same Thomas did not appear, that if the same Thomas shall not have appeared before the said council within the 14 weeks next and immediately following to answer to this matter, and see further process in the same case, that then the same William Smith shall be restored to possession of the said Manor with appurtenances without further delay, etc. And because the said Thomas did not appear, therefore it was decreed by the said Council, in accordance with the power of the said decree. And a commission was issued to the sheriff of the county of Wiltshire to put the aforesaid William Smith in possession of the aforesaid manor, as is more fully contained in the same Commission.* Warrant to ye Sheriff to put the plaintiff in possession of the manor.* [Req. 1/1/14r]

21 February 12.H.7. The Provost of Cambridge has to appear next Friday in person or by an adequate deputy, to answer to a bill of complaint proposed against him by Henry Looke, and this under penalty of 40 pounds. [Req. 1/1/14v]

[fo. 50v (p. 14)]

On the same day. Thomas Gurney being sworn says, in virtue of his oath, that on last Ash Wednesday past, he delivered to the wife of Henry Knolton a certain writ of Privy Seal directed to the same Henry, to appear before the Lord King's council immediately on sight, under penalty of allegiance,[1] and then left the said writ in the said Henry's house. And because the same Henry did not appear, it was decreed by the said Council that a privy seal should be directed to the sheriff of Hertford county to attach and keep securely the said Henry's person until etc. [Req. 1/1/14v]

3 March 12.H.7. Robert Birt is allowed to appear before the Lord King's Council by Robert Samson and John Patten his attorneys in a certain case moved against him by John Garland. And the same Robert promised before the said Council that he would have right, willing, stable and steadfast all and whatsoever etc. by his said Attorneys, in the mentioned case under penalty of 100 pounds to be raised etc. [Req. 1/1/15r]

[fo. 51r]

*3 March 12.H.7. William Gray, plaintiff, against Thomas Bassingborne, defendant, for [£]5. 13[s.] 4[d.] debt without Specialty:

---

[1] *Subpoena legeanciae*: if Knowlton was a tenant-in-chief owing knight's service, the allegiance was a condition of his tenure. Otherwise this would refer to his common allegiance as a Crown subject.

decreed to give a sufficient securitie to the plaintiff content, to pay the said some with 13 Shillings 4 pence more for expenses. fol. 22.[1] [Req. 1/1/16r]

[fo. 50v (p. 14)]

21 March 12.H.7. Henry Knolton and Thomas Gurney appeared and have to appear next Thursday at [St.] Paul's, before the President of the lord King's Council *President of the lord King's council* to see further process in the same case. And this under penalty of 40 pounds. [Req. 1/1/18v]

On the same day. In the case which is pending before the Lord King's Council between John Love, party plaintiff, against Thomas Maidford, party defendant, of and concerning the title and possession of certain lands and tenements in dispute between the aforesaid parties: it was decreed by the Lord King's Council, by agreement of the parties, that this case should be committed to the investigation of Masters Yauxley and Frowicke, Sergeants at law to examine and certify to the Lord King's Council according to their findings in the same before the next feast of the Pentecost. And the aforesaid parties meanwhile have to wait

[fo. 52r (p. 15)]

on and concerning the aforesaid Yauxley and Frowicke, together with their evidences concerning the aforesaid lands and tenements, and this under penalty of 100 pounds to be raised from the goods and chattels of the party delinquent in fulfilling the aforementioned conditions, for and on his behalf, for the use of the Lord King etc. [Req. 1/1/19r]

14 April 12.H.7. Thomas Hill appeared by virtue of a writ of Privy Seal directed to him, and has to appear before the Lord King's Council wheresoever next Tuesday under penalty of 200 pounds. [Req. 1/1/22v]

19 April 12.H.7. The King's Councillors were seated, sometimes at Greenwich, as often as elsewhere, and sometimes in the new monastery next to the Tower of London,[2] to wit, on the said day. [Req. 1/1/22v]

On the same day.[3] Henry Ughtrid, Joseph Ughtrid and Christopher Ughtrid each appeared, to whom individually it was enjoined under

---

[1] Thus J.C's foliation of Req. 1/1.

[2] A reference to a meeting held in the new monastery does not appear in the Order and Decree book until 20 April (fo. 24r).

[3] See *infra*, fo. 53r, *sub dat.* 9 February, 13.H.7.

penalty of 100 pounds that they should appear from day to day until etc., under the same penalty. [Req. 1/1/23r]

On the same day. In the case of Joanna Dardis against William Roper, the same William acknowledges expressly that title to tenements and a meadow with appurtenances, concerning which it is being complained by the said Joanna, belongs and should belong to the said Joanna. And it was enjoined to the same William that he should permit the same Joanna to use her peaceable possession of the same lands and tenements without interference to be made by him or another in his name, under penalty of 40 pounds: and the same William took it upon himself to keep peace with the said Joanna and all her friends, from this day henceforth, and this under penalty of 100 pounds. And further the same William freely swore that he would keep the aforementioned conditions. [Req. 1/1/23r]

26 April 12.H.7 at Greenwich. The Abbot of Fountain and William Gascoyne, knight, undertook, and each of them went bail under penalty of 100 pounds, that John Tomlinson and Henry Dickson will personally appear before the Lord King's council wheresoever before the Feast of the Pentecost to answer to charges against them etc. [Req. 1/1/25r]

[fo. 52v (p. 16)]

5 May 12.H.7. In the case of Agnes Wintre against John French, it is enjoined by the Lord King's Council to the said John that he should not prosecute further against the said Agnes in common law, until it shall have been seen otherwise by the said Council, in the same case, and this under penalty of 100 pounds to be raised from the goods and chattels of the said John, in case he shall have attempted anything in opposition, and that he should appear before the said Council on next Monday, under the same penalty, and to see further process in the same case, and thus from day to day until etc. [Req. 1/1/26v]

3 June 12.H.7. Thomas Hiberden and John Nash appear before the Lord King's Council by virtue of injunctions given to them, to answer of David Owen, knight, in a certain case of riot proposed against them, and have to appear before the said Council wheresoever the day after next All Souls' Day, to see further process in this case, and this under penalty to each of them of 100 pounds. [Req. 1/1/34r]

Actes, Orders, and Decrees made by the King and his Counsell,

13.H.7 remaining amongst the Records of the Court, now commonly called the Court of Requests.

25 January 13.H.7. In the case which is pending before the Lord King's Council between Hugh Carter and Thomas Wood the party plaintiff against Adam Chetwood, knight, of and concerning the disseisin of two acres of land in dispute between the same, this case concerning title and interest of the said acres of land should be committed to the investigation of Lord John Fyneaux chief Judge of the Lord King's Bench, and James Herbert Attorney of the said Lord King, to settle or otherwise

[fo. 53r (p. 17)]

to report to the said Council according to the findings in the same case. [Req. 1/1/46r]

5 Feb. 13.H.7. William Rowse was excused from personal appearance before the Lord King's council, in the suit of Margaret Barnabas, and it was decreed by the said council, that he should not be called in this case unless she first defrays expenses, previously had by the aforesaid William, with security to prosecute. [Req. 1/1/50r]

On the same day.[1] The Bishop of Bangor, the Bishop of London, the Dean of the Chapel, Doctor Nickes, Vicecount Wels, the Bishop of Durham, Doctor Dacres, Richard Poole, knight, and Sutton, learned in the law, were seated in the said council.

9 February 13.H.7.[2] Henry Ughtred and foure more were for a great riot committed by them in the Countie of Yorke, fined at five pound a piece to the King. [Req. 1/1/50r]

5 March 13.H.7. It was enjoined to Thomas Shyminge, mayor of the city of Rochester, under penalty of 100 pounds to bring forward into the Lord King's wardrobe silks seized by him because custom is not paid on them as it is presupposed, before next Thursday, [the silks] to remain in the same place until he shall have had otherwise in decrees of the said Council. *Silkes uncustomed brought into the King's wardrobe.* [Req. 1/1/53r]

4 April 13.H.7. It was decreed by the Lord King's Council that

---

[1] *Eodem die* is in fact a conflation of two days, neither of which is 5 February. On 7 February (Req. 1/1/49r) the Bishops of London and Bangor, the Dean of the Chapel, Doctor Nikke, Viscount Welles, and Richard Sutton [of the Council] learned in the law. On 9 February (Req. 1/1/50r) the Bishop of London, the Dean of the Chapel, Dr Nikke, Viscount Welles, and Sutton were joined by the Bishops of Durham, Dr Dacres, and Sir Richard le Pole.

[2] See *supra*, fo. 52r, *sub dat.* 19 April, 12.H.7.

John Winslow should be committed to the prisons of the Lord King's Porters, to remain in the same place until he shall have posted sufficient security for keeping peace with the Lord King's subjects. [Req. 1/1/56v]

28 May 13.H.7. The Bishop of London, the Dean of the Chapel, Robert Middleton, Robert Shirborne, Richard Hatton, Doctor Bambridge,[1] Lord St. John, Charles Somerset, and Richard Sutton, were seated in the King's Council. [Req. 1/1/62v]

Anno 14.H.7.[2]

[fo. 53v (p. 18)]

At Westminster 14. November 14.H.7. In the case of John Simpson against William Rowley of and concerning a certain bond of statute-merchant: The same William has to produce security to appear from day to day until etc., before next Friday, and this under penalty of 100 pounds, and on the same day to answer to the bill of complaint proposed against him. Which day arriving, the same William Rowley appeared and produced bond, and has to answer to a bill of complaint proposed against him and this under the same penalty. fol. 2. [Req. 1/2/2r][3]

On the same day the Abbot of Warden against John Dudley has day on Friday to reply to the replication[4] of the said John. fol. 2[r]

On the same day. Eleanor Cotton, widow, against Thomas Cotton, of and concerning the disseisin of the jointure of the said Eleanor, the same Eleanor has day on Friday to reply to the replication of the said Thomas. Let this case be committed to the investigation of Master Hutton and the Mayor of Cambridge. fol. 2[r]

On the same day. Joanna Spilman widow against John Hert of and concerning the disseisin of certain lands and holdings etc. The same John Hert has day on Friday to answer to the bill of complaint. fol. 2[v]

On the same day. Roger Walwein against Fulco Walwein of and concerning the disseisin of certain lands and holdings etc. The

---

[1] Bainbridge.

[2] Beginning with this regnal year and with a new Order and Decree book, J.C. includes foliation in his citations. The volumes were apparently unfoliated prior to J.C's use of them for *The Ancient State*, at which time he numbers the folios in his own hand.

[3] Req. 1/2/2r *et seq.* The following entries are found in Req. 1/2 unless otherwise indicated. The folio references appear at the end of the entries where J.C. had placed them.

[4] The 'replication' in this and subsequent entries seems to be the defendant's answer to the complaint.

same Fulco appeared by his son last Friday past, and had it in decrees to appear the next Monday or Wednesday, to produce security, that the same Fulco his father would fulfill all and everything alleged by him and to keep the ordinance of the lord King's council in the same case, but if on the other hand it was decreed by the said Council that the said Fulco be called by another Writ of Privy Seal under penalty of allegiance to personally answer: However he did not

[fo. 54r (p. 19)]

appear, nor did he produce security so that it was further decreed by the council that a Privy Seal should be made under penalty of allegiance because he did not fulfill the aforesaid decree. fol. 2[v]

On the same day. John Maismore against John Cassy of and concerning the disseisin of certain lands and tenements etc. The same John Cassy did not appear: on that account he has day on Friday to appear under peril of this case.[1] fol. 3[r]

16 November. The Master of Burton La Zaes[2] against John Sainton. The same John Sainton has to answer next Monday thereafter it was decreed, that a Privy Seal should be directed to the same John Sainton under penalty of allegiance because he did not appear by virtue of a Privy Seal under penalty of 100 pounds. fol. 3[r]

17 November. John Cressy sworn, says that on the twenty-sixth of July in the cemetery of the parish church of Wroxwardine he delivered to John Bishop, farmer of the fee of a farm of the same town, a certain Writ of Privy Seal under penalty of allegiance to appear immediately upon sight wheresoever etc. and because he does not appear, on that account it was decreed by the Lord King's Council that an attachment should be made by the sheriffs etc. to attach the person of the said John Bishop etc. until he shall have posted security etc. to personally appear wheresoever within 15 days etc. fol. 4[r]

26 November. Wisham and Wiseman against Dower, in term, by rejoinder have day on Wednesday to publish at Westminster. [Req. 1/2/10v]

On the same day[3]. In the matter depending betwixt the Lady

---

[1] *Sub periculo causae huiusmodi* . . . A formula indicating the loss of the action by default.

[2] Burton Lazars, Leics.

[3] See *infra*, fo. 55r, *sub dat.* 24 Feb., 14.H.7.

Darrel, and the Lord Delaware, for tenne pounds in joynture, it is by the said Lord Delaware agreed, etc. [Req. 1/2/11v]

30 November. In the case which is pending before the Lord King's Council between Robert Meke, party plaintiff, and William Jenny, party defendant, of and

[fo. 54v (p. 20)]

concerning right, title and possession of certain lands and tenements in dispute between the aforesaid parties: the circumstances of this case having been seen and understood by the said Council, and mature discussion having been held on that account, it was decreed that the same William Jenny should pay or cause to be paid to the aforesaid Robert Meke for the title and interest to the aforesaid lands five pounds, to wit, on next Christmas 20 s. etc. and the aforementioned Robert Meke will seal sufficient writings and evidences of and concerning the aforesaid lands for the aforementioned William Jenny as security for the aforesaid land, according as it will be seen to expedite by the Council of the said William, and will deliver to the same William all writings and evidences which the same Robert possesses, concerning the aforementioned lands and holdings before the said feast of St. Michael the Archangel. [NR]

[fo. 53r (p. 17)]

1 December 14.H.7. The Bishop of London, the Bishop of Rochester, the Dean of the Chapel, Martin Middleton,

[fo. 53v (p. 18)]

Nickes, Bambridge, doctors, and Sutton, learned in the law were seated in the King's Council. [Req. 1/2/14v]

[fo. 54v (p. 20)]

3 December. Hancocke against Compe the aforesaid parties have etc. to set forth everything. [NR]

6 February. Chaddreton, against Bullocke, to answer. This case is remmitted to the Lord King's Chancery where this case is suspended undecided. [NR]

Richard Spergor was allowed to appear by Robert Tredueke his attorney with a clause to have right and goodwill etc. and to abide in judgment and to pay charges, and this under penalty of 100 pounds. 23 February. [Req. 1/2/29v]

On the same day. Adam Chetwood, knight, was excused from personal appearance before the Lord King's Council in a case of riot moved against him by Philip Bothe, because the same Philip

shall not have proved this his case as far as a riot against the aforesaid Adam, and this case is remitted to common law to be decided
in the same place. fol. 33. [Req. 1/2/34r]

24 February. Colles against the Earl of Surrey. Colles has to prove
the promises held etc. for the payment of a certain sum for jointure
or dowry etc. and the same Earl of Surrey has to prove etc. [Req.
1/2/28v]

[fo. 55r (p. 21)]

On the same day[2]. In the case which is pending between Joanna
Darrell, widow, against Thomas West Lord de la Ware of and
concerning right, title and interest of 10 poundd in the name of
a jointure of the said Joanna of and concerning lands and tenements which recently came into the hands of the said Lord de la
Ware by reason of a grant to him of the same made by the Lord
King Henry the seventh, and formerly in the hands of James,
recently Lord of Audeley:[1] the circumstances of this case having
been seen and understood by the Lord King's Council, and because the same Thomas West, Lord De la Ware freely took a day
upon himself (to wit) and end-day of Hilary last past, to show
sufficient title in law to annul the said dowry or annuity of ten
pounds, but if on the contrary to pay in full the said annuity or
dowry of ten pounds together with arrears, for the time in which he
enjoyed the aforementioned lands and tenements, to which day he
has not given satisfaction: it was decreed that the same Thomas
West, Lord Delaware should pay or cause to be paid to the aforesaid Joanna the said annuity of 10 pounds together with arrears, and
this under incumbent peril, and it decreed that letters on this
account be made to the aforementioned Lord Delaware to fulfill
the things mentioned before. fol. 34 [Req. 1/2/35r]

[fo. 55r (p. 21)]

25 February. The case in dispute between the Mayor and inhabitants of the town of Exeter, against John Bonefante of and concerning the election made of the Mayor of the Staple, should be
committed to the examination of the Mayor of the town of Exeter,
and others of the 24 of the same town of common Council, and to
Robert Newton, John Donastre, and Ralph Pudsay to examine
whether the same John Bonefant is able to exercise the office of

---

[1] Audeley was Audelex in the printed edition but J.C. noted the error in the
table of faults (fo. 162r) and made the change by hand in his own copy.
[2] See *supra*, fo. 54r, *sub dat.* 26 Nov., 14. H.7.

Mayor of the Staple or not, and also [whether] the election thus held of the same John has been held according to the custom practiced there from ancient times, and to certify to the Lord King's Council according to the findings in the same. [Req. 1/2/35v]

27 February at Greenewich. Aylward against Spotell: In the term for replying to rejoining on next Friday
[fo. 55v (p. 22)]
the aforesaid parties have then to appear and to produce witnesses and evidences, and to see further process in the same case: and this under peril of this their case. [Req. 1/2/36r]

20 March. Pudsay against Lord Clifford: Lord Clifford has [until] next 15. Michaelmas to set forth all things to prove peremptorily by evidences, writings, witnesses or otherwise interest to lands and tenements in dispute between the aforementioned Richard Pudsay and the said Lord Clifford, and this under penalty of 40 pounds, and to see further process in the same case. [Req. 1/2/40v]

12 April. Robert Danet hath day to bring in all the evidences and writings that he hath in the matter of land that is depending against him on the behalfe of William Whiteborough, against him the 28. of this present moneth of Aprill. [Req. 1/2/44r]

1 May at Westminster. Lord Dacres of the South appears by virtue of a Writ of Privy Seal directed to him under penalty of 200 pounds and has to appear before the Lord King's Council wheresoever on next Friday to see further process in the same case, and this under the aforesaid penalty. Baldwin the other party.[1] [Req. 1/2/50r]

2 May. In the case of Christopher Judson against Robert Plompton knight of and concerning right, title and possession of certain lands and tenements in the town and fields of Plompton: the circumstances of this case having been seen and understood by the Lord King's Council it was decreed that the aforementioned Christopher Judson should enjoy possession of the aforementioned lands and tenements, without disruption, vexation or disturbance of the said Robert Plompton or of another whosoever of his agency, and this under inubent peril. [Ref. 1/2/50v]

9 May. In the case of William Lewyn against Anna Lewyn, widow,

---

[1] J.C. must have gone to the files of the cases to discover that Baldwin was the plaintiff. That information is not found in Req. 1/2.

of and concerning right, title and possession of certain lands and tenements, lying and situated within the parish
[fo. 56r (p. 23)]
of Burnham in dispute between the aforesaid parties: the circumstances of this case having been seen and understood by the Lord King's Council, it was decreed that the said Anna should enjoy possession of the aforementioned lands and tenements, both in fee tail and in fee simple for the term of the life of the said Anna without impeachment of waste or other alienation of any portion of the aforementioned lands and holdings until other effectual circumstances should be shown before the said Council by means of the said William and should be proved in the same place, by reason of which the said council may settle and decide otherwise in the same case. Always with the provision that right of reversion of the said lands and holdings will pass wholly to the aforementioned William Lewyn after the decease of the said Anna, and to the said William's heirs in perpetuity. [Req. 1/2/54r]
On the same day. Edward Wellesborne, clerk, appointed John Woodford, gentleman, his attorney in a case moved against him by Thomas Witnall with a clause to abide in judgement and to pay charges, to have and to have in future right, willing, stable and firm all and whatsoever etc. under pledge and obligation of all his goods, and promises with his plighted faith to fulfill this. [Req. 1/2/54r]
1 June at Greenwich. Nicholas Galon of Mallinge appears before the Lord King's Council by virtue of an order of the said Council by sergeant-at-arms, and has to appear before the said Council wheresoever next Monday to answer to a bill of complaint proposed against him by Nicholas Leche and thus from day to day until etc. and this under penalty of 100 pounds. [Req. 1/2/58r]
6 June. Lord King's Council held at Warderobe. [NR]
29 June. Lord King's Council held at Esthamsteede, and on the same day Richard Gilford, Thomas Lovell, Charles Somerset knights, Richard Mayo the Lord King's almoner, and Richard Hatton Doctor were seated. [NR]
[fo. 56v (p. 24)]
Council held at Beanlewe [sic] 3 August. [Req. 1/2/60v]
17 August at Newport on the Isle of Wight. In the case which is pending before the Lord King's Council between James Havilande of Pole, party plaintiff, against John Lee of the aforesaid Island,

gentleman, party defendant, of and concerning right, title, possession and interest of four acres of land lying in the aforesaid Island called Southfordell: the circumstances of this case having been seen and understood by the aforesaid Council, together with the evidences and proofs of the aforesaid parties, and mature investigation and deliberation having been held in the mentioned case, it was decreed by the aforesaid Council in form as follows (to wit) that the aforementioned James Haviland should enjoy possession of the aforementioned four acres of land called Southfordel, without any disruption, disturbance, vexation, harm or impleading elsewhere of the said John Lee or another whomsoever of his agency, until other effectual circumstances should be shown before the said Council by the party of the said John Lee in the same case and should be proved in same place: by reason of which the same Council may settle and decide otherwise in the same case, and this under penalty of 40 pounds to be raised from the goods and chattels of the said John Lee, in case he shall have attempted or shall have caused to be attempted anything in opposition to this judgment or decree. [Req. 1/2/61r]

Anno 15.H.7.

4 September. Lord King's Council held at Winchester. [Req. 1/2/61v]

18 March. Lord King's Council held at Baynard Castell [i.e. London.] [Req. 1/2/97r]

6 November. Malyn against Edward Stanhop, knight, has day to answer on Friday. [Req. 1/2/67r]

[fo. 57r]

*24 November 15.H.7, fol. 69. William George, plaintiff, against John Thorneborough, defendant, for a debt of 50 markes. Decreed to be payed. [Req. 1/2/70r]

[fo. 56v (p. 24)]

12 February. William Meux, knight, was excused from further

[fo. 58r (p. 25)]

appearance before the Lord King's Council in the case moved against him by Edward Anne, and this case is remitted to common law, to be decided in the same place because the aforesaid case touches lands and tenements etc. [Req. 1/2/94r]

11 March. The Bishop of London, the Bishop of Rochester *then president of the King's council, as it appears from the acts of the Star Chamber,* the Dean of the Chapel, the Dean of York, the

Lord King's Almoner, the Prior of St. John and Richard Sutton King's Councillors at Greenewich. [Req. 1/2/96r]

18 March. Thomas Reinold was excused from further appearance before the Lord King's Council in the case moved against him by Robert Turke, because the same Robert Turke does not prosecute his case against the said Thomas, and it was decreed that the said Thomas should not be called henceforth in the same case unless the expenses had in the same case are defrayed beforehand by the said Thomas. [Req. 1/2/96v]

6 May. Lord King's Council held at Canterbury.[1] [Req. 1/2/100r–100v]

21 May at Callis [i.e. Calais].[2] In the case which is pending before the Lord King's Council between John Michell and Margaret his wife, party plaintiff, against Robert Windebanke, clerk, and John Windebanke, party defendant, of and concerning right, title and possession of a certain tenement situated on le Green, near Winchester, and twelve acres of land pertaining to the same tenements, and formerly to Henry Yong deceased: the circumstances of this case having been seen and understood by the aforesaid Council, together with the testament of the said Henry Yong, in the presence of all of whom interest in this matter was presupposed, it was decreed that the aforementioned John Michell and Margaret should enjoy possession of the said tenement and twelve acres of land, according to the power, form and effect of the testament or last Will of the aforenamed Henry Young in perpetuity without any treacherous vexation or disturbance of the aforementioned Robert Windebanke, or another whomsoever of his agency, and this under penalty of 40 pounds. [Req. 1/2/104r]

[fo. 57r]

*3 June 15.H.7, fol. 100. Jone Clark widow, plaintiff, against John Turberville, knight, defendant Treasurer of Callice for a debt of 102 pounds uppon debentur.[3] [Req. 1/2/106r]

[fo. 58r (p. 26)]

6 July. Thomas Edmonde sworn says within the power of his

---

[1] The Court sat 4, 5, and 6 May in Canterbury before moving to its next meeting in Westminster, 9 May.

[2] Note the meeting of the Court in Calais where the members travelled with the King in his entourage.

[3] Plaintiff's action was an assumpsit laid against defendant for refusing to pay a debenture authorised by Council. The debenture to various treasurers, collectors, customers, etc. was a means of paying pensions and salaries directly from the Crown's revenue at its source rather than from Exchequer.

oath that on last St. Bartholomew's day past in the parish of Cilmeston in the county of Kent, he posted over the door of the house of John Harvy a certain Writ of Privy Seal directed to him under penalty of allegiance, to appear before the Lord King's Council wheresoever 15 days after last Trinity Sunday past. And because he does not appear it was decreed that another Privy Seal should be directed to the sheriff of the aforesaid County to attach the person of the said John Harvy, and keep him securely until etc. [Req. 1/2/110v]

Anno 16.H.7

16 November. At Woodstocke the case between Nicholas Leeche and Joanna his wife against Nicholas Galon, John Moore and others as far as title of lands and tenements in dispute between the aforesaid parties, and a breach of the peace related earlier in bills of complaint, is remitted to the Lord King's Council in the Star Chamber at Westminster where the same case is suspended undecided, to be decided in the same place, and as far as the riot supposed in the bill, the aforesaid parties have the day after the purification of the blessed virgin Mary next coming to prove the things alleged by them concerning the said riot wheresoever, and this under penalty to each of them of 110 pounds.[1] [Req. 1/2/120r]

15 January. Lord King's Council held at Langley. [Req. 1/2/122v]

22 January. Lord King's Council held at Warwicke. [Req. 1/2/123v]

27 January. Lord Kings Council held at Kenelworthe. [Req. 1/2/124v]

30 January. Lord King's Council held at Coventrie. [Req. 1/2/125r]

5 February. Lord King's Council held at Banbury. [Req. 1/2/126r]

15 February. Lord King's Council held at

[fo. 60r (p. 27)]

Windsor. [Req. 1/2/127v]

26 February. Lord King's Council held at Richmond.[2] [Req. 1/2/128r]

6 March. John Garnish appears by virtue of letters missive, at the suit of James Farmingham, and has to appear next Monday to answer to a bill of complaint proposed against him, and thus from day to day until etc., and this under incumbent peril. [NR]

[1] 110 pounds should read 100 pounds.

[2] The next entry in the Order and Decree book which bears any indication of location is 18 March at which time the Court sat 'at the signe of the Horn in Flete Strete'.

1 April. Lord King's Council held at Eltham. [Req. 1/2/134v]

3 May. Thomas, Bishop of London, Richard Mayo, Lord King's almoner, and John Wats, clerk, were seated in the King's Council. [NR]

*21 June 16.H.7, fol. 142. John Cartreton, plaintiff, against William Warres, knight, defendant, for an annuity of 40 shillings yerely issuing out of the manour of Eversley in Hampshire. [Req. 1/2/148v]

*5 July 16.H.7, fol. 146. John Wharton against the Lord Clifford, that the said Lord should discharge him of a bond of 100 pounds. Wherein he was bound as a suertie for the said Lord. [Req. 1/2/151v]

[fo. 60r (p. 27)]

5 July. John Denman appears by virtue of a Writ of Privy Seal under penalty of allegiance and has to appear by Richard Turner his attorney with the counsel of Ralph Rokeby of Lincoln's Inn, within the City of London. [Req. 1/2/150v]

7 July. It was enjoined to John Herper of Brisley under penalty of 40 pounds that he refrain from further persecution in common law against Robert Gogeney and John Athoo, while the case is suspended undecided before the Lord King's Council. [see Req. 1/1/39r]

Anno 17.H.7

25 October 17.H.7. Lord King's Council held at Greenewich.[1] [Req. 1/2/165r]

7 December: John Mortimer, knight, appears by virtue of a Writ of Privy Seal under penalty of 100 pounds and was allowed to appear by Richard Turner his attorney, with the counsel of a certain Arnold, learned in the law, in a case moved against him by Richard Acton, and Margery his wife, Humphrey Saunders, and Jocosa his wife, with a clause to abide in judgment and to pay charges, if etc., and this under penalty of 100 pounds. [Req. 1/2/170v]

4 February.[2] John Fawley sworn says within the power of his oath that on the next Monday after the last feast of the Lord's Epiphany

[fo. 60v (p. 28)]

past he was personally present within the manor of Lanfay when Jenkin Lluyn delivered to the bishop of Menevia a letter missive

---

[1] At Greenwich 25 and 26 October.
[2] See *infra*, fo. 60v, *sub. dat.* 2 March, 17.H.7.

of the Lord King directed to him, to fulfill as in the same, etc.
[Req. 1/2/175v]

5 February.[1] William Wilkins, attorney, and Edward Forman of the
Middle Temple counselor at law before the King's Council.
[Req. 1/2/175v]

11 February, S. Simeon, Richard Mayo, Hutton, Kidwelly and
Richard Sutton were seated in the King's Council at Richmonde.
[Req. 1/2/177v]

On the same day,[2] William Wilkins attorney, Robert Southwel
junior of Grey's Inn and Gregory Adgor of the Inner Temple,
counselors at law before the Lord King's Council. [Req. 1/2/177v]

14 February at Westminster. William Eaton and Richard Turnor
attorneys before the Lord King's Council. [Req. 1/2/178r]

On the same day,[3] Lawrence Fountain has to appear before the
Lord King's Council wheresoever the 15th day after next Easter,
to produce with him evidences, and writings favoring his interest
to lands and tenements in dispute between the aforementioned
Lawrence and the certain John Fountain, Thomas Fountaine,
John More and William Jackman, and this under penalty of this
his case etc. [NR]

20 February, Benedict Medley attorney before the King's Council.
[Req. 1/2/180v]

The last [28] of February, Robert Brudenell of the Middle Temple
counselor at law before the Lord King's Council, and John
Patten attorney. [Req. 1/2/182r]

2 March,[4] day was given to the bishop of Menevia in the month
of next Easter to prove bastardy alleged by him against John
Fawley, and this under penalty of this his case. [Req. 1/2/182v]

9 March. The bishop of Rochester president of the Council
president of the King's Council, the Dean of the Chapel, and
Richard Hatton, doctors, G. Burgeuenny,[5] Morgan Kidwelly and
Richard Sutton were seated in the King's Council. [Req. 1/2/184v]
[fo. 61r (p. 29)]

19 March. John Collens, attorney, before the Lord King's Council.
[Req. 1/2/186r]

13 April. The Lady Prioress of the house or Priory of Stratford

---

[1] William Lyndsey v. Ellen Johnson, widow.
[2] Thomas Bigge v. Thomas Fastalf.
[3] This was actually the next day, 15 February.
[4] See *supra*, fo. 60r, *sub dat.* 4 February, 17.H.7.   [5] i.e. Lord Abergavenny.

Bowe personally appearing before the Lord King's Council in the case moved against her by John Wilde, was allowed to appear in the same case by Robert Gayton her attorney, with a clause to abide in judgment and to pay charges etc., and this under penalty of 10 pounds. [Req. 1/2/187v]

On the same day John Morice attorney before the King's Council. [Req. 1/2/187v]

April 29 with G. Burgeuenny, G. Simeon, Doctor Morgan Kedwelly, Richard Sutton, King's Councillors sitting. It is decreed by the Kings most honorable Counsaile in a matter of variance depending before them betweene John Stokes the younger on the one partie plaintiffe, and Sir John[1] Beauchamp Knight Lord Saintmond and Robert Stilman partes Defendantes on the other partie, of and upon the right title, and possession of 3. meses, 30. acres errable lande, 6 acres medowe, 53. acres pasture, and the pasture of four Kine with the appurtenances, set, lying and being in Keuile within the Countie of Wiltshire, late appertaining to one John Stokes, father of the said John Stokes complainant: that the same John Stokes complanant, shall peaceably occupy and injoy, all the issues, profites and reuenewes of the said 3. meses with other the premisses, without impedement, or interruption of the said John Beauchamp or Robert Stilman, or either of them, or of any other person by their procuring or stirring, in as much as it euidently appeareth to the saide Counsell, as well by the testament of the said Stokes the father, approbate: as by other depositions, taken in that behalfe, that the said 3. meses with other the premisses ought rightfully to appertain, to the said John complainant, and nothing effectuall alleaged, and prooued to the contrarie by the said defen-

[fo. 61v (p. 30)]

dants. Prouided alwaies that if the said defendants or either of them on this side the utas of S. John Baptist next comming can lawfully proue any other testament or later wil of the same John Stokes the father or any other better title than as yet is proved, which should bee to the derogation of this decree, that thereupon such further direction to be taken as shall accord with right law, and good conscience, and in default thereof the saide Robert Stilman to be commanded by the said Counsel, to make an estate to the aforesaid John Stokes complainaunt, according to the said

---

[1] John Beauchamp to read Richard Beauchamp.

testament exhibited and approbate, and that upon paine of 100 lib. [Req. 1/2/192r]

6 May. Thomas Simpson, John Warren and John Roo, attorneys before the King's Council. [Req. 1/2/194v]

9 May. Richard Spenser sworn says that the custom of the diocese of London is and has been, that the custody of the fruits of vacant benefices pertains and should pertain to the bishop of London. [Req. 1/2/197v]

30 May. Term was given to William Warren, to produce evidences and other writings concerning lands and holdings in dispute between Thomas Simpson and the aforementioned William: as well as his petition by which he claims the said lands and holdings before the next octave of [St.] John, and this under peril of this his case. [Req. 1/2/197r]

10 June at Westminster.[1] John Skelton committed to the prisons of the Lord King's Porter. [Req. 1/3/2r]

29 June at Windsor.[2] Robert Vaux allowed to appear before the Lord King's Council by Roland Vaux his attorney with a clause to abide in judgment and to pay charges. [Req. 1/3/5r]

1 July.[3] In the matter of variance depending before the kings most honorable Counsell betweene Nicholas Lewes etc. [Req. 1/3/5r]

2 July.[4] Thomas Lister allowed to appear by Richard Lister his attorney of the Middle Temple with a clause to abide in judgment [fo. 62r (p. 31)] and to pay charges. [Req. 1/3/6v]

5 July.[5] Alexander Balam attorney before the Lord King's Council. [Req. 1/3/6v]

6 July.[6] Memorandum that in the matter betweene Sir Thomas Butler, Knight, on the one partie and Henry Risley, Esquire, on the other partie, for the tenure of the fourth part of a village called Culchethe in Lancashire etc. [Req. 1/3/7r]

13 July[7] at Windsor, in the case which is pending before the Lord King's Council between Thomas Simpson, party plaintiff, against William Mavin, party defendant, of and concerning right,

---

[1] An action concerning lands of Reginald Bray.
[2] John Hogan v. Robert Vaux.
[3] Nicholas Lewes and Katherine, his wife, v. William Crappet.
[4] Alice Johnson v. Thomas Lister.   [5] Richard Cook v. John Bruer.
[6] Defendant's rent was reduced by one-quarter because of the decreased value of the tenement.
[7] 13 July should read 8 July.

title and possession of certain lands and tenements stituated and lying within the territory or demesne of Maeke and Oye in the Marches of Calais which were recently in dispute between the aforesaid parties upon the death of John Orwell, the circumstances of this case having been seen and understood by the aforesaid Council, and mature deliberation having been held thereupon, and because the same William did not satisfy the decision assigned to him, it was decreed, that the same Thomas Simpson by right of his wife Elizabeth should have, enjoy and occupy possession of the aforementioned lands and tenements without treacherous vexation, disturbance or hindrance of the aforenamed William Mavin or another whomsoever of his agency, until other effectual circumstances should be shown before the said Council by the party if the said William and should be proved in the same place, by reson of which the same council may settle and decide otherwise in the same case. [Req. 1/3/8r]

21 July at Woodstocke. Robert Corbet, knight, was excused from further appearance before the Lord King's Council by virtue of an acknowledgement in which he is held to appear before the said Council from day to day etc., and this under penalty of 100 pounds, at the suit of William Charlton, etc., and moreover it was enjoined to the same Robert Corbet, knight, under penalty of 500 pounds that he shall keep and preserve the peace toward William Charlton, esquire, Robert Charlton and Richard

[fo. 62v (p. 32)]

Charlton, and the servants of the said Robert Corbet, [and] of his agency, shall keep and preserve the peace toward the said William Charlton etc. as above and this under the same penalty. [Req. 1/3/9v]

13 August. Lord King's Council held at Flaxley. [Req. 1/3/10v]

15 August. Lord King's Council held at Troy. [Req. 1/3/10v]

19 August. Lord King's Council held at Ragland. [Req. 1/3/11r]

Anno 18.H.7

Lord King's Council held at Beetley, August 30. [Req. 1/3/11r]

14 September.[1] Lord King's Council held at Fayerford. [Req. 1/3/13v]

18th October at Windsor. Thomas Goderd appears by virtue of an

---

[1] The Council appears to have met on 13 and 15 September at Fairford but not on 14 September according to the Order and Decree book.

injunction given to him elsewhere, and was allowed to appear by George Ashby his attorney with a clause to abide in judgment and to pay charges etc. [Req. 1/3/16v]

October 31 at Westminster[1] John Turner was allowed to appear before the Lord King's Council, in a case moved against him by Philip Courtney, by William Harris his attorney, with a clause to abide in judgment and to pay charges etc. [Req. 1/3/17r]

4 November. John Pawlin personally appearing before the Lord King's Council in a case moved against him by Philip Bene was allowed to appear in the same case by Richard Turnor his attorney, with the counsel of John Burgin of the Inner Temple, with a clause to abide in judgment and to pay charges if etc. and this under penalty of 40 pounds. [Req. 1/3/18r]

9 November. William Haydon attorney before the Lord King's Council. [Req. 1/3/18v]

On the same day *fol. 20* at Westminster in the case which is pending before the Lord King's Council between Agnes Donne, party plaintiff, against Griffethe Donne, party defendant, of and concerning right, title and possession of certain lands and tenements situated and lying within

[fo. 63r (p. 33)]

the demesne of Carmillan in Kidwelly County,[2] in dispute between the aforesaid parties. The circumstances of this case having been seen and understood by the aforesaid Council and because it is manifestly evident and certified to the same Council that the aforementioned Agnes Donne has recovered from the said Griffeth the aforementioned lands and tenements according to the laws and customs of the district in the same place, by the inquest of 12 jurors, that she herself should enjoy and have possession of the same according to the power, form, and effect of the said restoration, without any treacherous vexation, disturbance or disruption of the aforesaid Griffeth *This Court assisted the execution of a recovery at common Lawe* or another whomsoever in his name or agency, until other effectual circumstances concerning the aforementioned should be shown before the said Council by the

---

[1] J.C. appears to have consulted the papers concerning the case. The Order and Decree book has the cause moved by Turner against Philipp Courney, although the facts of the case are just the opposite according to J.C's report in this entry.

[2] *In Comitatu Kidwelly* does not refer to a county but to a lordship of the Duchy of Lancs. in south Wales.

party of the said Griffeth, and proved in the same place, by reason of which the same Council may settle and decide otherwise in the same case. [Req. 1/3/19r]

16 November. Henry Salcoke appears by virtue of a Writ of Privy Seal under penalty of 100 pounds at the suit of Richard Stevens, and has to appear next Friday before Richard Guilford, Controller of the Lord King's Household,[1] and other officials of the same, and thus from day to day until etc. under the same penalty. [Req. 1/3/19v]

21 November.[2] William Wilkins attorney before the Lord King's Council. [Req. 1/3/21v]

23 November.[3] Thomas Homwood attorney before the Lord King's Council. [Req. 1/3/21v]

6 December. In the matter of variance depending before the King and his Counsel, betweene Anne Pickering, widow, complainant, and Adam Mulcaster, Alexander Mulcaster, and John Mulcaster, defendants, of, and upon a forcible entrie and riote, supposed to be made by the saide defendants upon certaine lands, called Stone-flats, parcell of the mannour of Salesbie, the which she affirmeth to be her right inheritance, it is decreed by the King by the advise of his Counsell, and by the assent of

[fo. 63v (p. 34)]

the Lord Dacre, that if any riot or forcible entrie be confessed, or hereafter proved against the saide defendants, or any of them, whereby fine shall be sessed upon them, that then the said Lord Dacre to pay the same, or els to bring in the bodies of them before the King and his Counsell within six weekes next, and immediately ensuing the feast of the purification of our Ladie next coming, upon paine of fourtie pound, and in the meane time the same defendants and everie of them to be of good abearing toward the said Anne, and her tenants, and that every of them upon the pain of fourtie pound. [Req. 1/3/24v]

10 December in the case of John Warrant, party plaintiff, against William Dalton, party defendant, day was given to the aforementioned William Dalton on next Friday wheresoever [the Court may be] to produce evidences favoring his interest to lands and

---

[1] Controller of the Household is synonymous with Controller of the Wardrobe.
[2] Richard Mede v. Agnes Heyward, widow, and John Holbroke.
[3] 23 November should read 25 November. William Wady v. James Homwood, Sr. and James Homwood, Jr.

tenements in dispute between the aforesaid parties, and this under peril of this his case. Which day arriving, day was given to the aforementioned William Dalton peremptorily on the next octave of Hilary to produce evidences as above, under peril of this his case, and also to pay to the aforementioned John Warrant 2 s. for his expenses, because he did not satisfy the term assigned to him. [Req. 1/3/26r]

[fo. 64r]

*19 December, 18.H.7, fol. 28. John Baptista, Doctor of Medicine and tutor of John Boërius master of the house or hospital of the Blessed Virgin Mary of Bethlehem in the suburbs of London, plaintiff, against Henry Frank concerning the title, right and possession of a certain holding, etc. [Req. 1/3/27r]

*27 January, 18.H.7, fol. 30,[1] for money delivered by the father to the use of his children. [Req. 1/3/30r]

[fo. 63v (p. 34)]

8 February. The case between John Stanbridge against John Messenger is continued until 15 days after next Easter, and day was given to the aforesaid John Messenger on the said 15th day, to produce roles of court concerning lands and tenements in dispute, and at least 5 or 6 of them, and this under peril of this his case. And on this account let letters be made to the steward of the court in the same place to hand over the said rolls. [Req. 1/3/33r]

On the same day,[2] Walter Cokker attorney before the Lord King's Council. [Req. 1/3/33v]

10 February.[3] William Wistow attorney, etc. [Req. 1/3/34r]

[fo. 65r (p. 35)]

13 March. In the case disputed before the Lord King's Council between Richard Stavely, party plaintiff, and Henry Clifford, lord Clifford, and Westmerland, party defendant, of and concerning right, title and possession of one tenement etc., it was decreed, etc. [Req. 1/3/43v]

27 March. Richard Stable, clerk, and John Pennington appear by virtue of a Writ of Privy Seal under penalty to each of them of 100 pounds, at the suit of John Dowman, clerk, and have to appear

---

[1] Richard Houghton and Alice, his wife v. William Geine(?). The page is badly damaged and there is no file of documents regarding the matter. It appears though that the plaintiffs were under £40 penalty to appear in the Archdeacon of Bedford's court.

[2] The MS is too badly damaged to confirm this entry.

[3] *Ex parte* William Clerke *alias* Turner v. John Stepneth.

from day to day, until etc., and this under the same penalty, etc., and that they should refrain from further process in common law, while the case is suspended undecided before the said Council, and this under the aforesaid penalty. [Req. 1/3/47r]

5 May. Richard Carew, knight, appears by virtue of a Writ of Privy Seal etc. to the suit of Agnes Smith, widow, and has to appear from day to day, until, etc. under the same penalty. [Req. 1/3/50v]

20 May. Thomas Roderam appears before the Lord King's Council by virtue of the Sergeant at Arms, to the suit of Oliver Buckbere, and has to appear from day to day until, etc. [Req. 1/3/55v]

21 June. It was enjoined to Henry Coote under penalty of 40 pounds that he should refrain from further process in common law against John Dunning, and Elizabeth his wife, while the case between the aforesaid parties is suspended undecided before the Lord King's Council. [Req. 1/3/63r]

4 July[1] Lord King's Council held at Coliweston. [Req. 1/3/67v]

31 July.[2] Nicholas Birome, knight, appears by virtue of a Writ of Privy Seal etc. to the suit of John Bothe knight, and has to appear from day to day until etc. [Req. 1/3/69v]

[fo. 64r]

*18 August, 18.H.7. The Priour and Carmelite Friers of Notingham for a yerely annuity of 5 markes out of a mill and fisshing given by the Lord Grey, against Thomas Leeke, gentleman. [Req. 1/3/71v]

[fo. 65r (p. 35)]

Anno 19.H.7.

1 September.[3] William Ingram, attorney, etc. [Req. 1/3/73r]

6 September.[4] William Wolfe, attorney, etc. [Req. 1/3/81r]

[fo. 65v (p. 36)]

8 November. John Patten attorney etc. [Req. 1/3/82r]

15 November. In the case moved by William Clerk,[5] party plaintiff, against John Stepnethe, party defendant, of and concerning right, title and possession of certain lands and tenement in dispute between the aforesaid parties, as it appears more fully in their bills:

[1] And 6 July also.   [2] The MS is too badly damaged to confirm this entry.
[3] *Ex parte* Thomas Cutherd v. Henry Hebzaed.
[4] *Ex parte* John Honey v. William Rotman (or Lotman – both spellings appear in the MS).
[5] *alias* Turner.

day was given to the aforementioned John Stepnethe on the 29th
day of the present month to prove that feoffment was made to the
use of Robert Parker, and payment of money for the same, and
this under peril of this case, and meanwhile that he should refrain
from further process in common law concerning land in dispute
while the case is suspended undecided before the said Council etc.
[Req. 1/3/85v]

17 November.[1] Owin Holland attorney, etc. [Req. 1/3/86r]

18 November.[2] Richard Snede attorney before the Lord King's
Council and John Hasilwood likewise. [Req. 1/3/86v]

25 November.[3] Alexander Balam attorney etc. [Req. 1/3/89r]

3 February.[4] Thomas Chamond, attorney, etc., [Req. 1/3/99v]
and William Rudhale and Richard Fletcher likewise.[5] [Req.
1/3/100v]

5 February.[6] John Pecocke Attorney etc. [Req. 1/3/100v]

14 February. Roger Litchfield was excused from further appearance
before the Lord King's Council, in the case moved against him on
behalf of William Rudland, because the same William shall have
alleged or proved nothing effectual against the said Roger, and
because it is evident to the said Council that the said Roger is
excused from the impeachment of the aforementioned William
in the court of Chancery in the same case. [Req. 1/3/105r]

26 February. In the matter of variance depending before the
Kings honourable Counsell, betweene Richard Westley, plaintife,
and Sir Richard Fowler, knight, defendant: It is decreed by the
sayd Counsell, in maner and forme folowing, that is to say, that
where the sayd Richard Westley was indited of felony, and ac-
quited of the same: That therefore the sayd Sir Richard Fowler
shall restore, and

[fo. 66r (p. 37)]

deliver or cause to be restored and delivered, before the feast of
the Annunciation of our Lady next comming, unto the aforesayd
Richard Westley, all such oxen, kine, steeres, heifers, sheepe and
calves, or the price of them, and al other goods, and cattels, that

---

[1] *Ex parte* John Hall v. Robert Dighton.
[2] *Ex parte* Richard Halome v. Richard Peeke, clerk. And *Ex parte* Robert Jeff v.
John Crabenthorpe.
[3] *Ex parte* Thomas Brofield, Jr. v. Thomas Brofield, Sr.
[4] The MS is too badly damaged to confirm this entry.
[5] *Ex parte* Thomas Welby v. William Welby.
[6] *Ex parte* William Smythe v. Alicia Laurence.

the said Sir Richard, or any other in his name or by his commaundement tooke out of the possession and keeping of the said Richard Westley, upon paine of 200 libri to be forfeited to the King's grace. [Req. 1/3/108r]

7 March.[1] Matthew Standish attorney etc. [Req. 1/3/111r]

15 March.[2] Richard Lloyd attorney etc. [Req. 1/3/113r]

6 May. Robert Ellerkar was excused from further appearance before the Lord King's Council in the case moved against him by the party of Thomas Gase, because the same case is suspended undecided before the Judges of the lord king in common bench at the suit of the aforesaid Thomas Gase. [NR]

14 May.[3] Leonard Spenser attorney etc. [Req. 1/3/117v]

20 May. The case moved before the king's Council between Walter Mower, party plaintiff, and William Shelliston and Robert Shelliston, [defendants] is remitted to common law because it concerns lands and tenements and thus the same William and Robert were excused from further appearance in the same case before the said council. [Req. 1/3/120v]

24 May. The case which is pending before the Lord King's Council between John Roice, party plaintiff, and Christopher Browne and other parties defendant is adjourned until the octave of next Trinity. On which day, the aforesaid parties have to appear wheresoever to see further process in the same case. And meanwhile it was enjoined to the same Christopher etc. that he should not interfere by himself or by any other of his agency, with the person of the said John, but that he should allow him to enjoy his liberty without any treacherous vexation, disturbance or hindrance of the said Christopher or another whomseoever, while the case is suspended undecided. *a priviledge of protection during a sute.* [Req. 1/3/121r]

7 June. Thomas Stephan appears by virtue of a command of the Lord [fo. 66v (p. 38)] King by the sergeant at arms, at the suit of Robert Turke, and has to appear before the Lord King's Council at Richmond within the 2 days next and immediately following after the arrival of the said Lord King at Richemond, and to answer to a bill of complaint proposed against him, etc. [Req. 1/3/121v]

---

[1] Joan Pickering v. Richard Baron.
[2] *Ex parte* James Framlingham v. Elizabeth Bardwell, widow.
[3] The MS is too badly damaged to confirm this entry.

12 June. Henry Glene and John Bristoll appear by virtue of a command of the Lord King's Council by the sergeant at arms under penalty of 100 pounds at the suit of William Wright. And the case concerning lands and tenements in dispute between the aforesaid parties is remitted to be decided according to the custom of the Manor of John Risley, knight, lord of that fee etc. [Req. 1/3/122v]

15 July. Robert Heydocke, clerk, appears by virtue of a Writ of Privy Seal under penalty of 100 pounds, at the suit of the Lady[1] Elizabeth Nevill, widow, and has to answer to a bill of complaint proposed against him next Monday, and thus to appear from day to day etc. [Req. 1/3/130r]

24 July. It was enjoined to Richard Blunt esquire under penalty of 100 pounds that he as well as his servants of his agency shall keep and preserve the peace toward William Awbrey and his servants, while the case between the aforementioned Richard and William is suspended undecided. In like manner it was enjoined to William Awbrey under the aforesaid penalty that he as well as his servants should keep the peace toward Richard Blunt etc. [Req. 1/3/131r]

Anno 20.H.7.

18 October.[2] Edward Dudley Lord King's Councillor. [Req. 1/3/135v]

4 November.[3] William Sergeant attorney etc. [Req. 1/3/135v]

15 November.[4] William Heydon attorney etc. [Req. 1/3/143v–144v]

[fo. 67r]

*13 December 20.H.7, fol. 143. Elizabeth Butler, widoe, plaintiff, for a certain chest with goods, jewels, plate apparell & other stuf against David ap. Henry, defendant. [Req. 1/3/152v]

[fo. 66v (p. 38)]

30 January.[5] John Baker, Stephen Terry etc. were allowed to appear before the Lord King's Council etc. by Richard Turner their attorney together with the counsel of Ralph Rokeby of Le Lincolns Inne, with a clause, etc. [Req. 1/3/155v]

On the same day,[6] William Hamond was allowed to appear etc. by

---

[1] J.C. transcribed *dominae* as *domini* in the text.
[2] Dudley is appearing for Edward Donne in his action against John Verney.
[3] Richard Herdman v. John Ratcliffe.
[4] No legible entry is available to confirm this entry.
[5] Thomas Edmonde was the plaintiff.   [6] Christian Baker was the plaintiff.

[fo. 68r (p. 39)]

Richard Turner attorney etc. with the counsel of John Rooper of the King's bench with a clause. [Req. 1/3/155v]

1 February.[1] John Drew, of the inn of Le Greys Inne attorney before the Lord King's Council. [Req. 1/3/157r]

The last of February.[2] Richard Walenger attorney etc. [Req.1/3/166r]

3 May. John Arden was excused from further appearance before the Lord King's Council in the case moved against him by the party of John Knight, because this case is suspended undecided in common law. [Req. 1/3/188r]

4 June.[3] William Woulfe attorney etc. [Req. 1/3/199r]

6 June.[4] John Roo attorney etc. [Req. 1/3/199r]

20 June.[5] Thomas Hurte attorney etc. [Req. 1/3/201r]

21 June. The Earl of Essex appears by virtue of a Writ of Privy Seal under penalty of 100 pounds and has to appear from day to day until etc. [Req. 1/3/201r]

William Kempe and Nicholas Wrene attorneys before the Lord King's Council June 27.[6] [Req. 1/3/203r]

15 July. Day was given to John Hayworthe to personally appear before the Lord King's Council in the case moved against him by the party of Hugh Creshawe the day after next All Souls' Day, and meanwhile it was enjoined to the same John that he should restore to the said Hugh without delay all tithes owed by him to the same Hugh as farmer of the parish church of Whitehampstead, and also that he should warn all the parishioners in the same place to fulfill the abovementioned things for and by their parties in all things, without deceit or treacherous influence in opposition, and this under penalty of 100 pounds. [Req. 1/3/207r]

16 July.[7] Richard Clerke attorney, etc. [Req. 1/3/209r]

Anno 21.H.7.

13 October,[8] at Reding. William Belhouse, attorney before the Lord King's Council. [Req. 1/3/212r]

---

[1] *Ex parte* Joan Martin, wife of Walter Martin v. Robert and Edmund Yeo.

[2] *Ex parte* Thomas Tagell v. Thomas Morefield and William Rawlin.

[3] 4 June should read 6 June. *Ex parte* William Hasilden v. William Pynke and John Belle.

[4] No entry is available to confirm this note. See 29 November, 21.H.7, wherein John Roo appeared as attorney.

[5] *Ex parte* Randolph Todde v. William Hurt (or Hunt).

[6] *Ex parte* Richard Genowe v. John Pygott.

[7] *Ex parte* Thomas Tymynge, clerk, and Christopher Cooke v. John Dunham.

[8] William Tychener and Isabella, his wife v. John Bogger.

3 November. William Harper of Rushall in Stafford County appeared before the Lord King personally by virtue

[fo. 68v (p. 40)]

of a certain bond in which the aforementioned William, together with others, is held to a certain William Smith, sheriff of the aforesaid county, to appear on the same day, and thus by the command of the said Lord King the forementioned William Harper is remitted to appear before the Lord King's Council learned in the law[1] at Westminster. [NR]

22 November. In the matter of variance betweene Elizabeth Palmer, complainant, and Hughe Wilford, defendant. It is decreed, that the same Hughe upon Monday next comming shall bring two sureties, to be bounde with him by recognizaunce, or otherwise in the summe of 40 lib. to prove by wrightings or witnesses sufficient by the utas of the purification of our Lady next comming that the lands in controversie betweene the same parties [having] beene intailed to the auncesters of the same Hughe, and to whom he is next heire, or els to avoid his possession, and claime of the said lands, and to suffer the said Elizabeth, and her assignes peaceably to enjoy and possesse the same with the arrerages of the rentes of the same: and also in the meane time, not to meddle with the rentes nowe being in the hands of the tenants of the same, and until the right be determined, to whom the same lands, and rentes rightfully ought to appertaine. [Req. 1/3/214v]

22 November, at Westminster. G. Simeon,[2] E. Vaughan, Richard Hatton, Robert Drury knight, Richard Sutton esquire, King's Councillors. [Req. 1/3/215r]

29 November.[3] Nicholas Kirkham was allowed to appear before the Lord King's Council in the case moved against him by the party of John Way, by John Roo of Le Greys Inne, and Charles Hopping of Le Lions Inne jointly and separately, with a clause to abide in judgment and charges are to be paid. This under penalty of 100 pounds etc. [Req. 1/3/216r]

29 March. Thomas Pole appears by virtue of a Writ of Privy Seal under penalty of 100 pounds[4] at the suit of the Abbot of

---

[1] For a discussion of the role of the council learned and its members see R. Somerville, 'Henry VII's "Council Learned in the Law"', *English Historical Review*, 54 (1939).

[2] J.C. took these names from the margin.

[3] 29 November should read 26 November.   [4] 100 pounds to read 200 pounds.

Chester, and has to answer to a complaint bill proposed against him [fo. 70r (p. 41)] next Wednesday and thus to appear from day to day until etc. under the same penalty. [Req. 1/3/225v]

25 May. George Kirkeham clerk of the Lord King's Hanaper,[1] Richard Pinfolde and Richard Copcote attorneys[2] before the Lord King's Council. [Req. 1/3/232v]

27 May. In the matter of variance depending before the Kings most honourable Counsell, betweene Robert Ballard, partie complainant, and Robert Blundell, partie defendant, of and for the inclosure of the third part of the Waste ground, within the Lordship of Joyce Blundell: It is decreed etc. [Req. 1/3/233r]

28 May, in the case of John Adams and others against the duke of Buckingham, term was given on Friday, to wit the 19th of June, next coming, to appear to see further process in the same case, and this under incumbent peril. [Req. 1/3/233v]

2 June at Richmond. Robert Jervis and John Willianson appear by virtue of a Writ of Privy Seal under penalty of 100 pounds at the suit of Richard Nix bishop of Norwich, and have to appear from day to day until, etc, and this under the aforesaid penalty. [Req. 1/3/234r]

[fo. 69r]

*26 June 21.H.7, fol. 218. William Stevenson an executor to Margaret Gateley enforced by decree to deliver to Nicholas Burghe, plaintiff, all such apparell & other goods come to his handes from his testatrix left with her as a pawne for 7 libri. [Req. 1/3/238v]

*The same fol. 219. The Administrators of John Morgan late Bisshop of St. Davids deceased sued David ap. Owen for a debt of [£] 7. 16[s]. 3[d]. due to the said Morgan. [Req. 1/3/238v]

[fo. 70r (p. 41)]

27 June. John Fitz-James Junior as counsellor of William Lord Storton and for the same appears by virtue of letters missive at the suit of Thomas Estcourte, and has to answer to a complaint bill proposed against the said Lord Storton on next Wednesday, and thus to appear from day to day, etc. [Req. 1/3/238v]

On the same day, William Gravile, sergeant at law, appears by

---

[1] *Ex parte* John Evyn v. William Warren and John Susan.

[2] *Ex parte* Randolph Freeman and John Freeman v. John Wastet, clerk, of the parish of Dunstable, and Henry Hunt.

virtue of a Writ of Privy Seal at the suit of John Arderne etc.
[Req. 1/3/238v]

3 July.[1] Thomas Henage, and John Beldon,[2] attorneys before the
Lord King's Council. [Req. 1/3/241v]

7 July. In the case of the Abbot and Convent of the Monastery
of St. Gerberga in Chester against Thomas Pole, esquire, term
was given to the aforementioned Thomas Pole, under penalty of
500 pounds, to personally appear wheresoever etc. [Req. 1/3/242v]

9 July. John Roos was allowed to appear before the Lord King's
Council

[fo. 70v (p. 42)]

in the case moved against him by the party of William Keby, by
Richard Turnor his attorney, with the counsel of Robert Sheffield,
knight, and George Emerson of Le Lincolnes Inne, with a clause
to abide in judgment and to pay charges and this under penalty of
40 pounds. [Req. 1/3/247r]

Anno 22.H.7.

7 September.[3] Lord King's Council held at So[[m]]ninghill.
[Req. 1/3/245v]

10 September. Lord King's Council held at [W]Oking. [Req.
1/3/245v]

13 September.[4] Lord King's Council held at Walington. [Req.
1/3/245v]

14 October. John Shaa appears by virtue of a Writ of Privy Seal
under penalty of 100 pounds at the suit of Robert Banister, and
this case is remitted to the Chancellor of the Duchy of Lancaster.
[Req. 1/3/247r]

On the same day. Thomas Mountagu appears in the name of proxy
for the Abbot of Peterborough, and says that the aforesaid Abbot
restricted and attached the goods specified in the bill as the goods of
John Trigge outlaw, as it is clear by the record, etc. [Req. 1/3/248r]

15 October. Henry Kerkeby appears by virtue of a Writ of Privy
Seal under penalty of 100 pounds at the suit of Lord Ogle, and
has to appear from day to day until etc. [Req. 1/3/248r]

14 December.[5] William Wolfe attorney etc. [Req. 1/3/259r]

---

[1] *Ex parte* Richard Smewen v. William Blaknall and Robert Blaknall.
[2] *Ex parte* John Talbot v. William Everard.
[3] 7 September should read 9 September.
[4] 13 September should read 13 October.
[5] *Ex parte* Isabelle Gorton v. Robert Reynolds (or Richard Reynolds – both
names appear in the MS).

20 January at Greenewich, Peter Wright appears etc. by R[ichard] T[urner] with the counsel of William Eliot, sergeant at law. [Req. 1/3/260r]

27 January.[1] William Bonds attorney etc. [Req. 1/3/260v]

On the same day the Abbot of the new Monastery appears by virtue of a Writ of Privy Seal under penalty of 500 pounds and has to appear from day to day until etc. under the same penalty. [Req. 1/3/261v]

On the same day. James Homewood appears by virtue of a Writ of Privy Seal at the suit of the Abbess of St. Bridget of Sion, and has to appear from day to day etc. [Req. 1/3/261v]

[fo. 71r]

*28 January, 22.H.7[2] [Req. 1/3/262r] and 29 January, fol. 242.[3] [Req. 1/3/262v] Causes of annuities decreed and the arrerages thereof.

[fo. 70v (p. 42)]

29 January. John Wood in the name of proxy for Lady Katherine Langley, widow, appears by virtue of a Writ of Privy Seal

[fo. 72r (p. 43)]

directed to the same Katherine, at the suit of Thomas Regwin, etc. [Req. 1/3/262r]

8 February. Thomas Grisacre, clerk, was allowed to appear by Henry, etc. in the case moved against him by the Abbot Meny etc. [Req. 1/3/269r]

11 February. Thomas Marston, fellow-monk and bursar of the Monastery of the Blessed Virgin Mary of the Fountains, appears in the name of proxy for the Abbot of the same monastery by virtue of a Writ of Privy Seal at the suit of Robert Fisher clerk etc. [Req. 1/3/270r]

[fo. 71r]

*11 February 22.H.7, fol. 249.[4] For certain services, sute of Court and other amerciaments. [Req. 1/3/271r]

[fo. 72r (p. 43)]

21 April. George Langton appears by virtue of a Writ of Privy

---

[1] *Ex parte* John Chapman v. William Goring, Richard Goring and Robert Carter.

[2] John Hunt and Agnes, his wife, Nicholas Daley and Joan, his wife and v. Isold Puttocke, widow.

[3] John Fylot, clerk, recluse in the Charterhouse at Shene v. Reginald Fylot, his brother.

[4] Christopher Hyde and Margaret, his wife v. Robert Jakes, Steward to William Hastings, esquire.

Seal under penalty of 100 pounds at the suit of the Lord Pope's Polidor[1] in England, etc. [Req. 1/3/284v]

28 April.[2] Richard Bray, attorney etc. [Req. 1/3/285v]

On the same day. Thomas Molens in the name of proxy for the Abbot of Abbotsbury, and for the same, appears by virtue of a Writ of Privy Seal under penalty of 500 marks, at the suit of Thomas Alexander etc.[3] [Req. 1/3/286r]

Robert Brudewell, attorney etc. April 30. [Req. 1/3/287v].

On the same day.[4] In the matter depending before the Kings most honourable Counsell betweene Robert Belwood, etc. [Req. 1/3/288r]

6 May. In the case moved by Simon Robinson against Ralph Chamberlaine it was enjoined to both the same Ralph and Simon Robinson to refrain from all further prosecution of their cases or pleas before judges whomsoever, or in courts whatsoever, while this case is suspended undecided before the Lord King's Council, and this under penalty to each of them of 40 pounds etc. [Req. 1/3/289v]

7 May. It was enjoined to Simon Harcourte that he should not withdraw without special permission of the Lord King's Council, and until the case in dispute between a certain William French and the aforementioned Simon should be fully decided, and meanwhile that the same Simon should refrain from all further process in common law against the said William, and this under penalty of 100 pounds. [Req. 1/3/290r]

19 May. It was enjoined to Christopher Banister under penalty of 100 pounds that he himself shall keep and preserve the peace, and his servants shall keep and preserve the peace, and any one of them shall keep and

[fo. 72v (p. 44)]

preserve [the peace] toward Richard Ellis and his servants. And it was enjoined likewise to Richard Ellis under the same penalty. [NR]

15 June.[5] Thomas Archer attorney etc. [Req. 1/3/293v]

[1] 'The Lord Pope's Polidore' was Polydore Vergil whose official duties in England were papal collector and nuncio. There are no extant papers relating to this case but it is possible that Vergil was suing to collect a papal obligation in the Court of Requests.

[2] *Ex parte* John Hicke v. John Copyngton.

[3] *Ex parte* Giles Winchester and Adam Splene v. Edmund Brykwell.

[4] Robert Belwood and Agnes, his wife v. Stephen Hatfield and Elizabeth, his wife, in the right of Elizabeth's three daughters by a previous marriage.

[5] 15 June should read 25 June.

2 July. Thomas Hopton was excused from further appearance before the Lord King's Council in the case moved against him by the party of John Crice, because this case is suspended undecided in common law, and thus he has withdrawn free without day. [Req. 1/3/294v][1]

13 July. Lady Anna Grisley, widow, was excused from further appearance before the Lord King's Council, in the case moved against her by Richard Grisley etc., because it appears by the certification of John etc. that the aforementioned Richard has no just case against the said Anna etc. [Req. 1/3/300r]

Anno 23.H.7.

23 October, at Hanworthe. John Bonway appears by virtue of a Writ of Privy Seal under penalty of 100 pounds at the suit of the Lord King, and has to appear from day to day etc. and this under the aforesaid penalty. [Req. 1/3/302v]

24 October, at Westminster. The Abbot of Fountains and William Ratcliff appear by virtue of injunctions given to them by the Lord King's Council, at the suit of Robert Fisher, clerk, and have to appear from day to day until etc. [Req. 1/3/302v]

25 October. William Damet was allowed to appear before the Lord King's Council in a case moved against him by the party of William Packard, by Robert Damet his attorney of Cliffords Inne, with a clause to appear in judgment and to pay to the person awarded if, etc. [Req. 1/3/303r]

28 October.[2] In the cause of variance moved afore the Kings Counsell by Robert Male, Richard Whele, and other against Richard Bastarde: It is enjoyned to the saide Richarde, that he proceed no further in any actions, taken in the common plees against them, but to remaine in such state as they now be unto the 15. of Saint Hillarie, next coming, and that upon paine of 40 lib.

4 November. Richard Copcote[3] and John West,[4] attorneys, before the Lord King's Council

[1] There is a Deputy Keeper's note on Req. 1/3/296v indicating that this folio and several others were brought into the P.R.O. as a part of the Star Chamber papers (STAC). They were subsequently removed from STAC.2/25 and placed in their proper position in Req. 1/3.

[2] There have been orders from the Court not to initiate Common Law actions and there have been releases from the Court in cases where a Common-Law action has been in progress. This is, however, the first instance selected by J.C. of Requests suspending further action at common law, in an action already started, pending a future appearance in the Court of Requests.

[3] William (?) Hallam and Agnes, his wife v. John Goodwin and Elizabeth, his wife.   [4] John Hills v. Robert Turgis.

[fo. 73r (p. 45)]

with a clause to appear in judgment and to pay to the person awarded. [Req. 1/3/305r]

18 November. In the case of William Jeffrey against William Cobb: it was enjoined to the same William Jeffrey under penalty of 100 pounds that he should refrain from having all further process in common law against the aforesaid William while the case is suspended undecided before the said council, and until he shall have had otherwise in commands by the said council. [Req. 1/3/309v]

25 November. Agnes Sordich, widow, was excused from further appearance before the Lord King's Council in the case moved against her by the party of Lady Joanna Kidwelly, widow, concerning a certain farm called Legats situated in Watford, because the aforementioned Lady Joanna Kidwelly has, on the days assigned to her, [not] prosecuted her case against the aforesaid Agnes, neither by herself nor by her authorized attorney, and thus the said Agnes has withdrawn, free from further impeachment of the said Lady Joanna in the same case, without day.[1] [Req. 1/3/311v]

29 November. Lady Margaret Carew, widow, was excused from further appearance, etc., in the case moved against her by Richard Androes etc. [Req. 1/3/313r]

14 February.[2] In the matter of variance depending etc. betweene Joane Garraway, plaintiff, and the Reverend Father in God Silvester, Bishop of Worcester: it is decreede etc. [Req. 1/3/328r]

18 February,[3] the Abbot of the Monastery of Biland appears by virtue of an injunction, etc. in the case moved against him by Robert Warcup, etc. [Req. 1/3/329r]

At Greenewich, March 31.[4] Thomas Nelson attorney before the Lord King's Council in the case moved by John Irton against Richard Kelton, with a clause to abide in judgment and to pay charges. [Req. 1/3/331r]

4 April. Roland Morton attorney in like manner. [NR]

6 May. Robert Egerle attorney in like manner. [NR]

---

[1] In Req. 1/3/311v the *minime* which Caesar struck out was part of the text which accounts for the negative syntax in the rest of the entry.

[2] 14 February should read 16 February.

[3] 18 February should read 23 February.

[4] From 31 March, 23.H.7 until 7.H.8 there are no surving Order and Decree books. The cases that have been found have come from the class Req. 2, Proceedings in the Court of Requests.

10 May. Nicholas Hudson and John Breus, attorneys in like manner. [NR]

On the same day, Lady Joanna Mountgomery appears by Blunte of the Middle Temple, at the suit of Roger Parker etc. [Req. 2/17/33]

15 May. Thomas Leigh was allowed to appear in the case moved against him by the party of Peter Asheton, by William Danby of Le

[fo. 73v. (p. 46)]

Cliffords Inne with the counsel of William Fairefax, sergeant at law etc. [NR]

On the same day John Beldon and Roger Whetely, attorneys before the Lord King's Council, with a clause to abide in judgment and to pay charges. [NR]

19 May. Bartholomew Harwood appears by virtue of a Writ of Privy Seal under penalty of 100 pounds at the suit of the Abbot of Egliston etc. [NR]

On the same day Lionel Fowle appears as proctor for the Abbot of Whalley by virtue of a Writ of Privy Seal etc. at the suit of the Abbess of Sion etc. [NR]

20 May. John Forde attorney etc. [NR]

2 June. A.B. allowed to appear etc. with the counsel of William Grevile sergeant at law. [NR]

4 July. Nicholas Chokke, in the case moved against him by the party of John Chokke, was allowed to appear by Richard Turnor, with the counsel of John Roo with a clause to. abide in judgment and to pay charges. [NR]

Anno 24.H.7.

25 October. Robert Porter attorney etc. [NR]

[fo. 74r]

*23 November, 24.H.7, fol. 73. The case of Richard Hatton clerk, provost of King's College within the University of Cambridge, and the scholars of the same on the one hand, and Elizabeth Holland, recently wife and executrix of Roger Holland deceased of these parts on the other, concerning arrears of the rent of the Priory of St. James near the city of Exeter appropriated to the provost and scholars of the same college. [NR]

[fo. 73v (p. 46)]

3 February. William Bounde, attorney with a clause to abide in judgment and to pay charges. [NR]

6 February. The Prior of Berleche was allowed to appear before the Lord King's Council, in the case as far as riot [i.e., concerning riot] moved against him by the party of William Rouswell, by William Hewet his attorney, with a clause to abide in judgment and to pay charges, and the case as far as a tenement [i.e., concerning a tenement] is remitted to common law, to be decided in the same place. [NR]

13 March. John Newdigate Attorney etc. [NR]

23 April. Thomas Chowe appears as proctor for the Abbot of Hayles by virtue of a Writ of Privy Seal, and has to appear from day to day until etc. [NR]

Anno Primo H.8.

[fo. 74r]

*9 July, 1.H.8. fol. 103. John Bountaine, gentleman, plaintiff, Sir John Chock, knight, defendant, touching certain obligations in variaunce betwene them.

[fo. 73v (p. 46)]

19 October. John Chorman appears as proctor for Herrald Staunton by virtue of a Writ of Privy Seal and the same John says

[fo. 75r (p. 47)]

within the words of his priesthood that the said Harrald is detained by such infirmity etc. [NR]

8 November. Anthony Fitzherbert of Le Greys Inne, attorney, before the Lord King's Council with a clause to abide in judgment and to pay charges. [NR]

19 November. John Stepneth appears by virtue of a Writ of Privy Seal etc. [NR]

5 February. Thomas Moreton, attorney, etc. [NR]

Anno 2.H.8.

12 June. Agnes Buckley, widow, was excused from further appearance before the Lord King's Council in a case moved against her by the party of William Marcham, haberdasher of the City of London, because this case between the aforesaid parties is suspended undecided in common law, and thus the said Agnes withdrew free without day from further impleading of the said William before the said Council etc. [NR]

[fo. 74v]

*2 October, 2.H.8., fol. 147. Sir Edmond Lucy, knight, plaintiff; Thomas Wheler and Thomas Linnall, priests of the Chauntery

of Hampton, defendants, for an annuel rent of 16 shillings issueng
out of certain meadowes and pastures, etc. [NR]
[fo. 75r (p. 47)]
30 October at Richmond, John Towneley, knight, appears by
virtue of a judgment exacted before the Earl of Salop etc. [NR]
7 November. Thomas Hampton attorney etc. [NR]
16 December. In the case which is pending before the Lord
King's Council between Robert Arderum and Joanna his wife,
party plaintiff, and John Barton, clerk, party defendant, of and
concerning right, title and possession of the Manor of Blakborne,
in the county of Lancaster with appurtenances in dispute; the
bills, answers, replies and rejoinders of the aforesaid parties
having been heard by the aforesaid council, and mature deliberation having been held thereupon; it was decreed that the aforesaid Robert Arderum, by right and title of Joanna his wife and
mother of the aforesaid John Barton, should have, enjoy and
possess all revenues and profits in any way regarding or pertaining
to the said Manor of Blackborne, with its appurtenances, during
the life of the said Joanna, without any disturbance, disruption,
vexation or hindrance of the aforesaid
[fo. 75v (p. 48)]
John Barton or any other at his use or at his agency, and this
under penalty of 100 pounds to be raised from the goods and
chattels of the said John to the use of the said King, in case they
shall have attempted or caused to be attempted anything in
opposition to this decree. [NR]
30 January. Robert Bowring, attorney, with a clause to abide in
judgment and to pay charges. [NR]

Anno 3.H.8.

16 October. Richard Southwicke appears by virtue of an injunction given to him by Richard Wrettesley and Walter Leveson
esquires, under penalty of 100 pounds at the suit of Robert
Milleston and has to appear from day to day until etc. [NR]
27 October. Thomas Drake, clerk, rector of Lincoln College within
the University of Oxford, appears by virtue of a Writ of Privy
Seal, at the suit of the Provost and Fellows of a college called
Oriel College, within the same University, and the same Thomas
Drake was allowed to appear in the same case by Robert Claiton,
clerk, his attorney, with a clause to abide in judgment and to pay
charges, etc. [NR]

4 November. John Carile one of the Lord King's sergeants at law, and others appeared by virtue of a Writ of Privy Seal under penalty of 100 pounds, at the suit of John Hull, and have to answer to a bill of complaint proposed against them, next Thursday, and thus to appear from day to day until etc. Afterward, to wit on November 8, they were allowed to appear by R[ichard] T[urner] attorney etc. [Req. 2/10/56]

On the same day. Robert Ballard and others appear by virtue of a Writ of Privy Seal etc. at the suit of the Abbot of Battle, etc [NR]

6 November. Thomas Derham gentleman appears by virtue of a Writ of Privy Seal etc. at the suit of the Abbess of Denny in the county of Cambridge, etc. [NR]

28 November. In the cause of variance mooved afore the

[fo. 76r (p. 49)]

kings honourable Counsell, betweene Nicholas Reade of Aghton of Blackeburne shire in the Countie of Lancaster, complaiant, and Richard Heskethe and Sir Richard Sherborne, knight, defendants, of and for certein landes and tenementes set lying and being in Aghton aforesayd, called Lomycloughs in the sayd Countie, of the yerely value of 40 libri. Whereupon a commission under the kings letter, at the sute of the sayd Read, was directed unto the Abbot of Walley, and John Banester of Wadington, gentleman, for to examine, and certifie, the right, and title, of the said parties, of and in the premisses: upon whose certificate to the said counsell made, it appeareth that the very right, and title of the sayd lands and tenements, justly belongeth to a certain Chauntry, and towardes the finding of a Priest, to pray for the soule of one Alice Heskethe, mother of said Richard etc. Wherefore the said Counsell upon the consideration aforesaid etc. have awarded, ordered and decreed etc. [NR]

20 January. The Abbot of Darwelcresse appears by virtue of a Writ of Privy Seal etc, at the suit of Henry Piot, and has to answer etc. and to appear from day to day, until etc. [NR]

Afterwards, to wit on January 26, the aforesaid Abbot was allowed to appear before the said Council in the same case by Richard Turner his attorney, with the counsel of Anthony Fitzherbert, Lord King's sergeant at law, with a clause to abide in judgment and to pay charges, etc. [NR]

On the same day. Gerard Sotehill appears as proctor for the Lord of Clifford before the Lord King's Council, in a certain case moved against him by the party of the Abbot of St. Mary, of the city of York and has to appear from day to day until, etc., under penalty of 200 pounds. [NR]

On the same day. Robert ap Meredith appears before the Lord King's Council by virtue of a Writ of Privy Seal at the suit of the Bishop of Carlisle and has to answer etc. [NR]

[fo. 76v (p. 50)]

16 February. In the case which is pending before the King's Council between William Greene, party plaintiff, and John More-ton, party defendant, of and concerning right, title and possession of certain lands and tenements situated and lying in Sturminster Marshall, and elsewhere in the counties of Dorset and Wiltshire, in dispute between the aforesaid parties. The circumstances of this case having been seen, heard, and fully understood by the said council, and mature deliberation having been held thereupon, both upon sight of the evidences concerning the matter of the said lands and tenements yielded to the most Reverend Father in Christ John Moreton, recently Archbishop of Canterbury, and of other evidences yielded to Richard Moreton father of the afore-mentioned deceased, of the other part of the aforesaid lands, as well as of the indentures made between the aforementioned Archbishop and the aforenamed William Greene plaintiff, of the tribute of all lands in dispute, for which the said Archbishop, for the said William Greene, made satisfaction to the Lords of Sturton and of Audeley of 100 marks, as well as to other creditors of the said William to the sum of 60 pounds and more. And nothing effectual having been alleged or proved to the contrary by the party of the said William, it is decreed, that this case will be decided between the aforesaid parties according to the course or common law, and thus they have withdrawn free from further appearance before the said Council in the same case. [Req. 2/1/62]

Anno 4.H.8.

9 May at Greenwich. Bartholomew St. Leger was allowed to appear by R[ichard] T[urner] his attorney, with the counsel of Louis Pollard, sergeant at Law, with a clause to abide in judgment and to pay charges etc. [NR]

1 July. Robert Preston appears in the name of William Gascoine, knight, by virtue of a Writ of Privy Seal under penalty of 100 pounds at the suit of the Abbot of Cristall, etc. [NR]

[fo. 77r (p. 51)]

2 November. John Orenge appears in the name of the Abbot of Torbey by virtue of a Writ of Privy Seal etc. at the suit of John Dolman, and has to answer to a bill next Monday etc. [Req. 2/13/77]

12 November. Christopher Askewe appears by virtue of a Writ of Privy Seal at the suit of the Abbot of Welhowe and others and has to answer to a bill proposed against him next Friday, and thus to appear from day to day until etc. [NR]

29 January. Nicholas Williams of Lincoln's Inn appears as proctor for the Abbot of Tinturn before the Lord King's Council at the suit of John Care, and has to appear from day to day until etc. [NR]

18 April. William Wodde appears in the name of the Abbot of Ramsey, by virtue of a Writ of Privy Seal at the suit of Thomas Baron of Burwell, and has to answer to a bill on next Monday, and thus to appear from day to day until etc. [NR]

Anno 5.H.8.

From the 20th day of April in the 4th year until 3 May, 6.H.8, no act before the Lord King's Council is found in the register.

Anno 6.H.8.

18 September. In the matter of variance depending before the Kings most honourable Counsell, betweene Thomas Cooke clearke, vicar of Halberton, complainant, and Philip Courtney, gentleman, defendant, of and for the right, title & possession of 4. closures called the Vicars parkes, with a parcell of meddow, set and lying within the parish of Halberton, it is by the King's most honourable Counsell upon the sight etc. ordeined, awarded, and decreed etc. [NR]

26 October.[1] Edmund Riddale was allowed to appear in

[fo. 77v (p. 52)]

the case moved against him by the party of Robert Hoddes and others, by William Dobson his attorney with the counsel of Brian Palmes, sergeant at law, with a clause to abide in judgment and to pay charges. [Req. 2/10/20]

16 November. Henry Clifford, lord Clifford, Westmerland, and Vessy, Roger Tempest and John Bosome, gentlemen, appear by Writ of Privy Seal by Henry Rudley, junior their attorney, and

---

[1] Robert Hoddes was but one of twelve tenants of the manor who were suing for the custom of the manor.

were allowed to appear, by the party of Anna Warcup, widow, by John Lamberd of le Clements Inne, with a clause to abide in judgment and to pay charges. And thus the same John Lamberd has to appear in the same case from day to day until etc. [NR]

30 January. John Reade appears in the name of the Abbot of Kirkesteed by virtue of a Writ of Privy Seal etc. at the suit of Thomas Raviton etc. And he has to appear from day to day until etc. [NR]

4 March. Richard Eyre of Brampton in the county of Darby appears by virtue of a Writ of Privy Seal, etc., at the suit of Margaret, countess of Salisburie, etc. [NR]

March 30. In the case of Gregory Medley and Roger Mounday against Henry Keble, William Browne and others, term was given in the next month of Easter to the aforesaid parties to produce witnesses and by other grace of proofs to prove things alleged by them, and to see further process in the same case, and this under peril of this case: excepting only the profits to the defendant's party concerning the jurisdiction of the court of the Staple of Calais, because it is established that this case shall be decided in the same court. [NR]

Anno 7.H.8.

28 April.[1] The case specified in the bill of Roger Bostoke against Charles Memwaring and Izabella his mother, is remitted to the lords of the Lord King's Council in

[fo. 79r (p. 53)]

the Marches of Wales, to be decided in the same place, because it concerns lands and tenements being in the County Palatine of Chester, etc. [NR]

4 May. Nicholas Rugeley attorney etc. [NR]

12 May. Richard Bewley attorney etc. [NR]

The day after the Ascension, Walter Luke, attorney before the Lord King's Council, with a clause to abide in judgment and to pay charges. [NR]

15 May. In the matter of variance etc. Betweene John Shailerd the elder etc. and John Shailerd the younger etc. of and for the right, title and possession of a messuage and an hundred acres of land, twentie acres of medow, and twentie acres of pasture, set, lying

---

[1] Although the next several entries may appear in Req. 1/4 the volume is too damaged to be readable throughout. As the foliation is not sequential the earlier parts of the volume are in fact later than the parts which follow.

and being etc. after deliberate advise, & due examination etc. with such proofes and witnesses, as they for their title and interest would shew or declare, and forasmuch as it evidently appeareth etc. It is by the said Counsel ordered, adjudged, and decreed, that the saide John Shailerd the elder from henceforth shal have, possede [*sic*], and enjoy the said tenement and lands to him and his assignes without let, disturbance or impediment of the saide John Shailerd the yonger, or of any other person and persons by his procuring or stirring, unto the time he shall shew afore the said Counsell other matter effectuall for the proofe of his title, in derogation of this decree, etc. [NR]

9 June. The Dean of the Chapel of the Lord King, Lord King's Councillor, John Veysy LL.D. [NR]

10 June. The case between Henry Sawcheverel, knight, and Dionysius Lowe is committed to Lord Justice Reade, of the Lord King's common bench, to investigate and finally decide title of lands and holdings lately in dispute between the aforesaid parties. [NR]

28 June. Thomas Fitz-Hughe attorney before the Lord King's council with a clause to abide in judgment and to pay charges. [NR]

[fo. 78v]

*30 June, 7 Henry 8, fol. 241.[1] Thomas Magnus, clerk, and John Chackwray, plaintiffs. Sir Walter Calverley, knight, and Robert Calverley, his onkle, defendants concerning tithes and other duties and glebe landes belonging to the parsonage of Calverley.

[fo. 79r (p. 53)]

3 July. Thomas Rolfe, attorney before the Lord King's Council with a clause to abide in judgment and to pay charges. [NR]

[fo. 79v (p. 54)]

17 September. Thomas, Archbishop of York, Lord King's Councillor.[2] [NR]

15 October. John Vesy, Dean, John Gilbert, esquire, Rawlens, Almoner; King's Commissioners. [NR]

15 October. Robert Hege in the name of the Abbot of Bury St. Edmunds in the county of Suffolk appeared by virtue of a Writ of Privy Seal at the suit of Thomas Cler, and has to answer to a bill, etc. [Req. 1/4/3v]

---

[1] No such foliation exists in Req. 1/4. The reference may be from a missing volume or from Req. 1/4/24 which is entirely unreadable.

[2] This is the first appearance of Wolsey that J.C. notes in the collection.

20 October. Edward Gryvill, knight, appears by virtue of a Writ of Privy Seal etc. at the suit of the Bishop of Carlisle, etc. [Req. 1/4/4r]

24 October. John Wright attorney with a clause to abide in judgment and to pay charges. [NR]

2 November. Alexander Briggs, attorney, with a clause to abide in judgment and to pay charges. [NR]

4 November. Nicholas Speccot, gentleman, and Nicholas Badworthy appear by virtue of commands given to them by William Courtney and Edmund Larder, Lord King's Commissioners etc. [NR]

8 November. John Chamonde and John Arundell of Calverne, Commissioners, anything done before them was said done before the King's Council.[1] [NR]

12 November. Robert Wye and John Strange of the Inner Temple appear in the name of the Abbot of Malmesbury by virtue of a Writ of Privy Seal, etc. [Req. 1/4/5v]

16 November. John Waller and Thomas Hall, attorneys, with a clause to abide in judgment and to pay charges. [NR]

27 November.[2] In the matter of controversie depending afore the kings honourable Counsell betweene Richard etc. of and for the right or interest of a lease made, and granted etc.

1 December.[3] Robert Low, attorney, with a clause to abide in judgment and to pay charges. [Req. 1/4/8v]

23 January.[4] John Worshop, attorney, with a clause to abide in judgment and to pay charges. [Req. 1/4/11r]

On the same.[5] Roger Chomely, attorney, in like manner. [NR]

On the same.[5] William Coningesby, attorney, in like manner. [Req. 1/4/13v]

25 February.[6] Robert Norwich, attorney, in like manner. [Req. 1/4/14v]

10 April.[7] William Matthew, attorney, in like manner. [Req. 1/4/18r]

---

[1] Although the examination of witnesses by commissioners had been employed prior to the date of this entry, this was the first time that the authority of the commissioners was so explicitly spelled out.

[2] A very badly damaged folio. Richard Bageworth v. Richard Poole.

[3] Henry Knight v. Richard Caxton and Richard Rednesse.

[4] Richard Philipe v. John Dobbye.

[5] *Eodem die* is in fact after 28 January. Peter Martinson v. William Conningsby and Adam Palmer.   [6] Richard Waren v. Richard Lewes.

[7] *Ex parte* Thomas Austen v. Humphrey Brown.

Anno 8.H.8.

22 April.[1] Michael Middleton, attorney, with a clause to abide in judgment and to pay charges. [Req. 1/4/19r]

10 June. It is injoyned and injunction is given to Edward [fo. 81r (p. 55)] Willoughby, esquire, by the Kings Honourable Counsell, that he in no wise, ne, no other in his name, call upon the kings Justices, or any of them, for judgement to be given in the matter of variance betweene him and Martin Arden, *to stay after verdict and not to call for judgements* for the title of a lease of the farme place called the Heygate in the Countie of Staffordshire which of long time hath beene depending afore the sayd Counsell, and yet is undiscussed, unto such time, as by them other order and direction shalbe had, and taken, between the sayd parties, and that upon paine of three hundred poundes sterling, to be levied of the landes, goods, and cattels of the sayd Edward, to the use of our sovereigne Lord the King or his heires, if hee attempt the contrary of this order, and injunction aforesayd [Req. 1/4/22v]

[fo. 80v]
*10 June, 8.H.8, fol. 23. Agnes Andimor, widoe, plaintiff, [v.] David Lloyd and John Hume, defendants, for 16 shillings 8 d. yerely to bee payed out of a messuage and certain landes in Kingston in Surrey. [Req. 1/4/23r]

[fo. 81r (p. 55)]
1 July. Thomas Barnewell, in the name of the Abbot of St. Albans appeared by virtue of a Writ of Privy Seal, etc. at the suit of Gregory Creswell, etc. *fol. 25.* [Req. 2/12/211]

The same. In the matter of variance depending before the kings honourable Counsell betweene John Sanford, sonne and heire of Richard Sanford the yoonger, complainant, against Robert Sanford his uncle, defendant, of, for and upon the right, title and possession and interest of two tenements, etc. It is ordered, awarded, and decreed that the sayd Robert shall avoyd, amove and depart out and from the possession of the same, and every part thereof, by the feast of St. Michael the Archangell next, etc. And over and above this, it is further ordered, that if the sayd Robert be obstinate, and refuse to depart and avoyd from the said tenements, at the day afore specified, that then one of the Kings justices of peace there next and adjoining, by authoritie heereof, the morrow

---

[1] Robert Soham and John Bermingham v. Robert Sympson.

next after the sayd feast, to put the sayd John in peaceable possession of the same tenements, and the sayd Robert cleerly thereof
to expell and put out. *a warrant to the next Justice to put the
plaintiff into the possession of landes.* [NR]
4 July. Robert Holt, attorney, with a clause to abide in judgement
and to pay charges. [NR]
The same. Robert Porter, attorney, with a clause to abide in
judgement and to pay charges. [NR]
[fo. 81v (p. 56)]
The same. Injunction is given by the Kings honourable Counsell
to William Smith, late of London brewer, that he upon paine of
300 libri to be levied to the use of our sovereigne Lord the King,
surcease, and leave his sute made against John Wombewel, and
other, at the Common law and that hee also cause the exigent
against the same Wombewell taken to be put in suspense unto the
time, the matter now being afore the sayd Counsell, be ordered and
determined, by compromise, or otherwise, as by them shall be
thought consonant to right and good conscience. *fol. 27.* [Req.
1/4/27v]
10 November,[1] In the cause of variance depending afore the
Kings honourable counsell, betweene John Kent etc. of and for the
right, title, and interest of a lease etc. *for a lease.* [Req. 1/4/33v]
13 November.[2] In the matter of variance depending afore the
Kings honourable Counsell betweene Henry etc. of for and upon
the right, title and interest of an hundred acres, etc. [Req. 1/4/35r]
25 November. Where a matter of variance is depending afore the
Kings honourable Counsell, betweene John Fisher etc., complainant, against Gawin Ratclife, defendant, of and for a lease or
grant made to the sayd complainant, by the Abbot and Convent of
Fountaines etc. it is ordered and decreed etc. and in the meane
time the sayd Abbot to surcease all maner of processe by him taken
at the Common Law, against the defendant, and the sayd plaintifs
to enjoy the tithes aforesayd, according to the tenour of this
decree, upon paine aforesayd, untill such time as this decree be
adnulled by witnesse. [Req. 1/4/36v]
10 February. A decree made for the tenaunts and inhabitants of
Northumstan in the countie of Notingham, complainant, against

---

[1] John Kent *alias* Austen, the younger v. Robert, prior of Royston, and John
Kent *alias* Austen, the elder.
[2] Henry Trefyn v. Thomas Philip, William Chyroys and John William.

one Richard Skimshawe and others, defendants, touching the diking and stopping of a way thereabouts, leading to the Kings high way, that from thenceforth the sayd inhabitants should enjoy the sayd

[fo. 83r (p. 57)]

way, etc., without the let of the sayd Richard etc. [Req. 1/4/36v]

[fo. 80v]

*13 February, 8.H.8, fol. 45. Humfrey Stafford, esquier, plaintiff, [v.] John Butler, defendant, for the title and possession of 8 saltfats [sic] in Droitwhich in Worcestershire. [Req. 1/4/45r]

[fo. 83r (p. 57)]

16 March.¹ John Bury, attorney, with a clause to abide in judgment and to pay charges. [Req. 1/4/47v]

23 March.² William Esington, attorney, with a clause to abide in judgment and to pay charges. [Req. 1/4/47v]

Anno 9.H.8.

27 April.³ John More, sergeant of the Lords Privy Seal, attorney with a clause to abide in judgment and to pay charges. [Req. 1/4/49r]

11 May. Christopher Bradesey appeared by virtue of a Writ of Privy Seal at the suit of the Abbot of Furnes etc. [Req. 1/4/53v]

27 May, whereas matter of variance hath bene mooved afore the Kings honourable Counsell, betweene Izabell Eire, widow, complainant, and Sir Thomas Buckley, knight, defendant, of, for, and upon certeine lands and tenements being in the county of Yorke: and also of and upon the right, interest, title, use and possession of the same etc. It is decreed, ordered, and determined, that the sayd Izabel shall recovery have, and from hencefoorth quietly enjoy the sayd tenements and lands, above rehearsed etc. And over that it is ordered that the said Thomas shal content and pay unto the sayd Izabel Eire etc. 40 Shillings in ful recompense, and allowance of all costs and dammages susteined etc. for the trial of the right of the same lands: The sayd decree was exemplified under the privy seal, and signed by the hand of King Henry the eight, and is in the custody of one Bossevill, esquire, and is his evidence for this land, I did see it, and it was shewed by M. Thomas Seckeford, Master of

¹ Robert Gurnell, clerk v. Thomas Feteplace.
² John Wylde, Robert Walle and William Pynchbeck, clerks v. Lady Elizabeth Rede.
³ Philip Kenton v. Richard Drinkwater. John More may be Sir Thomas More's younger brother who also served as his clerk.

Requestes to the Queenes Majesty Queene Elizabeth. Richard Ostley.[1] And afterwards, viz. 20 October 11.H.8 the sonne of the sayd Sir Thomas, for disquieting her possession, was awarded to to pay her 40 libri and a new decree for the establishing of her possession. And he further injoyned not to interrupt, ne let the said complainent, her farmours ot [sic] tennantes, in the occupation or peaceable possession in the sayde landes, nor no further

[fo. 83v (p. 58)]
vexe, nor sue her for the same by any proces in the common law, nor never hereafter to bring any assise against her for the said lands etc. [Req. 1/4/62v–63v]

[fo. 82v]
*27 May 9.H.8, fol. 59. The Choristers of the Cathedral church of Sarum, plaintiff, [v.] John Ludlowe, gentleman, defendant, for 7 shillings yerely issueng out of certain landes of the said plaintiff, etc., given by his auncestors to the Choristers of the said Church for the maintenance of an antheime. [Req. 1/4/59r]

[fo. 83v (p. 58)]
15 June. The Abbot of the Monastery of Hilton etc. appears by virtue of a Writ of Privy Seal and has to appear from day to day until etc., at the suit of Thomas Rode etc. [Req. 1/4/64r]

20 June. John, Abbot of the Monastery of Chersey was allowed to appear before the Lord King's Council in the case moved against him by the party of Waren, by Pulsted his attorney with a clause to abide in judgment and to pay charges. [Req. 1/4/67r]

22 June. The Abbot of the Monastery of Notley was allowed to appear before the Lord King's Council in the case moved against him by the party of Thomas Cooke and other inhabitants of Notley, by John Basset his attorney, with a clause to abide in judgment and to pay charges. [Req. 1/4/67v]

*27 June, 9.H.8, fol. 70. John Goward and Elionor his wife, plaintiff, [v.] Richard Gery, gentleman, defendant. For certain evidences, escripts, charters and muniments concerning a tenement and certain landes. [Req. 1/4/70v]

[fo. 83v (p. 58)]
20 July. A decree by the kings honourable Counsell in the cause betweene Thomas Hall, parson of the parish Chuch [sic] of Crodwell, plaintife, and Richard, Abbot of the Monasterie of

---

[1] This was a margin note in Req. 1/4.

Malmesbury, defendant, against the Abbot. *for 2 oxen and a kowe taken from them by the Abbot as a mortuary.* [Req. 1/4/77r]

9 February. The Abbot of the monastery of Bildwas appears before the Lord King's Council in the case moved against him, by the party of John Bennet, and has to appear from day to day until he should have otherwise in commands by the aforesaid council, and this under penalty of allegiance. [Req. 1/4/87r]

12 February. The Abbot of Bildwas was allowed to appear before the Lord King's Council in the case moved against him by the party of John Benet, by Roger Trentham his attorney, with a clause to abide in judgment and to pay charges. [Req. 1/4/89r] [fo. 82v]

*12 February. 9.H.8, fol. 88. Jone Jourden, widow, executrix, to Henry Jourden her late husband, plaintiff, [v.] John Whitehall, defendant, for certain goods, implements and howseholdstuf and 40 shillings due to her late husband as executor to Jane Morice, creditor to the said defendant. [Req. 1/4/88v] [fo. 83v (p. 58)]

Anno 10.H.8.

17 June.[1] Thomas Hacche, attorney, with a clause to abide in judgment and to pay charges. [Req. 1/4/98r]

24 June. Thomas Lovet appears by virtue of a Writ of Privy Seal at the suit of the Abbot of Betlesdon etc. and gave answer, and upon this was allowed to appear before the Lord King's Council [fo. 85r (p. 59)] in the said case, by Edward Warner of the Middle Temple with a clause to abide in judgment and to pay charges. [Req. 1/4/98v]

8 July. William Addingegrove appears by virtue of letters missive, etc. [Req. 1/4/99v]

18 November.[2] The Abbot of the Monastery of Chersey appears by virtue of letters missive at the suit of John Pigion, and has to answer to a bill, etc., and to appear from day to day until etc. [Req. 1/4/114v]

On the same. The Abbot of the monastery of Dale appears by virtue of a Writ of Privy Seal at the suit of Alice Rawson, and has to answer to a bill etc. and to appear from day to day until etc. [Req. 1/4/115r]

---

[1] James Williams v. Thomas Chapleman, William Dewneman, Thomas Beard.
[2] This MS is too badly damaged to confirm this entry.

On the same.¹ William Hall, attorney, with a clause to abide in judgment and to pay charges. [Req. 1/4/115r]
[fo. 84v]
18 November, 10.H.8, fol. 112. John Waldorne of Belbroughton in Worcestershire, plaintiff, against Philip Cachemay and 6 other defendants for the attachment or seisure of 4 tonnes of iron seized by the Sherifs of Glocester at the sute of the said defendant alleadging that no smitheholders on the overside of the wood in the forest of Deane should carry or sell any iron further then Glocester, etc. [Req. 1/4/112r]
*The same, fol. 113. John Reve of London, Inholder, plaintiff, and William Mede of the same Citie, bruer [i.e. brewer], defendant, for 12 clothes called Northeren dozens of the goods of one Rowland Walker left in the custodie of the said plaintiff safely to bee kept to the use of the said Walker, the which clothes afterwards at the request of the said defendant were delivered to one William Cooke of Cottington in Hertfordshire, draper, for whom the said defendant undertooke as suretie and to the save the said plaintiff harmeles for the said delivery. [Req. 1/4/113r]
*The same. Agnes Beall, widoe, plaintiff, William Walreme of Brenkworth in Wiltshire, defendant, for the unlawful taking away of 3 kine and 3 calves belonging to the said plaintiff, etc. [Req. 1/4/113v–114r]
[fo. 85r (p. 59)]
24 November. Whereas variance of late hath bene moved afore the kings honourable counsell, betweene John Chamberlaine etc. and William Terill, gentleman, etc. the said Terrill claiming to be seassed of the said Chamberlaine and his auncestors as villaines, and nefs regardants² unto the sayde manour: Forasmuch as the said Chamberlaine, hath shewed a sufficient and lawfull manumission sealed with the seal of the auncestors of the said Terrell, owner of the manour etc, it is ordered, and decreed, that the saide Terrell from henceforth, shall not onely peaceably permit and suffer the said John Chamberlaine, and his heires, tenants and assignes to have, hold, occupie, and injoy the said messes, and landes aboue specified etc. but also suffer him to goe at his free

---

¹ William Gysnam v. Thomas Colson, clerk, and Gerard Ornell.
² I.e. niefs regardants. 'Niefs' were bonds-women and 'regardants' referred to the responsibility to perform all base services within the manor. See J. Cowell, *A Law Dictionary* (edition of 1727) *sub* 'Niefs' and 'Regardant'.

libertie without seasure of his bodie, lands, goods, cattels etc. [Req. 1/4/116v]

On the same. In the cause of variance depending afore the kings most honourable Counsell etc. betweene Richard Waren plaintife against Sir Richard Fitz-lewes, Knight, etc. *fol. 117 the plaintiff an administrator for 6 featherbeds with theire bolsters & 5 horses etc.* [Req. 1/4/117v]

17 December, 15.18. [i.e. A.D. 1518] (10.H.8) in the King's house at Greenwich, the Florentine citizens Pietro de Bardis and Barnardo Cavalcanti being personally before us in a certain suit and case between the aforesaid pending before the honorable King's Council: the said Pietro, plaintiff and suer, sought

[fo. 85v (p. 60)]

that surety of abiding in judgment and paying charges should be given to him by the said Barnardo. Which Barnardo called and brought before us the prudent man Giovanni Cavalcanti, Florentine citizen and merchant. Which Giovanni indeed by all better means etc. promised to the process [or presence] and suit, and stood as surety of abiding in judgment and paying charges for the said Barnardo to the same Pietro in the aforesaid case, in the presence of all the aforesaid separate men, Master Pietro Torrisano,[1] Florentine sculptor, and Richard Manchester, Englishman, as witnesses etc. [Req. 1/4/119v]

January 31. The Abbot of Boxley etc. appear by virtue of a Writ of Privy Seal and have to answer to a bill etc. and thus to appear from day to day etc. [NR]

16 February. Where matter of variance hath beene had, and mooved afore the Kings honourable Counsell between James Gangrain of the Isle of Garnsey, mariner, gardian of the daughter of John Viner of the sayd Isle, marchant, complainant, against Thomas Fevir and James Fevir executor of the last will and testament of John Fevir their father for the sum of 108 libri sterling, left in the handes and custodie of the sayd John Fevir deceased, safely to bee kept, to the use and behoofe of one Thomasin, one of the daughters of the sayd John Viner, *Money left in trust to the use of children* towards her preferment in mariage, the which summe so left, as afore is rehearsed, the sayd Thomas Fevir and James by their aunswere remaining afore the sayd Counsell, have alledged, declared and sayd was redelivered by their testator in his

---

[1] Probably this was Pietro Torrigiamo, the sculptor of Henry VII's tomb.

life to one John Martin at the desire of the sayd complainant; whereof they have made no such proofe by witnesse, ne otherwise afore the Commissioners assigned for the hearing of the same, ne yet in the 15. day of February last past, to them by the sayd Counsell also assigned for proofe of the same. In consideration whereof, and forasmuch as it evidently appeareth, by the othes of certain credible persons, that the sayd 108 libri was in the chest, and keeping of the sayd John Fevir their father, afore

[fo. 87r (p. 61)]

and after his decease, to whome the sayd Thomas and James bene [being] executours, leaving aswell in their possession and keeping the foresayde summe of 108 libri as much other great substance and goods. It is ordered and decreed by the sayd Counsell, that the sayd Thomas and James Fevir upon the sight heereof, or within the space of sixe dayes next ensuing, shal deliver or cause to be delivered to the said James Gangrain or to Henrie Beauvoir atturney to the sayd James, the foresayd summe of 108 libri without any further delay therein to be made, upon pain of 200 libri to be levied of the landes, goodes, and cattels of the said Thomas and James Fevir, to the use of our sovereigne Lord the king, if they truely content and pay not the same as afore is specified. [Req. 1/4/135r]

27 February. Philip Clerk of the island of Jersey, clerk, appears by virtue of a Writ of Privy Seal under penalty of 100 pounds at the suit of John Salmon, and because the bill of the said John concerns lands lying in the said island, therefore it is remitted by the Lord King's Council to the King's Jurats of the said island to administer justice to the parties according to the customs practiced in the same place. [Req. 1/4/135r]

[fo. 86v]

*27 February, 10.H.8, fol. 135. Julii Nethermill of the city of Coventrie, draper, plaintiff, [v.] Rafe Wats of London, defendant, for 16 broade White Wollen clothes Wourth 53 libri 6 shillings 8d. sent to the said defendant by reason of a forged letter written in the name of one William Wats father to the said defendant and delivered to the said defendant by Robert Kervyn the carrier, etc. [Req. 1/4/136r]

[fo. 87r (p. 61)]

14 March, at Greenewich.[1] Memorandum, that in the cause of

---

[1] J.C. entered this date in the Order and Decree book in his own hand. The date

complaint of William Crecheley and his wife etc. against John Marshall, esquire, on the other party, for and upon the right, title, use and possession of certaine landes, and tenements etc. it is enacted, sentenced, and finally decreed, aswell by the right honourable Counsell, with the advise of John Erudley, knight, chief Justice of the kings Common banke, and Richard Brooke, sargeant at the Law, required by the sayd counsel to give their advise in that behalf, as by the assent of both the sayd parties etc. *the Kings chief Justice of the common plees & servient Brooke enjoined by the kings counsell of this Court to give their advise.* [Req. 1/4/137r]

Anno 11.H.8.

9 May. James Gerard, attorney, with a clause to abide in judgment and to pay charges. [Req. 1/4/137r]

10 May. William, Abbot of Dieulacres, appears by virtue
[fo. 87v (p. 62)]
Writ of Privy Seal at the suit of Henry Piot etc. and has to appear from day to day until etc. [Req. 1/4/139v]

11 May.[1] Robert Sowne appears by virtue of an injunction given to him by the sheriff of Sussex, and has to answer to a bill etc. on next Friday, and thus to appear from day to day etc. [Req. 1/4/142v]

The same, William Spicer appears by virtue of a command given to him by the assigned Commissioners in a certain case moved against him by the party of Gregory Weldon and has to appear from day to day until etc. [Req. 1/4/143r]

12 May. Roger Bellingham, knight, appears by virtue of a Writ of Privy Seal etc. at the suit of William Middleton, and has to answer to a bill on next Saturday, and thus to appear from day to day until etc. Afterwards this case is remitted to the Star Chamber because it concerns a riot. [Req. 1/4/144r]

On the same. John Seddenham appeared by virtue of a command given to him by the Lord King's Council in a certain case moved against him by the party of John Millet etc., and was allowed to appear by Radford his attorney with the counsel of John Porteman. [Req. 1/4/144v]

17 May.[2] Baldwin Porter of the Inner Temple, attorney with a clause to abide in judgment and to pay charges. [Req. 1/4/146v]

immediately before was 22 March and the date immediately after was 24 February.
[1] *Ex parte* Richard Kayen and (?) Senllingham v. Robert Sowne.
[2] *Ex parte* William Dulcoke v. Joan Mitton.

On the same.[1] Christopher Conies of Lincolns Inne, attorney, with a clause to abide in judgment and to pay charges. [Req. 1/4/146v]

On the same.[2] Robert Warner, attorney, with a clause to abide in judgment and to pay charges. [Req. 1/4/146v]

On the same.[3] Roger Cholmeley, attorney, with a clause to abide in judgment and to pay charges. [Req. 1/4/147r]

19 May.[4] Robert Caldwell, attorney, with a clause to abide in judgment and to pay charges. [Req. 1/4/147r]

20 May.[5] Edward Warden, attorney, with a clause to abide in judgment and to pay charges. [Req. 1/4/148v]

23 May at Westminster. In the mater of variance etc. betweene Alice Rawson, plaintiff, against the Abbot and Convent of Dale, defendant, etc., for 11 oxgangs of land etc. *a lease.* [Req. 1/4/150v]

On the same. Thomas Heth appears by virtue of letters missive at the suit of Edward Haseley and upon answer being presented the aforesaid Thomas was allowed to appear by John Radford his attorney with a clause to abide in judgment and to pay charges. [Req. 1/4/152v]

On the same. Robert Bolt and John Witford appear in the name of Richard Odeby

[fo. 89r (p. 63)]

by virtue of letters missive, and have to answer to a bill the day after next Ascension. George Treherne councillor. [Req. 1/4/152v]

[fo. 88r]

*25 May, 11.H.8, fol. 154. Pietro de Bardis, plaintiff, [v.] Barnardo Calvacanti, defendant, for 19 libri parcel of a greater somme due to the plaintiff from the defendant by reason of an arbitrament, etc. [Req. 1/4/153r]

[fo. 88r]

*26 May 11 H. 8. fol. 153.[6] John Bird of London, plaintiff, [v.] Sir John Arundel, knight, defendant, for 40 pieces of tinne

---

[1] *Ex parte* Thomas Smalpage v. John Thometon.
[2] *Ex parte* Thomas Bywater v. Thomas Doddington.
[3] *Ex parte* John Sylle v. Thomas Wentworth.
[4] *Ex parte* John Russell v. Thomas Grameley.
[5] *Ex parte* Simons Purden. Warden should read Warner.
[6] The original arbitration was made by the Council of Florentine Merchants in London.

valued at 218 libri of the goods of the plaintiff left in the hands of
one John Husy of [South] Hampton, marchant, to the use of the
plaintiff and delivered afterwards by the said John Husy to the
said defendant by reason of the kings letters. [Req. 1/4/154r]
[fo. 89r (p. 63)]
28 June. John Thornston appeared in the name of the Abbot of the
Monastery of St. James of Northampton by virtue of a Writ of
Privy Seal, at the suit of William Cooke, and has to answer to a
bill on next Monday and thus to appear from day to day etc.
[Req. 1/4/162r]
The same. William Fleshmonger, clerk, Dean of Chichester,
appeared in the name of the Reverend Father, the Bishop of
Chichester, by virtue of a Writ of Privy Seal under penalty of
allegiance, and has to answer to a bill proposed against him by
John Underhill on next Friday and thus to appear etc. until he
should have otherwise in commands by the King's Council etc.
[Req. 1/4/162v]
5 July. Robert Thruston appeared by virtue of a command given to
him by the assigned Commissioners, and has to appear from day to
day until etc. [Req. 1/1/169r]
6 July.[1] William Andrewe appears etc. and upon answer being
presented he was allowed to appear by Peter Barnes his attorney
with a clause to abide in judgment and to pay charges. [Req.
1/4/169r]
13 July. Memorandum that in the cause etc. by William Selwyn,
complainant, against William Lord Sturton, defendant, for the use,
and occupation of the manour of Aston Grey with the appurtenances in the Countie of Wiltshire etc. it is awarded ordered and
decreed, by the said counsell, that the said Lord Sturton shall
permitte and suffer the said William Selwyn his heires, executors
and assignes to enter into the said Manor at the feaste of Saint
Michaell the Archangel next after the date hereof, and therein to
continue etc. [Req. 1/4/170r]
[fo. 88r]
*13 July, 11.H.8, fol. 171. Thomas Strachey, plaintiff, Robert
White, Priour of Roiston, defendant, for the taking away of certen
corne and other goods. [Req. 1/4/171v]
[fo. 89r (p. 63)]
13 October. John Sampson, clerk, appeared by virtue of a Writ

---

[1] William L'Ayland v. William Andrewes.

under the King's signet at the suit of Richard Hawson, and has to appear from day to day until he should have otherwise in commands by the Lord King's Council. [Req. 1/4/174v]

17 October. Lady Elizabeth Delnes, widow, appears by virtue of letters missive at the suit of Curton, and has to

[fo. 89v (p. 64)]

answer to a bill on next Tuesday, and thus to appear from day to day etc., and upon answer being presented, the aforesaid Elizabeth was allowed to appear before the Lord King's Council by Roger Cholmeley, her attorney, with a clause to abide in judgment and to pay charges. [Req. 1/4/176r]

On the same. Thomas Brook, Lord of Cobham appears by virtue of a Writ of Privy Seal under penalty of allegiance, and has to answer to a bill proposed against him at the suit of Edmund Langley on next Friday without further delay, and thus to appear from day to day until etc. [Req. 2/3/140]

21 October. Thomas Everarde etc., gentleman, being personally before the Lord King in his Chancery, acknowledged that he owed to the same Lord King 40 pounds to be paid at the feast of St Nicholas bishop next coming etc., and unless etc. then etc. The condition is for the standing to an arbitrament, etc. [Req. 1/4/178v]

4 November. The Abbot of Dora was allowed to appear before the Lord King's Counsel in the case moved against him by the party of Katherine Williams, by George Treherne, his attorney, with a clause to abide in judgment and to pay charges. [Req. 1/4/183v]

On the same. Richard Alderich appears by virtue of a command given to him by Robert Fulwood, and other assigned commissioners in a certain case moved against him by the party of John Alderich, and has to appear from day to day until etc. [Req. 1/4/183v]

7 November. David Mores, rector of the church of Richardes Castle in Hertford County, being personally before the Lord King in his Chancery, acknowledged that he owed to the same Lord King 40 marks to be paid at the feast of St. Andrew Apostle next coming, and unless etc. then etc. the condition is for the standing to the awarde, and the arbitrament of certaine arbitrators. [Req. 1/4/184r]

14 November. The cases between William More, plaintiff, and Agnes Ligon, widow, defendant, and also between Thomas Romney, plaintiff, and William More and John More, defendants, are

remitted to the Lord King's Councillors in the Marches of Wales to
[fo. 90r (p. 65)]
examine and administer justice to the parties etc. [Req. 1/4/187v]
23 November. Memorandum, that in the cause of variance brought
afore the kings honourable Counsell, by Robert Edmoundes, complainant, against Robert Sludham nowe Abbot of the Monasterie
of Barmondsey, defendant, the said counsel have decreed that the
said Abbot without any further delaie shall content and paie to the
complainant etc. *for 15 libri due to the plaintiff uppon a bill of
debt signed by the defendant* [Req. 1/4/191r]
[fo. 88r]
*28 November. 11.H.8, fol. 195. Anthony Complay of Ipswich in
Suffolke, plaintiff, William Browne, Priour of the monastery of
St. Peter in Ipswich, defendant, for a lease of a mese and garden.
[Req. 1/4/195v]
[fo. 90r (p. 65)]
18 October. Be it remembered that in the cause of variance
brought afore the kings honourable Counsell, by Hugh Hickeman
etc. with divers and many other inhabitants, dwellers and tenants
of our soveraine Lorde the king in the towne, and parish of
Patingham in the Countie of Stafford complainant, *decreed for
the tenants against the Lord for common of pasture* aswell upon
the behalf, and in the right of our said soveraigne Lord the king,
as in their owne right, as his tennants of Patingham aforesaid
against Sir William Molmeris, Knight, defendant, of and for, the
occupation and usage in the common of 350 acres of lande and
hethe within Rugge within the Countie of Salop etc. The said
Counsel hath now decreed, that all the saide Complainants, and
their heires, tenants of our soveraine Lord the king in the said
towne and parish of Patingham from hencefoorth shall use and
have common of pasture for their beasts and cattell in all and
every of the foresaide pastures in common time of the yeere, as of
olde time it hath beene used and accustomed, without let or disturbance of the said Sir William etc, and further Sir William to pay
etc. 4 libri for costes etc. [Req. 1/4/193r]
28 November.[1] Henry Bury, attorney, with a clause to abide in
judgment and to pay charges. [Req. 1/4/194v][2]

[1] A very damaged folio. *Ex parte* Thomas Smyth v. Byrde (?).
[2] There is no further record until 20 January, 14.H.8. From the citation of fol. 9
in J.C's work we can determine that a new volume was begun but the new
volume no longer survives.

28 January. Lady Elizabeth Robbisherte, widow, appears by virtue of a Writ etc. at the suit of Richard Hardeson, and has to appear from day to day until etc. Afterwards, upon answer being presented, the aforesaid Lady was allowed to appear before the Lord King's Council etc. by Gregory David of le Lincolns Inne, her attorney, with a clause to abide in judgment and to pay charges. [NR]

[fo. 90v (p. 66)]

On the same. Matthew Standish in the name of Thomas, Earl of Derby appears by virtue of a Writ of Privy Seal at the suit of John Hopwood, and has to answer to a bill on next Friday and thus to appear from day to day until etc. [Req. 2/5/217]

29 January, fol. 11. Richard Beaneley in the name of the Abbot of Newminster, sworn, says within the power of his oath, that Gerard, Abbot of Newminster, is detained by such great infirmities that he cannot appear except with grave danger to his body. Therefore he was allowed to appear before the Lord King's Council by the aforesaid Richard Beaneley with a clause to abide in judgment and to pay charges. [NR]

3 February, fol. 13. Thomas Audeley, attorney, with a clause to abide in judgment and to pay charges. [NR]

5 February, fol. 14. In the case between Henry Trevins, plaintiff, and Martin Thomas, defendant, it was decreed that a Privy Seal should be directed to the Sheriff of the county of Cornwall to deliver possession of lands, lately in dispute between the aforesaid parties, to the aforementioned Henry. [NR]

10 February. Alice Rawson, widow, was allowed to appear before the Lord King's Council in the case moved against her by the party of the Abbot of Dale, by Lawrence Holonde of le Greys Inne, her attorney, with a clause to abide in judgment and to pay charges. [NR]

[fo. 88r]

*10 February, 11.H.8, fol. 16.[1] Robert Breydon, plaintiff, Bartholomew Collins, defendant, for 10 libri paid by the said plaintiff into the Exchequer as suertie for the said defendant to keape the kings peace, which the defendant broke. [NR]

[fo. 90v (p. 66)]

13 February, fol. 18. In the Cause depending etc. betweene Robert Hawking, plaintiff, and Thomas Everard, gentleman, defendant,

[1] This is from a missing volume of the Order and Decree books.

of and upon the demande of 10 libri due to the said Robert by reason of certaine ruines, decaies and hurtes, done upon the free Chapple of Saint John Baptist in Hungerford in the Countie of Wiltshire, and other houses thereunto belonging: it is awarded ordered and decreed etc. *dilapidations.* [NR]

Anno 12.H.8.

23 April, fol. 24. Alexander Tailor, attorney, with a clause to abide in judgment and to pay charges. [NR]

25 April, fol. 26. John Whiddon of the Inner Temple, attorney, with a clause to abide in judgment and to pay charges. [NR]

On the same, fol. 29. Henry Amphill, Monk, in the name [fo. 92r (p. 67)] of the Abbot of St. Albans appeared by virtue of a Writ of Privy Seal etc. at the suit of Ralph Watforde, and sworn upon his corporal oath that the said Abbot is detained by such old age (to wit of 84 years), that he cannot appear except with grave danger to his body, and therefore he was allowed to appear by Richard Bellamy, his attorney etc. [NR]

On the same. Lady Margaret Girlington appears by virtue of a Writ of Privy Seal etc. to appear from day to day etc. [NR]

6 May, fol. 38. Bartholomew Prouz of the Inner Temple, attorney, with a clause to abide in judgment and to pay charges. [NR]

16 October, fol. 51. Thomas Pultney, esquire, and John Wiggeston, gentleman, appear by virtue of a Writ of Privy Seal at the suit of David Cecill, etc. [NR]

10 November, fol. 62 & 63. Henry Bury, Ralph Caldewall, and William Richarde, attorneys, with a clause to abide in judgment and to pay charges. [NR]

12 November, fol. 64. Francis Calthrop etc. was allowed to appear etc. by John Walter and William Robartes, his attorneys, with the counsel of Edward White etc. with a clause to abide in judgment and to pay charges. [NR]

The same. Richard Bellamy appears in the name of the Reverend Father Richard, Bishop of Norwich, by virtue of a Writ of Privy Seal. [NR]

The same, fol. 65. Robert Miles appears by virtue of a Writ under signet etc., and was allowed to appear by Thomas Audeley of the Inner Temple, his attorney, with a clause to abide in judgment and to pay charges. [NR]

28 November, fol. 65. John Bristowe of Croston in Cumberland

County, gentleman, being personally before the Lord King in his Chancery, acknowledged that he owed to the same Lord King 100 pounds to be paid at the next feast of the Purification of the Blessed Virgin Mary etc. and unless etc. then etc. The condition of this recognizance is that if the above named John Bristow be and personally appeare afore the kings Counsell at Westminster in his Court of Requests in the 15. of Pasche next comming, and then, and there pay and content all such summes of money, as by the kings Counsell there shall be founde due and owing unto Thomas Wrotsley, otherwise called Garter, concerning the cause of variance [fo. 92v (p. 68)] afore them remaining in writing, that then etc. [NR]

23 January, fol. 72. Richard Lawe appeared in the name of Elias, Abbot of Croxton by virtue of commands given to him by Maurice Barkeley and other assigned Commissioners, in a certain case moved against him by the party of John Melling: and the said Richard says upon his oath, that the said Elias is detained by such old age that he cannot appear on the day assigned to him; therefore he was allowed to appear by Thomas Witherby, his attorney, with the counsel of John Audeley, and with a clause to abide in judgment and to pay charges. [Req. 2/6/237]

On the same folio. William Malevery and Marmaduke Constable, knights, etc. [NR]

28 January, fol. 76. John Pennington, clerk, appears by virtue of letters missive at the suit of Doctor Lynacre etc.

Afterwards the said John was allowed to appear before the Lord King's Council, in the case moved against him by the party of the said Linacre, by Henry Bury, his attorney, with a clause to abide in judgment and to pay charges. [Req. 2/10/64]

4 February, fol. 86. John Grove appeared by virtue of a Writ of Privy Seal etc. at the suit of Windsor College, and has to appear from day to day until etc. [NR]

7 February, fol. 88. Edward Bugges, etc. being personally before the Lord King in his Chancery admitted that he owed to the same Lord King etc. The condition of this recognizaunce etc. for the standing to an arbitrament of etc. touching the causes of two severall billes etc. depending before the kings counsell in his Courte of Requests etc. [NR]

15 February, fol. 92.[1] A Decree for Agnes Sweeting, complainant,

---

[1] The only remaining document is the initial petition addressed to Wolsey.

against John Sampford, Abbot of Coggyshall, defendant, of and for the occupation and possession of a tenement etc. [Req. 2/2/41] [fo. 91v]

*15 February, 12.H.8, fol. 93. Joan Sowter, widoe, executrix of Edmond Wilkinson, plaintiff, Robert Heyward, defendant, to whom shee had delivered an obligation in trust, to the end hee should have saved the said Hayward and his executors harmeles for certain dilapidations, which hee not doing, the plaintiff redemaundeth her obligation or to bee so saved harmeles etc. Decreed for the plaintiff. [Req. 2/10/196]

*The same, fol. 94. For a lease of an howse and 100 acres of land and 6 acres of meadowe with the appertenances for 3 lives, the lease being in wrighting and uppon a good consideration of ready money payed for the same. [NR]

[fo. 92v (p. 68)]

21 February, fol. 96. Where matter of controversie hath bene mooved afore the kings honourable Counsel between the Masters and Fellowes of the Universitie Colledge of Oxford, complainant, against John Mordant, etc., defendant, of, for, and upon the right, title, interest, use and

[fo. 93r (p. 69)]

possession of three acres of lande etc. the said counsell have thereupon awarded and decreed that etc. [NR]

15 April, fol. 98.[1] David Lewes appeared by virtue of a Writ of Privy Seal etc. Afterwards, to wit on the 25th day of the said month, the aforesaid David was excused, because the plaintiff's party does not prosecute his case, and because he did not appear by himself or by his attorney. [Req. 2/8/51]

16 April, fol. 99. Baldwin Porter of the Inner Temple, attorney, with a clause to abide in judgment and to pay charges. [NR]

17 April, fol. 103.[2] John Lucas and Richard Charr, appear by virtue of a Writ of Privy Seal; they were allowed to appear by John Springonell, the attorney of the same, with the counsel of master White of the Inner Temple with a clause to abide in judgment and to pay charges. [Req. 2/7/76]

On the same, fol. 104. The Abbot of Brendon appeared by virtue of a Writ of Privy Seal, etc., at the suit of the Dean of Windsor, and

---

[1] John Edwards and Agnes Edwards, his wife v. David Lewes and Alice Lewes, his wife.

[2] John Rodley and Avyce Rodley, his wife v. John Lucas and Richard Charr.

has to answer to a bill on next Friday and thus to appear from day to day until etc. [NR]

Anno 13.H.8.

24 April, fol. 110. William Spare of the Inner Temple, attorney, with a clause to abide in judgment and to pay charges. [NR]

[fo. 94r]

*24 April, 13.H.8, fol. 112. For the right, title, interest and possession of parcel of a copyhold land. [NR]

[fo. 93r (p. 69)]

1 May, fol. 116. John Stoffolde appeared by virtue of a command given to him by the messenger of the Chamber and has to answer etc. *for a debt of 97 pounds due uppon accoumpt for monies received by the defendant to the use of the plaintiff.* [NR]

[fo. 94r]

*1 May, 13.H.8, fol. 119. For 14 libri due to the plaintiff by the defendant uppon accoumpt for monies received by the said defendant for the use of the said plaintiff. [NR]

*On the same, fol. 120. Katherin Alat, widoe, plaintiff, Richard Nowel and Richard Harecourt, defendant, for certain landes leased to her uppon a rent for terme of her life by the said Harecourt and afterwards without any cause of forfeiture given by her, newely leased and graunted to the said Nowel for terme of his life. Decreed for her. [NR]

*4 May, 13.H.8, fol. 123. Doctor Linacre, executor of William Grocyn, late Master of Maidestone Colledge,[1] plaintiff, the present Master thereof, defendant, for halfe a yere's pension due from the said colledge to the said late Master thereof. [NR]

*On the same, fol. 124. Edmond Lentoll of Mounton in Devon and Margaret, his wife, plaintiff, John Windover, defendant, for the beating, hurting, and wounding of the said plaintiff. [Req. 2/2/66]

[fo. 93r (p. 69)]

12 May, fol. 129. Memorandum, that the Kings Counsell the day aforesayde, have enjoyned, and streightly commaunded John Bound of London, gentleman, that he upon paine of 40 libri to be levied of his goodes for the Kings use in his Eschequer, from hencefoorth utterly surcease his sute taken against Jenin Canoncle one of the kings house, and no further proceed in the same, untill such time he have sufficiently answered the bill of the sayd

---

[1] I.e. Master at All Hallows, Maidstone. See D.N.B.

Canoncle, remaining afore the sayd Counsell. Afterward the 11 of July following, the sayd Counsell, in consideration
[fo. 93v (p. 70)]
that the foresayd Bond hath not exhibited, ne brought his aunswere, but continually hath prosecuted his sute and actions against the foresayd Jenin, not regarding any commandement to him given by the Kings messengers, sent at the commandement of the sayd Counsell, but contemptuously hath disobeyed the same in every thing to him commaunded, they have therefore commaunded him to the Fleet *one committed to the Fleete for a contempt* there to remaine untill such time he hath submitted himselfe to the kings commandements, and his Counsell, against whome he had, and spake many unfitting wordes and language, as by the certificate therof made by Brome the Messenger, taken upon his othe, more evidently it appeareth. [NR]

16 May, fol. 132. John Holte of Clerkinwel in the County of Middlesex, gentleman, appeared personally before the Lord King's Council and acknowledged that he owed to the same Lord King 40 pounds to be paid at the next feast of Pentecost etc. and unless etc. then etc. The condition of this recognisance is such, that if the forsayd John Holte doe personally appeare afore Master John Stokesley, Clerke, *John Stokesley one of the king's honorable counsell* one of the Kings honourable Counsell, in St Stevens chappell at Westminster, or in his lodging at Warwickes Inne in the city of London, upon Wednesday now next comming after the date hereof: and so from thenceforth every Friday and Wednesday, till the 7 of June then immediately following, then this recognizance to be voide, and had for nought. [NR]

6 June, fol. 137. William Knight of Reding appeared at Westminster before the Lord King's Council, at the suit of Reginald Horseley, and has to answer etc. [NR]

On the same. Richard Clerke of Compton appeared at Westminster at the suit of the King, and has to appear before the Lord King's Council from day to day until etc. [NR]

10 June, fol. 138. Robert Lethely appeared at Westminster
[fo. 95r (p. 71)]
by virtue of a Writ of Privy Seal under penalty of 100 pounds at the suit of Richard Lethely etc. and has to appear from day to day etc. [NR]

11 June, fol. 139. Thomas Wilson and Roger Geffrison appear by

virtue of a Writ of Privy Seal etc. at the suit of James Meadow, and have to answer to a bill etc. Afterwards upon answer being presented, the case between the aforesaid parties was remitted to the Chancellor of the duchy of Lancaster, because it concerns lands in the county of Lancaster. [Req. 2/10/28]

13 June fol. 144. John Rudding of Martins Hussintree in the county of Wiltshire, gentleman, personally appeared before the Lord King's Council at Westminster and acknowledged that he owed to the Lord King 40 pounds to be paid at the feast of St. John the Baptist next coming, and unless etc. then etc. The condition of this recognizance is such that etc. [NR]

18 June, fol. 145.[1] Thomas Swenerton of Hilton in Stafford county, gentleman, appeared personally before the Lord King's Council at Westminster, and acknowledged that he owed to the said Lord King 40 pounds to be paid at the feast of St. John the Baptist next coming, and unless etc. The condition of this recognisance is such, that etc. [Req. 2/6/34]

On the same, fol. 147. John Pigot of Sudington in the county of Leicester, gentleman, appeared personally before the Lord King's Council at Westminster, and acknowledged that he owed to the said Lord King 40 pounds sterling to be paid at the next feast of the nativity of St. John the Baptist and unless etc. then etc. The condition of this recognisance is such, that if the said John Pigot for his part well and truely obey, perfourme, and fulfill the awarde, order and judgment of Master John Stokesley, clerke, *John Stokesley one of the kings Honorable Counsell.* one of the Kinges honourable Counsell in the cause against him, moved by Nicholas Miller now remaining afore the said Counsell, then this recognisance to bee voide, or els to stand in full strength and vertue. [NR]

[fo. 94r]

*20 June 13.H.8, fol. 148. A farmor of a manour sued by the plaintiff for 5 libri 8s 4d as an annuity due to the said plaintiff out of the said manour. The like 11 July, the same year, fol. 158 and 28 October, the same, fol. 178. [NR]

[fo. 95r (p. 71)]

1 July, fol. 152. Thomas Wetherby, attorney, with a clause to abide in judgment and to pay charges. [NR]

4 July fol. 155. Raymond Harfleete was allowed to appear

1 John Haley v. Thomas Swynnerton.

[fo. 95v (p. 72)]

before the Lord King's Council by William Dobson, his attorney, with the counsel of Master Browne of the Inner Temple, with a clause to abide in judgment and to pay charges. [NR]

5 July fol, 156. Robert Hegge of the Inner Temple, attorney, with a clause to abide in judgment and to pay charges etc. [NR]

On the same, fol. 157, Thomas Michelborne commaunded by the Counsell that he from henceforth be of good, and honest bearing in his deedes and words against Thomas Sherley etc. *good behaviour* [NR]

15 October, fol. 170. Roger Lukenor, Knight, of Sussex county personally appeared before the Lord King's Council at Westminster, and acknowledged that he owed to the said Lord King 40 pounds sterling, to be paid at the next feast of the Lord's nativity, etc. The condition of this recognisance is such, that if the aforesaid Sir Roger do personally appeare afore the Kings Counsell in the day after the purification of the Blessed Virgin Mary next comming, and then directly make answere unto such things as are alleaged against him afore the saide Counsell, by William Stavely, etc. [NR]

On the same, fol. 171. Thomas Allen appeared before the Lord King's Council by virtue of a Writ under penalty of 100 pounds, at the suit of the Master of Queen's[1] College in the University of Cambridge, etc. [NR]

16 October, folio 171.[2] In the cause depending betweene William Lee, plaintife, and the Abbot of Berdisley, defendant, etc. The Counsell awarded five pounds to the Abbot, for his expenses and costs in that suite etc. *costes to the defendant after sentence.* [Req. 2/7/35]

24 October, fol. 176.[3] It is ordered, and awarded, by Master John Stokesley, clerk, one of the Kings honorable Counsellers, that William Salford, clerke of the Kings signet, shal upon Tuesday next after the date hereof in the presence of the under Bailiffe of Barnet, John Radclif, and Henrie Bellamie deliver unto the handes of Julian Baker, all such implements, goods, and stuffe of houshold, as the saide *goods distreined for rent*

[fo. 96r (p. 73)]

William lately tooke in liew of distresse for rent, to him due as he

[1] In original *Reginae*.
[2] William Lee v. Abbot of Bordesley, Richard Kottyssey, Humphrey Fielde and Harry Baker.
[3] Julian Baker, widow v. William Baker.

saith: And that to doe, as hee is commanded upon paine of forfeiture of such summes as are comprised in his bond obligatorie,
wherein he is bound to the performance of this awarde to be made,
by the saide Master Stokesley. [Req. 2/7/30]

[fo. 94r]

*24 October, 13.H.8, fol. 176. For 40 libri due to the plaintiff from
the defendant uppon 2 severall obligations ordered that the
defendant shalbee bound to the plaintiff in Statute Marchant for
the payment of 20 libri, etc. [NR]

[fo. 96r (p. 73)]

8 November, fol. 184. In a cause depending before the Kings
honourable Counsell betweene Robert Waren, plaintife, against
Sir William Clopton, knight, defendant, touching certaine lands
holden by copy of court roll of the predecessour of the Reverend
Father in God, John, now Abbot of St. Edmundesburie etc. It was
ordered that the saide Reverend Father, etc., shall at the next
court of the saide mannor to bee holden after the demonstration of
this decree to him made by the saide complainant, restore and put
him in peaceable possession of the saide lands, according to the
custome of the said Mannor etc. [Req. 2/8/47 (petition) and Req.
2/2/147 (answer)]

11 November, fol. 186. The Kings Honourable Counsel by the
advise of the Kings Counsell learned in the lawes *a difference
apparant betwene the Kings Honorable Council and the Council
learned in the lawes.* have decreed etc the possession of a garden
ground, against one Thomas Greneway, pretending title by gift
amongst other lands to him made by the King till such time as the
said Thomas hath sufficiently proved the Kings title therein to bee
good, and effectuall in lawe and conscience, etc. [NR]

13 November, fol. 187. A decree made for Robert Fisher, and
Margaret, his wife, complainant, against John Grendon, gentleman, defendant, whereby the possession of certaine landes is
awarded unto the said complainant, notwithstanding continuance
of possession in the defendant by the space of 40 yeeres, which was
thought no sufficient discharge nor barre to defeate the complainant
from their title in the said lands, seeing their claime proved continually to bee made by their auncestors as by certificate it appeared, etc. until such time as the said defendant shal prove afore

[fo. 96v (p. 74)]

the said Counsel, a good and sufficient title in Lawe and conscience to the said lands etc. [Req. 2/11/148 and Req. 2/13/112 (another petition).

On the same, fol. 189. The possession, rents, and profites of a Chantrie decreed to certaine copartnors etc. giving further commandement, to all the tenants pertaining to the said Chantrie, to obey and fulfill this decree as much as in them is etc. [NR]

On the same, fol. 194. The possession of certaine landes decreed by the Kinges honourable Counsell, to Agnes Stirling against the Abbot of Abindon and his Monasterie etc. till he have sufficiently disproved, the title of the complainant, etc. [Req. 2/12/112 and Req. 2/12/185]

24 January, fol. 199.[1] Richard Curtes of Norfolk county, yeoman, appeared before the Lord King's Council etc., and by the mercy of the court, day was given to the aforesaid Richard to answer to a bill on next Monday. [Req. 2/3/239]

6 February, fol. 214. James Gerard, attorney, with a clause to abide in judgment and to pay charges. [Req. 3/29/214][2]

On the same, Robert Chideley, attorney, with a clause to abide in judgment and to pay charges, etc.

Anno 14.H.8.

5 May, fol. 226.[3] William Astell, attorney, with a clause to abide in judgment and to pay charges etc. [NR]

On the same. Thomas ap. Madoke, clerk, appeared at Westminster by virtue of a Writ of Privy Seal etc. [NR]

9 May, fol. 235, Thomas Sidenham, attorney, with a clause to abide in judgment and to pay charges. [NR]

[fo. 97v]

10 May, 14 H. 8. fol. 237. Touching certain injuries done to the plaintiff by the defendant.

[fo. 96v (p. 74)]

15 May. William Cocke, enjoyned by the Kings Counsell to appeare before them at a day certaine, there to abide such open punishment and correction, as by them shalbe devised, for his

---

[1] The commission, which is the only document in the file, makes no reference to Curtees of Norfolk, simply Curtees.

[2] This folio was found among the Request Miscellany (Req. 3). Fos. 210–216v, as numbered by J.C., were found in this class and were lost from the original volume which no longer remains.

[3] These cannot be identified but Req. 3/8 yields one gathering which probably contains the entries for 5 and 9 May. The folios are too badly damaged to clearly identify the dates. The gathering contains fos. 220r–237v (15 February, 13.H.8–10 May, 14.H.8.).

craft, and untrueth committed, and done contrarie to the Kings Lawes in that behalfe which was in forging of a deed etc. [NR]

21 May. folio 246, John Franke was allowed to appear by Henry Bury, his attorney, with a clause of land being decreed and judgment made by the Lord King's Council etc. [NR]

[fo. 98r (p. 75)]

30 May, folio 252. Robert Heyward of Hungerford in the county of Berkshire, yeoman, appeared by virtue of an attachment directed to the sheriff of the aforesaid county, at the suit of Joanna Sowter, widow, and has to appear before the Lord King's Council from day to day until he should have otherwise in commands by the aforesaid Council, and this under penalty of 200 pounds and also under penalty of forfeiture of a certain bond, in which he is held by the said sheriff to appear before the said council, on the day set in the King's Writ. [Req. 2/10/196]

[fo. 97v]

*31 May, 14.H.8, fol. 254. For certain wages due to the plaintiff and factor for the defendant for a certain voyage undertaken and performed by him into Iseland and for his service and labour there taken. [NR]

*3 June, 14.H.8, fol. 256. One mans executor against the executor of an other for 20 corves[1] of wheate due by the testator of the one to the testator of the other uppon a bargaine and sale. [NR]

[fo. 98r (p. 75)]

25 June, fol. 263.[2] Robert Yeo, etc. was allowed to appear by Robert Chideley, his attorney, with the counsel of Master Roo, sergeant at law, with a clause to abide in judgment and to pay charges. [Req. 3/27/263v]

On the same, fol. 266. John Mature appeared in the name of Thomas Laken at Westminster by virtue of a Writ under penalty etc., at the suit of Ralph Poiner, and upon his oath he says that the said Thomas cannot ride of late because of a fracture of his shin, and therefore the aforesaid Thomas was allowed to appear by Richard Foster his attorney with a clause to abide in judgment and to pay charges. [Req. 3/27/266r]

On the same. John Hawkins appeared etc, and upon answer being

---

[1] Corves is from the Medieval Latin corus being a measure of grain or a quarter of grain.

[2] Badly damaged folios from Req. 3. (?) Martin v. Robert Yeo.

presented, he was allowed to appear by Thomas Wetherby, his attorney, with a clause to abide in judgment and to pay charges. [Req. 3/27/266v]

2 July, fol. 276. Lady Margaret Marren, widow, appeared at Westminster by virtue of a Writ etc. at the suit of William Everarde etc. and has to answer to a bill etc. and to appear from day to day etc. [Req. 3/27/276r]

On the same, fol. 277. Christopher Nores appeared at Westminster by virtue of a Writ under penalty of 100 pounds, etc., and afterwards upon answer being presented, he was allowed to appear by Christopher Conies, his attorney, with a clause to abide in judgment and to pay charges. [Req. 2/1/8]

9 July, fol. 281. John Prendergest, gentleman, appeared at Westminster etc. and upon answer being presented he was allowed to appear by William Somester of le Stronde, attorney, with a clause to abide in judgment and to pay charges etc. [NR]

11 July, fol. 288. Memorandum, that in the matter of variance [fo. 98v (p. 76)]

moved and brought afore the Kings honourable Counsell, betweene Richard Marble, etc., and Christian his wife, complainants, against William Carkeke of London, Scrivener, and his wife, defendant, for the witholding and keeping of certain evidences, deedes and writings by the saide Christian delivered to the saide An Kerkeke concerning certaine lands and tenements, in Southwarke, and Newington, is by the Kings said Counsell upon proofe before them remaining in writing reciting in effect that the same Christian in her widowhood made a state of the same landes in the same deedes comprised to one Thomas Seymor and others to the use of the saide Christian for terme of her life, and after her decease to her children, wherof An, nowe the wife of Thomas Mascall, is one. And to the intent that those uses should be assuredly performed, the said Christian delivered the deeds indented to An, the wife of the said Carkeke declaring the said uses safely to be kept by the saide An Carkeke to the behoofe of the children of the said Christian, and in the answere of the sayd Carkeke and An his wife is specified more at large. Ordered, awarded and decreed that the said evidences for the causes afore rehearsed shall remaine and continue in the keeping of the said Carkeke and his wife to the use of the said An Mascall, daughter and heire apparant of the said Christian without any further trouble or sute for them to be made by the said Marble and his wife, which nowe maketh request for the same, onely as it appeareth, to make alienation and sale of the saide lands contrary to the uses in the same deedes mentioned, and that upon paine of payment of such costs, as by the said Counsell shall bee awarded and given to the aforesaide defendants, at such time as the saide Marble shal hereafter make any further suite against them for that cause, which now be dismissed and cleerly discharged of any time or day of appearance hereafter to be made, at the sute or request

[fo. 99r (p. 77)]

quest [sic] of the said complainants. [NR]

14 July, fol. 289. Forasmuch as it is apparent unto the kings honorable Counsell sitting in his Court of Requests etc. [NR]

18 July, fol. 297. In the cause betweene Peter Grey, complainant, against Roger Barrowe, defendant, the kings honorable Counsell have streightly charged the said Barrow, that he upon pains of etc. doo surcease his sutes and actions taken against the said Peter and his sureties etc. *for 17 libri 8s. 6d. due uppon a bargaine* [Req. 2/12/118]

18 July, fol. 298. Divers variances and debates depending before the kings most honorable Counsell betweene John Ellis, and Elizabeth, his wife, plaintife, and Richard Bowes, and Jone, his wife, defendant, are referred to John, Abbot of Rysby, whome the kings Counsell prayeth, desireth and also requireth to take these paines, and labours upon him, as he tendreth the good advancement of Justice, and the quietnesse of his poore neighbors, to Gods pleasure and the kings etc. [NR]

16 October, fol. 308. Adam Holling etc. allowed to appear before the Lord King's Counsel by Nicholas Hare of the Inner Temple with the counsel of Master Mountforde and with a clause to abide in judgment and to pay charges. [NR]

The same, fol. 309.[1] Lady Margaret Rede, widow, appeared by virtue of a Writ under penalty of 100 pounds etc. at the suit of Thomas Waker etc. and has to appear from day to day etc. [Req. 2/3/106 and Req. 2/11/88]

The same, fol. 310. Thomas Horfall appeared by virtue of a Writ of Privy Seal etc. at the suit of James Alger etc. and has to appear from day to day etc., and afterwards upon diverse considerations being shown, he was allowed to appear before the Lord King's

[1] The defendant is Lady Elizabeth Reade rather than Lady Margaret Reade.

Council in the said case by James Jerrard, his attorney, with a clause to abide in judgment and to pay charges. [NR]

26 October, fol. 314. Thomas Abbot of Gareydon in the county of Leicester appeared before the Lord King's Council by virtue of an injunction given to him by Richard Sacheverel and others in a certain case moved against him by Bartholomew Lee, and has to answer to a bill on next Friday and

[fo. 99v (p. 78)]

to appear from day to day until etc. [NR]

4 November, fol. 316. Thomas Roo etc. appeared before the Lord King's Council etc. at the suit of John Drewe etc. and has to appear from day to day etc.; and afterwards (to wit) on the 14th day of the present month, because the party plaintiff did not appear by himself or by his attorney, nor was any bill returned on the designated day, therefore the aforesaid Thomas was allowed to appear by John Fleming of le Stronde Inne, his attorney, with a clause to abide in judgment and to pay charges, etc. [Req. 2/11/88]

29 November, fol. 320. Where matter in controversie etc. depending afore the Kinges Honourable Counsell between Thomas Game, complainant, against Ele Elwin, widow, defendant, etc. as in the bill and replication of the sayd Thomas to the Kings grace presented, onely upon consideration of povertie, it is declared more at large: upon which his request, in that behalfe made, the Kings highnesse committed the hearing and determination of the same to his foresayd counsellers etc. [NR]

29 November, fol. 323. Thomas Sheming appeared before the Lord King's Council etc. in a certain case moved against him by the party of James Likebarough, and by their consent the case is adjourned until the next 15th of St. Hilary, on which day the aforesaid James has to appear by James Jerrard, his attorney, and the said Thomas in his own person, if meanwhile agreement shall not have been had in the same case, and this under penalty of 40 pounds. [Req. 3/27/323v]

5 February, fol. 14. Henry Cowper etc. appear at Westminster before the Lord King's Council by virtue of an injunction etc, and because certification was not returned on the designated day, therefore the parties defendant were allowed to appear before the Lord King's Council by John Wistowe, their attorney, with a clause to abide in judgment and to pay charges etc. [Req. 1/5/14r]

22 April, fol. 18.[1] Thomas More, knight, appears before the Lord King's Council at Bridewell by virtue of a Writ of Privy Seal under penalty of 100 pounds at the suit etc. and has day given to him

[fo. 100r (p. 79)]

to answer to a bill on next Monday and thus to appear from day to day until he should have otherwise in commands by the aforesaid council; and this under the aforesaid penalty. [Req. 1/5/18r]

Anno 15.H.8.

9 November, fol. 21, at Woodstocke. Where matter of variance dependeth afore the Kings honourable counsell betweene John Paine of Melles, yeoman,[2] plaintiff, and John Horner, defendant, for and upon the right, title, interest, use and possession, of a capitall Messuage with all the lands, etc. The sayd counsell have awarded, ordered and decreed that the sayd John Paine shall from thenceforth suffer the sayd John Horner to have, and peaceably to injoy and occupy the said farme place, and other the premisses etc. This decree subscribed with the hands of the foresayd counsell, etc. [Req. 1/5/21r]

Anno 16.H.8.

10 May. fol. 21, Thomas Corby and Joanna, his wife, and Nicholas Strowde of the county of Kent, appear before the Lord King's Council at Westminster, by virtue of letters missive, at the suit of Joanna Silvestre, widow etc. [Req. 1/5/21v]

20 November, fol. 22. In the cause depending etc. betweene Nicholas Monke, plaintiff, and William Lane defendant for certain lands etc. Forasmuch as after deliberate hearing of the said cause, in former time it was decreed against the said Nicholas: which decree the sayd Nicholas hath broken etc. It is therefore in consideration of the misdemeanors done by the said Nicholas in resisting the former directions and conditions in the former decree concluded etc. Ordered that he from henceforth in no maner of wise shall present or bring any bill, or other matter to the

[fo. 100v (p. 80)]

kings Grace or counsell touching the same upon paine of imprisonment, etc. [Req. 1/5/22r–22v]

---

[1] This entry is properly a part of 15.H.8 because the regnal year changed 22 April.

[2] Plaintiff was a Yeoman of the Crown, thus establishing the Court's jurisdiction in this matter.

Anno 17.H.8.

12 June, fol. 23. This bill made the said day and yere witnesseth that I, Robert Yeo, esquier, have authorised and put in my place John Roo, Sergeant at the Lawe, and William Honychurch and every of them to be mine assignes and counsell to appeare before Master Ingelfield and Master Doctor Wolman the twelveth day next ensuing the feast of Holy Trinitie next comming after the date hereof, and there to plead, confes, save, and get, in my name and behalfe the right, title, possession, use and inheritance of a mise of 160 acres of land called Woodwill within the parish of Bediforde within the Countie of Devon; and which mise, and land, one Walter Martaine and Joan, his wife, claimeth and pretendeth title to by the way of petition before the said Master Ingelfielde and Master Doctor Wolman, Counsellours to our said Soveraigne Lord the King. In witnesse whereof I, the said Robert Yeo, have sealed and subscribed this letter of atturney with my hand the day and yere above written. *Ingelfield and Wolman, Counselors to the King*[1] [Req. 1/5/24r]

[fo. 101r]

*23 June, 17.H.8, fol. 24.[2] For the lease of a farme to the which the plaintiff pretended interest for certain yeres yet to come. [Req. 1/5/26r]

*27 June, 17.H.8, fol. 25.[3] For the use and Possession of a parsonage with all the tithes and profits thereto belonging. [Req. 1/5/27r]

[fo. 100 v. (p. 80)]

4 February, fol. 26. John Brereton of Duleancre in the County of Stafford, esquire, complainant, against Thomas Alben of the said Countie, yeoman, defendant, etc. The King's Counsell having the advise of divers persons learned in the Kings lawe have determined, etc. [Req. 1/5/28r]

9 December, fol. 28, at Windsor. Where matter of variance dependeth before the King's Honourable Counsell between Richard Tate, gentleman usher of the Kings most honorable chamber, plaintiff, and John Audelet, gentleman, defendant, touching the right, title, and interest of a lease of the mannour of Wolleighe with

---

[1] Fo. 23, which J.C. cites, is loose in the volume and is foliated by some other hand.

[2] John Warde and his wife, Joan v. John Wyke.

[3] Roger Hatchman, King's Yeoman of the Guard v. Thomas Bradshaw, clerk, Thomas Bolt, William Bolt.

the appurtinances in the Countie of Berkshire, etc. *a lease.* [NR]
[fo. 102r (p. 81)]

Anno 18.H.8.

9 November, fol. 31. Edward Pomerey, knight, was allowed to
appear before the Lord King's Council in the case moved against
him by the party of Thomas Bilford and Margery, his wife, by
William Dobson, his attorney, with the counsel of Master Collis,
and Syddenham of the Inner Temple with a clause to abide in
judgment and to pay charges. [Req. 1/5/33r]

Anno 19.H.8.

24 January, fol. 36. Walter Griffin, knight, appears before the
Lord King's Council at Westminster at the suit of the Master
Dean of the King's Chapel, by virtue of a certain Writ of Privy
Seal, and it was enjoined to the said Walter by the aforementioned
Council that he should appear from day to day, up to the time
when and until he should have otherwise in commands etc. [Req.
1/5/38r]

Anno 20.H.8.

18 June, fol. 39. Memorandum, that the King's Counsel have continued the cause of variaunce afore them brought by William
Covell, plaintiff, against William Permeter now Mayor of Notingham, defendant, unto the morow after the feast of al sowles next
comming: for that the sayde Covel hath not manifested, ne declared that the said Permeter at the time of his sute commensed,
was Mayor, ne so named him in the kings Privy Seal by colour
whereof he intended, and craftily did deceive the said counsell
therein, which having therof knowledge woulde not awarde any
processe againe the sayd Mayor during the time of his office.
*proces for appearance not to be awarded against a mayor during
his office.* [Req. 1/5/41r]

[fo. 101v]

*4 December, 20.H.8, fol. 40. Simon Tod, clerk, plaintiff, against
Richard Benson, clerk, parson there for a vicaredge and the profits
and tithes to the same belonging. [Req. 1/5/42r]

[fo. 102r (p. 81)]

28 January, fol. 41. Hereafter foloweth the names of such Counsellours as be appointed for the hearing of poore mens causes in the
kings Court of Request. *Counselors appointed to heare poore
mens cases in the Court of Requests.* [Req. 1/5/43v][1]

[1] See also *supra*, fo. 3v.

The Bishop of Lincoln, the Deane of the kings Chappel,
[fo. 102v (p. 82)]
Dr. Wolman, Dr. Rouland, vicar of Croydon, Dr. Lupton, Dr.
Cromer, Sir Thomas Nevel, knight, Dr. Suliard, Dr. Saint Jermine, Thomas, Abbot of Westminster, the Bishop of St. Asaph,
the Lord of St. Johns Jerusalem: Sir John Hussey, Sir William
Fitzwilliams, Sir Roger Townsende, Knights. [NR]
[fo. 101v]
*15 February, 20.H.8, fol. 44.[1] For a possession of a tenement
chalenged by the plaintiff by a lease parole. [Req. 1/5/46r]
[fo. 102 v (p. 82)]

Anno 21.H.8.

26 April, follio [*sic*] 48. William Wake of Hertwel in Northampton
county, gentleman, personally appeared before the Lord King's
Council at Westminster on the said day and year, and acknowledged that he owed to the said Lord King 40 pounds to be paid
by the feast of the nativity of St. John the Baptist next coming
etc. and unless etc. then etc. The condition of this recognisance is
such, that if the aforesaid William Wake from the date hereof
during the space of 3 yeares next, and immediately following, and
fully to bee complete and ended, bee of good and honest bearing
aswell against Ralfe Addington, and all other persons nowe
keepers and walkers of the Forest of Whiteleywoode in the
Countie aforesaide, and also other keepers and walkers there for
the time beeing; And also during the same time doe not kill ne
destroy by himselfe, nor his servantes by his procuring any of the
kings deare, or game in the same Forest, then this recognizance to
bee void and of no force, or else to stand in full strength and
vertue. [Req. 1/5/50v]
2 June, fol. 51.[2] Thomas Woodman appeared etc. he was allowed
to appear by John Hichcoke, his attorney, with the counsel of
Master White of the Inner Temple, with a clause to abide in
judgment and to pay charges. [Req. 1/5/53r]
On the same. William Hawkins appears etc. at the suit of William
Baylie, Knight, etc. [Req. 1/5/53v]
7 June, fol. 52. Roger Colverhouse etc. appears etc. at the suit of
Luke Langland, esquire etc. [Req. 1/5/54v]
11 June, fol. 54. Thomas Knight of the city of London, personally

---

[1] William Hayes v. The Prior of St. Bartholemews.
[2] William Canon v. Thomas Woodman.

[fo. 104r (p. 83)]

appeared at Westminster before the Lord King's Council by virtue of a Writ of Privy Seal. And he acknowledged in the same place that he owed to the said Lord King 40 pounds sterling, to be paid at the feast of the nativity of St. John the Baptist next coming, etc. And unless etc. then etc. The condition of this recognisance is such, that if the aforesaid Thomas Knight daily make his personall apparance before the Kings Counsell in White Hall at Westminster, or els where the said Counsell shalbe commaunded to sit, and keepe Court during the time, the cause against him moved by William Smith shal bee in traverse, and not determined, then this recognisance to be voide..[Req. 1/5/56r]

[fo. 103r]

*30 June, 21.H.8, fol. 56.[1] For 10 libri delivered in trust by the plaintiffs wife to one Nightingal, of whose executors goods the defendant is administrator. [Req. 1/5/58v]

*6 July, 21.H.8, fol. 58. Robert Fox, plaintiff, Thomas Portington, late Sherif of Lincolne, defendant, for 40 shillings received by the defendant of the plaintiff for his acquitall uppon an untrue enditement of felony against him conspired and decreed for the plaintiff to have restitution of his 40 shillings. [Req. 1/5/60v]

*10 July, 21.H.8, fol. 59. Thomas Pichar, plaintiff, William Compton, Abbot of the monastery, etc., defendant, for the reversion of the scites [sic] of 2 manours to the said monastery belonging, graunted to the plaintiff by the said Abbot and Convent under the Convents seale. [Req. 1/5/61r–62v]

[fo. 104r (p. 83)]

20 November, fol. 66. In the cause depending etc. betweene Henrie Sylby of the towne of Thingdon in the countie of Northampton, as all other customarie tenants and copyholders there complainants against one John Mulsho, Esquier their landlord, Defendant, touching such excessive, and great fines, which they affirme to be demanded of them, by the said John Mulsho contrarie to their olde and ancient custome etc. It is now by the said Counsell ordered etc. that the same Mulsho, and his heires from henceforth etc. shal use the seasing of the same fines reasonably, according to his customarie court rolles and presidents. And if the saide tenants, and the saide Mulsho and their heires cannot heerafter reasonably agree upon the asseasing of the said fines; It is by

---

[1] Andrew Simpson v. John Selle and William Nightingale.

the said Counsell further ordered for the reliefe of the said tenants, that then the tenants so grieved, shal resort to the Steward there for the time being, hee according to his learning to assesse the same after such forme and maner, as may stand to be consonant to Equitie, right, and good conscience, as he will answere afore the Counsell for the same etc. *decreed for the tenants against the Lord for the reasonable sessing of fines.* [Req. 1/5/68r]

4 February, fol. 75.[1] Nicholas Cadman etc. was allowed to appear etc. with the counsel of Master Goodale of the Inner Temple. [Req. 1/5/77r]

[fo. 104v (p. 84)]

12 February. In a cause etc. betweene Thomas Tong, clerke, parson of the parish church of Medill in the countie of Salop, plaintife, and Richard Banester of the same parish, Esquier, defendant, touching the taking, and withholding of certain oblations and tithes etc. ordered for the plaintife, against the defendant etc. [Req. 1/5/77v–78r]

Anno 22.H.8.

6 May, fol. 79. William Sparry of the Inner Temple, in the name of John, Prior of Studley, personally appeared as attorney of the said Prior, etc. [Req. 1/5/82r]

18 May, fol. 81. In the cause etc. betweene William East, complainant, and the Reverend Father in God, John, Abbot of the Monasterie of Charlesley, defendant, touching 39 libri foure shillings due for 28 quarters of wheate, and 28 quarters of barley etc., the said Counsell have awarded, that the said Abbot shall pay the said money etc. [Req. 1/5/84r–84v]

21 June, fol. 84.[2] Ralph Bland appeared at Westminster etc. and upon answer being presented he was allowed to appear by Michael Purfrey, gentleman, with the counsel of Master Bromeley of the Inner Temple with a clause to abide in judgment and to pay charges. [Req. 1/5/87v]

28 June, fol. 86.[3] Robert Currant etc. was allowed to appear by Francis Thirkill, his attorney, with the counsel of Master Hare of the Inner Temple, with a clause to abide in judgment and to pay charges etc. [Req. 1/5/89r]

18 October, fol. 91. Where matter of controversie etc. between the

---

[1] Richard Tinton v. Nicholas Cadman.
[2] Richard Ward and Isabell, his wife v. Ralph Bland.
[3] Robert Carter v. Robert Currant.

Master and fellowes of Universitie Colledge in Oxford, complainant, against Robert Mordant, sonne and heire of William Mordante, esquire, deceased, defendant, for, and upon the right, title, interest, use, and possession of three acres of land etc. *University Colledge against the Lord Mordant for land.* [Req. 1/5/94v]

10 November.[1] Richard Sampson, Dean etc. King's Councillor. [Req. 1/5/94v]

[fo. 105r]

*10 November, 22.H.8, fol. 94.[2] For the non performance of certain covenants and agreements specified in a paire of indentures dated, etc. [Req. 1/5/97v]

[fo. 106r (p. 85)]

18 November, fol. 96. William Covell of the town of Notingham and Thomas Warcup etc. acknowledged that they owed to the Lord King 10 pounds etc. under the condition that Alice Andrew will prosecute her case against John Cooke moved before the King's Council, and will pay expenses in case she shall have been penalised. [Req. 1/5/99v]

27 January, fol. 105. John Sprige etc. was allowed to appear by Master Warner and William Saunders of the Inner Temple etc. [Req. 1/5/108r]

8 February, fol. 108. John Browne of Langley in Hertford County appeared personally at Westminster before the Lord King's Council, and acknowledged that he owed to the said Lord King 100 pounds sterling etc. The condition of this recognizaunce is such, that if the aforesaid John Browne surcease his sute, and action, which he now hath depending in the Common plees against one Jeffrey Hill, concerning an obligation of the summe of 100 markes, and therein no further proceed, unto such time the kings Counsell have otherwise determined in the cause afore them depending then this recognizance to be voyd. [Req. 1/5/111v]

Anno 23.H.8.

11 May, fol. 121.[3] William Brykenshawe was allowed to appear etc. by William Dobson, his attorney, with the counsel of Master

---

[1] There is nothing under this date to indicate Sampson's connection but on fo. 93v a margin note appears: 'per Ric. Sampson, Dec[anus]'. This refers to his cancelling a recognizance. J.C. may possibly have the wrong folio and date.

[2] Robert Brightman v. John Hunt.

[3] *Ex parte* Agnes Worcester, widow v. William Brykenshawe.

Bosse, and Master Bradshawe of the Inner Temple with a clause to abide in judgment and to pay charges. [Req. 1/5/124r]

June 29, fol. 137. In a matter now depending afore the King's honourable Counsell in his Courte of Requests betweene Thomas Rothwood, plaintiff, against William nowe Abbot of Stratford etc. [Req. 1/5/140r]

[fo. 105v]

*20 May, 23.H.8, fol. 124.[1] For certain plate to the valewe of 40 libri delivered by the plaintiffs father in trust to the said defendant due to this plaintiff as his fathers administrator. [Req. 1/5/125v]

*28 June, 23.H.8, fol. 134.[2] For a legacy of 100 libri due unto the plaintiff and withheld from him by the said defendant by couler of a forged will. [Req. 1/5/137v]

*29 June, 23.H.8, fol. 137.[3] For a copyhold. [Req. 1/5/140r]

[fo. 106r (p. 85)]

26 January, fol. 153. George Willoughby, esquire, appeared personally etc. at the suit of Thomas Smith etc.; he was allowed to appear by William Dobson, his attorney, with the counsel of Master

[fo. 106v (p. 86)]

Audley, and Master Willoughby, sergeant at law, and Richard Heydon of Lincolns Inne with a clause to abide in judgment and to pay charges. [Req. 1/5/156v]

7 February, fol. 159. In the cause of variance brought afore the King and his honourable Counsell by William Wrenche etc., plaintiff, against Thomas Shephard, defendant, etc. [Req. 1/5/162r]

On the same, fol. 160. In a cause moved and brought afore the king and his honourable Counsell in the Courte of Requests, by Thomas Canston etc., plaintiff, and James Osborne etc., defendant, etc. [Req. 1/5/163r]

Anno 24.H.8.

4 May, fol. 174, in a cause depending etc. betweene Thomas

---

[1] William Walker, yeoman v. John Brightwell, ironmonger. The formula which opens this decree is markedly different from its predecessors in J.C's collection: 'whereas cause of variance . . . hath byn moved and brought afore the Kings Honorable Counsaill *in his Courte of Requests* . . .' (emphasis is J.C's). If one follows along through the next several folios one finds that, initially, the 'Court of Requests' designation was used more often with paupers' cases while the old style was employed with the other cases (e.g. Req. 1/5/129r 138v–140r).

[2] Christopher Middleton v. John Obyn.

[3] Thomas Rothewood v. Abbot of Stratford.

Hawkings, sonne and heire of James Hawkings, complainant, against Dame Katherine Pakingham, widow, defendant, etc. [Req. 1/5/177v]

27 June, fol. 186. John Grevell etc. acknowledged that he owed to the Lord King 40 pounds, etc. with condition to appear from time to time, in White Hall at Westminster during the time that the cause against him mooved by Margaret Arches, widow, remaineth indiscussed etc. [Req. 1/5/187r]

4 July, fol. 186. Thomas Parker of Northmulton in Devon County appeared personally before the Lord King's Council at Westminster by virtue of a Writ of Privy Seal etc. at the suit of Lord Zouche, and has day given to him to answer to a bill on next Monday, and thus to appear from day to day etc. [Req. 1/5/189r]

The same, whereas upon the examination of a cause brought afore the kings honourable Counsell touching the title and possession of 5 acres of land etc. whereof Thomas Smith and Rose, his wife, suppose them to be disseased by one John Browne etc. It is ordered that such interest, and title, as in that matter is declared and supposed to be betweene John Jermy, and George Willoughby esquires be wholly remitted to the common law, there to be determined according to the course of the same, which

[fo. 108r (p. 87)]

both parties are sufficient and able to followe, and trie, there [sic] substance in lands and goods well considered and knowne etc. [Req. 1/5/189r]

10 July, fol. 189.[1] In a cause of variaunce depending in the Court of Requests before the Commissioners there etc. *for certain Wollen clothes sued for by an executrix.* [Req. 1/5/193v]

13 July, fol. 192. In a cause depending etc. betweene Richard Robinson, citizen and broderer of London, plaintiff, against Thomas Yong of the same Citie, broderer, defendant, etc. touching one boothe in Sturbridge faire besides Barnewel in the Countie of Cambridge etc. [Req. 1/5/196v]

[fo. 107r]

13 July, 24.H.8, fol. 191.[2] For an office of portership of a monastery gate graunted by the Abbot etc, defendant. To the plaintiff. [Req. 1/5/195v]

---

[1] William Cowell and Thomas Warcup v. Alice Andrews. See *supra*, fo. 106r, *sub dat* 18 November.

[2] Hugh Pigot, Yeoman of the King's Guard v. John, Abbot of Chester.

[fo. 108r (p. 87)]

19 November, fol. 201. Robert Alot of Emley etc. acknowledged that he owed to the Lord King etc. The condition of this recognizance is such, that if the foresayd Robert Alot from henceforth, at no time hereafter, neither by himselfe, ne any other person by his assent, procuring, or assisting do not inquiet, nor trouble, vexe nor sue, by the order or course of the Kings Common lawes, or otherwise, William Smith, and William Capell, ne none of their tenaunts, as to them are adjudged, by order of a decree, thereof made by the Kings Counsell, contrary to words and matter therein conteined, that then this recognizaunce to be void, etc. [Req. 1/5/205v]

25 November, fol. 202. Thomas Whitney, Abbot of the monastery of Dulacresse, was allowed to appear before the Lord King's Council in a case moved against him by the party of Peter Willot, because the same did not appear before the said Council, by Master Flowre, his attorney, with a clause to abide in judgment and to pay charges, etc. [Req. 1/5/206r]

22 January, fol. 206.[1] Richard Williams etc. was allowed to appear etc. by William Dobson, his attorney, with the counsel of Master Brooke of the Inner Temple with a clause to abide in judgment and to pay charges etc. [Req. 1/5/210r]

1 February, fol. 208. Anthony Benet was allowed to appear by John Dion of Clements Inne, his attorney, with the counsel of Master Moyne of the Inner Temple with a clause etc. [Req. 1/5/212v]

12 February, fol. 210. In a cause depending and brought

[fo. 108v (p. 88)]

before the Kings honourable counsell by a bill of complaint to the Kings grace, presented by Thomas Asheley of Melton, constable in the county of Norfolke, esquire, complainant, against the now Prior of Christchurch in the city of Norwich etc. *for a mill, and a mildam.* [Req. 1/5/214v]

16 February, fol. 226. In a cause depending etc. betweene John Stanbanke and Margaret, his wife, sometimes the wife of Thomas More, deceased, plaintife, against John More, sonne and heire of the sayd Thomas More and Margaret, his wife, defendant, touching the joynture to the sayd Margaret plaintife, assigned and appointed. It manifestly appeareth unto the said Counsell, aswell upon view and sight of a booke heeretofore made by Sir William

[1] Robert Warde v. Richard Williams.

Paulet, knight, now Controller of the King's honourable housholde and by indenture of award since that time made by certaine arbitratours, that the sayd Margaret should have and enjoy for terme of her life all such lands and tenements as be written with the hand of the sayde Sir William Paulet in a leafe of the said booke, for and in the name of her joynture to her belonging by force of the gift of her sayd late husband, Thomas More, as by the sayd booke, and the sayd indenture more plainly appeareth etc. *William Poulet, knight, Controller of the king's household. [Req. 1/5/231v]

[fo. 107r]

*22 March, 24.H.8, fol. 215. For goods to the valewe of 60 libri. Whereof the plaintiff was cosoned and deceived by overmuch trust given to 2 chapmen by the defendants credit and wordes to the plaintiff of theire honestie and habilitie. Dismissed. [Req. 1/5/219r]

[fo. 108v (p. 88)]

Anno 25.H.8.

April 30, fol. 216.[1] Edward Fabian, etc. was allowed to appear etc. by William Dobson, his attorney, with the counsel of Master Baldwine, Sergeant at Law, with a clause to abide in judgment and to pay charges, etc. [Req. 1/5/220v]

23 May, fol. 222.[2] Richard Woleman and William Suliard of the Kings Counsell. [Req. 1/5/227r]

[fo. 109r]

*24 May, 25.H.8, fol. 223.[3] For restitution of or satisfaction for certain plate delivered uppon the defendants letter to the valewe of 40 libri. [Req. 1/5/228r]

*26 June, 25.H.8, fol. 230.[4] For a tenement with the appurtenances graunted in mariage to the plaintife. [Req. 1/5/235r]

[fo. 108v (p. 88)]

8 July, fol. 237. John Lambert etc. personally appeared before the Lord King's Council at Westminster etc. and acknowledged that he owed to the said Lord King 40 pounds sterling, etc. The condition of this recognizance is such, that if

[fo. 110r (p. 89)]

the Maior of the towne of Hull etc. the Aldermen and Comminality

[1] Thomas Mowle v. Edward Fabian.
[2] *Ex parte* John Coke [infant] v. Bartholemew Edwards.
[3] John Veysy v. John Vesy, clerk.
[4] Anne Bulkeley, widow of Lewes Bulkeley v. John Bulkeley.

of the same, doe send up and cause to appeare afore the Kings counsell at Westminster on the day before All Soul's Day next comming, one person as atturney sufficiently authorised under their common seale to make aunswere unto such a bill as is exhibited afore the sayde Counsell in the name of divers of the inhabitants of the township of Leistof[t]e in the county of Suffolke, then this recognizaunce to be voyde, or els to stand etc. [Req. 1/5/242v]

16 October, fol. 240.[1] John Thirlby etc. was allowed to appear etc. by Simon Sampson etc., his attorney, with the counsel of Master Wingfield and John Baron of the Temple, with a clause to abide in judgment and to pay charges. [Req. 1/5/245v]

[fo. 109r]

*4 November, 25.H.8, fol. 243.[2] For a mill. [Req. 1/5/248v]

[fo. 110r (p. 89)]

17 November, fol. 245. The Bishop of Landaffe personally appeared at Westminster in the name of the master, the brothers and sisters of St. Katherine near London at the suit of John Allen knight, and upon answer being presented, and an oath being taken thereupon, he was allowed to appear etc. by William Dobson, his attorney, with the counsel of Master Maudline of the Middle Temple with a clause to abide in judgment and to pay charges. *Bishop of Llandafe, Master of St. Catherine.* [Req. 1/5/250v]

23 January, fol. 1.[3] Thomas Watson of Staunford appeared personally before the Lord King's Council at Westminster by virtue of an Writ of Privy Seal under penalty of 100 pounds at the suite of Richard Cecill, gentleman, etc. [Req. 2/11/17]

30 January, fol. 5.[4] Memorandum, that William Werrall hath contented and payde afore the kings Counsell in the White-hall at Westminster to the use of Master Coppinger the summe of thirtie shillings etc. [Req. 2/3/97]

[fo. 109r]

*4 February, 25.H.8, fol. 6. Injunction to the defendant not to alter, alienate or cause anie estates to bee made of the manour in

[1] Anthony Cloughte v. John Thirlby.
[2] Thomas Langford v. Sir Nicholas Stylvley.
[3] Richard Cecil v. Francis Browne. The complaint is missing and thus the full list of defendants, including Thomas Watson, cannot be verified. But the locus of the litigation is Stamford.
[4] John Coppinger v. William Wirrall.

question, to the prejudice or hurt of the plaintiffs title, neither to commit wast uppon the said manour, neither in decay of howsing ne felling of timber, till the Court take further order. [NR] [fo. 110r (p. 89)]

Anno 26.H.8.

4 May, fol. 14.[1] Edward Don, knight, defendant etc. [Req. 2/12/175]

12 May, fol. 16. Afore the kings counsel in the White-Hall at Westminster etc. [NR]

18 May, fol. 17. Memorandum, that it is ordered by the kings [fo. 110v (p. 90)] honorable Counsell that no privy seal be directed to the Prior of Norwich at the sute of Denis Fuller, but that the sayd Prior be admitted to appeare by his atturney. [NR]

On the same, fol. 18. A cause touching the title of a messuage etc. remitted to the common law, with injunction that neither of them shall use any dilatory plea etc. [NR]

[fo. 111r]

*18 May, 26.H.8, fol. 17. Decreed against 2 defendants to save harmeles the plaintiffs who were bound in 2 several recognizances as sureties for theire appearance at the Assises in 60 libri which recognisances, uppon the defendants nonappearance, were forfeited and the plaintiffs sued. [NR]

*20 October, 26.H.8, fol. 27. For 40 shillings arrerages of the rent of a tenement in the possession of the defendant. [NR]

[fo. 110v (p. 90)]

6 November, fol. 30. A cause decreed for the freedome and liberty of William Netheway, challenged by Sir Edward George, knight, for his bondman etc. [Req. 2/5/21]

24 November, fol. 33. Elizabeth Corogouse bound in recognizance etc. for to keepe etc. the award, order and determination of Master Woleman and Master Suliard, two of the Kings counsellors, in the cause depending before them in the Requestes etc. See 12 February fol. 41. [NR]

[fo. 111r]

*28 November, 26.H.8, fol. 35. Decreed against the parson of St. Margarets Moyses in Friday Streete in London to pay a pension of 5 markes yerely to the Priour and Convent of St. Faiths in Horsham in Norfolke. [NR]

---

[1] Agnes Bate, sometime wife to William Darrell v. — —.

[fo. 110v (p. 90)]

Anno 27.H.8.

30 November, fol. 59. In Whitehall Westminster a decree touching a statute bond etc. whereof there could be no execution by the rigour of the law. [NR]

30 November, fol. 60. A decree in confirmation of a former decree made by Thomas, Archbishop of Yorke, later Lord Chanceller and his coassistants etc. *in Whitehall 19 November, 10.H.8.* [NR]

31 January, fol. 67. Master Doctor Wolman, and Master Suliard, two of the kings honourable counsellors etc. [NR]

Anno 28.H.8.

25 May, fol. 77. In awarding of possession of lands, a provision made for the carriage away of the corne already sowen, etc. [NR]

8 November, fol. 85. Thomas Richards and others etc., upon divers considerations being shown to the aforesaid Council, were allowed to appear by Richard Flowre, their attorney, with the counsel of Master Mountague, Serjeant at law etc., with a clause to abide in judgment and to pay charges. [NR]

[fo. 112r (p. 91)]

Anno 29.H.8

6 June, fol. 102.[1] William Essex, knight, personally appeared at the suit of the bishop of Chichester. [Req. 2/3/136]

23 January, fol. 115. Heereafter followe the names of the commissioners appointed to sit in the court of Requests in the Whitehall at Westminster: First, the reverend father in God Richard, the Bishop of Chichester, Nicholas Hare, Thomas Thirleby, Edmond Boner, and Edward Carue. [NR]

4 February, fol. 118.[2] Thomas Monning personally appeared, and day was given to the defendant's party to answer, on which day he satisfied the limit, and the plaintiff's party says nothing in answer for 10 days, therefore the aforesaid Thomas was allowed to appear by Simon Sampson his attorney, with the counsel of master

---

[1] Richard [Sampson], Bishop of Chichester v. Sir Edward Essex. This is the same case as J.C. reported from the Order and Decree books. Either he made an error in transcribing Edward Essex as William Essex or there were several defendants and different ones were noted in each place.

[2] George Braunche v. Thomas Manning. This may be the correct case. It was sued at the proper time, the complaint having been made to Lord Audley, the Lord Chancellor. A commission was issued 8 November, 33.H.8. The complaint does seem to be addressed more to Chancery than either to Requests or Council.

Wingfield, with a clause to abide in judgment and to pay charges etc. [Req. 2/2/169]

10 February, fol. 119.[1] Day given to Thomas Arthur to answer to a bill etc. without delay, and also to bring with him an indenture lately in dispute. [Req. 2/4/351]

[fo. 113r]

Anno 30.H.8.

*15 May, 30.H.8, fol. 124. An executor of an executor sued for divers moveable goods, plate and other marchandises due to the father of the plaintiff. [NR]

[fo. 112r (p. 91)]

28 May, fol. 128. Causes depending before the Lord Privy Seale, or at the common law etc. [NR]

[fo. 113r]

*31 May, 30.H.8, fol. 129. Concerning the bargaine and sale of a tenement. [NR]

[fo. 112r (p. 91)]

2 June. Touching the title and interest of certaine landes betweene etc. It is ordered and decreed by the Kinges honourable counsell etc. [NR]

26 June, fol. 133. Thomas Atkins appeared personally in the name of Joanna Haines, widow, and says upon his oath that the said Joanna is detained by such infirmities and old age that she cannot appear. Therefore it is granted by the court that Nicholas Poines, and Walter Denis, knights, should have power to receive answer, and to certify etc. [NR]

The same, fol. 134. A pledge having been made of the infirmities of Thomas Tirrell,

[fo. 112v (p. 92)]

knight, it is granted to him, we gave power directed to John Springe etc. to receive answer and to certify etc. [NR]

The same. Thomas Hilton, attorney, with a clause to abide in judgment and to pay charges. [NR]

[fo. 113r]

*5 July, 30.H.8, fol. 140. For nonperformance of covenants. [NR]

[fo. 112v (p. 92)]

6 July, fol. 141. A certificat written to the Lord Bishop of West-minster by Master Nicholas Hare, touching a decree made and signed by him at Court in a cause depending betweene A.B. etc. [NR]

---

[1] Thomas Arthur and Anne, his wife v. John Dassett.

16 October, fol. 144. John Atmore etc. allowed to appear by Simon Sampson, his attorney, with the counsel of Masters Gaudy, Carell and Suliard of the Inner Temple, with a clause to abide in judgment and to pay charges. [NR]

The same, fol. 145.[1] Sir Richard Brereton, knight, complainant, etc. [Req. 2/12/184]

2 November, fol. 146. The Ladie Rose Wallop, widow, complainant etc. [NR]

4 November, fol. 5. A day peremptorily given to the Lord of Rutlande to make answere to the complaint of Curtes, etc. [Req. 1/6/7r][2]

6 November, fol. 149. Jone Tyler, plaintiff, and Robert Souche,[3] defendant, etc. The defendant dismissed, and she charged and commaunded that she sequester and utterly leave rayling and unfitting wordes speaking hereafter against the defendant upon paine of imprisonment, and such other punishment that thereof may follow and ensue etc. [Req. 2/3/218]

The same, fol. 151. Where cause of contention etc. hathe bene moved before the Kings most honourable Counsell etc. touching the title, interest and possession of certaine landes etc. where the titles on both sides are examined and decreed for the plaintiff both for possession and title, against the defendant, till the defendant shal shew better matter for his title either afore the sayde counsell, or otherwise by course of the Kings common lawes. [NR]

[fo. 113r]

*6 November, 30.H.8, fol. 149. An executor sued for a legacy of 20 libri the like 27 October, the same year, fol. 151 [NR]

*15 November, 30.H.8, fol. 156. Touching a lease of 8 acres of land, etc. [NR]

[fo. 112r (p. 91)]

1 February, fol. 10. Jeffery Downe, plaintiff, and the Abbot of Reading, defendant, etc. [Req. 1/6/13v]

[fo. 113r]

*4 February, 30.H.8, fol. 169. To bee restored to the possession of certain tenements and landes held in lease by the plaintiff for an yerely rent and expulsed therefrom by the defendant injuriously

---

[1] Sir Richard Brereton [Bruton], knight v. John Lancastre, Prior of Launde, Leics.

[2] Req. 1/6 is an Order book only. It is foliated but not by J.C. The original book from whence J.C. took his references is no longer extant.

[3] The commissioners' certificate refers to the defendant as Robert South.

and without just cause: and decreed for the plaintiff against the defendant. [NR]

*5 February, 30.H.8, fol. 169.[1] Collectors of Fifteenthes for the King, plaintiff, against Thomas Derham, gentleman, defendant, they exacting more then his landes were aforetime set at, and hee proving by auncient presidents that hee should pay for his said land but 31 shillings 2 [pence] which hee offered unto them, hee was dismissed from further appearance in this court. [Req. 2/9/131]

[fo. 114r (p. 93)]

Anno 31.H.8.

22 June, fol. 194. John Sewall etc. was allowed to appear by William Dobson, his attorney, with the counsel of Master Porter of the Inner Temple with a clause to abide in judgment and to pay charges. [NR]

[fol. 113v]

*23 June, 31.H.8, fol. 196. An executor sued for the arrearages of such landes as descended to the plaintiff and were received by the testator who married the plaintiffs mother; beesides for 80 wether shepe and ewes valewed at 6 libri; 2 melche kine at 26 s. 8 d; one horse at 16s.2d; 2 oxen at 20 s, etc. 15 libri decreed for and to the plaintiff. [NR]

[fo. 114r (p. 93)]

28 June, fol. 198. Robert Parker personally appeared before the Lord King's Council at Westminster by virtue of a command given to him by the messenger of the Chamber of the said Lord King at the suit of Henry Draper etc. [NR]

[fo. 113v]

*5 July, 31.H.8, fol. 228. Tenants of Chawworth in Nottingham-shire, plaintiff, Rafe Rolston, defendant, for the inclosure of a common by the defendant. Decreed for the plaintiff against the defendant, that the same shall remain common still. [NR]

[fo. 114r (p. 93)]

6 July, fol. 201. William Curtes of London, Tallowchaundler, complainant, against the Earle of Rutlande, defendant, touching the right, title and possession of an house and certaine lands, and decreed against the said Earle. [NR]

10 October, fol. 203.[2] George Columbell etc, allowed to appear by

---

1 John Atkyn and Robert Collyn, the younger, Collector of Fifteenths and Tenths in Norfolk v. Thomas Derham. See also Req. 2/10/244.

2 Christopher Browne and Margery, his wife v. George Columbell and John Sheffield, executors of Margery Columbell. See also Req. 2/1/43.

John Dion of the Inner Temple with a clause to abide in judgment
and to pay charges. [Req. 2/5/368]
22 October, fol. 210. The keeping of a Parke etc. adjudged to a
servant against his master upon the graunt of an annuitie unto him
by the said master to continue till matter sufficient to discharge the
saide servant compl. bee shewed before the kings Counsell. [NR]
25 October, fol. 213. The possession of an yeerely rent of iii.
shillings adjudged, but the title, and right to the land, left to the
triall of the kings common lawes. [NR]
[fo. 113v]
*25 October, 31.H.8, fol. 211. For the restitution of certain goods,
howseholdstuf and rentes deteyned by the defendant, being a
guardian, from the plaintiff, an infant. Decreed for the plaintiff
against the defendant to accompt and satisfie. [NR]
*26 October, 31.H.8. Fol. 213. For a legacy being a cup wourth 6
libri, decreed either the cup to bee delivered or 6 libri to bee paid
for the same to the plaintiff and 4 nobles for costes of sute. [NR]
*On the same, fol. 214. For the lease of a farme. The like, 6
November, the same year, fol. 217. [NR]
[fo. 114r (p. 93)]
18 November, fol. 223. Fourtie shillings for costs awarded to a
defendant to be paide to him or his assignes when and as soone as the
said complainant shall hereafter [l]itigate, sue, vexe, or trouble, the
said defendant touching the title, and interest of the premisses or
any parcell thereof. *costes to the defendant after sentence* [NR]
[fo. 113v]
*23 November, 31.H.8, fol. 224. For a watermill, a garden, a
pond, etc. and the way to the same belonging. Decreed to the
plaintiff. [NR]
On the same, fol. 225. For the breach and nonperformance of
certain covenants specified in a paire of indentures, etc. [NR]
[fo. 115r]
*25 November, 31.H.8, fol. 227. Launcelot Alford, Grome of the
Kings Wardrobe and Beds and Margaret, his wife, late wife and
executrix of John Parmenter, deceased, plaintiff, against, Richard
Smith, executor of Thomas Smith, defendant, touching the debt of
229 libri due to Thomas Smith uppon divers billes and specialties
to him made by the said Parmenter, late husband to Thomasin,
daughter to the said Thomas Smith. Which debtes were remitted
to the said Parmenter by the said Smith in his life time in regard of

the good usage used to the said Thomas Smith and his daughter Thomasin, by the said Parmenter, her husband. XX libri decreed against the plaintiff to the defendant in satisfaction of all debtes, etc. and all the said billes and specialties to bee delivered to the said plaintiff. [NR]

[fo. 114r (p. 93)]

27 November, fol. 229. Richard Flower and John Suaynton, attorneys, with a clause to abide in judgment and to pay charges. [NR]

[fo. 115r]

*28 November, 31.H.8, fol.   . A lease of a parsonage and prebend with the portions and tithes thereto belonging. Decreed to the plaintiff against the defendant. [NR]

[fo. 114r (p. 93)]

6 February, fol. 238. John Cheinty personally appeared before the Lord King's Council by virtue of a Writ of Privy Seal under penalty of allegiance to answer to certain articles objected against him by the party of the Lord King, and has day given to him etc., and has to appear from day to day

[fo. 114v (p. 94)]

until etc. [NR]

[fo. 115r]

*6 February, 31.H.8, fol. 238. A cause of legacy and other debtes. Decreed to a greate valeue against an executor. [NR]

[fo. 114v (p. 94)]

8 February, fol. 46.¹ The execution of a former order staied till the matter be further heard and determined etc. [Req. 1/6/49r]

[fo. 115r]

*13 February, 31.H.8, fol. 239. For a copyhold. [NR]

[fo. 114v (p. 94)]

21 April, fol. 49.² upon considerations shewed to the Counsell by the Master of the Rolles, etc. [Req. 1/6/52v]

28 April, fol. 2.³ John Newman allowed to appear before the Lord King's Council at Westminster etc. by Richard Flower, his attorney, with the counsel of Master Weston of the King's Bench with a clause to abide in judgment and to pay charges. [Req. 1/7/4r]

¹ — — Duffield v. — — Webbe.
² Henry Ilen v. Dame Elinor Kempe.
³ *Ex parte* Thomas Colyn v. John Newman. This entry is properly a part of 32.H.8 as the regnal year changes 22 April.

Anno 32.H.8.

8 June, fol. 11. William Weston, knight, complainant, against Simon Smith, defendant etc. [Req. 1/7/12v]

On the same, fol. 12. Matthew Smith of Brasennose in Oxford University appeared personally before the Lord King's Council at Westminster by virtue of a Writ of Privy Seale at the suit of William Abley, and has to answer to a bill on next Saturday and thus to appear from day to day etc. [Req. 1/7/13v]

[fo. 115r]

*20 June, 32.H.8, fol. 14.[1] For a lease of a farme and the landes and tenements thereto belonging. Decreed. [Req. 1/7/15r]

* 22 June, 32.H.8, fol. 16.[2] For a debt of 14 libri 10s. [Req. 1/7/17r]

[fo. 114v (p. 94)]

2 July, fol. 20.[3] Richard Norwich of Westley personally appeared etc.; afterwards, upon answer being presented, because the plaintiff's party desisted and did not appear, therefore the aforementioned Richard was allowed to appear in the aforesaid case by William Dobson, his attorney, with the counsel of John Adington, with a clause to abide in judgment and to pay charges etc. [Req. 1/7/21r]

3 July, fol. 21.[4] In the matter depending etc. and it is nowe by the Kings most honourable Counsell ordered etc. [Req. 1/7/22r]

8 July, fol. 23.[5] Where there hath bene long variance depending before the kings most honourable Counsell betweene William Warren, plaintiff, and Walter Allen, defendant, etc. [Req. 1/7/24v]

[fo. 115r]

*11 July, 32.H.8, fol. 28.[6] For a debt of 11 libri v.s. and 6 loades of hey. [Req. 1/7/29r]

*On the same.[7] For an annuity of 26 s. 8d. [Req. 1/7/29v]

[fo. 114v (p. 94)]

8 November, fol. 34.[8] Richard Gurney appeared, etc. and because the plaintiff's party did not appear on the day previously ap-

---

[1] John Bodenham v. Stephen ap Parry and his wife, Joan, and Wat Grey.
[2] Richard Duffeld v. Richard Hurting.
[3] William Breten v. Richard Norwich.
[4] John Bowman and his wife, Etheldrede v. John Cornell.
[5] William Warren v. Arthur [not Walter] Allen and Fulke Banker.
[6] Roger More, gentleman v. Thomas Calxson and his wife, Joan.
[7] Margaret Robyns, widow v. John Hall (?).
[8] *Ex parte* William Love and Edmund Rice v. Richard Gurney.

pointed for them, therefore the aforementioned Richard was allowed to appear by William Dobson, his attorney, with the counsel of Michael Malet of the Inner Temple with a clause to abide in judgment and to pay charges. [Req. 1/7/34r]

23 January, fol. 38. Lady Alice More, widow, personally

[fo. 116r (p. 95)]

appeared before the Lord King's Council at Westminster by virtue of a Writ of Privy Seal etc. at the suit of Christopher Newton, and has to answer to a bill on next Monday, and thus to appear from day to day until etc. [Req. 1/7/39v]

[fo. 115v]

*4 February, 32.H.8, fol. 43.[1] For a copyhold. [Req. 1/7/44v]

*10 February,[2] 32.H.8, fol. 48.[3] For the withholding of a lease from the plaintiff. [Req. 1/7/46r]

[fo. 116r (p. 95)]

12 February, fol. 46[4]. The Ladie Margaret Marques Dorcet, defendant, etc. and 1 July 33.H.8, fol. 8. [Req. 1/7/11r]

Anno 33.H.8.

25 May, fol. 62.[5] A matter of promise upon mariage and of legacie decreed. [Req. 1/7/62r]

[fo. 115v]

*25 May, 33.H.8, fol. 63.[6] For a mill and wast groundes thereto belonging. Ordered for the plaintiffs possession of the premises quietly without the interruption of the defendant or by his meanes, etc. [Req. 1/7/63r]

[fo. 116r (p. 95)]

29 May, fol. 66.[7] A decree against Sir Raphe Langford, knight for payments of 38 libri etc. for distreining and carying away of certaine cattell whereunto he had no interest, by colour of an extent upon a statute delivered then unto him as Sheriffe of Notinghamshire. [Req. 1/7/66r]

22 June, fol. 73. William Mantell and John Golding scholars of the college of Vause appear personally before the Lord King's Council

[1] William Simon v. William Astell ap Baker, William Wraske, James English.
[2] 10 February should read 12 February.
[3] William Pryseley v. William Adams.
[4] William Ashley *alias* Hyching v. Lady Margaret, Marques of Dorset, George Medley, Thomas Dygby. See *infra*, fo. 115v, *sub dat.* 1 July, 33.H.8.
[5] Mary Everyngham v. John Leyke, esquire.
[6] Richard Gilbert v. John Aston.
[7] John Thorpe and Ralph Spalton v. Sir Ralph Langford.

at Westminster by virtue of a Writ of Privy Seal etc. at the suit of Richard More clerk etc., and have to answer to a bill etc. and to appear from day to day

28 June, fol. 64. A decree subscribed by the Bishop of Westminster, Robert Southwell and John Tregonwell of the kings honourable Counsell etc [Req. 1/7/69v]

[fo. 115v]

*28 June, 33.H.8, fol. 64.[1] For an annuity of xx shillings. [Req. 1/7/64r]

*1 July, 33.H.8, fol.[2] 80. For rent of certain landes. Decreed for the plaintiff. [Req. 1/7/78v]

*3 July, 33.H.8, fol. 81.[3] For deteining from the plaintiff of a deede indented, sealed, etc. [Req. 1/7/81r]

*5 July, 33.H.8, fol. 83.[4] For the possession of a manour place and the landes, tenements, etc. thereto belonging, leased by Indenture to the said defendants wife and her former husband by the plaintiffs father. The lease adjudged voide and the possession of the premises decreed to the plaintiff [Req. 1/7/83r]

*6 July, 33.H.8, fol. 85.[5] For 129 libri, paid by the plaintiff for the rannsome of the defendant and for his diet being taken prisoner by the Scots. [Req. 1/7/85r]

[fo. 116r (p. 95)]

24 October, fol. 92.[6] Edmund Bonor, Bishop of London, complaint etc. *one of the judges of the court plaintiff in the court.* [Req. 1/7/90v]

6 November, fol. 93.[7] Thomas, Lorde Bishop of Westminster, one of the Kings most honourable Counsell in the White-hall etc. [Req. 1/7/90v]

10 November. The same folio, Lord Henry Morley was allowed to appear before the Lord King's Council in a case moved against him by the party of William Norf, by Simon Sampson his attorney,

---

[1] Richard Watkins, gentleman v. John Lyngham, esquire.

[2] Thomas Astley *alias* Hyckling v. Lady Margaret, Marques of Dorset, George Medley, esquire, Thomas Dygby, Arthur Laurence. See also Req. 1/7/11r and see *supra*, fo. 116r, *sub dat.* 12 February, 32.H.8.

[3] William Colfer v. William Polstead.

[4] Robert Morgayn v. Thomas Cowper and Elizabeth, his wife, and Alexander Hoskyns, her son.

[5] Leonard Morton v. Thomas Husting.

[6] Edmund Bonner v. John Symons, clerk.

[7] Thomas Thirlby, created 1540, translated to Norwich 1550. The diocese of Westminster was established in 1540 and merged into the diocese of London upon Thirlby's translation.

with the counsel of Master Browne, Serjeant at law, with a clause to abide in judgment and to pay charges. [Req. 1/7/91v]
On the same, fol. 96 and 97.[1] Certaine witnesses punished by
[fo. 116v (p. 96)]
the Kings most honourable counsel for their untrue depositions before them made in a matter depending betweene John Stephen etc., plaintiff, and Edward Shelley etc., defendant, by imprisonment etc. [Req. 1/7/95v–96r]
[fo. 115v]
*20 November, 33.H.8, fol. 96.[2] For a yerely rent of 40s issueng out of a tenement. [Req. 1/7/95r]
[fo. 116v (p. 96)]
10 February, fol. 124.[3] A decree all in latine by Thomas, Bishop of Westminster, Robert Southwell, knight, and John Tregonwell, esquire, all three the kings Counsellors in his court of White-Hall and sealed with their seales. [Req. 1/7/122v]
[fo. 115v]
*11 February, 33.H.8, fol. 106.[4] For the performance of certain covenants specified in a paire of indentures dated, etc. 10 libri decreed to the plaintiff. [Req. 1/7/105r]
[fo. 116v (p. 96)]
14 March, fol. 109. In the cause of David Sissell of Witham in the countie of Lincolne, plaintiff, against Richard Sissell, his brother, Yeoman of the kings robes, for certaine landes being in Staunford in the sayd Countie of Lincoln *and for a lease of the landes or manor of Tinwell in the countie of Rutland* etc. dismissed by kings most honourable Counsell etc. and David injoyned to leave his clamour further to be made to the kings grace, touching the premisses upon paine of imprisonment etc. [Req. 1/7/108r]

Anno 34.H.8.

6 May, fol. 118.[5] A decree against the master of an apprentise in London for the restitution of money received with him etc. *For a prentise against his master* [Req. 1/7/117v]
[fo. 117r]
*6 May, 34.H.8, fol. 117.[6] For copyhold landes. [Req. 1/7/116r]

---

[1] John Stephen and Nicholas Stephen v. Edward Shelley and James Skynner.
[2] Paul Tanner v. William Hargill.
[3] The foot of the folio is too damaged to identify the litigants.
[4] John Bradstreet, Roger Bradstreet and William Birche v. Robert Bradstreet.
[5] Baldwin Marwood and his son, Barnard v. Robert Harris.
[6] Henry Freland v. John Freland.

*On the same day.[1] A suretie to bee saved harmeles by the princi-
pall for a debt paid by him and his charges of sute spent for
defence of the cause. Decreed for the plaintiff. [Req. 1/7/116v]

Sir Humfrey Stafford,[2] knight, plaintiff, George Butler, etc.,
defendants, for the possession of 8 saltfats [sic] with sailes kept
from the plaintiff by the defendant with the profits of the
same. Decreed for the plaintiff, 20 May, 34.H.8, fol. 122. [Req.
1/7/121r]

[fo. 116v (p. 96)]

10 May, fol. 120.[3] Thomas Maleverer, gentleman, defendant, etc.
[Req. 1/7/120v]

[fo. 117r]

*13 May, 34.H.8, fol. 123. Memorandum, that a petition was
heard, etc., be it ordered, adjudged and decreed by the reverend
father in Christ, Thomas, Bishop of Westminster, Robert Southwell, knight, and John Tregonwell, gentleman, the lord Kings
Counsellors in the said Lord Kings Court of Whitehall, etc.
Decreed for copyholders against theire Lord wherein theire services, whereto they shalbee after tied, are particularly expressed,
the plaintiff being the tenants of Beaulines in Wiltshire, and
Edward Capell, esquier, defendant. [Req. 1/7/122r]

[fo. 116v (p. 96)]

10 October, fol. 130.[4] John Benge of Pepingbury in Kent county
appeared personally etc. by virtue of an injunction given to him by
Thomas Darell and Roydon, esquires, and because no certification was sent back on the day designated by the writ, therefore he
was allowed to appear by William Dobson, his attorney, etc.
[Req. 1/7/129r]

14 October, fol. 130.[5] Thomas Egerley etc. Afterwards, to wit on
the 18th day of the said month, the bill in the aforesaid case is
remitted to the Lord King's general overseers [i.e., the court of
General Surveyors] to hear and decide etc. [Req. 1/7/129 v]

[fo. 117r]

*21 November, 34.H.8, fol. 135.[6] For 20 libri in money and certain

---

[1] Thomas Wolley v. Reginald Davy.
[2] Sir Humphrey Stafford, knight v. George Butler and John Butler. J.C. has not
   made his usual annotation to set this apart as a separate entry although clearly
   it is.
[3] Propositor of Cambridge v. Thomas Maleverer.
[4] Purnell Bourage v. Nicholas Crocke and John Benge.
[5] Robert Tomlinson v. Thomas Egerley.
[6] Thomas Chaude [or Chande] v. Bernard Goolde.

jewels borrowed by the said defendant of the nowe wife of the said plaintiff in her widowehood. [Req. 1/7/134r]

[fo. 116v (p. 96)]

25 November, fol. 137. In the cause depending betweene Parnell Bowdo, plaintife, against Peter Bowdo her husband

[fo. 118r (p. 97)]

defendant, who had put her away, for maintenance during his absence from her, it was decreed etc. That she should have xx. d. a weeke out of his fee of xvi. d. a day, till either hee were reconciled unto her, or coulde prove sufficient matter of divorce by order of the Law. [Req. 1/7/137v]

23 January, fol. 146. James Coffin, esquire, appeared etc. at the suit of Maurice Donat, doctor of medicine, etc. [Req. 1/7/139r]

On the same.[1] Thomas Charleton appears in the name of Matthew Browne, knight, etc. And upon his oath he says that the said Matthew is detained by such infirmities and old age that he cannot appear on the day set for him, therefore a commission is granted to John Skinner etc. to receive answer etc. And to certify etc. [Req. 1/7/139v]

3 March, fol. 156.[2] A decree for a poore woman against certaine Church-wardens in London for a messuage and implements therein, with respite of taxation of charges, till the Counsell might perceive what towardnes there is in the defendant, for the accomplishment of this order, which if they refuse to doe, then the costs to be taxed to the uttermost charge approved due etc. [Req. 1/7/150r]

12 April, fol. 162. Thomas, Bishop of Westminster, and Thomas Dacres, Esquier, two of the Kings honorable Counsell etc. [Req. 1/7/156v]

Anno 35.H.8.

30 May, folio 170.[3] William Whiting etc. allowed to appear etc. by William Dobson, attorney, with the counsel of Master Harris, Serjeant at law, with a clause to abide in judgment and to pay charges. [Req. 1/7/170v]

[fo. 117v]

*31 October, 35.H.8, fol. 176.[4] For a debt of 45 libri. [Req. 1/7/165v]

---

[1] Henry Ashely v. Sir Matthewe Browne, knight.
[2] Alice Dacres, widow v. Thomas Gonne and others, wardens of the Fraternity of Our Lady, St. Stephen, and St. Gabriel in St. Sepulcre's parish, Middlesex.
[3] John Morie v. William Whiting.
[4] Henry Wyke v. Giles Doddington and John Bulbage.

[fo. 118r (p. 97)]

15 November, fol. 176. The day of St. Michael held at the town of St. Alban's, where the court held by the Lord King's Council is called Whitehall, and 24 November 34.H.8, fol. 178 etc. [Req. 1/7/166r]

20 November, fol. 178.[1] A cause of legacie decreed etc. [Req. 1/7/168r]

[fo. 118v (p. 98)]

21 February, fol. 188. Nicholas Alcocke, ordered to paie Margery Alcock his wife xx. s. towards her sustentation etc. [Req. 1/7/178r]

Anno 36.H.8.

14 May, fol. 198.[2] Thomas Packington, etc. allowed to appear etc. by Edward Gleyn, his attorney, with a clause to appear in judgment and to pay to the person awarded etc. [Req. 1/7/187r]

[fo. 119r]

*17 May, 36.H.8, fol. 198.[3] For a yerely stipend for the finding and sustentation of a priest to sing, etc. [Req. 1/7/187v]

[118v (p. 98)]

25 June, fol. 208.[4] A decree for awarding of charges and costs for the breach or not performance of a bargaine in communication etc. [Req. 1/7/196r]

[fo. 119r]

*28 June, 36.H.8, fol. 208.[5] For 2 yeres arrerages of the rent of a mill waters and fisshings thereto belonging. [Req. 1/7/196v]

*30 June, 36.H.8, fol. 209.[6] Touching a lease of a manour made and graunted first by the Right Honorable Sir Thomas Broke, late Lord Cobham, deceased and afterwardes renewed by the right honorable George, nowe Lord Cobham, etc. [Req. 1/7/197v]

*5 November, 36.H.8, fol. 216.[7] For a petition of landes to bee made betwene the plaintife and defendant done by commission, certified and decreed. [Req. 1/7/202v]

---

[1] Christopher Hall and Thomas Benson v. Jane Erley, executrix of late Thomas Erley.

[2] William Packington v. Thomas and William Packington.

[3] Richard Wyke and Miles King in the name of the inhabitants of the town of Okeham, co. Rutland v. John Wymark, clerk, deceased.

[4] Thomas Warde v. William Blaknall.

[5] John Newynton v. George Bulstrode and Thomas Bulstrode.

[6] Thomas Richards v. William Crabb, Henry Crabb and Maude, his mother.

[7] John Brown, for and in the name of Joan Mychecrofte *alias* Brown, his mother v. Sir Anthony Hungerford.

[fo. 118v (p. 98)]
11 November, fol. 220.[1] Forasmuch as it appeareth before the Kings Counsell in the honourable court of White Hall at Westminster etc. [Req. 1/7/206v]
25 November, fol. 223. Sir Arthur Darcey, knight, complainant, against John Martin of Ware, yeoman, for the not performance of a bargaine for 120 quarters of malte etc. [Req. 1/7/208r]

Anno 37.H.8.

27 April, fol. 235.[2] Baldwin Sheldon was allowed to appear etc. by Richard Flowre his attorney, with the counsel of Master Walle of the Inner Temple with a clause to appear in judgment and to pay to the person awarded etc. [Req. 1/7/223v]
30 April, fol. 236. A decree against Sir Thomas Wentworth, knight, Lord Wentworth, defendant etc. for the payment of a certain annuitie, and the arrerages of the same then unpayd etc. to one Edward Glemham and Mary, his wife, complainant etc. [Req. 1/7/224v]
[fo. 119r]
*12 May, 37.H.8, fol. 238. The customary tenants of the manour of Bradford in Somersetshire, plaintiff, William Francis and Richard Warre, esquiers, defendants, for the enjoyeng theire customes as in former time, and for the certeintie of theire fines, and for the plaintiffs for the enjoyeng of theire customary tenements. [Req. 1/7/226r]
[fo. 118v (p. 98)]
15 May, fol. 240.[3] A decree upon the interest, right and title of certaine messuages, lands, and tenements, in Abbots Ripton in the county of Huntingtonshire etc. [Req. 1/7/228v] The like decreed,[4] Sir Foulke Grevile, knight, being complainant 16 November 37.H.8, fol. 248. *touching landes in the isle of Gernsey* *A decree touching landes in the Isle of Gernsey.* [Req. 1/7/236r]
12 November.[5] Nicholas, Bishop of Worcester, plaintiff etc. [Req. 1/7/234r]

---

[1] There does not appear to be any particular reason for citing this style as it had been used before.
[2] *Ex parte* John Marshe v. Baldwin Sheldon.
[3] Simon Kent, William Byrde, Thomas Rogers, William Stokesley v. Sir John St. John and Oliver St. John, his son and heir.
[4] Sir Fulke Greville and his wife, Elizabeth v. Nicholas Fashyn, gentleman.
[5] Nicholas Heath v. (?) John Roberts. The folio is too badly damaged to clearly identify the defendant.

[fo. 120r (p. 99)]

27 November, fol. 251.[1] A decree touching the stopping of a watercourse to a mill, etc. [Req. 1/7/239r]

22 December, fol. 251.[2] The Right Honourable earle of Oxford, defendant, etc. and the possession of a manour decreed for the plaintiff against the sayd Earle. [Req. 1/7/239v]

28 January, fol. 258. John Powes, gentleman, appeared, etc. at the suit of the Lord of Derby, etc. [NR]

1 February, fol. 260. Where, upon variance mooved and depending before the Kings most honourable counsel, in the Whitehall at Westminster, betweene Richard Wike, plaintife, and the Lady Honor Lisle, late widow to the right honourable Arthur Plantagenet, late Viscount Lisle etc. Being a servants sute against his Lady for an annuity granted by her late husband, etc. [NR]

10 February, fol. 263.[3] Sir Philip Hobby, knight, plaintiff, etc.[4] [Req. 3/14/263r]

Anno 38.H.8.

1 June, fol. 269. The Kings most honourable counsell of Whitehall having a respect to a former order and decree made by the Kings most honourable counsel in the Starre Chamber at Westminster. *touching copyhold landes holden of the manour of Normington in Darbyshire.* [Req. 3/14/269r][5]

4 [[July]] *June* D. fol.[6] A decree touching the forfeiture of certaine wheate seised by the bailifes of Oxford from a Baker as forfeited, etc. [Req. 3/14/269v]

On the same day, fol. 271.[7] A decree for an Almesmans place in the Cathedrall Church of Westchester.[8] [Req. 3/14/271r]

[fo. 119v]

*4 June, 38.H.8, fol. 270. Henry Knight, plaintiff, Henry Wats, defendant, for certain conveyances for and in consideration of a pretensed mariage uppon a affiance and contract made betuene the

---

[1] John Celroger v. William Carvanell.

[2] Edward Bowland and Thomas Pierson v. Earl of Oxford.

[3] Sir Philip Hobbey v. William Tattarsall, gentleman.

[4] This citation, and several which follow, are taken from a gathering from an Order and Decree book now missing in its entirety. The foliation is in J.C's hand and the gathering was found among the Requests Miscellany (Req. 3).

[5] Thomas Gyles and Elizabeth, his wife v. Godfrey Foljambe, gentleman. Half of this folio is missing.

[6] John Lewes v. Bailiff of the City of Oxford.

[7] William Wederall v. John Moyle.

[8] This is either Winchester or Westminster.

said plaintiff and Elizabeth the daughter of the said defendant by indentures of covenants concerning a joynture as also other deedes indented of lease etc. Decreed that the plaintiff at his being out of prentisehood shall marrie the said Elizabeth or give her 20 markes for her advauncement, etc. [Req. 3/14/270r]

[fo. 120r (p. 99)]

6 June, fol. 274. Forasmuch as John Bird, the elder, and John Bird, the younger, complainants, against John earle of Bathe, defendant, for and concerning a seisure of certain goods and cattals, taken by the officers of the said earle, claiming the same to be due unto him, as the goods and cattals of villains regardants to the mannour of Holne in the county of Devon: and upon answere, replication and rejoynder, touching the same, the sayde complainants during the

[fo. 120v (p. 100)]

space of two yeres and more, nothing have further sayd ne done for trial of their liberty, wherfore the said counsell have now dismissed the sayd earle out of this court, and remitted the matter to be tried according to the due order and course of the Common lawes, where all such causes ought to be heard and determined. [Req. 3/14/274r]

[fo. 119v]

*29 June, 38.H.8, fol. 276.[1] For a yerely rent of 26 shillings 8 d. issueng out of certain landes of John Loddington in Huntington-shire. Decreed for the plaintiff. [Req. 3/14/276v]

*8 July, 38.H.8, fol. 279.[2] For the pulling downe and carrieng away of a tenement called Walkhamstowe parsonage in the county of Essex. [Req. 3/14/279r]

[fo. 120v (p. 100)]

14 July, fol. 287.[3] A decree touching certaine lands assured away by fine and recovery: but under certaine conditions, not performed, as the plaintiff prooved, and thereupon had reliefe for the value of the land, but not it, etc. [Req. 3/14/287v]

29 July, fol. 285.[4] Agreed betweene H.F. and N.L. to make humble sute to the Kings honourable counsell attendant upon his person and commonly sitting in the Kings Majesties court of Whitehall at Westminster. [Req. 3/14/285v]

[1] Randolph Durden, Alice Harrys, Katherine Durden v. Thomas Moddy.
[2] John Wastell v. Paul Wythyrpolle.
[3] Thomas Halman, son and heir to John Halman v. George Harper.
[4] Humphrey Fitzherbert v. Nicholas Lowe.

25 September, fo. 280. An order and finall end taken and made by the right reverend father in God, Nicholas, Bishop of Worcester, and Sir Nicholas Hare, knight, of the Kings most honourable Counsell betweene Henry Vyne, gentleman, and Thomas Thaccumbe, etc. [Req. 3/14/280v]

17 October, fol. 286. In the matter of variance depending before the kings honourable counsell: betweene Sir Nicholas Hare, knight, complainant, and John Willoughby, esquire, defendant, etc. *touching a free rent issueng out of certain landes etc. Decreed with the plaintiff.* [Req. 3/14/286v]

20 November, fol. 291.[1] Sir Richard Cholmely, knight, defendant, etc. [Req. 3/14/291r]

26 November, fol. 292.[2] The most reverende father the Archebishop of Yorke, defendant, etc. *For the tithes and other profits of the parsonage of Bentham in Yorkeshire. Decreed for the plaintiff.* [Req. 3/14/292v]

Anno 1.E.6.

4 February, fol. 298. The right honourable Sir John Russell, knight, Lord Russell and Lord Privie Seale, defendant etc. *The plaintiff an executor for howseholdstuf and other goods belonging to his testator. Decreed with the plaintiff.* [NR]

6 February, fol. 298.[3] The Reverende Father in God, Robert, Bishop of Carlisle, defendant, etc.

[fo. 121r]

*8 February, 1.E.6, fol. 299.[4] The tenants of Noweland Carleton in Notinghamshire against Richard Whalley, esquier, touching certain enclosures and other wronges supposed to bee done by the defendant to the said plaintiff. [Req. 2/3/108r]

[fo. 120v (p. 100)]

15 May, fol. 2. Robert Kirkham allowed to appear etc.

[fo. 122r (p. 101)]

by William Dobson, his attorney, with the counsel of master Stapleton with a clause to abide in judgment and to pay charges. [NR]

[1] Gabriel Proctor v. Sir Richard Chomeley.
[2] John Anderson, Joan Anderson and Alice Anderson v. Edward [Lee] Archbishop of York and Robert Grave.
[3] Robert Aldrich, Bishop of Carlisle.
[4] William Stirtivant, John Johnson, William Cutbert, etc., tenants of the King's Lordship of Norwell and Carleton-upon-Trent, co. Northumberland, for all the tenants v. Richard Whalley. J. C. transcribed the manor incorrectly.

22 May, fol. 3. John Burrell, mayor of the town of Berwike, personally appears etc. and has to appear from day to day to the time when and until he has permission to withdraw. [NR]

[fo. 121r]

*27 June, 1.E.6, fol. 8. For an annuity of 40 s. yerely out of a manour. Decreed for the plaintiff. [NR]

[fo. 122r (p. 101)]

28 June, fol. 9. Edward Glenham, esquire, and Mary, his wife, plaintiff, and the right honorable Sir Thomas Wentworthe, Lord Wenworth, defendant, etc. A rent of 20 libri a yeere decreed against the said Lord. *a rent* [NR]

[fo. 121r]

*29 June, 1.E.6, fol. 9. Concerning the taking and withholding of 23 tod[1] of woollen yarne to the valeue of 23 libri from the plaintiff by the defendant. Decreed for the plaintiff with 3 libri for costes. [NR]

*28 June, 1.E.6, fol. 10. The plaintiff an executor for 3 libri, 6 s viii d. Decreed for the plaintiff. [NR]

[fo. 122r (p. 101)]

5 June, fol. 3.[2] Anthonie Belasses, clerke, Master of the Hospitall of Sherbourne House in the County of Dorset, defendant, touching an annuitie pretended to have bine graunted by Doctor Leigh alias Sir Thomas Leigh, knight, late Master of the said Hospitall, and the Cobrethren of the same etc. *annuity.* [Req. 2/17/79]

18 October, fol. 14. Lord Scroupe was allowed to appear etc. by Ralph Scroupe with a clause to abide in judgment and to pay charges. [NR]

[fo. 121r]

*26 November, 1.E.6, fol. 19. Certain groundes called Grenehill, parcell of the demesnes of the prebend called Netherbury in terra otherwise called the manour of Yendover, which the plaintiff chalengeth by reason of a lease from the Lord Edward Seymour, prebendary of the foresaid prebend: Decreed for the plaintiff to have the possession thereof. [NR]

[fo. 122r (p. 101)]

27 November, fol. 20.[3] A cause examined by the right honorable the Earle of Southampton late Chauncelour of England: betweene

---

[1] A 'tod' was a weight used in the wool trade usually being equal to two stones or 28 pounds.

[2] Edward Morley and Margaret, his wife v. Anthony Bellasse.

[3] Richard Buttell and John Knotting v. Henry Wyndbourne.

John Knitting etc., complainant, and one Henry Windborne, defendant, was reexamined by the Kings Counsell in his court of Requests: and the partie committed to the Fleet by the said Lord Chaunsellour, was discharged upon sureties by the saide Counsell, till againe hee was committed by them upon the hearing of the cause. *a discharge from commitment to the prison of the Fleete.* [Req. 2/17/24]

Anno 2.E.6.

30 January, fol. 26.[1] Robert Brandling, knight, plaintiff, etc. [Req. 2/18/72]

On the same, fol. 27. Lord Windesor, plaintiff, etc. [NR]

January 31, fol. 29. A decree for and touching a clame made and pretended to a common high way etc. [NR]

3 February, fol. 6. The Lord Scroupe, defendant. [NR]

4 February, fol. 29.[2] A decree against Richard Jervis, Sheriffe of London, for deteyning a gelding, as goods feloniously

[fo. 122v (p. 102)]

taken and stolen: and he inforced to pay to the plaintiff v. libri for the same, and xx. shillings for sadle, and harnesse etc. [Req. 2/15/51]

8 February, fol. 9. George Lusher, gentleman, defendant etc. [NR]

9 February, fol. 30. A decree for the tenantes of a mannor against the Lord thereof for the usage of the Common at times accustomed etc. *for the tenants against the Lord for common.* [NR]

[fo. 121v]

*9 February, 2.E.6, fol. 31. For the discharge of a rent charge out of the manour of Winterborne in Dorcetshire, awarded by a former decree: The decree confirmed and the plaintiff condemned to pay the defendant 40 s. for costes of his wrongfull vexation. [NR]

[fo. 122v (p. 102)]

13 February, fol. 32. An Injunction to stay the suite of a bonde in the king bench, etc. [NR]

20 April, fol. 35. A decree for possession for the plaintiff and the defendant condemned in xx. shillings for costes of sute. [NR]

[fo. 121v]

*4 May, 2.E.6, fol. 42. For certain sommes of money received by the said defendant etc. Decreed for the plaintiff. [NR]

---

[1] Sir Robert Brandling and Thomas Scott v. Lewis Sergeant and Cicely, his wife. See infra, fo. 126r, sub dat. 24 April, 5.E.6.

[2] William Denys v. Richard Gervys, Sheriff of London.

[fo. 122v (p. 102)]
12 May, fol. 41. Restitution of goods, seazed of under pretence of felony, decreed. *for the plaintiff with 20 shillings 8 d. costes* [NR]

[fo. 121v]
*14 May, 2.E.6, fol. 42. One executor, plaintiff, against an other for the division of certain moneis received by the defendant. [NR]

[fo. 122v (p. 102)]
9 June, fol. 52. The President and fellowes of Corpus Christi Colledge in Oxford ordered to make a lease of certaine lands etc. [NR]

[fo. 121v]
*15 June, 2.E.6, fol. 50. To save the plaintiff harmeles of 2 obligations wherein hee standeth bound for the defendant for the payment of certain money. [NR]

*20 June, 2.E.6, fol. 53. For recompence of a false and wrongfull imprisonment, the plaintiff a poore parson of a church against Sir Nicholas Pointz, knight, defendant. The defendant condemned in 5 libri to the plaintiff. [NR]

[fo. 122v (p. 102)]
22 June, fol. 54. A testamentarie cause remitted to the kings delegates where it depended by appeale from the Prerogative Court, before any suite commensed for the same, before the kings Counsel, etc. [NR]

23 November, fol. 63. A decree touching a copiholde in a mannor belonging to the Bishop of Worcester. The copy whereof passed by these wordes to be had and held to himself and his people according to the custom of the manor and the meaning of the saide wordes, there set downe to containe onely terme for the tenantes life etc. and their possession and fourtie shillings for costes of suite awarded to the plaintiff, etc. *to himself and his people according to the custom of the manor.* [NR]

28 November, fol. 62.¹ A decree against Sir Fraunces Leeke, knight, for and touching a lese of certaine tithes, and 6 libri awarded and decreed against him to the complainant for the costes, and expenses of the suite. [Req. 2/15/74]

[fo. 121v]
*27 January, 2.E.6, fol. 72. For copihold landes. Decreed for the plaintiff. [NR]

¹ Richard Shyrbroke v. Sir Francis Leke.

[fo. 122v (p. 102)]

Anno 3.E.6.

23 January, fol. 65. John Hall allowed to appear by Richard Oseley, his attorney, with the counsel of Master Chidley and John
[fo. 124r (p. 103)]
Browne with a clause to abide in judgment and to pay charges. [NR]
On the same. Leonard Welbecke, etc. allowed to appear, etc. by Richard Osely, his attorney, with the counsel of William Latton of the Inner Temple, with a clause to abide in judgment and to pay charges. [NR]
30 January, fol. 69.[1] William Laxton, knight, plaintiff, etc. [Req. 2/18/1]
8 May, fol. 75. Richard Osely and Robert Dale, attorneys, with a clause to abide in judgment and to pay charges. [NR]
9 May, fol. 77.[2] Lady Blanche Forman was allowed to appear etc. by Richard Osely, her attorney, with the counsel of Master Atkins, and Master Hadley, with a clause to abide in judgment and to pay charges, etc. [Req. 2/15/96]
20 May, fol. 82. A cause of tythes remitted to the Judges ecclesiasticall to bee determined according to the lawes there, for that by a late statute made in that behalfe, the causes of tythes is thereto be determined, and not elsewhere. [NR]
[fo. 123r]
*20 May, 3.E.6, fol. 82. For and touching the non performance of an award, decreed for the award. [NR]
*The same, fol. 83. Edmond Clerk, gentleman, one of the clerks of the Kings Privy Seal, plaintiff, and Sir John Gresham, knight, defendant, touching a claime made by the saide plaintiffe to the offices of Bailiwick of Westerham and Edenbridge: decreed for the plaintiff. [Req. 2/14/182]
*22 May, 3.E.6, fol. 85. For recompense of the late tenant for certain dilapidations of some tenements committed by him: decreed for the plaintiff against the defendant. [NR]
*31 May, 3.E.6, fol. 86. Administrators, plaintiff, for a debt due to the deceased by the defendant, decreed aswell for the defendant as for the plaintiff. [NR]
[fo. 124r (p. 103)]
1 June, fol. 89. Touching the usage of a Common leased to Henry

---

[1] Sir William Laxton v. Robert Edolf.
[2] Robert Morgan v. Lady Blanch Forman, widow.

Drake etc. amongst other things, by the Abbot, and Convent of the late Monastery of Buckeland in the Countie of Devon etc. [NR]

[fo. 123r]

*1 June, 3.E.6, fol. 87. The plaintiff a farmor of a parsonage for certain tithe corne. [NR]

*The same, fol. 90. For the making of a lease promised by the defendant to the plaintiff. [NR]

*2 June, 3.E.6, fol. 92.[1] For the possession of the parsonage howse of Dunchurch in Warwick with landes thereto belonging. [Req. 2/17/29]

*The same, fol. 93.[2] For the tithes belonging to the parsonage of Hunstanworth in Durham; decreed for the plaintiff. [Req. 2/14/116 and Req. 2/14/157]

[fo. 124r (p. 103)]

4 June, fol. 94.[3] A decree touching the demaunde and interest of a Stewardship and Bailifwike of the Manor of Condover in the Countie of Salop. etc. [Req. 2/18/65]

28 June, fol. 99.[4] Edward Manwaring was allowed to appear by Richard Osely, his attorney, with the counsel of Master Woode of the Inner Temple with a clause to abide in judgment and to pay charges, etc. [Req. 2/14/96]

8 July, fol. 102.[5] A decree against William Howard Lord Howard defendant for the payment of 12 libri for certaine wares received of the complainant, etc. *for a debt.* [Req. 2/18/73]

[fo. 123r]

*8 July, 3.E.6, fol. 102. For the performance of a lease promised to bee procured to the plaintiff upon the p[ayment] of 30 libri which was paid accordingly by the plaintiff and the lease not procured by the defendant: decreed that the defendant should either procure the lease for the plaintiff or repay to him his money. [NR]

[fo. 124r (p. 103)]

15 October fol. 105.[6] John Kingston was allowed to appear etc. By George Forman his attorney with the counsel of James Smith of

---

[1] John Fanne v. Thomas Haloway, and others.

[2] William Eglestone v. William Farewell. The documents in these two files are parts of the same action and should be incorporated under one reference number.

[3] Robert Jevans v. Robert Long.

[4] Alice Polson, widow v. Edward Maynwaring and Alice, his wife.

[5] Katherine Phillips v. William, Lord Howard.

[6] Elizabeth Whytwell v. John Kingston.

the Temple called the Steire Temple, with a clause to abide in judgment and to pay charges etc. [Req. 2/16/106]

28 November, fol. 115. a cause of legacie decreed etc. [NR]

[fo. 124v (p. 104)]

Anno 4.E.6.

26 January, fol. 118. The Reverend Father in Christ the bishop of Peterborough, plaintiff etc. [NR]

29 January. If the defendant in this court have (being also defendant at the common law) waged his law, then he is to be dismissed out of this court. [NR]

[fo. 125r]

*6 February, 4.E.6, fol. 120. An award ratified and confirmed and both parties plaintiff and defendant enjoyned to performe the same. [NR]

*On the same day. An administrator, plaintiff, for restitution of 360 sheepe delivered to the defendant by the deceased as a stock with a farme and for the rent of the said farme behind, unpayed. Decreed with the plaintiff. [NR]

*8 February, 4.E.6, fol. 121.[1] The tenants of Livermere in Suffolke, being 35 persons, plaintiffs, for the use, occupieng, grasing and pasturing of certain wast groundes in Livermere, enclosed by the defendant with great dikes and pondes to the greate hinderance of the said tenants: decreed that the said groundes shalbee layed open as before etc. and further that the defendant shall pay to the plaintiff 4 marks for costes, and 13 February, 5.E.6, fol. 157, Richard Coddington, esquire, plaintiff. [Req. 2/17/73]

[fo. 124v (p. 104)]

11 February, fol. 122.[2] A decree for and touching the turning of the water course of ancient and long time running and comming to the mill called Menmots mill in the county of Notingham.

April 30. Dame Elizabeth Constable, plaintiff, etc. [NR]

18 May. A decree against the Right Honourable Thomas Lord Howard, for the restoring the possession of a tenement to one John Freeman etc. 22 October fol. 132. [Req. 2/15/115]

24 October, fol. 133. Forasmuch as upon the cause brought etc. at the sute of Thomas Ivery, by the onely procuring of his wilful wife, for the title of a mease with the appertenances, etc. [NR]

---

[1] Hamond Claxton and others, inhabitants of Great Livermere, Suffolk v. Richard Coddington.

[2] Ralph Chadwick v. John Byron.

8 November, fol. 136. Ralph Bulmer, knight, was allowed to appear before the Lord King's Council etc. by William Dobson, his attorney, with the counsel of Master Rokesby and with a clause to abide in judgment and to pay charges. [NR]

[fo. 125r]

*10 November, 4.E.6, fol. 138. For a debt a 40 marks uppon a sale of certain landes made to the defendant by the plaintiff. [NR]

*11 November, 4.E.6, fol. 138. For a debt of 40 marks uppon a sale of certain landes made to the defendant by the plaintiff. [NR]

[fo. 124v (p. 104)]

12 November, fol. 139.¹ John Weving committed to the Marshalsea for the breach of an injunction. [Req. 2/17/104]

23 November, fol. 140. A decree for the performance of an arbitrament, *with an interpretation of the said award* [NR]

[fo. 125r]

*23 November, 4.E.6, fol. 141. An administrator, plaintiff, for the withholding and cancelling of a lease by the defendant belonging to the deceased: decreed that the defendant shall deliver the like lease to the plaintiff and pay likewise 40 s. for costes. [NR]

[fo. 124v (p. 104)]

24 November, fol. 143.² A decree for Thomas Boraston and Constance, his wife, late the wife of William Goodyere, complainant, against Nicholas Goodyere, defendant, for a cottage with a garden thereunto adjoyning set, lying, and being in Edgware in the county of Middlesex, next the mansion of the vicar there on the South part etc. [Req. 2/18/2]

26 November.³ Sir Humfry Browne, knight, one of the Justices of the Common Plees etc. *defendant.* [Req. 2/16/114]

[fo. 125v]

*27 November, 4.E.6, fol. 145.⁴ The copyholders of the manour of Wellowe in Somersetshire, plaintiff, against William Crouche, defendant, for that the defendant hath made a conigree in the common where the copyholders did use to pasture theire sheepe: Decreed for the copyholders against the defendant that they shall

---

¹ John Weyving v. Bennet Jaye.

² Thomas Boraston, Yeoman of the Crown, and Constance, his wife v. Nicholas Goodyere and Henry Page.

³ Elizabeth Woodliff, executrix of late William Woodliff v. Sir Humphrey Browne. See *infra*, fo. 126v., *sub dat.* 30 May, 6.E.6.

⁴ William Worey, and others, copyholders of the manor v. William Crouche.

enjoy theire common for pasture according to theire copies as before time. [Req. 2/16/116]

*On the same day. For a copyhold: decreed for the copyholder with caution that shee shall not, under paine to forfait her copyhold, fell anie timber, woods or underwoods growing uppon the copyhold without the Lords licence [NR]

[fo. 126r (p. 105)]

16 January. In default of the appearance of the defendant an injunction for possession of landes awarded to the plaintife etc. [NR]

Anno 5.E.6.

24 January, fol. 150. Edward Marvin, knight, and one of the justices of the Lord King's Bench, appears personally at Westminster by virtue of a Writ of Privy Seal under penalty of 100 pounds at the suit of John Crobeke, and has day given to him to answer to a bill on next Monday, and thus to appear from day to day until, etc. [NR]

[fo. 125v]

*13 February, 5.E.6, fol. 157. [NR]

*16 February, 5.E.6, fol. 156. For certain copyhold landes: decreed for the copyholders, plaintiff. [NR]

[fo. 126r (p. 105)]

24 April.[1] Sir Robert Branling, knight, etc.

April 30. A decree for the possession of an office of Bailiwike etc. [NR]

[fo. 125v]

*9 May, 5.E.6, fol. 173. For a debt of [£] 20. 11 [s] 5 [d] due to the plaintiff from the defendant uppon a bargaine and sale of 23 quarters *et de.* of wheate after 17s. 6d. the quarter, etc. Decreed for the plaintiff. [NR]

*10 May, 5.E.6, fol. 169. Touching the lease of a tenement with the apurtenances. [NR]

*11 May, 5.E.6, fol. 174.[2] For the office of Hundredership and Bailiwick of the libertie of St. Albons: decreed for the plaintiff. [Req. 2/18/64]

[fo. 126r (p. 105)]

13 May, fol. 175.[3] A decree for the felling and carrying away of

---

[1] See *supra,* fo. 122r, *sub dat.* 30 January, 2.E.6.

[2] Robert Brande v. Sir Richard Lee.

[3] Robert Lamplugh, and others v. John and Eleanor Dalston, heirs to Thomas Dalston; and Christopher Fisher and other tenants of Flymby Manor, co. Cumberland.

5000 Okes in Flemby Parke in the Countie of Cumberland etc.
[Req. 2/14/155]
[fo. 125v]
*14 May, in the same year, fol. 176.[1] Concerning certain landes
pretended to belong to the hospitall of St. Laurence nere Canterbury. [Req. 2/16/5]
[fo. 126r (p. 105)]
20 November, fol. 187. Edmund Ashefielde, esquire, personally
appeared etc. at the suit of the Dean of Christ College, Oxford,
etc. [Req. 2/16/93 and Req. 2/17/88]
23 November, fol. 190. A decree for a parson for certaine glebe
landes belonging to the parsonage. [NR]
26 November. A cause dismissed by the kings Counsell sitting in
his court of Requests for that the parties are dwelling within the
liberties of the counsel at Yorke, etc. [NR]
[fo. 125r]
*30 November, 5.E.6, fol. 194. For a lease of a parsonage and for
the felling and carrieng away of a plot of wood. Decreed for the
plaintiff [NR]
[fo. 126r (p. 105)]

Anno 6.E.6.

29 January.[2] Commissioners appointed to sit in the court of
Requests (viz.) Thomas Bishop of Norwich, William May, deane
of Paules, Sir Nicholas Hare, knight, Sir Richard Rede, knight,
John Cokkes, esquire, John Lucas, esquire, John Tregonwell,
esquire, and William Cooke, esquire. [Req. 1/9/9v]
[fo. 127r]
*8 February, 6.E.6, fol.[3] . An administratrix of a lessee for
yeres by a bill of revivor: and decreed for the plaintiff. [Req.
1/9/11r]
*On the same day, fol. 12.[4] The Kings Majesties Counsell in the
Whitehall at Westminster ordered the defendant to restore such
monies as hee received with the daughter of the plaintiff whom hee
married, for that the mariage was dissolved by the court ecclesiasti-

---

[1] Amy Lewis, Prioress of the Hospital of St. Lawrence near Canterbury v.
John Culpeper.
[2] The list of commissioners has no date attached but it faces Req. 1/9/10 r which
contains the entry for the opening of Hilary Term [29 January] 6.E.6.
[3] Alice Walley, widow of Humphrey Walley v. Margery Nelson, widow of
Richard Nelson.
[4] Richard Fisher, gentleman, and his wife Anne v. Nicholas Adams.

call and unlawefull, shee to release all her interest in the defendants landes by reason of the said mariage. [Req. 1/9/12r]

*10 February, 6.E.6, fol. 13.[1] The defendant put in trust by a Bisshop to pay 80 libri to the plaintiffs wife at the day of her mariage, refused the payment thereof being demaunded and therefor ordered to enter with 2 sufficient sureties into bond of 200 markes for payment of the said 86 libri to the said plaintiff and 6 libri for costes. [Req. 1/9/13r]

*11 February, 6.E.6, fol. 15.[2] The copyholder, plaintiff, against his Lord, defendant, for 2 tenements, into which hee was admitted by 2 copies of Court rolle. Decreed for his quiet possession against the defendant and the defendant condemned to pay 14 libri to the plaintiff for costes. [Req. 1/9/15r]

*12 February, 6.E.6, fol. 19.[3] For certain copyhold and customary landes: Decreed for the plaintiff [Req. 1/9/19r] And the like,[4] 31 May, in the same year, fol. 32. [Req. 1/9/32r]

*23 May, 6.E.6, fol. 36.[5] An arbitrament confirmed by this Court and the parties injoyned to performe the same. [Req. 1/9/36r]

[fo. 126r (p. 105)]

26 May. Forasmuch as it is sene to the kings Counsel upon

[fo. 126v (p. 106)]

sight and hearing of the complaint of James Hawes, defendant, against John Butlocke, plaintiff, that they be persons of abilitie in substance and lands: therefore the said counsel have remitted them with their cause to bee determined and ordered according to the course of the common lawes. [Req. 1/8/20r]

30 May, fol. 40[6]. In the cause of variance depending, etc., betweene Elizabeth, widow, plaintiff, and Sir Humfrey Browne, knight, one of the justices of our Soveraine Lord the kings Majestie of his Common Plees, for and concerning certain wares etc. *Debt for wares. A justice of the Common Plees, defendant* for which goodes divers sutes were had and mooved betweene William Woodlife, late husband of the said widow, and the said Sir Humfrey Brown in the Kings highnesse court of Chauncerie, which sute there depending by the space of twelve yeere, and before any end there

---

[1] Mathew Hull and his wife, Joan v. William Leveson, clerk.
[2] Henry Williams v. Thomas Compton.
[3] John Rumbalde and his wife, Joan v. Edward Whale.
[4] Elen Harte, widow v. Thomas Harte.
[5] John Standerwicke and Alice Standerwicke v. John Halswell.
[6] See *supra*, fo. 124v., *sub dat.* 16 Nov., 4.E.6.

made, the said William died, after whose death the poore widow considering the long delayes before used by the said Sir Humfrey Browne did exhibit her supplication unto the kings majestie, etc. appointed the premisses to be duely examined in this court etc. It hath appeared etc. that the said parties had submitted themselves to the awarde, of the right honourable Sir William Paulet, knight of the noble order of the Garter, Lord Saint John, Earle of Wiltsheire, Marques of Winton, and Lord Treasurer of England: then Lord great Master of the Kings Majesties most honourable houshold, and then Lord Keeper of the great Seale of England, etc. According to whose awarde, it is ordered and decreed that the said Sir Humfrey Browne shall forthwith pay etc. the summe of twentie pound etc. and also sixe pound for charges of suite, etc. *The Lord Treasurer Poulet* [Req. 1/8/40r]

28 June, fol. 35.[1] William Barbor, of Ipswich, was permitted to appear by Robert Dale, his attorney, with the Counsel of Master Sackford, etc. [Req. 1/8/35v]

[fo. 127r]

*2 July, 6.E.6, fol. 43.[2] For a copyhold. Decreed for the plaintiff. [Req. 1/9/43r]

[fo. 128r (p. 107)]

5 July, fol. 44. The kings moste honourable Court of Requests etc. *for a copyhold* [Req. 1/9/44v]

7 July. In the cause of one Pollerd, plaintiff, against Foxley, defendant, for the interest and title of certain tenementes and houses in London: for that Foxley hath utterly refused to stand to such end and direction as was thought reasonable by the kings Counsell. The sayde Counsell considering his wilfulnesse therein have nowe remitted the parties to take their remedies according to the course of the Common law etc. [Req. 1/8/30r]

[fo. 127v]

*10 July, 6.E.6, fol. 52.[3] For an annuity of 10 libri decreed for the plaintiff. [Req. 1/9/52v]

*The same, fol. 55.[4] The tenants of Teukesbury in Glocestershire against Sir John Ribalt, knight, and William Reede, esquire, defendant, for the injoyning of a common. Decreed for the plaintiff. [Req. 1/9/55r]

---

[1] John Howes v. William Barbour.   [2] William Mitchell v. Humphrey Watkins.
[3] Christopher Gerard v. William Wilford.
[4] Seventeen tenants of Tewkesbury Manor, Glocs. v. Sir John Rigbalt and William Reede.

[fo. 128r (p. 107)]
27 October, fol. 76.¹ A question arising whether that a lease of a parsonage then in question were made good by the statute of 28.H.8² for the satisfaction of the defendant in this behalfe. The said counsell have caused the question of the said lease to be mooved unto the Kings Majesties Justices of the Common Plees at Westminster, who upon the deliberate hearing thereof have fully resolved that the saide lease is good, by vertue of the same statute, for that the saide yeerely rent is within fourtie shillings of the saide summe and value contained in the Kings books, etc. *touching the lease of a parsonage: decreed for the plaintiff with 4 libri costes to bee paid if the defendant shall molest the plaintiff with any neue sutes touching this cause* [Req. 1/9/76r]

3 November, fol. 71. A commission directed into Lincolnshire etc, to Richard Cecill, Robert Wingfielde, Henry Digby etc, esquires, etc. *touching custumary landes held by copy of Courtrolle.* [Req. 1/9/70v]

4 November, fol. 88.³ A decree of injunction or inhibition, that a testament prooved in the Prerogative Court of Canterbury in England should not be called in question in any forraine courte out of this lande, etc. nor anything done, etc. to the violation of the intercourse or treaty between the Kings Majestie of England and the Emperour, etc. [Req. 1/9/88v]

7 November, fol. 70.⁴ Ralph Flaxeley, the mayor of Oxford, appeared in person, etc. and upon answers made he is to appear by Richard Oseley, his attorney, with counsel of Master Poisdon, etc. [Req. 1/8/70r]

[fo. 127v]
*14 November, 6.E.6, fol. 73.⁵ William Brakenbury, plaintiff, as in the right of Stephen Brakenbury for the lease of the parsonage of Litle Bursteed in Essex. Decreed for the said plaintiff and that the defendant shall yeald him the possession of the same and 5 markes for costes and damages. [Req. 1/9/73v]

---

¹ Erasmus Ford v. John Lewes, clerk, parson of Elsted.
² Or 27.H.8?
³ William Chester, London draper, and Fraunces Tempest, widow and executrix of Robert Tempest v. Thomas Harrison, London girdler, and his wife, Anne, sister to Robert Tempest See Req. 2/15/2 in which it states that a messuage in Antwerp was included in Tempest's estate.
⁴ *Ex parte* Michael Owen v. Richard Flaxeley.
⁵ William Brakenbury, in the right of Steven Brakenbury, v. John Richardson, clerk, and Thomas Richardson.

*22 November, 6.E.6, fol. 79.[1] For certain glebe landes belonging to the parsonage of Sibsdon in Leicestershire. Decreed with the parson being plaintiff. [Req. 1/9/79r]

[fo. 128r (p. 107)]

28 November, fol. 93.[2] A notable decree for the cancelling of a

[fo. 128v (p. 108)]

bonde and staing the suite thereof at the common law forced by a cruell master from his apprentice by long imprisonment, etc. [Req. 1/8/93r]

[fo. 127v]

*1 December, 6.E.6, fol. 92.[3] An executor of an executor sued for a legacy due by the will of the first testator and decreed for the plaintiff. [Req. 1/9/92v]

*9 December, 6.E.6, fol.   . The executor of an executor deceased before his testators will proved, sued by the administratrix of the said testator. [NR]

[fo. 128v (p. 108)]

Anno [[6]]*7**4E.6.

30 January, fol. 99.[5] Sir John Cheke, knight, plaintiff, etc. [Req. 1/9/99r]

1 February, fol. 100.[6] The Kings Majesties most honourable Counsel in the Whitehall at Westminster: where fourtie shillings costes was given to the defendant to be paid unto him when and at such time as the said plaintiff shall hereafter attempt or procure any further suite against the said defendant or his heires in any of the kings majesties Courts touching this mater. [Req. 1/9/100v]

[fo. 127v]

*6 February, 7.E.6, fol. 101.[7] For a chest with certain plate, gold and money therein, etc. Decreed for the plaintiff with 20 shillings for costes. [Req. 1/9/101v]

[fo. 128v (p. 108)]

8 February, fol. 105. Walter Chalcot, esquire, Sergiante at armes, plaintiff, against the right honourable Thomas, Lord Sandes,

---

[1] Thomas Tipping v. John Nowell and his wife, Anne, and Thomas Villars.
[2] Robert Harding v. Thomas Bartholomew and William Hatcher.
[3] William Halam and his wife, Agnes v. John Godyn.
[4] This was published '6.E. 6' but J.C. made a holographic correction to '7 E. 6'.
[5] Sir John Cheke v. John Gamblen.
[6] William Cutler and his wife, Ursula, daughter and heir to Richard Stote v. John Lewen.
[7] Ellis Shakelock v. Thomas Tyndale and his wife, Agnes.

defendant, for an annuitie. The saide Lorde ordered to pay 60 libri being the arrerages of the saide annuitie: which to be observed by the said Lord it is to him commanded upon the peril and danger that may follow and ensue. [Req. 1/9/105v]

19 February, fol. 121.[1] A decree for a Registers deputie and for the injoying of a house where the records of the said court did lie. [Req. 1/9/121r]

[fo. 129r]

*23 February, 7.E.6, fol. 114.[2] A defendant sued for to save harmeles the plaintiff for 2 oxen which hee has bought of the defendant for 8 libri which oxen had bene stolen and one of them nowe seized on to the use of the true owner. Decreed against the defendant to pay to the plaintiff for the same and damages and costes [£]10. 16[s]. 8[d]. [Req. 1/9/114v]

[fo. 129r]

*The same, fol. 117.[3] An administratrix and her husband, plaintiff, against divers tenants for deteining and withholding from her divers landes and tenements leased unto the deceased by the king whereof divers yeres were yet to come, belonging to her as administratrix of his goods and chattels. Decreed for the plaintiff and the defendant commaunded presently to avoide from the possession of the said landes and to suffer the said plaintiff to enjoy the same during theire terme. [Req. 1/9/117r]

[fo. 128v (p. 108)]

1 April:[4] An obligation made by Robert Hethe to John Cocks and John Lucas, esquires, in 300 libri in the cause in suite betweene him and one William Pantrye: the condition of this obligation is such that if the abovebound Robert Hethe on this side of the 16 day of June next comming after the date above written shall not disprove in the Kings court of his Requests by the order of the same court, one order and decree already had and made in the same Court for the part of William Pantrie and Mary, his wife, against the said Robert Hethe and Percivall Hethe, his brother, or else if the said Robert Hethe and Percival, his brother, or one of

[1] John Chetham v. Edward Planckney.
[2] George Middleton v. William Roake.
[3] Robert Robotham and his wife, Grace, administratrix of the goods of Robert Bull, her late husband v. Thomas Blackbourne, Cuthbert Codname and Thomas Bannister.
[4] The reference cited is to the 'order and decree already made in the same Court [of Requests]'.

them before the said 16 day of June do not con-

[fo. 130r (p. 109)]

tent or pay etc. unto the said William Pantrie etc. the mony awarded etc. by and in the said decree etc. if then the said Robert Hethe doe personally appear before the Masters of the Requests made unto the kings majestie to be and remaine prisoner in the prison of the Fleete, from whence (to the intent this condition should bee truely perfourmed) he is delivered, that then this obligation be voyd etc. [Req. 2/14/49]

6 April, fol. 127.[1] Leonard Perpoint, gentleman, appears in the name of the most reverend in Christ Thomas, Archbishop of Canterbury, before the Lord King's Council at Westminster, by virtue of a Writ of Privy Seal at the suit of Thomas Chiney knight, and has day given to him to answer to a bill etc., and thus to appear from day to day until he should have authorization to desist etc. [Req. 1/9/127r]

8 May, fol. 134. Ordered and decreed by the kings most honourable Counsell in his Court of Requests etc. [NR]

10 May, fol. 153. The right honourable William, Lord Windsor, against Elizabeth Porter, widow, for the right, title and interest of a Mannour called Walters Hey etc. in the countie of Worcester etc. and he condemned in fourty shillings to her payable at his next commensing of any sute against her touching the premisses. [Req. 1/9/135r]

15 May, fol. 139.[2] The right Honourable An, Countesse of Oxford, defendant, etc. condemned to pay the arrerages of the profites of certaine landes, and in fault of performance v. libri costes etc. [Req. 1/9/139r]

[fo. 129r]

*8 June, 7.E.6, fol. 152[3] (and 28 November, 1 and 2.P.andM., fol. 270).[4] The tenants of Easthatch in Wiltshire, plaintiff, against Sir John Mervyn, knight, defendant, touching a common of pasture. Decreed for the plaintiff. [Req. 1/9/152v]

---

[1] Thomas [Cranmer], Archbishop of Canterbury, defendant.

[2] Katherine Shouldham, widow to Edward Shouldham v. Anne, Countess of Oxford. See also *infra*, fo. 129v, *sub dat*. 28 November, 1. Mary, and 18 June, 2&3.P&M.

[3] Thomas Sanger, Maude Davis, widow, Robert Gerrard, Thomas Bent v. Sir John Marvin.

[4] Same as n. 3, but dealing with the limitation placed upon the number of grazing head on the contested common.

[fo. 130r (p. 109)]

12 June, fol. 154,[1] John Cockes and John Lucas, esquires, masters of the Requests to the kings majestie. [Req. 1/9/154r]

22 June, fol. 157. The ladie Margary Acton, plaintiff, against Sir Robert Acton, knight, her husband defendant complaining of his absence from her etc. hee ordered to pay her for her maintenance for five yeeres past 30 libri and for the time comming 30 libri yeerely during his life if shee so long live etc. And if the said Sir Robert upon the sight hereof

[fo. 130v (p. 110)]

doe or shall refuse to obey, fulfill and perfourme this saide order, that then hee shall immediatly without any delay in proper person appeare before the kings majesties Counsell attending upon his royal person etc. [Req. 1/9/157r]

[fo. 129r]

*24 June, 7.E.6, fol. 160.[2] For the lease of certaine landes belonging to a prebend in Salisbury called Yeatmister Prima without Upbury, let by the then prebend with the consent of the then Bishop. Decreed that the plaintiff shall admit the defendant at his next Court to certain landes aforementioned to holde them by copy of a court rolle for terme of his life according to the custome of the manour and that the defendant shall pay unto the plaintiff for a fine 14 libri. [Req. 1/9/160v]

[fo. 130v (p. 110)]

Anno 1.M.

October 31, fol. 177. Sir William West, knight, plaintiff etc. *touching certain covenants and conditions reciting in effect the bargaine sale wardship and marriage of one Edward Rie, esquire* [Req. 1/9/177r]

[fo. 129r]

*6 November, 1.M., fol. 176.[3] An award for the appeasing of a controversie amongst certaine parishioners of one parish, ratified, confirmed, and decreed by this court accordingly. [Req. 1/9/176r]

[fo. 130v (p. 110)]

10 November. Forasmuch as upon opening of the cause betweene Richard Fielde, plaintiff, and Edmond Brudenell, defendant, it

---

[1] John Barnaby v. Parnall Lentall, widow.

[2] Anthony Delaber, errant of his Majesty v. John Winterhaye. See *infra*, fo. 135v, *sub dat.* 28 January, 3&4.P&M.

[3] Richard Stratton, vicar v. Anthony Middleborough and John Scott, churchwardens.

appeareth that the same is concerning title of lande, which ought not to bee determined in this Courte etc. therefore by the said Counsell it is remitted to the Common law etc. [Req. 1/8/121r] 19 November, fol. 178.[1] Sir Thomas White, knight, and John Throgmorton, esquire, Masters of the Requests ordered touching a tenemente demaunded by the plaintiff that a commaundement should be geven to the steward of the saide Mannour, that hee at the next Courte to bee holden at the said Mannour should admitte the said plaintiff tenant to the premisses, to hould to him and to his heires after the custome of the Mannour aforesaid paying the fine accustomed etc. *for the admission of a tenant by the Steward of a manour.* [Req. 1/9/178v]

[fo. 129v]

*28 November, 1.M., fol. 187.[2] The executors of certain patentees from the King ordered to passe an estate over to some others, who paid for a moyetie of the landes granted in the said booke, albeit the names of the patentees were onely used in the said booke according to some agreements passed betwene them and the plaintiff. [Req. 1/9/187v]

*The same, fol. 190.[3] Anne, Countess of Oxford, sued by the executors of Edward Shouldham, esquier, for divers parcels of plate, goods, chattels, etc. graunted by deede of gift from the said Countesse to the said Shouldham. Found that the said Shouldham was servaunt to the said Countesse and that the said deede of gift was to her owne use and not to his: and therefor decreed that the plaintiff should redeliver the said deede to the defendant to bee cancelled and that the defendant should pay 100 libri to the plaintiff, whereof 80 libri should bee aunswered by the plaintiff to the use of the testators children. [Req. 1/9/190v]

[fo. 130v (p. 110)]

26 January, fol. 197.[4] Francis Stradling etc. personally appeared etc. by virtue of an injunction given to them by John Saintlow, knight, and other assigned commissioners in a certain case moved

---

[1] The names of the Masters of Requests were noted at the top of the folio and J.C. included them in the entry for this case. Robert Colcocke v. William Colcocke.
[2] Marmaduke Wardrepe and his wife, Anne, late wife of Thomas Tymwell v. Edmund Tymwell, Christopher Nedeham, and William Chester. See also Req. 2/21/4 – a paper decree regarding defendants Nedeham and Chester.
[3] Executrix is Katherine Shouldham, plaintiff, for her children Thomas and Anne. See *supra*, fo. 130r, *sub dat.* 15 May, 7.E.6.
[4] John Collis v. Francis Stardling and John Mellus.

among them by John Collis, and have day given to them to answer on next Monday and thus to apperr etc. ([Req. 1/9/197v]

On the same, fol. 197.[1] Memorandum, that where matter of controversie doeth depend in the Queenes Majesties Court of Requests in the White-hall at Westminster, before her Hignesse Commissioners there in the same court etc. [Req. 1/9/197v]

25 April, fol. 207. John Walter personally appears etc.

[fo. 132r (p. 111)]

by virtue of an injunction given to him by the Commissioners etc., and was allowed to appear by Robert Dale, his attorney, with the counsel of Master Sackvile of Greys Inne, with a clause to abide in judgment and to pay charges. [Req. 1/9/207r]

On the same. Thomas Smith, knight, plaintiff. [NR]

26 April. Whereas sute and contention hath bene mooved in the Queenes Majesties Court of Requests by Rafe Kingston, plaintiff, against Richard Sampford the older etc., defendant, for a certaine lease for terme of yeres etc. It is seen to her Majesties honourable counsell of her said court, that the matter is determinable at the Common lawe, and that the sayde parties be men of wealth and abilitie to sue and prosecute the same there, and neither of them the Queenes Majesties servant; wherefore the said counsell have dismissed the sayd parties out of this court etc. [Req. 2/17/101][2]

28 April, fol. 207. John Lane, merchant of the city of London, personally appears by virtue of a command of the said council sent to him by the messenger of the chamber etc. [Req. 1/9/207r]

7 May, fol. 219.[3] The Queenes most honourable counsel in her court of Requests etc. *for the herbage of a parcell of wood being custumary landes* [Req. 1/9/219v]

On the same, fol. 221.[4] A cause touching tithe corne etc. dismissed out of this court, for that both the sayd parties be men of good livings and dwelling within the county of Chester and able to pursue, and trie their rights and titles in and to the premisses by the common lawe of this Realme etc. *Chester.* [Req. 1/9/221r]

28 May, fol. 228.[5] A cause depending in this court touching cer-

---

[1] John English v. Thomas Fitzwilliams, Lord of manor of Kempton.

[2] The original petition is marked 'dysmyssed' on dorse. Other writing is either faded or damaged but appears to note the award of a Privy Seal to the defendant rather than noting the reasons for dismissal.

[3] Joan Hooper, widow v. John Drake, esquire.

[4] Robert Manweryng, one of Her Majesty's Gentlemen at Arms v. Sir Thomas Holcrofte.   [5] Anne Whyte v. Thomas Warren.

taine lands and tenements within the franchise and liberties of the Cinque ports to be dismissed out of this court, and the complainant to sue for his remedie before the Lord Warden in his court of Chancery there: and thereupon John Web, gentleman, steward to the sayd Lord Warden there, being called into this court, hath faithfully promised, that the sayd complainant shall there have justice with expedition, and shalbe admitted *in forma pauperis* [fo. 132v (p. 112)] and for lacke of justice the sayd sutes and matters to be called againe into this court here to be further ordered by the same. *note that this court supplieth the want of justice in other courts.* [Req. 1/9/228r]

1 June, fol. 229. Sir Thomas Smith, knight, Deane of Carleil, plaintiff, etc. [Req. 1/9/229r]

Anno 1&2P.&M.

16 October, fol. 246.[1] 40 s. costs given against the plaintiff for suing a cause in this court after judgement given against him in the same cause at common law, payable when the plaintiff shall againe commense any sute touching the same cause against the defendant. [Req. 1/9/246r]

19 October. A cause for and concerning certain tithes, land and pasture referred to the ecclesiastical court as a matter meerely determinable by the order of the ecclesiastical lawes. [NR] [fo. 129v]

*20 October, 1&2.P&M, fol. 247.[2] For the office of underkeapership of the litle parke of Toplif in Yorkeshire. [Req. 1/9/249v] [fo. 132v (p. 112)]

25 October, fol. 249.[3] The Kings and Queens most honourable counsell in their Graces Court of Requestes, etc. and 1 February, fol. 295. *Executors sued by a legatary.* [Req. 1/9/249r]

17 November. The cause at the sute of Edward Keble, clerke, plaintiff, against Richard Bellamy, defendant, is now dismissed out of this court to the common law forasmuch as the said matter in concerning an obligation which is determinable by the same lawe. [NR][4]

---

[1] Thomas Fox v. John Plantree.
[2] Edward Norton v. Henry Jackson and Richard Norton.
[3] Mary Goughe, widow v. Peter Whitehorn and Paul Whitehorn, gentlemen.
[4] Although there is no clear reference the following documents bear on the cause: Req. 2/20/85 (vellum petition) and Req. 2/23/141 (paper petition). In neither case is there anything to indicate the dismissal to which J.C. makes reference.

[fo. 129v]

*20 November, 1&2.P&M, fol. 264.¹ For the performance of a promise. [Req. 1/9/264v]

[fo. 132v (p. 112)]

21 November, fol. 265.² The King and Queenes most honorable Counsell in the Whitehall at Westminster [Req. 1/9/265v] and 4 February, fol. 291. *for a mill with all commodities thereto belonging.* [Req. 1/9/291r]

[fo. 129v]

*22 November, 1&2.P&M, fol. 267.³ For a lease of a vicaredge, etc. [Req. 1/9/267r]

*23 November, 1&2.P&M, fol. 276. Sir William Suliard, about 23 years past was a Master of Requests. [Req. 1/9/276v]

[fo. 131r]

*24 November, 1&2.P&M, fol. 282.⁴ An injunction to stay execution of common lawe uppon a bond after judgement in the common plees and the defendant committed to ward for taking out execution contrary to that injunction and hee was not discharged out of prison till hee had discharged the said plaintiff out of execution. [Req. 1/9/273v]

[fo. 129v]

*24 November, 1&2.P&M, fol. 268.⁵ For slaundering the plaintiff to bee a coyner of money. Decreed against the defendant to pay 4 libri to the plaintiff and to aske him forgivenesse publickly. [Req. 1/9/268v]

[fo. 131r]

*24 November, 1&2.P&M, fol. 282.⁶ For the lease of a parsonage graunted to the plaintiff by Sir Thomas Smith, knight, Provost of Eaton Colledge, and the fellowes of the same colledge for 30

¹ Elizabeth Yarwood, widow, executrix to John Yarwood v. Robert Perte.
² John Wall, one of her Majesty's Butlery v. Richard Chroste, esquire.
³ John Westcote, Yeoman of her Majesty's Guard v. William Roberts, Christopher Roberts, William Mores, Robert Walker and Thomas Hawkins.
⁴ John Albertson *alias* Acollyn v. Lionell Arnold, Peter Parson, Walter Sherwood, Katherine Arnold, widow, executrix to Lionell Arnold, Reinyse Williams *alias* Williamson, factor and attorney to Henry Lullyns, a son of Lionell.
⁵ Because Thomas Shepherd *alias* Shefford had sued and harrassed Henry Milward in the Court of Requests and had caused him injury and costs and because he had slandered him with charges of being a coiner of money, for these reasons a decree was made that Shepherd should be bound to pay £4 costs and damages to Milward.
⁶ George Ireland, Yeoman of her Majesty's Guard v. Richard Faldowe and Margaret Faldowe.

yeres for the rent of 6 libri and 15 quarters of wheate yerely. [Req. 1/9/282v]

*28 November, 1&2.P&M, fol. 273. Thomas Smalebone, plaintiff, and the executors of William Benson, clerk, late Deane of Westminster, defendant, for the restitution of 60 libri paid by the plaintiff to the said Benson for that hee should procure him a lease of certain landes under the chapiters seale, which for that Benson did not, etc. It was decreed against the defendant to repay the said 60 libri to the said plaintiff. [Req. 1/9/273v]

*30 November, 1&2.P&M, fol. 279. A decree partly for the plaintiff and partly for the defendant, with theise wordes, ordered, adjudged and decreed by the Kings and Queens Majesties Counsell of the Court of Requests, or by the said Counsell and Court of Requests, etc. till by the lawes of this Realme, in this Court, or anie other the King and Queens Court of Record, etc. [Req. 1/9/279r]

[fo. 132v (p. 112)]

20 January. *Sir* Thomas White and Master John Throgmorton, Masters of the Kings and Queens Majesties Court of Requests. [NR]

[fo. 131 v]

*1 February, 1&2.P&M, fol. 295.¹ Touching a deede of gift of all the goods and chattels of the plaintiff made to the defendant in trust to the plaintiffs use to the ende to defraude the plaintiffs creditors. The defendant entered uppon the plaintiffs goods and chattels by vertue of the said deede contrary to the trust. And decreed for the plaintiff that the defendant should restore unto him all the goods and chattels and 5 markes for costes. [Req. 1/9/295r]

[fo. 132 (p. 112)]

5 February, fol. 292.² The right honorable Sir John Nevill, knight, Lord Latimer, defendant, etc. And decreed against the said Lord. *for an annual rent charge of 20 nobles.* [Req. 1/9/292r]

[fo. 131v]

*10 February, 1&2.P&M, fol. 298.³ The defendant charged with the stealing of 2 maires, for which hee had obtained the Queens Majesties pardon and afterwards sued the plaintiff in the Kings

---

¹ James Hovell v. Thomas Barnes, gentlemen.
² Anne Eglenby, widow v. Sir John Nevill, Lord Latymer.
³ Walter Nicolson and his son, Robert v. William Bott.

Bench in an action uppon the case supposing the same was a slaunder. The defendant adjudged to pay 20 nobles to the plaintiff for the 2 maires and no further to proceade in his action uppon the case at common lawe and also to pay to the plaintiff for costes 40 s. [Req. 1/9/298v]

*On the same day, fol. 299.[1] An executrix and her husband, plaintiff, against Anne, Countesse of Oxford, for the performance of a lease promised by her to the testatrix, in regard of 12 libri received of the said testatrix. And for that the said Countesse had since devised the said landes by lease unto an other, it was ordered and decreed this present day, being the 10 of February in the 1 and 2 yeres of the reignes of our Souverain Lord and Lady, Philip and Mary, by the Grace of God King and Queen of England, France, Naples, Jerusalem and Ireland, Defendors of the Faith, Princes of Spain and Sicill, Archedukes of Austria, Dukes of Millane, Burgundy and Brabant, Countes of Ausburgh, Flaunders and Tiroll, that the said countesse, her executors or assignes shall pay to the said plaintiff for that shee cannot make a lease according to her promise.

[fo. 131v]

and faithfull assumption and for costes the somme of 15 libri 20 April next following and so the said Countesse to bee discharged from making any such lease. [Req. 1/9/299v]

[fo. 132v (p. 112)]

6 May, fol. 312.[2] A recognisance taken in Chancerie for the appearance of Richard Blike, etc. before the Kings and Queens most

[fo. 134r (p. 113)]

honorable privy Counsell etc. [Req. 1/9/312v]

7 May, the same folio. Richard Albery etc. appear personally before the Lord King and Lady Queen's Council at Westminster, by the command of Master Throgmorton one of the Masters of Requests, at the suit of Thomas Milles etc. [NR][3]

[fo. 133r]

*25 May, 1&2.P&M, fol. 317. Thomas Milles, plaintiff, Richard Albery and Andreue Clerk, defendants. That Agnes the plaintiffs wife, by the procurement of the said defendants, tooke suretie of peace of her husband, and that the said defendant and one Thomas

---

[1] Gregory Lovell and his wife, Joan v. Anne, Countess of Oxford.
[2] 6 May should read 9 May.
[3] Req. 1/9 stops with fo. 316v. See also Req. 2/2/34 for Clerk's countersuit.

Stelman carried the plaintiff to Mr. Lovelace, Justice of Peace in Barkshire, who bound the said plaintiff to the peace and for lack of suerties delivered a mittimus to the said Andrewe Clerk, being then Constable, to carry the said plaintiff to the gaole and that immediately after the said defendant became bound with sureties in 40 markes for the keaping of the peace; and so departed taking with them the said mittimus by color whereof they threatened to carry him to prison if hee would not be contented to bind his land to save them harmeles from theire said recognizance. Whereuppon the plaintiff being carried by them as a prisoner to London, did there by a bargaine and sale passe and assure over certain his landes to them and theire heires for ever simply and without condition; and for the rest of his landes made an assurance by theire meanes and enforcement to the said Stelman to the use of his wife, the said plaintiff being unlettered. Decreed that the said plaintiff shall have and enjoy his said landes, that the said deedes and conveyances passed to the said defendant and Stelman shalbee cancelled, that they shall restore to the plaintiff the meane profits, make releases of theire interests, etc. as by the said decree (worthie the reading) more largely doth appeare. [NR]

[fo. 134r (p. 113)]

29 May.[1] The Right Honorable Henrie, Lord Stafford, defendant etc. [NR]

18 June, fol. 332. Ordered, that an extent be directed forth under the privie seale to the shirifes of the said counties of Brecknocke etc. to levie, and take up of the landes, goods and cattales that be nowe, or were in the possession of the said Robert Thomas Vaughan defendant or any other for him, or to his use, sithence the feast etc. the summe of 34 libri 3 s. 4. d. and to deliver the same to the saide John Rawlins, plaintiff, or his assignes, immediately upon the levying and taking up of the same etc. *quod nota.* *execution of a decree uppon landes goodes and catals* [Req. 2/24/22]

[fo. 133v]

*18 June, 1&2.P&M, fol. 331. For the tithes and other goods of a late incumbent in a benefice carried away by others, sued for by the said incumbents executor: Decreed for the plaintiff against the bodie and goods of the defendant. [NR]

[fo. 134r (p. 113)]

1 July. A cause for copiholde land dismissed, for that it is de-

1 See also Req. 2/25/278 for the relevant interrogatories.

terminable in the Lords court of the mannour, and no partialitie laide nor alleadged against the said Lord, nor steward there. [NR]
[fo. 133v]

*5 July, 1&2.P&M, fol. 342.[1] For a Serjeantship or Bailiship of the Honor of Wigmor in the Countie of Hereford. [Req. 2/23/6]
[fo. 134r (p. 113)]

Anno 2.&3.P.&.M.

17 October, fol. 2. In the matter of variance before the King and Queens Majesties in their court of Requests etc., for that appeareth unto the King and Queens Majesties Counsell of that Court, that the defendants have vexed and sued the said complainant at the common law, without any just cause so to doe, It is ordered, that the said defendant, shal forthwith stay and surcease to prosecute their said sute at the common lawe, against the said complainant and further suffer them to have, holde, occupie, possesse, and quietly enjoy all their said tenements, and farmeholdes, without the let or interruption of the said defendant or any other for them, by them, in their names, or
[fol. 134v (p. 114)]
by their procurement to the contrary, untill such time as the said defendant shall have proved their titles to the premisses, etc. before the Lord President, and other the Kings and Queenes Majesties Commissioners in the North partes, etc. [NR]

7 November, fol. 5.[2] Ordered etc. that a letter shalbe written to the steward of the mannor of Langham, etc. to bring into this Court the Court rolle, made etc. and that in the meane time, the saide defendant etc. shall not fell, cut downe, or carie away any wood being or growing in and upon the ground in variance, but onely for reasonable fewell, until such time as further order be therein taken, etc. [Req. 2/22/29] And 23 November, fol. 16 [Req. 1/10/16r][3] and 27 November, fol. 17 [Req. 1/10/17r][4] where wood may be felled etc. for fensing or inclosing the said ground.

8 November.[5] Ordered that the defendant shall make no answere

---

[1] William Froysell v. John Bray.

[2] Robert Myles and others v. John Craddocke.

[3] This folio is too badly damaged to check anything more than the date.

[4] — — Plummer v. John Craddocke. A largely illegible folio because of damage. Plummer was another tenant of Craddocke's bringing action against his lord. This refers to the same court-baron of the manor of Langham to which reference was made *supra, sub dat.* 7 November.

[5] This entry is probably the same as that case which is recorded on a vertical half fragment found in Req. 1/10. (?) Stourton v. (?) Alford.

to the complainants bill untill such time as the said complainant have paid unto the defendant 7 libri according to a former decree in this Court. [Req. 1/10/5v]

On the same, fol. 9.[1] The Kings and Queens most honourable Counsell, in their Majesties Court of Requests, etc. [Req. 1/10/8r] And 28 November, fol. 18. [Req. 1/10/18r]

15 November, fol. 14. A cause betweene William Elkins, plaintiff, and Sir Anthony Kingston, knight, defendant. For that it is matter touching the Queenes Majesties title, dismissed out of this Court, to the Exchequer [Req. 1/10/14r]

17 November, fol. 16.[2] A defendant enjoyned in open Court not to attempt any action, or suite against the plaintiff at the Common law. [Req. 1/10/16r]

24 November.[3] Sir John *Bourne*, knight, one of the two principall Secretaries to the Kings and Queens Majesties, plaintiff, etc. [Req. 2/22/73]

26 November, fol. 17.[4] A cause dismissed to the common lawe, because there properly determinable, and for that the defendant hath continued his possession in the landes in question, by the space of fourtie yeeres. [Req. 1/10/17r]

[fo. 135r (p. 115)]

3 February, fol. 28.[5] A cause of legacie dismissed to the spirituall law as determinable there, by ecclesiasticall Judges, etc. [Req. 1/10/28r]

10 February,[6] fol. 32.[7] An injunction granted against a defendant to stay his suite at common lawe, etc. [Req. 1/10/32r]

On the same, fol. 34. A Commission directed to John Widdon one of the Kings and Queens Majesties Justices of their Bench and, others, to heare and determine the cause betweene A.B., plaintiff,

1 The *eodem* is incorrect. The date was 5 November not 8 November.

2 John Underhey and his wife, Joan v. John Southerote and Thomas Southerote.

3 Sir John Bourne v. the inhabitants of Ripple, Delford, Bessford and Croome, co. Worcester. This may not be the same suit to which J.C. made reference but the plaintiff is the same and is identified as one of the two Principal Secretaries.

4 John Perkins v. Lawrence Gascoyn.

5 This folio is too damaged to read in any detail.

6 The date, 10 February, seems wrong. The following day in Req. 1/10 is 7 February and the preceding day in the volume is 6 February. This is probably 6 February also but there are instances of irregular dating and J.C's transcription may be correct.

7 — —Bainbridge v. John Keble, gentleman. Req. 1/10/32r is virtually too damaged to read.

and C.D., defendant, if they can, or else to certifie into this Court at next Easter Term, etc. [Req. 1/10/34r]

27 April, fol. 42. Lord Robert Dudley, defendant, etc. [Req. 1/10/42v]

On the same, fol. 43.[1] A cause appointed to be hearde, at the Temple Church in the after noone. [Req. 1/10/43r]

1 May, fol. 43.[2] If the plaintiff bee necessarily attendaunt here, though the land in question lie in the Marches of Wales, and the defendant dwell there, they may bee called up hether, otherwise not [Req. 1/10/45r]: and 27 April, fol. 43, etc.[3] [Req. 1/10/43r]

6 May, fol. 52. An injunction for staying a sute commensed at the Common law by the defendant against the plaintife. [Req. 1/10/51v][4]

[fo. 135r (p. 115)]

16 May, fol. 57.[5] John Tailor, defendant, punished in the Gatehouse at Westminster for his contempt in the breach of an injunction. [Req. 1/10/57r]

8 June, fol. 67.[6] An affidavit for the excuse of a contempt of a defendant in refusing to perfourme a decree of court refused to be taken in consideration of the youth of the servant who did offer to sweare, and the contempt, the said defendant, etc. [Req. 1/10/67r]

On the same, fol. 71.[7] An injunction for stay of a sute at Common Law, etc. [Req. 1/10/71r]

12 June, fol. 79. The King and Queens most honourable counsel in their Graces court of Requests at Westminster. [Req. 1/10/79v]

14 June, fol. 72.[8] A cause dismissed for that fine and recovery had therein passed the common law. [Req. 1/10/72v]

18 June, fol. 82.[9] Katherine, Countesse of Oxford, called by mes-

[fo. 135v (p. 116)]

senger into the court, appeared by one Foster, esquier, etc.

---

[1] The tenants of Yeatminster v. Anthony Dalaber. See *infra*, fo. 135v, *sub dat.* 28 January, 3&4.P&M.

[2] Richard Lawrence and his wife, Elizabeth v. Hugh Dryhurst and Henry Conway. See also Req. 2/24/72 (the defendants' answer).

[3] — —Bayles and — — Hunt v. — — Cartwright and — — Hurst. A badly damaged folio. See *infra*, fo. 135v, *sub dat.* 25 January, 3&4.P&M.

[4] This is a virtually illegible folio.   [5] Margery St. John v. John Taylor.

[6] Modwyn Venables, widow v. Henry Vernon, esquire.

[7] Elizabeth Lawrence, widow v. James Durant, attorney to Rowland Durant.

[8] Thomas Adams *alias* Adamson and his wife, Elizabeth v. Richard Albery.

[9] The names should read: Anne, Countess of Oxford and Katherine Shouldham. See *supra*, fo. 130r, *sub dat.* 15 May, 7.E.6. and other references there noted.

Ordered that either she should presently pay to the plaintife the money ordered by a former decree, or els to bee and appeare 18 Michaelis next in the saide Court, etc. [Req. 1/10/82r]

Anno 3&4.P&M.

24 October, fol. 101.[1] A cause touching title of an annuitie claimed by the plaintife during her life beeing matter determinable at the Common Law is dismissed out of this court, the parties being able to prosecute their sute at the common law 25 October. [Req. 1/10/101r]

25 October, fol. 110.[2] A cause against Hugh Perrin of Roshal in Jersey, defendant, ordered and decreed in this court. [Req. 1/10/110r]

9 November, fol. 113.[3] Ordered that a cause should bee deteined in court, notwithstanding the parties defendant inhabit within the commission of the Marches of Wales, etc. For that the plaintife was one of the officers of the Queens Majesties pantrie. [Req. 1/10/113r] 10 November, fol. 116 [Req. 1/10/116v][4] and 25 January, fol. 140. [Req. 1/10/140r][5]

25 November, fol. 128.[6] A cause referred to the arbitrament of Sir William Cecill, knight, Valentine Dale, Doctor of the Civill Law. Gilbert Gerard, and Robert Manwood, Esquiers, they to determine the same if they can and if they cannot then John Boxall, clerke, one of the Queens Honorable Counsell of the Court of Requests to be umpire, and if he can make no order etc, then the cause to be heard eftsoones openly in this court. [Req. 1/10/128v]

27 November, fol. 133.[7] An injunction to stay the defendants proceedings at Common Lawe. [Req. 1/10/132v]

28 January, fol. 143.[8] A cause once againe heard, notwithstanding the same had bene already decreed. [Req. 1/10/143r]

9 February, fol. 148. In the cause in contention betweene Thomas

[1] Alice Browne, widow v. Rowland Browne.
[2] Defendant must seek remedy in Jersey courts having received his decree in the Court of Requests.
[3] Humphrey Dimmock, gentleman v. Thomas Balle.
[4] Dimmock's affidavit.
[5] Thomas Baylies (?) and Isabell Hunt, widow v. John Cartwright *alias* Bolter and Raynes Hurste. See *supra*, fo. 135r, *sub dat.* 27 April (fol. 43) 2&3.P&M.
[6] Adam Aldaye, gentleman v. —— —— Rolfe, esquire.
[7] Henry Hurford, Richard Hurford and Joan Hurford v. Erasmus Pym.
[8] 'The cause late in contencion betwixt the tenants of Yeatminster, complainants, and Anthony Dalabar, defendant, is by the Counsaill yet once agayne (notwithstanding the same order alredy decreed) appoynted to be herde upon the second days of the next terme.' See *supra*, fo. 129r, *sub dat.* 24 June, 7.E.6.

Southall, etc, plaintife, against Sir George Blunt, knight,
[fo. 136r (p. 117)]
defendant. Forasmuch as the said defendant alleadgeth himselfe to
be at great charge by reason of his attendance heere with his
retinue it is ordered by the Counsell that he shal from henceforth
appeare by his lawfull atturney sufficiently authorised and instructed concerning this matter: And he, the said defendant, to
stand to and abide by that his atturney shall doe in the same at all
times. [Req. 1/10/148r]
10 February, fol. 148.[1] A compulsorie decreed for witnesses *ad
informandum conscientiam*. [Req. 1/10/148v]
5 May, fol. 168.[2] A cause merely determinable at common lawe,
helde in the Court of Requests, for that the parties plaintifes
were very poore persons and not able to recover their right
at common lawe and for want of Justice in the law court. [Req.
1/10/168v]
6 May, fol. 158.[3] After publication past, and the matters divers
times heard the plaintiff licensed to bring into the court such witnes
and proofes as they coulde to informe the Counsels consciences in
and concerning their title claimed. [Req. 1/10/158v]
13 May, fol. 161.[4] An injunction to staie the defendants sute at
Common lawe [Req. 1/10/161v] and 14 May, fol. 162[5] [Req.
1/10/162v] and 19 May, fol. 164,[6] where the defendant was enjoyned further not to depart out of the towne without license first
obtained of the Kings Counsell. [Req. 1/10/164r]
21 May, fol. 164.[7] A day appointed for the bringing in of all witnesses and proofes or els the cause to bee heard as it appeareth in
the Court at their perils. [Req. 1/10/164v]
21 June, fol. 188.[8] Forasmuch as the landes in variance doe lye
within the city of Worcester and the said citie hath cognizance of

---

[1] John Dowson and his wife, Joan v. Richard Hamonde. See *infra, sub dat.*
6 May.
[2] Edward Durueford and his son, Nicholas v. Elys Churchill.
[3] John Dowson and his wife, Joan v. Richard Hamonde. See *supra, sub dat.*
10 February.
[4] Frauncis Coxe, officer of Her Majesty's Pantry v. William Grey, gentleman.
[5] Margaret Cotton, widow, and her son John Cotton v. William Rede. See
infra, fo. 136v, *sub dat.* 19 November, 4&5.P&M.
[6] John Warren and his wife, Margaret v. John Boyer, gentleman. See *infra,*
fo. 136v, 24 November (fol. 264) 4&5.P&M.
[7] George Adam v. William Skevington, esquire.
[8] Anne Norton, widow v. John Steyner.

the plea within the same, it is therefore dismissed out of this Court, etc. [Req. 1/10/188r]

2 July, fol. 195.[1] An injunction to stay the proceeding at Common law. [Req. 1/10/195r]

19 June, fol. 198. The King and Queens most honourable Counsell [fo. 136v (p. 118)]
in their Court of Requests, etc. [Req. 1/10/198r]

29 June, fol. 204. The Kings and Queens Majesties most honourable Counsell attendant upon their royall persons in their Court of Requests, etc. [1/10/104r]

5 July, fol. 216.[2] A complaint remaining of recorde in this Court. [Req. 1/10/216r]

6 July, fol. 222.[3] Tenantes sueing their Lord for common of pasture and certaine copiholdes, etc. [Req. 1/10/222r]

Anno 4&5.P&M.

27 October, fol. 229.[4] A letter of atturney to a Stewarde to keepe Courtes, receive money, etc. [Req. 1/10/229r]

3 November, fol. 231.[5] Sir Thomas White, knight, of the King and Queenes Counsell. [Req. 1/10/231v]

5 Movember [*sic*], fol. 232. A cause of the Queenes tenants, plaintiff, against the Mayor of Duchued in Cornwal, heard in this Court. [Req. 1/10/232v]

On the same, fol. 233.[6] An injunction for stay of proceeding at common law. [Req. 1/10/233r]

18 November, fol. 249. A cause of tythes deceed [*sic*].[7]

19 November, fol. 257.[8] Execution of a judgement at common

---

[1] Richard Cole v. Richard Mayowe.

[2] — — Sprackett v. — — Wolrond. These folios are very badly damaged at bottom and the references cannot be fully confirmed.

[3] Richard Bydwell, Thomas Clerke, Thomas Collin, *et al.*, inhabitants and tenants of Leighton Bromwewolde, Hunts. v. Sir Robert Tyrwhit.

[4] This is an unusual entry: the letter of attorney was entered in Req. 1/10 by order of 'Counceill'. Richard Brent, esquire, of Cosington, Southants, grants his stewardship in the manor of — — to his brother-in-law John Denham, gentleman. This folio is badly damaged at the foot and is very difficult to fully check.

[5] Richard Tattell v. James Davers. Sir Thomas White granted an injunction against defendant requiring his appearance.

[6] Thomas Froste v. John Phetyplace.

[7] This folio is too badly damaged to make a complete identification.

[8] Margaret Cotton, widow, and her son John Cotton v. William Reed. The reference to Req. 2/23/60 is included because Req. 1/10 is so badly damaged that reference to the draught copy of the decree was necessary. See *supra*, fo. 136r, *sub dat.* 14 May, 3&4.P&M.

lawe in an action of trespasse stayed by decree of this Court. *stay after judgement at common lawe.* [Req. 1/10/253v and Req. 2/23/60]

23 November, fol. 235.[1] Witnesses brought into the court to be examined *ad informandum conscientias consilii*. [Req. 1/10/235r]

24 November, fol. 237.[2] An answere put in for an infant defendant by his gardian. [Req. 1/10/237v]

On the same, fol. 264.[3] An injunction to stay further proceeding at common lawe with v libri charges given against the defendant for proceeding formerly therein. [Req. 1/10/261v]

27 November, fol. 264. Sir John Williams, knight, Lord Williams of Thame, defendant, etc. [Req. 1/10/264v]

27 January, fol. 270.[4] Possession awarded to the plaintiff for negligence in the defendants not answering. [Req. 1/10/270r]

[fo. 137r (p. 119)]

On the same day. An injunction to stay the proceeding at the Common lawe. [NR]

5 February, fol. 280. A decree against Sir John Nevill, knight, Lord Latimer, defendant. [Req. 1/10/280v]

10 February, fol. 276.[5] A copiholde cause sent to bee tryed in the Court of the mannour, for that the plaintiff alledged no partialitie in the Lady of the manour nor in her Steward there. [Req. 1/10/276v]

15 February, fol. 277.[6] Ordered etc. that the defendant shall no further proceed in sute neither himselfe, nor by his atturney or atturneis, at the common law, against the said complainant neither shall molest him by indictment or otherwise for the occupation of the premisses. [Req. 1/10/277v]

4 May, fol. 4. Sir Thomas White, knight, and John Throgmorton, esquire, Masters of the King and Queenes Majesties Requests. [NR]

9 May, fol. 14. A cause heard, and decreed in Court of Requests for that the plaintiff was a poore man, and not allied nor friended in the countie where the lande in question lieth and for that the defen-

[1] Martin Buckman, *et al*. v. Richard Buckman.
[2] George Wood v. John and Mary Cowstock. Mary Cowstock was a minor and leave was given to her father-in-law, John Cowstock, to appear for her.
[3] John Warren v. John Boyer. The text of the injunction appears Req. 1/10/264r. See *supra*, fo. 136r, *sub dat*. 19 May, 3&4.P&M.
[4] Vincent Fullwood v. Francis Lowe and Jasper Lowe.
[5] Agnes Sterkey, widow to Henry Sterkey v. John Denton.
[6] Parties' names are destroyed.

dants were men of great wealth and greatly alied and friended in the saide Countie and greatly borne by the Jurors and ringleaders of the same shire, etc. [NR]

12 May, fol. 16. Decreed that the defendant being Lord of the Mannour shall admit the saide plaintiff tenant of the twelve acres of land in question, etc. [NR]

23 May, fol. 24.[1] A decree against the defendant for enlargeing of a prisoner without sufficient warrant. [Req. 2/23/80]

On the same day, fol. 25. The possession of landes in question decreed to the plaintiff but the defendant licensed to take and carie away the corne sowen by them on the premisses. [NR]

17 June, fol. 33.[2] Sir Ralph Bulmer, knight, defendant, alleadging that hee could not presently answere for lacke of his evidence was ordered to come into the Court and there to sweare that his allegation was true. [Req. 2/22/6]

20 June, fol. 33. Sir Gilbert Dethicke, knight, Principall king [fo. 137v (p. 120)] of Heraldes, defendant. [NR]

24 June, fol. 35. For that both the Plaintiff and the defendant are rich men and of great wealth able to try their cause, either in the Citie of London or elsewhere, therefore the Counsell dismissed them out of this Court. [NR]

Anno 5.&6.P.&M.

20 October, fol. 56.[3] A notable decree against the Bailiffes of Northampton for a wilfull escape of a prisoner uppon debt, and for other injustice. [Req. 2/20/165]

7 November, fol. 53. Whereas a Privy Seal of allegiance is directed forth to Richard Toplif the younger for his appearance at the sute of John Toplif and others, forasmuch as the right honourable Henry, Lord Willoughby hath by his corporall othe in open court declared, that the defendant was so sick that he was not able to have appeared according to the tenor of the first Privy Seal without danger of life: it is therfore ordered that a *dedimus potestatem* under the Privy Seal be directed to certain commissioners to take the aunswere of the said defendant notwithstanding the said Privy Seal of alleagiance. [Req. 2/22/105]

---

[1] John Hodges v. Gilbert Archibold and William Atter, bailiffs of Northampton town. See *infra*, fo. 137v, *sub dat.* 20 October, 5&6.P&M.

[2] John Thomas and his wife, Ellen v. Ralph Bulmer.

[3] John Hodges v. Gilbert Archibald and William Atter. See *supra*, fo. 137r, *sub dat.* 23 May, 4&5.P&M.

14 November, fol. 55. Severall causes dismissed to the common law out of this court for that severall verdicts had passed therein. [NR]

Anno 1.Eliz.

25 January, fol. 58. The names of the Queen's Majesties Counsel of her Court of Requests: Walter Haddon, esquire, Doctor of Law and Thomas Seckford, esquire, learned in the common lawes of the Realme. [NR]

15 February, fol. 73. Thomas, Lord Wharton, defendant, Thomas Chamberlain and others his tenants, plaintiffs. And decreed against his Lordship for the plaintiffs for the use of their Common. [NR]

[fo. 138r (p. 121)]

23 February, fol. 77. The Reverend Father in God, John, Abbot of the Monastery of Saint Peter of Westminster, defendant. And decreed against the Abbot. [NR]

27 April, fol. 83.[1] Bee it remembred that this present day one Robert Nele, gentleman, was by the Queen's Majesties Counsell of her court of Requests, committed to the keeping of the warden of the Fleete for his contempts grievously comitted against the Queen's Majestie in troubling, and attaching one of her Majesties Sergiants at Armes for that the same Sergiant at the commaundement of the Counsel of the late Queen Mary, of her Honourable Court of Requests did (for divers contempts against the saide Queen by the said Nele committed) attache the same Nele. *attaching a Sereiant at armes.* [Req. 2/23/27]

2 June, fol. 102. A cause clerely dismissed out of this Courte aswel for that the defendant inhabiteth in the Kings towne [i.e. Kingston] upon Hull where the Mayor and Shreifes of the same towne have power and authoritie to hold plea of all landes lying within the saide towne: as also for that the plaintiff is not of the Queenes Majesties houshold, nor by any meanes so attendant but that he may from time to time at his libertie pursue for his right before the said Mayor and Sheriffes, or else at the Common lawe, and for that also the matter is determinable at and by the said Common law. [NR]

5 June, fol. 103. Fourtie shillings given to the defendant for expences *retardati processus* to be paid by the plaintiff immediately upon the sight of this order. [NR]

---

[1] John Hastings v. Robert Neale. These are interrogatories and depositions only which were taken 4&5.P&M.

10 June, fol. 107. An injunction to stay the defendants proceeding at common lawe. [NR]

15 June, fol. 108. An injunction to the tenant of certaine groundes that hee nor any for him, etc. shall make any strip, waste, fell, cut downe, carry away nor otherwise to spoile any maner of wood or underwoode growing or being upon the premisses. [NR]

10 October, fol. 128. Forasmuch as the Lord Zouche being cal-

[fo. 138v (p. 122)]

led into this court by Richard Marler, and others, can not appeare by occasion of sicknesse, but hath sent a servant of his to make an affidavit for him, it is therefore nowe ordered etc. that the said Lord Zouche shall by atturney effectually sue out a *dedimus potestatem* for the taking and receiving his answere and procure the same to be returned in *Crastino animarum proximum* without delay, or els the Lord Zouche to pay to the plaintiff such costes as by the said Counsell shall be taxed. [NR]

18 October, fol. 130.¹ Henry, Lord Barkeley, defendant. [Req. 2/57/46]

19 October, the same folio. Possession awarded against the defendant for not bringing his answere into the Court. [NR]

20 October, fol. 131. A messenger sent unto the defendant to give commandement unto them in the Queenes Majesties name not to vexe, sue, nor trouble the complainant but suffer him to come and goe freely to this Court, untill such time other order be by the Counsell of the saide Court taken therein. And 25 October, fol. 132. [NR]

7 November, fol. 147. Whereas Richard Tisdale, yeoman Cutter of the Queens Majesties great Warderobe, exhibited his bill of complaint to the Queens Majestie against John Bridges, taylor, for and concerning certain injuries and wronges by the sayd John done to the sayd plaintiff in the execution of his office of Yeoman Cutter, aforesaid, and disturbing of the said plaintiff in doing of his offices there, etc., ordered, etc., that the benefites of the said office shall be devided betweene them. [NR]

¹ William Bridges v. Henry, Lord Berkeley, and others. This appears to be the cause that J.C. was citing because the complaint was endorsed as received 30 May, 1.Eliz. and the return day given was the quindene of Michaelmas within which 18 October falls, the date upon which the defendant was admitted to answer the plaintiff. The matter was still active 4 February, 25.Eliz. when an exemplification under Privy Seal was issued.

11 November, fol. 130. In the cause of John Seimor, gentleman, against Peter Wentworth, defendant. It is by the Counsell ordered that forasmuch as the said defendant hath not brought into this court his answere to the plaintiffs bill according to an order therein heretofore taken the sixth day of this insant moneth, therefore the saide defendant shall pay twelve pence every day unto the said plaintiff from this present day for costes untill the day that hee shall bring in

[fo. 139r (p. 123)]

that answere. And 22 November, 2 Elizabeth, fol. 138, two shillings per diem allowed in like case. [NR]

Anno 2.Eliz.

1 February, fol. 167. An injunction for stay of the defendant's proceeding at the Common Lawe. [NR]

5 February, fol. 167. Possession awarded to the plaintiff for the defendant's contempt in not answering. And *similiter*,

2 May, fol. 183. [NR]

4 May, fol. 185. Sir William Huet, knight, Lord Mayor of London, plaintiff, against Peter Silvester, defendant. [NR]

10 May, fol. 188. Possession of the land in question awarded to the plaintiff for default of the defendant's answere. [NR]

13 May, fol. 200. A cause touching an extent upon a statute heard and determined, and commanded to be perfourmed under paine of 100 markes to bee paide by the defendant to the plaintiff, his executors, administrators or assignes by the name of a fine. [NR]

21 May, fol. 201. A decree touching the lease in question, the rent whereof was reserved to the corporation of Christ Church in London. [NR]

27 May, fol. 204. A decree upon an assumpsit. [NR]

The same day, fol. 207. A decree against an executor for charges disbursed in the intertainement of his father the testator, and companie by the plaintiff. [NR]

28 May, fol. 207. A decree for repaiment of money unduly payd. [NR]

31 May. A cause of possession notably decreed. [NR]

17 June, fol. 210. The cause dismissed for that both parties dwell within the Commission of the Marches of Wales. And 18 June, fol. 211. [NR]

18 June, fol. 212. A cause dismissed upon the parties assent to

[r]eferre the same to the right honourable Sir Nicolas Bacon, knight, Lord Keeper of the Great Seale of England and Sir Robert Cattlin, knight, Lord Chiefe Justice of England. [NR]

[fo. 139v (p. 124)]

10 October, fol. 219. John Silvester, etc. appeared personally, etc., at the suit of William Huet, knight, Mayor of London and he was ordered to give 2 shillings a day not to depart etc. and to appear from day to day as long as and until, etc. [NR]

16 October, fol. 220. Master Dale, Attorney, before the Queen's Counsell. [NR]

The same day, fol. 221. Injunction given to the defendant to permit the plaintiff to followe his sute without arrest etc. upon paine of an hundreth pound. [NR]

5 November, fol. 227. Injunction to stay the defendant's proceeding at the Common Law. [NR]

12 November, fol. 230. A cause dismissed, for that the land in variance lieth within the precinct of the Marches of Wales, and both parties inhabiting there. [NR]

16 November, fol. 231. Possession of the landes in question granted to the plaintiff for default of the defendants answere. [NR]

Anno 3.Eliz.

26 November, fol. 232. Edmond Gest, Bishop of Rochester, plaintiff, against Richard Spillisburie, defendant. [NR]

6 February, fol. 259. The Deane and Chapter of Glocester, plaintife, against John Kirby, defendant. [Req. 2/117/50]

10 May, fol. 292. An injunction to stay the proceeding at Common Lawe and 16 May, fol. 296, the same. [NR]

19 May, fol. 297. In the cause betweene the right honorable Sir Ambrose Cave, knight, one of the Queen's most honorable privie Counsell, and Chancelour of the Dutchie of Lancaster, plaintife, and Thomas Bracebridge, Esquier, defendant, an injunction granted to stay the proceeding at Common Lawe, the defendant committed for breache thereof to the Fleete, and afterwardes licensed to proceede to the triall of his right in this Court, and decreed 3 June following. [Req. 2/78/24]

The same fol. 299. For that this sute dependeth at the com-

[fo. 140r (p. 125)]

mon law, and the plaintifs be of sufficient abilitie, to sue at the common law, and are none of the Queen's Majesties ordinary servaunts, nor meete to be received into this Court, as it seemeth to her Majesties Counsell of this court, therefore it is cleerely dismissed. [NR]

13 October. Possession of the landes in question given to the plaintife for want of the defendant's answere. [NR]

14 October, fol. 365. The defendant enjoyned to surcease, and no further to proceede in his sute or recoverie had against the plaintife at common lawe. [NR]

15 October, fol. 343. Ordered that forasmuch as the plaintife had exhibited his bill of complaint into this court, before that the defendant had proceeded in his sute at Common Lawe against the said plaintife to the utlawrie, that therefore the said defendant shall bring into this court, a full and sufficient answere to the plaintifes bill by Friday next etc. [NR]

20 October. The Ladie Margerie Acton, defendant, licensed to goe to triall and judgement at common law, but enjoyned to stay execution, etc. *injunction to stay execution at common lawe.* [NR]

23 October, fol. 348.[1] A defendant enjoined to stay execution after judgement, etc. *the like* [Req. 2/62/51]

24 October, fol. 348. The Atturney of the defendant called into this court, and enjoyned to stay the defendant proceeding at common law against the plaintife, etc. [NR]

13 November, fol. 355. The Lord Robert Dudley, plaintife, against the Earle of Cumberland, defendant. [NR][2] The same, The Master and Fellowes of Gunwell [i.e. Gonville] Hall, and Caius Colledge in Cambridge, plaintifes, against Thomas Wall, defendant. [NR]

Anno 4.Eliz.

18 November, fol. 358. A defendant in this court condemned by decree to pay a summe of money to the

[fo. 140v (p. 126)]

plaintife, tooke the prison of Ludgate, where he went abroade with his keeper, and sought not to agree with the said plaintife, upon information whereof it was further decreed by this court, that a Serjeant at Armes shal apprehend and take the body of the said defendant at any time that he may be found abroade out of the same prison [o]f Ludgate, and bring him to any such other prison, as by this court shalbe nominated, and appointed, there to remaine

---

[1] Roger Southall v. Margery, Lady Acton, widow, and Henry Acton, her son.
[2] See *infra*, fo. 140v, *sub dat.* 3 February, 4.Eliz.

without bale or liberty, or to go abroad any more, untill such time he shall have observed the sayd decree. [NR]

26 November. A cause of dower decreed for the plaintiff in the thirds of her late husbands lands. [NR]

10 December, fol. 363. Depositions taken before the Counsell, having relation to facts and words committed and spoken upon the sea, forborne to be published. *depositions extramarine forborne to bee publisshed.*

23 January, fol. 1.[1] Decreed that the defendant shall not be compelled to answere the bill of the plaintiff being excommunicate, till [s]he be absolved. [Req. 1/11/1r]

24 January. Edward Steward, gentleman, was for his contempt (in causing Randolph Hall, gentleman, to be arrested by bil of Middlesex, having sute in this court against the sayd Steward) committed by the counsell of this Court, to the keeping of the Warden of the Fleet. *the priviledge of a sute.* [Req. 1/11/1v]

30 January.[2] A defendant in this court notwithstanding he had the plaintiff in execution after judgement upon a *nihil dicit* at the Common Pleas, refusing to stand to the order of this Court, was committed to the Fleet, fol. 4. *commitment to prison for refusing to stand to the order of this Court.* [Req. 1/11/3v]

3 February, fol. 6.[3] The Lord Robert Dudley, plaintiff, and Henry, Earle of Cumberland, defendant. [Req. 1/11/6r]

6 February, fol. 8. The Bishop of Norwich, plaintiff, against Richard Wie, equire, defendant, and injunction granted to stay the defendant proceeding at the Common Law. [Req. 1/11/8r]

12 February, fol. 11. The Lady Elizabeth Stafford, plaintiff, against Sir Humfrey Stafford, her husband, defendant. [Req. 1/11/11r]

[fo. 141r (p. 127)]

1 June, fol. 50. Memorandum that Edmund Lucas, Gentleman, was this present day committed to the keeping of the Warden of the Fleet, for that hee being enjoyned by the Queens Majesties counsel of this court, not to have proceeded in his sute at common lawe, against Robert Chalice, did notwithstanding the same injunction to him given, proceede therein, in contempte of this

---

[1] The volume, Req. 1/11, is in very good condition and covers the years 4. Eliz.–8. Eliz. This entry concerns Alice Duncombe, widow v. William Skipworth, esquire.

[2] Thomas Taylor, *et al.* v. Hugh Taverner.

[3] See *supra*, fo. 140r, *sub dat.* 13 November, 3.Eliz.

sayde court. *commitment to the Fleete for proceeding at common lawe contrary to injunction.* [Req. 1/11/50r]

14 June, fol. 58.[1] Be it remembered, etc. that the order made 16 October. Last concerning certaine lands and tenements etc. in the cause betweene Sir Thomas Standley, knight, plaintiff, and Redman Clerke and others, defendant, is this present day made frustrate and voide in all respectes, for that it appeared to the sayd Counsel of this court, by a record to them shewed, that the Queenes Majestie was intitulated to the premisses by information in the court of Exchequer. [Req. 1/11/58r]

Anno 5.Eliz.

8 May.[2] The Lady Carew, late wife to Sir Wimond Carew, knight, enjoined to stay her proceeding at the Common Law, upon a bond against Penruddocke, plaintiff. Fol. 148. [Req. 1/11/148r]

Anno 6.Eliz.

3 February, fol. 205. Term was held at Hertford. [Req. 1/11/205r]

9 May, fol. 231. Thomas Bracebridge, plaintiff, against the Right Honourable Sir Ambrose Cave, knight, one of the Queenes Majestes honourable Counsell and Chanceller of her Majesties Duchy of Lancaster, defendant. [NR] Vide, 16 June, 5 Elizabeth, fol. 197. [Req. 1/11/198v]

10 May. Robert Davie, plaintiff, against the Earle of Worcester and Thomas Clerke, defendants. [NR]

12 May, fol. 142.[3] Sir Ambrose Cave, aforesayd, answered the [fo. 141v (p. 128)]

plaintiffs bill, upon his othe, notwithstanding his honourable places. [Req. 1/11/242r]

5 June, fol. 275. Mathew Becke, one of the yeomen ushers of the Queenes Majesties chamber, plaintiff, against James Harrington, esquire, defendant, touching a graunge called Pipwell graunge, with the appurtenances in the county of Lincolne. [Req. 1/11/275v]

14 October, fol. 284. Edward Filtmersh, plaintiff, against Henry, Lord Aburgavenny, defendant. [Req. 1/11/284v]

6 November, fol. 299. Oliver Denham, gentleman, plaintiff, against Sir Richard Sackevile, knight, defendant [NR] Sir Richard

---

[1] Thomas Standley, knight v. John Redman, clerk, *et al.*
[2] George Penruddock and his wife, Anne v. Dame Martha Carew.
[3] fol. 142 should read fol. 242.

then being a Privie Counseller, as appeareth fol. 307,[1] concerning the detention of an obligation. [Req. 1/11/307v]

Anno 7.Eliz.

5 February.[2] Edward Filtmersh and Frideswith, his wife, plaintiff, against the right honourable Henrie Nevill, knight, Lord Aburgavenny, defendant, concerning the right, title and interest of one messuage and 60 acres of land, and decreed against the said Lord. fol. 371. [Req. 1/11/372v]

22 June, fol. 425.[3] Masters of Requests, Bishop of Rochester, Walter Haddon, Doctor of Civil Law and Thomas Seckford, gentleman, [of the Counsel] learned in the law. [Req. 1/11/425r]

16 October, fol. 483. In the cause at the sute of Thomas Hill, plaintife, against William Arundell, gentleman, defendant. It is by the Queenes Majesties Counsell of this court ordered, that if the said complainant doe not bring into this said court good suerties upon the Friday next (at the sitting of the Court) to be bound for the said complainant that hee shall fully prove the materiall allegations of his bill of complaint exhibited into this court, by witnesses or otherwise to bee true by the Utas of Saint Hillarie next comming, then the same matter bee dismissed. The sureties were brought into this court, according to the order, whose

[fo. 142r (p. 129)]

names follow: viz., Thomas Hill of Taunton, marchant, and John Come, of the same place, mercer. [Req. 1/11/483r]

Anno 8.Eliz.

29 January, fol. 558. Roger Askham, equire, and Sir John Browne, defendant, the defendant enjoyned to bring in his answere by a day limited under paine to pay such costs, as this court shall award. [Req. 1/11/558r]

7 March, fol. 600. Thomas Thurland, clerke of the Queenes Majesties closet, plaintiff, William Whitacres, and Ralph Day, defendant. Whereas the plantiff is committed to the Fleete by the Justices of the Common Plees, upon an execution of 600 libri the meere debt being but 300 libri etc. Forasmuch as it hath bene given to this Court to understand by divers of the Queenes

---

[1] The reference to Privy Council in this entry is based upon the use of the style 'Rt. Hon'.

[2] See *supra, sub dat.* 14 October.

[3] J.C. took this from a clerk's notes at the head of the folio which recorded the opening of Trinity Term, 7.Eliz.

highnesse most honourable Privie Counsell, that her Majesties pleasure is to have and use the present and speedie travell of the saide Thomas Thurland, in and about divers her Highnesse weightie affaires in divers and sundrie places of England and Wales for and about minerall causes there, to the very likely commoditie and benefite of her Majesty and al her subjects. It is therfore presently ordered and decreed by her Majesties Counsel of this court, that the said Thomas Thurland shall and may with his kee-

[fo. 142v (p. 130)]

per, appointed by the Warden of the Fleete, travell into any partes of the saide Realme etc. about the affaires aforesaid, without the disturbance, let or interruption of the said defendant, etc. and to that purpose an injunction granted against the said defendant their atturneys, solicitors etc. in 1000 libri and likewise that neither they nor any of them shall vexe, sue, trouble or molest or impleade etc. the said plaintiff or Richard Tirell, Esquier, nowe Warden of the Fleete, or any other person whatsoever, for the travelling, or departing of the saide Thomas Thurland, from the saide prison of the Fleete, with his keeper appointed as aforesaid etc. from the day of making this decree untill the feast of All Saintes next insuing if the said plaintiff so long shal have cause to attend about the affaires. [Req. 1/11/600r]

one committed from the common plees upon an execution was by this court for a time licensed to travell into the countrie with his keeper.

2 May, fol. 1.[1] Masters of Requests, the Bishop of Rochester, Walter Haddon and Thomas Seckeford. [NR]

5 June, fol. 57. An admirall cause committed by the Lords of the Queens Counsell to Master Thomas Seckeford, decreed in this court and ordered, bonds to be taken of the defendant in England to the friends of the plaintiff for keeping the peace on the sea, etc. [NR]

16 November, fol. 93. William Dungate, plaintife, the Lord Aburgavenny, defendant. The defendant licensed to amend some words mistaken in his answers. [NR]

Anno 9.Eliz.

28 November, fol. 105. In the cause of the Lord Strange, ordered

---

[1] See Req. 1/107/1r for a similar entry *sub dat.* 1 May, 8.Eliz.

that he being plaintiff shal procure and cause, that Charles Price and others shalbe brought into this court, on this side the last day of this moneth to be examined on the part and behalfe of the said defendant or els then the matter to be dismissed. [NR]

Fol. 108, 22 October. *RR Elizabethae* 8, Richard Pigot, plaintiff, the Lord Willoughby, defendant. The plaintiff sued for an amerciament to be pardoned, imposed upon him in the said Lord's court, the defendant being by proces called to make answere, promised upon his honor, not to take any benefite or advantage of the said amerciament: Thereupon ordered that the said matter should be dismissed. [NR]

20 November. fol. 121. John Thorman, plaintiff, the Lord Hastings of Loughborough, defendant. The defendant injoined to restore to the plaintiff a tenement and landes seased on for the felonie of the Plaintiff's father: upon the opinion of the Justices of the Common Plees, that the attainder of the father

[fo. 143r (p. 131)]

was no forfeiture of the estate of those in the remainder. [Req. 2/56/26r]

3 February, fol. 162. The Lord Strange, plaintiff, and Andrew Vavasor, defendant. The plaintiff praying longer time to examine witnesses, and the defendant alleadging that it was but onely for delay of paiment of the 300 libri to the saide defendant, which the said defendant had recovered against the said plaintiff at the common lawe. Therefore ordered with the assent of the said plaintiff that hee the saide plaintiff before the last day of this terme shall become bound with one sufficient suretie to Richard Oseley, Esquier, clerke of this court, by obligation in the summe of 400 libri that he the saide plaintiff shall bring into this court 300 libri in currant money of England, or els sufficient pawne of plate or other thing or things of golde and silver, or one of them for the saide summe, etc. and if the saide complainant refuse, or make default to put in surety etc. then the matter cleerly to be dismissed with expenses. [NR]

18 April, fol. 173. For the said Lord *not* performance of the former order, ordered the cause to be dismissed with 4 marks for costs of suite, to be paid to the defendant. [NR]

25 October, fol. 263. The Lord Gray, plaintiff, William Crowder, defendant, an injunction graunted to stay the defendant proceeding at the Common Law. [NR]

Anno 10.Eliz.[1]

26 January, fol. 311. The Lord Wentworth, plaintiff, Henry Baker, defendant, ordered the cause to be dismissed, unlesse the plaintiff shew good cause on Saterday next etc. [Req. 2/71/82r]

27 January.[2] Henry Moyse committed to the Fleete for disobeying a decree, etc. fol. 312. [Req. 2/97/39r]

17 May, [fol.] 363. John Lorcomb, plaintiff, the Lady Edith Horseley, defendant. The defendant ordered to stay her suite at common lawe, untill the plaintife have examined his wit-

[fo. 143v (p. 132)]

nesses in this Court. [NR]

1 June, fol. 409. Memorandum, that this present day, order was by the Queenes Majesties Counsell of this Court taken, that when any matters shall be upon a day appointed by the said Counsell to be heard, no order shall bee made nor any person heard, that shall bee made nor any person heard, that shall moove the Court for the same, until such time as the matters appointed to be heard shalbe throughly heard.

no motion till hearings bee past. [NR]

6 July, fol. 410.[3] Thomas, Lord Wentworth, plaintiff, Henry Baker, defendant. [NR]

13 October, fol. 450. Reynold Warcup, plaintife, the Lord Latimer, defendant, one Edmond Adamson, gentleman, Atturney in the Court of Kings Bench, touching an action of debt for the saide Lorde, against the said plaintiff is this present day enjoyned by the Queenes Majesties Counsell of this Court, to surcease and stay his action alreadie commensed against the said plaintiff untill the saide Lord shall by himselfe or his atturney sufficiently authorised and instructed, have made his full and perfect answere to the plaintiffs bill. [Req. 1/12/450v]

Anno 11.Eliz.

18 November. Robert Lloyd, plaintiff, Sir Edward Bray, knight, defendant. Richard Quarles, a messenger, sworne that he served the injunction on the defendant, who at the receipt of the injunction and sight of the decree, saide at the first that he would be con-

---

[1] Req. 1/12 contains the entries for 10.Eliz. and 11.Eliz. but the volume is in a shambles, its folios ravaged by rot and decay. This condition accounts for the scant references which are found below.

[2] John ap Rice v. Henry Moyse.

[3] See *supra*, fo. 143r, *sub dat.* 26 January, 10.Eliz.

tended to obey any thing that the Masters of Requests had done therein; and foorthwith the Lady, his wife, came to him and did stand with him, and immediately hee changed his former speaking, and saide that hee would pay no money, hee did know the worst, it was but to lie in the Fleete, etc. and thereupon 21 November (as appeareth in the booke of Proccs [sic] that yeere) an attachment was awarded to the Sherife of the Countie of Surrey to attach the body of the said Sir Ed-

[fo. 144r (p. 133)]

ward Bray, knight, defendant. [NR]

24 January, fol. 1. Bishop of Rochester, the [Queen's] Almoner, Walter Haddon, Doctor of Lawe, and Thomas Seckford, Esquire, sate Judges in this Court. [NR]

9 May, fol. 33.[1] This present day one Hales, Serjeant at Armes, was given by the Queenes Majesties Counsel of this Court sent to fetch and bring before the sayd Counsel the body of William Golightly, Serjeant Ferror, for divers great contempts by him committed against the Queens Majestie and her said Counsell. [Req. 2/74/38]

23 June, fol. 62. Lord Viscount Bindon, plaintiff, Henry Rogers, etc., defendants. This present day Richard Calmadir, Atturney at the Common Lawe, for Henry Rogers was in open Court enjoyed neither by himselfe nor by any other atturney by his means to proceed any further at the Common Law in a manner there depending, betweene the said plaintiff and defendants untill the sayd defendants have personally appeared in this Court, and made answere to the bill of the said plaintiff and thereupon further order taken, etc. [NR]

Anno 12.Eliz.

8 May, fol. 111. In the cause depending in this Court betweene George Stowe, plaintiff, and William, Lord Willoughbie, defendant. It is decreed, that if the said defendant doe not cause his sufficient answere (whereby his title to the landes in variance may appeare) to bee put into this Court by the eight day of the next terme, then a decree to bee made against the said Lord Willoughbie, for the plaintiff to have the possession of the lands in variance, according to a former decree, etc. [NR]

14 November, fol. 161. John Goly, plaintiff, the earle of Southampton, defendant. [Req. 2/41/100 and Req. 2/33/1]

---

[1] William Golightlie, Sergeant Ferrier to the Queen v. Thomas Sheerer.

[fo. 144v (p. 134)]

Anno 13.Eliz.

31 January, fol. 188. Sir James Crofts, knight, Controller of the Queens Majesties housholde, plaintiff, Alexander Scoffeld, defendant, shall by or before Saturday next bring into this court all such evidences as hee hath in his custodie and possession touching the landes nowe in question betweene the said parties and also then shew good and sufficient matter why the same should not be forthwith delivered to the sayd plaintiff or els then order to be taken for the restoring of the same to the sayd plaintiff without further delay. [NR]

2 July, fol. 250. John Cob, plaintiff, William Leake, defendant, this present day, Robert Marshall, solicitor for the sayd defendant at Common Law against the sayd plaintiff is in open court enjoyned to surcease and stay his sute at Common law until such time as other and further order shalbe therein made by the Queenes Majesties counsell of this court. [NR]

4 July, fol. 251. Memorandum, that upon such information as was this present day made by the Wardens of the Fleet to this court, for divers contempts heretofore by John Taylor, marchant, committed against the Queenes Highnesse and the sayd court: it is ordered that the sayd Warden of the Fleet shal apprehend and take into his prison and custodie the body of the sayd John Taylor wheresoever he may be found, the same to be kept there until such time as the sayd Counsell shall have taken further orders for the same. [NR]

23 October, fol. 297. Nicholas Bush, plaintiff, Thomas Strachi, defendant, the cause decreed against the sayd defendant and at the date of this decree the sayd defendant being in open court was injoyned upon his allegeance to performe the same which he faithfully promised to do without fraud or deceit. [NR]

12 May. A warrant for a privy seale signed by Thomas Wilson, Doctor of Law, Master of Requests. [NR]

[fo. 145r (p. 135)]

Anno 14.Eliz.

6 February, fol. 13. Robert Watman, plaintiff, the Lord St. John, defendant, ordered that the sayd defendant shall examine all such witnesses as he intendeth to use before the 4 day of the next terme without delay. [NR]

12 February, fol. 17. The Ladie Anne, countesse of Sussex,

plaintiff, Augustine Grafigina, defendant, ordered that if the sayd plaintiff do not reply by the first of next terme, then the matter to be dismissed. [NR]

28 April, fol. 46. Robert Watman, plaintiff, the Lord Marques of Winchester, defendant. [NR]

1 May, fol. 50. Memorandum, that Robert Spencer of Lincolns Inne, esquire, being this present day called into this court, at the sute of Edward Skegs, Sergeant of the Powltrie, was enjoyned upon his allegeance, to surcease all such sutes as he hath now depending at the Common law against any the assignes and servants of the sayd Skegges for the manurance and carrying away of the hay, late growing upon a certaine parcell of medow being customery landes etc. untill order shall be therein made by this court. [NR]

13 May, fol. 58. The earle of Lecester, plaintiff, William Savell, esquire, defendant, ordered that the defendant shall make a better and more perfect answere and have libertie to take his first out of the court. [NR]

24 June, fol. 99. The earle of Warwicke, plaintiff, John Worlt, esquire, defendant, ordered that the defendant shall before the 2 day of the next terme, bring into this court all such evidences and conveyances, as he now hath in his custody and possession, touching the inheritance of the manour of Rookby in the county of Warwicke, and also all such bondes, estatutes, and defeazances made upon any statutes, or other bondes for the performance of any bargaine and sale made by the sayd plaintiff to the sayd defendant

[fo. 145v (p. 136)]

of the saide mannour, to the ende that upon the sight thereof the Queenes Majesties Counsell of this Court may take further order. [NR]

9 October, fol. 124. Memorandum, that the body of Nicholas Sherewood, who appeareth by force of a Proclamation of rebellion, is by order of the Queenes Majesties Counsell of this Court, committed to the custodie William Walker servant to George Rogers, Sherife of the Countie of Somerset, in whose warde he now remaineth as a prisoner, to the ende he may give his attendance in this Court from day to day, etc. [NR]

11 November, fol. 141. A deede enrolled concerning the scite of the monastery of Wimoneham granted to Sir Henry Cobham,

knight, and Anne, his wife, late wife of Walter Haddon, Master of Requests, etc. [NR]

Anno 15.Eliz.

17 April, fol. 252. Memorandum, that this present day John Rice being of the age of 14 yeeres and more, soone of Robert Rice of Thaxteede, deceased, came into this Court with his Counsell learned, and desired that William Staines, his grandfather, might be his Gardian, and have the education of him during his nonage. Whereupon the Queenes Majesties said counsell have appointed the said William Staines to be gardian to the said John Rice. [Req. 2/65/85]

12 November, fol. 366. William Raines, gentleman, plaintiff, the Lord Aburgavenny, defendant. [NR]

Anno 16.Eliz.

26 November, fol. 372. Patrick Goughe, plaintiff, Elizabeth Daniel, widow, defendant, one Russell, gentleman, atturney at the Common Lawe for the said defendant against the said plaintiff *injunction to stay execution at common lawe.*

[fo. 146r (p. 137)]

being this present day called into this court, is by her Majesties sayd Counsell of the same, injoyned not to cal for execution in the said cause untill the end of this present terme. [NR]

28 November, fol. 404.[1] William Raines, plaintiff, Henry Lord Aburgavennie, defendant. A commission awarded by the Lordes of her Majesties most honourable privie Counsell, to certaine gentlemen to sequester the corne in question, during the dependencie of the controverse aforesaid, and to examine witnesses, and finally to order and determine the same cause if they could or els to certifie their proceedings into her Majesties Court of Requests, to her Counsell there, etc. and with a certificate made, and thereupon a day of hearing appointed at that day. The Queens Majesties Counsell of the said Court, for the better proceeding according to law and equitie: if any doubt or ambiguity should happen to arise: did in her Majesties name desire Richard Harper, one of the Justices of the Common Plees, *one of the Justices of the common plees sat with and assisted the [*sic*] Majesties Counsell of this Court* to sit with them and assist them with his opinion for matters in lawe if need should require; who came and sate in the said Court accordingly, etc. and ordered for the said plaintiff

---

[1] See *supra*, fo. 145v, *sub dat.* 12 November, 15.Eliz.

against the said Lord and his Lordship injoined in 500 libri (being present in person at the hearing of the said cause) to performe this order and decree in every behalfe, etc. [NR]

28 November, fol. 433. Rose Bone, widow, and others coheires of John Harington, deceased, plaintiff, and Walter Leveson, esquire, defendant, touching one messuage or tenement with the appurtenances lying and being in Wolverhampton in the Countie of Stafford, etc. And further shewed that Sir Richard Leveson, knight, deceased, father to the sayd defendant, etc. decreed for the said defendant against the plaintiff. [NR]

1 May, fol. 499. Be it remembered that in the cause at the sute of the right honourable Gregory Lord Dacres of the South and Roger Manwood, esquier, one of the Justices
[fo. 146v (p. 138)]
of the Common pleese, plaintiff, against Thomas Michelborne and others defendant. Master Bell, Master Colby, and Master Fetiplace, are by order of her Highnesse Counsell of this court assigned to be of Counsell with the saide Thomas Michelborne and others the defendants. [NR]

22 May, fol. 512. Memorandum, that this present day a Pursuivant was by the Counsell of this court commanded to fetch in John Heyward of London, Imbroderer, to answere to such things which on the behalfe of Nicholas Brooke should be objected against him concerning the purusing of a sute at the common lawe against the said Nicholas touching a tenement called the Swanne in Tottle-streete in Westminster, which the said Heyward pursueth by force of a letter of Attourney, to him made by one Richard Banester. [NR]

15 June, fol. 572. The right honourable Philip, Earle of Surrey and Dame Anne, his wife, plaintiff, against William Musgrave and Isabell, his wife, defendant. It is by the Counsell ordered that if the said plaintiff doe not upon Thursday next sitting of the court shewe in this court good and sufficient matter in maintenance of this cause, then the same to be dismissed, and 17 June, fol. 592. [NR]

22 June, fol. 579.[1] Memorandum, that this present day upon motion made unto the Queenes Majesties counsell of her honourable court of Requests, on the behalfe of John Rice an infant within age (*viz.*) of 16 yeeres, it is by her Majesties said Counsell ordered,

---

[1] See *supra*, fo. 145v, *sub dat.* 17 April, 15.Eliz.

that one Richard Wilde of Edelmenton in the county of Middlesex, who taketh upon him as gardian in socage to the saide Rice and is thereby to disburse and lay out certaine summes of money for fines and other assurances of certaine landes and tenements to the use of the said John Rice of all such summes of money as he shall disburse and lay out, for and to the use and benefit of the said infant during his nonage, for

[fo. 147r (p. 139)]

the assurance of his sayde landes, in such sort, as by her Majesties sayd Counsell, at the age of the sayd infant[1] shal be adjudged and thought meet.

26 June, fol. 580. Francis Pope, plaintiff, William West, Lord Delaware, defendant. And 29 June, fol. 608, the sayd defendant condemned to pay 12 libri 15 shillings parcell of a greater summe recovered against him by the sayde plaintiff by judgement at the common law. *This court giving assistance to the execution of a judgement at common law.* [NR]

Anno 17.Eliz.

18 November, fol. 7. Memorandum, that this present day one William French, a solicitor, in the matter in variance betweene A.B., gentleman, plaintiff, and C.D., defendant, was committed to the prison of the Fleet, for that hee in contempt of the Queen's Majestie, and this court, did contrary to an injunction delivered by the sayd plaintiff touching the same, cause proceede in a *nisi prius* at the last assises in the countie of Norfolke. *a sollicitor committed to the Fleete for proceading at common lawe contrary to an injunction.* [NR]

23 April, fol. 65. Memorandum, that this present day John Bearden, citizen of London, was for divers his contempts committed to the keeping of the Warden of the Fleet, at the sute of Henry Shaw. [Req. 2/38/8]

13 May, fol. 92.[2] Thomas Higgins, gentleman, plaintiff, the reverend father in God, Richard, Bishop of Chichester, defendant, and 22 June, fol. 108, ordered that the sayde defendant shall make a better and more perfect answere to the plaintiffs bill and subsign the same with his proper hand, or els a *dedimus potestatem* shalbe

---

[1] I.e. when the individual reaches maturity, as probably determined by an appearance *aspectu corporis* before the court. This would substantiate of record the claim of maturity or reject such a claim.

[2] Richard Curteys, Bishop of Chichester, defendant.

foorwith awarded to a certeine gentleman of worship for to receive his answere upon his othe, etc. [Req. 2/103/46]

Anno 18.Eliz.

24 January, fol. 171. Memorandum, that the whole pleadings of the matter in variance betweene John Keiser, plaintiff,

[fo. 147v (p. 140)]

and John Smith, defendant, were delivered by commaundement from the lordes of her Majesties most honourable privie Counsel to Serjeant Lovelace, to make report out of the same of the whole state of the matter to them and thereupon the same matter of pleadings delivered by like commandement to the Clerkes of the Privie Counsell, there to remaine untill the said lordes should take order therein, at the sute as well of the said Keiser, as of Doctor Huicke now defendant therein, where the bookes doe still remaine. [Req. 2/121/18]

12 February, fol. 194. William Chainell and others, plaintiff, Thomas, Lord Howard, Viscount Bindon, defendant, and decreed for the plaintiff against the defendant. 2 July, fol. 305. [Req. 2/79/38]

9 May, fol. 212. Memorandum, that Mary Puttenham, the wife of Richard Puttenham, esquire, hath this day in open court received the summe of 13 shillings 8 d. due unto her for the halfe yeeres paiment of one yeerly annuitie to be taken and issuing out of the rentes, revenues, and profites of the said Richard, her husband, by force of a decree heretofore in that behalf made by her Majesties Counsell of this Court, the same being due at the Annunciation of our Lady last past, and attached and defalked by Spencer, esquire, one of her Majesties Serjeants at Armes, by order of this Court, upon the last day of Aprill last past, out of such summes of money as were tendered upon Chawcers tombe within the cathedrall church of St. Peter in Westminster, by Robert Cheynie, Citizen of London, and there paied to the use of the same Richard Puttenham. *annuity issueng out of land* [NR]

10 May, fol. 230.[1] The inhabitants of Surry, plaintiff, against

---

[1] 'The inhabitants of Surry' are inhabitants of various parishes and townships in the county. The decree requires the defendant to go to King's Bench and plead trespass against plaintiffs who are in turn to plead justification based upon the traditional use of the lane in question as an open highway. Defendant then to take issue with this justification. Court of Requests will either enforce King's Bench judgment of fact or, should defendant not go to King's Bench, regard this as a default and find for plaintiffs.

Christopher Mellershe, defendant, for and concerning the stopping up of a certaine high way within the said Countie. See 3 July, fol. 308. *stopping of an highway* [Req. 2/134/14]

25 May, fol. 264. Richard Swift, plaintiff, Gregory Pourmount, defendant, the cause referred to the hearing ordering, and fully deter-

[fo. 149r (p. 141)]

mining the Right Honorable Sir Thomas Smith, one of the Queenes Majesties principall secretaries and of Thomas Seckford, esquire, and Thomas Wilson, Doctour of Law, the Queenes Majesties Counsell of the Court. [NR]

1 November, fol. 329. Giles, Lord Paulet, plaintiff, Nicholas Bier, Defendant. [NR]

Anno 19.Eliz.

25 January, fol. 383.[1] Thomas Higgons, plaintiff, the Bishop of Chichester, defendant, and ordered against the defendant for the plaintiff. 4 February, fol. 389. [NR]

15 November, fol. 1. Thomas Seckeford, gentleman, and Valentine Dale, Doctor of Law, the Queenes Majesties Counsel in the Court of Requests. *Thomas Seckford, gentleman, Valentine Dale, Doctor of Law.* [NR]

Anno 20.Eliz.

19 November, fol. 4. The tenants of Boldsoner, plaintiff, against the Right Honourable the earle of Shrewesburie, defendant. [NR]

8 February, fol. 61. The Right Honourable Gregorie, Lord Dacres, plaintiff, and Herbert Pelham, esquire, defendant. [Req. 2/34/49]

[fo. 148v]

*11 February, 20 Elizabeth. An enrolment of a certificate and a schedule taken before John,[2] Bisshop of London, Sir Christopher Wray, Lord Chiefe Justice of England, Sir William Cordel, knight, Master of the Rowles and John Southcot, one of the Justices of the Kings Bench touching the assurance past from her Majesty to Sir Christopher Hatton, knight, the captain of the gard, of Elie Howse in Holborne. Were theise wordes amongst others are expressed; and of all such losses as he hath presently susteined to certifie us in wrighting tripartite, indented and sealed with your seales, the one part thereof to remaine with our selfe to be inrolled in our Court of Requests, the second to be delivered to our said servaunt, etc. fol. 36. [NR]

---

[1] See *supra*, fo. 147r, *sub dat.* 13 May 17.Eliz.   [2] John Aylmer.

[fo. 149r (p. 141)]

2 May, fol. 85. John Walton, plaintiff, Edward Sherington, defendant. The defendant enjoyned not to call for judgement in an action of *ejectione firmae*, depending at the common law etc. [NR]

3 May, fol. 85. George Ashby, esquire, plaintiff, William Rolfe, defendant. An injunction awarded against the defendant etc. not to prosecute or proceede any further at the Common lawe, which injunction being by the procurement of the said Rolfe disobeyed, it is now ordered that Francis Whitney, esquire, Sergeant at Armes, shall by warrant and authoritie here of apprehend and arrest al and every such person and persons, as shall be found to prosecute the sayd cause for the sayde defendant, contrary to the sayde injunction, and after their apprehension, to commit them

[fo. 149v (p. 142)]

to the safe custodie of the Warden of the Fleet, there to remaine untill order bee taken for their deliverie by her Majesties counsell of this court. By authority wherof the sayde Rolfe was apprehended and committed to the Fleet for his contempts. Afterwards, in further contempt of this court, the sayde Rolfes atturney at Common Law did prosecute a *nisi prius*, before Sir Christopher Wray, knight, Lord Chiefe Justice of the Queens Bench, against the sayde plaintiff in Guildhall in London, which sayd atturney was then and there presently taken from the barre by the sayd Sergeant at armes and committed to the Fleet. *An atturney committed to the Fleete for proceading at common lawe contrary to an injunction.* [Req. 2/25/34]

31 May, fol. 125. The right honorable Thomas Wilson, one of her Majesties principall Secretaries, plaintiff, William Drowt, defendant, *and 28 October, 22.Eliz., fol. 28. *for a quitrent issueng out of certain land due to St. Catharines Hospitall.* [NR]

17 June, fol. 137. Henry Bettes, plaintiff, William Ancher, defendant. The defendant is injoyned in open court forthwith to make answere to the plaintiffs bil, and not to depart out of this towne, until he be licensed so to do by her Highnesse most honourable privie counsell. [NR]

Anno 21.Eliz.

23 January, fol. 179. Peter Elliot, plaintiff, John Cheston, defendant. The defendant enjoyned upon paine of his allegiance to attend from day to day, until further order be made, etc. [Req. 2/35/83]

9 May, fol. 225. Thomas, Lord Buckhurst, plaintiff, Anthony Smith, defendant. The defendant enjoyned to stay his proceeding at common law. [NR]

On the same day, fol. 226. John Wentworth, gentleman, atturney at the common law, was called into this Court, at the sute of John Revet, plaintiff, against Katherine Morse, defendant, and enjoyned not to call for execution, etc *injunction to stay execution at the common lawe* ([NR]

15 May, fol. 230. Henry, earle of Huntington, plaintiff, Laurence Levet, esquire, defendant. [NR]

[fo. 150r (p. 143)]

On the same day, fol. 235. John Parker, plaintife, Henrie Buckfold, defendant: one Stampe, gentleman, atturney at the common law, for the said defendant being this present day called into this court, was then, and there by her Majesties Counsell of the same court injoyned to surcease and stay, and no further to prosecute, an action of debt commensed by the said defendant against the saide plaintife upon an obligation of thirty pound for the paiment of twentie, untill such time as he the said defendant shal put in sufficient baile to answere the saide plantife at the common lawe unto certaine actions there to be commensed against him upon two severall obligations remaining in the hands of the said plaintiff and have also made answer to the plaintiffs bill in this court. *this court assisteth the Common lawe.* [Req. 2/91/15]

20 October, fol. 303. Memorandum, that Richard Gooch hath before Master Velentine Dale, esquier, Doctor of Lawe, one of her Majesties Counsell of this court acknowledged himselfe to owe unto the Queenes Majestie the summe of 40 pound etc. The condition is, that whereas the said Gooch hath committed severall contempts, and nowe being brought into this court by the Shirife of London by vertue of an attachment: if he the saide Gooche doe from day to day make his personall appearance in this court, and not depart without license, untill the same matter shall here have received hearing, and also abide and performe such order as shalbe herein taken, then this recognisance to be voyde. [NR]

Anno 22.Eliz.

26 November, fol. 318. Memorandum, that this present day Sir William Gerrard, knight, Lord Chancelour of Ireland, was presented and did sitte in her Highnesse Court of Requests with Master Thomas Seckford, esquier, and Master Valentine Dale,

Doctor of Law, upon her Ma-
[fo. 150v (p. 144)]
jesties pleasure signified by the honourable Thomas Wilson, one of
he[r] Highnesse principall Secretaries letter being extant in this
court in forme following. After my very heartie commendations,
these are to advertise you that the Queenes Majestie hath appointed the Lord Chancellour of Ireland to be one of the Masters
of her Court of Requests, at his last being in England, at what time
he tooke his othe afore the Lords [of the Council] and therefore if
he doe come to sit in the court, I am to require you in her Majesties
behalfe, that he may be received with all favour. Thus in haste
fare you heartily well. At the Court, this 23 of November 1579.
Your most assured loving friend, Thomas Wilson. To the right
worshipfull my very loving friends the Masters of Requests, and
to either of them. [NR]
30 January, fol. 357. A recognisance taken before Thomas Seckford, gentleman, and Valentine Dale, Doctor of Lawe, in these
words: Memorandum, that Henrie Corne of the parish of Saint
Martin at the Three Cranes of the Vintree, tailer, doeth knowledge
himselfe to owe unto the Queenes Majesty the summe of 100 libri,
etc. The condition of this recognisance etc. for apparance before
the Lords of her Majesties most honourable Privy Counsell, etc.
[NR]
9 February, fol. 362. Richard Francklin, plaintife, the Lord
Cromwell, defendant. [NR]
4 May, fol. 392. The inhabitants of Browby Knecton, plaintifes,
against the Reverend Father in God, Richard, Bishop of Durham,
defendant. A commissioner refusing to subscribe the returne of
the Commission, is required by a letter from her Majesties Counsell in this court to certifie the same commission with speede. [NR]
4 June, fol. 421. John Sadler, plaintife, and Thomas Smith,
defendant. The said defendant was this day committed to the
Fleete for disobeying a decree made by the Counsel of this court
betweene him and the plaintiff. *commitment to prison for dis-
obeyeng a decree.* [Req. 2/72/8]
[fo. 151r (p. 145)]
20 October, fol. 4. William Baker, plaintife, John Poole, defendant.
The defendant being brought into this court upon an attachment,
was this day committed (for his contempts) to the keeping of the
Warden of the Fleete. [NR]

28 October, fol. 28. The Master, brethren and sisters of St. Katherins, plaintifes, William Drought of London, Baker, defendant, for a yeerely rent of xxiii shillings ii pence, issuing and growing out of a messuage or tenement with the appurtenances, situate and being in the parish of St. Benedict Grace Church in the Bridge Warde of London, knowen and lately called by the name of The Shippe, payable at foure feastes in the yeere etc., the saide rent, and the arrerages thereof adjudged and decreed to the said Master, brethren and sisters, and their successors for ever. *a quitrent due to St. Catharins* [NR]

Anno 23.Eliz.

28 January, fol. 51. Thomas Eaton, plaintife, John Tomlinson, etc. defendants. The saide defendants are this present day enjoyned in open Court upon their alleageance, and also Thomas Swinton, gentleman, atturney at the common lawe for the saide defendant was likewise enjoyned to surcease and stay their proceedings at the common lawe against the said plaintife, and not to call for judgement, or execution therein, untill further order be taken by this court, and 11 February, fol. 56. *injunction after triall at common lawe to stay judgement and execution.*[1] [Req. 1/39 (*sub dat* 28 January, 23 Eliz.)]

26 May, fol. 106. Thomas Seckford, gentleman, Valentine Dale and David Lewes, Doctors of Law, the Queens Majestys Counsel in the Court of Requests.

Anno 24.Eliz.

29 January, fol. 182. Sir James Croftes, knight, Controller of her Majesties most honourable house[hold], plaintiff, against

[fo. 151v (p. 146)]

Walter Vaughan, esquire, defendant. [Req. 1/39 (*sub dat* 29 January, 24 Eliz.)]

21 June, fol. 262. Thomas, Lord Buckhurst, plaintife, John Stonden, defendant. The defendant enjoyned to stay his proceedings at the Common Law against the said plaintife. [NR]

6 November, fol. 301. Michaelmas Term held at Hartford. [NR]

Anno 25.Eliz.

27 April, fol. 276. John Joy, plaintife, John Androwes, Customer of Bristoll, defendant. The defendant is this present day commited

---

[1] This and subsequent entries are found only in Req. 1/39 which is a draught Order book. The book is not foliated and dates are the only available correlations.

to the custodie of the Warden of the Fleete, for contempts by him committed touching the same matter. [NR]

On the same day, Hugh Beston, plaintiff, Dorothy Downes, defendant. Robert Younger, gentleman, atturney at the common law for the said defendant is enjoyned in open Court to surcease the defendants suite at common law against the plaintiff and not to call for judgement or execution, etc. [NR]

1 May, fol. 397. A matter of adulterie examined in this court. [NR]

4 June, fol. 418. Nicholas Wright, plaintiff, against the right honourable the Lord Morley, defendant, it being a cause consisting upon accompts, is referred to Commissioners indifferently named by both parties. [Req. 1/39 (*sub dat* 4 June 25 Eliz.)]

17 June, fol. 431. Thomas Gray, plaintiff, Francis Burnell, defendant. The defendant enjoyned to stay execution against the plaintiff and not to vexe him by meanes of any judgement or execution heretofore had or obteined against him at common lawe in the same cause. *injunction to stay execution at common lawe.* [Req. 2/58/8]

25 October, fol. 8. William Russell, etc., plaintiff, John Fielde, defendant. This present day John Field being present in court was by her Majesties Counsell enjoyned upon paine of his allegiance to appeare in the Court of Starchamber up-

[fo. 152r (p. 147)]

on Wednesday next, to answere to such things as shal be there objected against him. [NR]

On the same day, fol. 9. Magdalene Middleton, plaintiff, the right honourable Henry Lord Cheiney of Tuddington, defendant, at the common law, one Swane, gentleman, atturney there for the plaintiff is this present day in open court enjoyned to stay his proceeding against the said Lord Cheiney at the common law, untill the sayd Magdalene have made answere to the bill of the sayd Lord Cheiney being plaintife in this court. [Req. 2/121/60]

Anno 26.Eliz.

14 May, fol. 96. Henry Seckeford, esquire, one of the Groomes of her Majesties Privie Chamber, plaintiff, William Cowper of London, Marchand, defendant. The defendant this present day in open court was upon his allegeance enjoyned to attend in this court from day to day untill hee be otherwise licensed etc., and

further that from hencefoorth he shall surcease and stay and no further prosecute or proceed in any action, at and by the order of the common lawes against the sayd plaintiff, etc. [NR]

25 June, fol. 124. The Lord Buckhurst, plaintiff, John Fray, defendant [Req. 1/13/121r]

8 July, fol. 132. Thomas Braken, gentleman, plaintiff, Hugh Fairecloth, defendant: the defendant enjoyned not to call for judgement or execution in his cause depending at common law against the sayd plaintiff. *injunction to stay judgement and execution at common lawe.* [NR]

5 November, fol. 182. Hugh Wilsdon, plaintiff, Walter Heale, defendant. See touching an injunction. [NR]

11 November, fol. 165. John Leeke, esquire, plaintife, Humfrie Clerke, esquire, defendant: the defendant committed to the keeping of the Warden of the Fleet for divers contempts by him committed against her Majestie and her Counsell of this court. [Req. 2/40/104]

[fo. 152v (p. 148)]

Anno 27.Eliz.

19 November, fol. 168. Simon Perin, plaintife, John Reade etc., defendant. One Pearsall, gentleman, Marshall of the Kings Bench, being called into this court, is by her Majesties Counsell of the same, commaunded to restraine the sayd Read (being now a prisoner in his custodie) of his libertie, and not to suffer him to goe abroad with his keeper, untill such time as he, the sayd Read, shall dutifully submit himselfe to the order of this court, touching the aforesayd cause, and stay his sute at the common law according to the affect of an injunction under her Majesties privie seale to him, the sayd Read, and others in that behalfe awarded, for that it is informed to this court that all to whom the sayd injunction apperteineth (the sayd Reade onely excepted) do forbeare to prosecute the sayd sute at the common law, and the sayd Read onely with his keeper doth contemptuously pursue the same. [NR]

23 January, fol. 197. Named to the Council of our Lady, Queen Elizabeth, in the Court of Requests: Thomas Selford, gentleman; Valentine Dale, Ll.D; and Ralph Rokeby, gentleman who lived, judged, and remained in the said court until the year 1596; at which time (after John Herbert, gentleman, and William Aubrey, Ll.D) Julius Caesar for five full years had judged.

[fo. 154r (p. 149)]

21.H.7.

The oth given to the Kings Counsell Judges of this Court.

Yee shall be faithfull and true Counsellour to our Soveraigne Lord, Henrie by the grace of God, etc. and to his Counsell shall bee diligently attendant, and due and diligent attendance ye shall give to the same, and in every matter touching our sayd Soveraigne Lord his honourable suretie, or profit that shall come to your knowledge, or that shall be commoned or treated in his Counsell, ye shall to the best of your wisedome give plaine and true counsell; Not letting so to do for meed, dread, favour or affection, of any person of what degree or condition soever he be. The Kings counsell, as long as it is ordeined to be counsell yee shall conceale and keepe secret, without disclosing it to any person though he be of the same Counsell, if it touch him and that he have not bene made privie thereto. And if there shall come any thing to your knowledge that may be hurtfull, prejudicial or dishonourable to our sayd Soveraigne Lord ye shall let it to the best of your power, and assoone as yee goodly may, shew it to our sayde Soveraigne Lord, or such of his Counsell, as ye shall thinke will shew it to him: All which premisses, and every of them, ye shall well and truely keepe and observe, so God you helpe and all the Saints, and by his holy Evangelists by you bodily touched. Fol. 56. In an olde booke of Presidents remaining amongst the Records of this Court.

[fo. 174r]

The copie of mine oath when I was
sworne Master of Requests. 10 January 1591

You shall sware to be a true Counsellor to the Queenes Majestie (as one of her Masters of Requests); you shall not knowe or understand of any manner of thing to be attempted done or spoken against her Majesties honor, crowne or- dignitie royall; but you shall lett and withstand the same to the uttermost of your power. And neither doe or cause it forwith to be revealed either to her Majesties self, or to the rest of her Privie Counsell. And you shall to your uttermost beare faith and true allegeaunce to the Queenes Majestie, her heires and lawfull successors, and shall assist and defend all Jurisdictions, preheminences and authorities graunted to her Majestie and annexed to the Crowne, against all forreyne princes, persons, prelates or potentates, etc. by Act of

Parliament or otherwise. And generallie in all thinges, you shall doe as a true Counsellor ought to doe to her Majestie. So God you help and the contentes of this booke.

Done at Richmond the day and year aforesaid, then and at the same place present: Sir Christopher Hatton, Lord Chauncellor; William, Lord Burghley, Lord Treasurer; Charles, Lord Howard, Lord Admirall, Henry, Lord Hunsdon, Lord Chamberlaine; Thomas, Lord Buckhurst; Sir Thomas Henneadg, knight, Vicechamberlaine; Mr. Wolley and Mr. Fortescue, esquires, of her Majesties most honorable Privie Counsell. And Mr. Anthony Ashley, Clerk of the said Counsell.

[fo. 154v (p. 150)]

5.E.6.

A Privie Seale to give the partie possession of the lands of a man that doeth disobey all kind of processe to make the partie grieved satisfaction of his due.

Welbeloved, we greete you well, letting you weet [sic.], that John Perkins alias Wolman, late of Farneborough in our Countie of Kent, which not only for his great and urgent contempts by him committed and done, as well in disobeying our letters under our Privie Seale, upon penalties of great summes of money, faith, and allegiance, attachments, proclamations, with writs of rebellion; but also a decree, and all our orders by our Counsell made and determined for the quieting and pacifying of the cause in traverse betweene him and Robert a[p] Rice, was committed to the prison in the Fleete, where he yet remaineth and of long time hath done according to his desertes yet neverthelesse he being called afore our sayd Counsell, and being by them advertised for his conformitie to be had in that behalfe, in no wise would bee perswaded thereunto. Wherefore wee considering his obstinacie and disobedience, and fully perceiving his perverse mind to continue in prison rather then to performe the decrees and orders of our sayd Counsell, being thereunto gently perswaded, will that ye by authoritie of this our expresse commandement, for that ye bee Steward and Bailiffe in the hundred and liberties called Rokesby hundred, that immediately with convenient celeritie yee resort and goe to the tenement called the signe of the George in Farneborough and all other lands belonging to the sayd Perkins alias Wolman, and of the same to put the plaintife in full and quiet possession, so that they

may therein peaceably continue and have
[fo. 156r (p. 151)]
the same, until the whole rents thereof shall amount and extend to
the summe of 15 pound specified and recited in the decree, thereof
made, and the arrerages that is and shall be due by force of the
saide annuitie, and unto such time they shall have received,
collected, and taken 15 pound with the summe of xx. shillings
awarded for the processe and writts sued by the said Robert, with
other great charges for execution of the same, and the arrerages
which is, and shalbe due by force of the saide annuitie: without
failing the due execution hereof, upon paine of 100 pound, and as
ye will further answere at your utmost perill. Yeoven under
our Privy Seale, and directed to our welbeloved I.L., Steward and
bailife of the hundred and liberties called Rokesby hundred in our
Countie of Kent. Fol. 71, in an old booke of Presidents of this
court.

An extent

Trustie, etc., signifying unto you that upon matter of controversie
and debate brought afore our Counsell by John Marwood the
elder against John Watts, it was after deliberate hearing and examination of the title of certaine lands and tenements specified in
their pleadings, perceived and seene aswell by evidences and witnes,
as other good and apparent matters that the said Watts had good
and just title to the same, as by a decree made by our Counsell,
reciting the whole interest of the parties titles at large in writing
subscribed with their hands plainely may appeare. In the which
decree amongst other things it is ordered that the said Marwood
should in recompence of such costs, hurts, and dammages as the
said defendant had susteined by reason of taking the rents and
profits by the space of three yeeres, truely content and pay to the
said Watts [£]6. 13[s] 4[d] at times in the said decree specified,
which the saide Marwood
[fo. 156v (p. 152)]
hath not accomplished ne done notwithstanding our severall
letters to him directed under our Privy Seal for the same, but
fraudulently at al times hath refused to accomplish all reasonable
orders therein made. Wherefore we will and commaund you, that
ye by warrant of these our letters repaire unto the dwelling house
and landes of the said John Marwood, and there make levie of his

goods and cattals amounting to the summe aforesaid, and of the same indifferently praised, to make the saide Wattes due deliverie, without other delay made to the contrarie, as ye will answere unto us at your utmost perill. Yeven, etc. to our trustie, etc. The Shirife of our countie, etc. Fol. 81, amongst the presidents of this Court.

1&2.P&M.
An Attachment and Extent

Trustie, etc. Whereas wee heertofore have addressed to you aswell our severall letters of attachment, as Proclamations of rebellion for the punishment of such contumacie and rebellious misbehaviours as have bene committed and done by one William Holmes dwelling and resiant within your franchise and liberties of Farthingbridge, for most obstinate breach and disobeying not only of our processe aforesaid, but also of such orders and decrees as have bene made by our Counsel: not a litle marveiling that such a rebellious person persisting in his obstinacie can or may by any meanes bee suffered to tarie or abide in your libertie, or els where in this our realme: wee willing such disobedience not to passe unpunished, will and require you, and in the streightest wise charge and command you, that ye with convenient celeritie repaire to the dwelling house of the saide Holmes, and in case he be found

[fo. 157r (p. 153)]

within the same or elsewhere, that ye then apprehend and take him and send him to our Counsell in our court of Requests in the 15 [i.e. quindene] of St. Michael the Archangel next comming and if the sayd Holmes cannot be found aforesaid, that then ye by warrant hereof enter into his sayd house, taking an Inventorie of all his goods and chattels, and the same to commit to safe and sure keeping. And also that ye receive and take the rents of all his lands and tenements comming and growing of the same, not suffring any other man to entermeddle therewith, untill such time ye shall receive from us and our sayd Counsell otherwise in commande-ment: Willing and commaunding you further certifie us and our sayd Counsell in our court of Requests at the sayd 15 day [i.e. quindene] of St. Michael next coming if all your doings herein, with a true Inventorie of the sayd goods and chattels and rents by you attached and perceived not failing the due execution hereof, as ye will answere at your utmost perill. Yeoven under our

Privie Seale etc in an old booke of Presidents of this Court. Fol. 82.

3&4.P&M.
An Injunction to a whole Towneship to restrein the abuse of their liberties.

It is shewed unto us and our Counsell on the behalfe of our loving subjects and tenants of our towne of S.S. in our Countie of Cornewall. That where wee of our especiall grace have unto you enlarged the incorporation of our towne of D. in the sayd Countie, that yee thereby presume not onely contrary to our sayd grant to make divers new found statutes and ordinances in the same, thereby daily molesting and vexing our sayd subjects and tenants [fo. 157v (p. 154)] inhabitants in the countrey neere thereaboutes, but also incroche upon our inheritance of our mannour of L. and upon certaine ground belonging to the poore lazarhouse of St. Leonard, standing within our mannour of L. and also that ye have imprisoned I.C.R.S. *cum multis allis*, the inhabitants of the countrey neere thereabouts comming to the markets there not shewing the cause wherefore. These therefore shall bee from hencefoorth most streightly too charge, commaund and enjoyne you and every of you upon paine of 500 libri to be levied of your landes, goods, and cattals in our Exchequer to our use, and upon paine of forfeiture of your liberties, neither to vexe, molest, imprison, sue, nor trouble, any of our saide tenants and subjects otherwise or in any other maner, then according to justice and due order of the Lawes of the Realme but to permit and suffer them in all lawfull maner, to have quiet agresse and regresse unto our saide towne of D. and that you doe not deteine, take from, nor witholde any of the duties from the poore lazarhouse aforesaide, which to them in any wise of right doeth appertaine, untill such time further order be by us and our said Counsell therein taken. And faile ye not hereof upon paine aforesaid, and further at your utmost perill. Given under our Privy Seal, 12 February, 3&4.[P&M] Signed by Thomas White and John Throgmorton. In an olde booke of Presidents of this Court. Folio 96.

2.Eliz.
An attachment to the Lord Warden of the Cinque Ports

Right trustie and welbeloved, we greet you well. And whereas heretofore for certaine contempts committed against us by James Justice, wee directed our letters under our Privy Seal to you, requiring you to direct foorth

[fo. 158r (p. 155)]

your accustomed letters of attendance to the sayd James Justice upon pain of his allegiance to have appeared afore us and our counsel in our court of Requests at Westminster, at the day and time therein limited and appointed, which he hath not done, but like a disobedient subject hath likewise disobeyed the same, notwithstanding that hee was duely advertised thereof by you and your Deputies there, as by your Certificate appeareth. Wherefore we eftsoons will and require you, that with all convenient speede ye doe arrest, or cause to be arrested, and put in sure Warde the body of the same James Justice wheresoever yee may finde him, and him there safely and surely to keepe, and so to remaine without baile of maineprise, untill such time hee hath found good and sufficient sureties before you to be bound in bondes obligatorie to our use be, and personally to appeare afore us and our sayd Counsell, in our sayd Court of Requests at Westminster, in the 15 [i.e. quindene] of Easter next comming, then and there to answere as well to his contempts committed and done, as also to all such other things as at his comming shall bee objected agaynst him, and faile yee not hereof as your [sic] tender our honours and the advauncement of Justice, which we specially regard. Geven under our Privie Seale at Westminster, 10 February, 2.Eliz. To our right trustie and welbeloved Sir William Cobham, knight, Lord Cobham, our Warden of our Cinque Portes, and in his absence to his Deputie or deputies there. In an olde booke of the Presidents of this Court, fol. 110.

[fo. 158v (p. 156)]

10.Eliz.

An Attachment with authoritie to breake open the doores
of a contemners house, and to bring him before the Counsell.

Wee greete you well: And where wee are credibly enfourmed that in a matter of variance of late depending in our Court of Requestes, betweene our welbeloved Margaret Cornewallis, widowe, late wife of Frauncis Cornewallis, Esquier, our groome Porter deceased, plaintife, and Edward Dickenson, defendant, for the possession of certaine houses scituate in Westminster, in our Countie of Middlesex, adjoyning to our Parliament house there, after orderly proceeding in pleading and due triall of the equitie of the cause by the said plaintife before our Counsell of our sayde Court, the same our Counsell made a decree for the saide plaintife expressed and published in writing under their handes, and sent certaine our messengers of our chamber at sundrie times, to seeke the saide Dickenson at his dwelling house, not onelie to give him notice thereof, but also to commaund him to have appeared before our sayd Counsell to understande further, what in equitie hee ought to doe: Forasmuch as the sayde Dickenson having had intelligence thereof at his saide house, given as well by our saide messengers of our Chamber, as also by the Bailife of Westminster, doeth wilfully withdrawe himselfe, and lurketh secretly in his saide house, shutting his doores fast, so as none of our Officers can come at him, to speake with him, meaning by such meanes in great contempt of us and our sayde Counsell, to infringe and defraude the true meaning

[fo. 159r (p. 157)]

of the saide decree, to the evill example of all others our subjects. Wee therefore minding the reformation of this his wicked and subtile practice, and to meete with such lewde examples hereafter, will and commaund you by authoritie hereof to make your undelayed repaire, to the dwelling house, or place wherein the saide Edward Dickenson dwelleth, or abideth now, and there to call for him to come foorth, and appeare before the said Counsell immediately, to understand our further pleasure touching the said cause. And if the same Dickenson shall still persevere in his wilfull disobedience and keepe his dorres shutte, and not come forth: then we wil that you doe foorthwith breake open the same doores, and enter into his saide house, and apprehend his person, and immediately bring him before our saide Counsell of our said Court to receive such condigne punishment as shall appertaine for this his contempt committed, and faile yee not hereof, as ye tender our pleasure and the advancement of Justice: and these our letters shall bee your sufficient warrant and discharge in that behalfe. Geven under our Privy Seal, 12 November 1568 and 10 Elizabeth and directed to our Bailife of our Citie of Westminster, or to his deputie, or deputies there. In an olde booke of the Presidents of this Court, fol. 225.

11.Eliz.

An execution upon the profites of lands and
goods for the performance of [[of]] a Decree

Trustie and welbeloved, wee greete you well. And whereas upon
the great contempts heeretofore by John Mounson of Offard
Darcie in our county of Hunting com-

[fo. 159v (p. 158)]

mitted aswell in disobeying our letters under our Privie Seale upon
penaltie of great summes of money, faith and alleageance, attachments, and proclamations of rebellion, as also all other orders by
our Counsell made for the quieting, and pacifying of the cause in
controversie betwixt him and our loving subject James Winne:
And for that also the said Mounson minding as it appeareth to continue this his perverse and obstinate dealing, hath fledde from
place to place, thinking by such meanes wrongfully and unjustly to
defraude our said poore subject James Win of his rightfull dutie
to his utter undoing, wee did direct our commission under our
Privy Seal unto you, commaunding you that by authoritie thereof immediately and with all convenient speede ye should resort and
goe to the Parsonage called Ossard Darcie in our saide countie of
Huntington and all other lands belonging to the same, and in case
he the said Mounson could be found within the same Parsonage,
or elsewhere, that ye then should have apprehended and taken
him, and after his saide apprehension to have kept and deteined
him under arrest and sure warde untill such time as wee shoulde
bee certified thereof, and thereupon should signifie our pleasure
what shoulde have beene further done for his due punishment in
that behalfe. And if the sayd Mounson could not be found, as
aforesayd, then ye should by warrant thereof enter into the sayd
Parsonage house and landes, taking an Inventarie of all his goods
and chattels, and also have seene the crop of corne and hay safely
Inned, and the same goodes, chattels, corne and hay, to have
committed to safe and sure keeping, untill such time as you shoulde
have received from us and our sayd Counsell otherwise in commaundement: Forasmuch now as ye have certified us, that ye
cannot as yet finde the body of the sayd Mounson, but that hee
still doeth withdraw himselfe, meaning to continue

[fo. 160r (p. 159)]

still in his perverse minde and dealings: and further, that yee can
finde no goodes within the sayde Parsonage to make an Inventory

of, but that ye have caused the croppe of corne and hay to be
Inned, which doeth remaine in and upon the sayd Parsonage:
Wee therefore will and desire you, and further streightly charge
and commaund you, that by authority heereof ye enter into
the sayd Parsonage house and landes, and the corne and hay by
you Inned, with all other his goods and chattels remaining in
and upon the sayd Parsonage house and grounds, or els where
they may be found within your liberties, forthwith by such
men as unto your discretion shall seeme meete, cause to be
praised and solde, and of the money thereof comming and arising,
to satisfie and deliver unto our loving subject James Winne the
summe of 26 libri. 13 s. 4 d. according to the decree made by our
sayd Counsell, betwixt him and the sayd Winne layed out for the
gathering and inning of the same corne and hay with 6 libri
13s. 4d. allowance unto our sayd subject James Winne for the
satisfying and discharging of the Parsons rent due at Michaelmasse
last past. And faile you not etc. Given under our Privy Seal at our
Castle of Windsor, 8 October in the 11th year of our reign. In an
olde booke of the presdients of this Court. Fol. 272.

¶ *Processe signed by the King.* *nota
A letter signed by Henry the 8 in a cause decreed by Dr. Richard
Woleman, one of his Counsell dayly attending upon his person,
Thomas More, grome Trayor of the Kings Celler, and Jone, his
his wife, plaintifes against William Hall and Henry Eve, executours of the testament of
[fo. 160v (p. 160)]
John Bird deceased, signed above by the King himselfe, and below
in the bottome of the letter by the sayd Richard Woleman,
directed to the sayd defendants, for the performance of the sayd
decree. Dated 8 October in the 20 yere of the Kings reigne, and to
be found annexed to an olde booke of presidents remaining in this
Court.

8.H.8.
A Commission to heare and determine, etc. for 25 messuages and
700 acres of lande betweene Henrie Piot, plaintife, and the Abbot
of Dilacres, defendant, signed by the King himselfe, and subscribed by Doctour Veisie, Deane of the Kings most honourable
Chappel. 8 May.

10.H.8.

A Commission to heare and determine etc., betweene John Waldron, plaintife, and Philip Catchmay, defendant, for foure tunnes of yron: signed by the King himselfe, subscribed by Doctor Veisie, Deane of the Chappell. 20 April.

9.H.8.

A Commission to heare and determine etc., touching a right of Common betweene the inhabitants of Shuckborough in the Countie of Warwicke, plaintife, and Thomas Shuckborough, defendant, signed by the king himselfe, and subscribed by the sayd Doctor Veisie. 12 June.

10.H.8.

A Commission to heare and determine, touching a messuage and 40 acres betweene John Nevell, plaintife,

[fo. 161r (p. 161)]

and John Aire, defendant, signed by the king himselfe, and subscribed by the sayd Doctor Veisie. 30 January.

10.H.8.

A Commission to heare and examine etc, touching an oratorie, betweene Richard Hill, plaintife, and John Speake, defendant, signed by the King himselfe, and subscribed by the sayd Dr. Veisie. 14 July.

10.H.8.

A Commission to heare and determine, etc. touching 10 libri lands and 20 libri sterling money betweene Richard Tipper, plaintife, and John Lorenge, defendant, signed by the King himselfe, and subscribed by Doctor Veisie the sayd Deane. 20 June.

15 March, Master Doctor Veisie, Deane of the Kings most honourable Chappell, and other of the Kings most honourable Counsell of his court of Requests, received the answere of Sir Richard Fitzlewes, knight, defendant, to the bill of complaint of Richard Warren, plaintife: amongst the records of this court in the rolles of 10.H.8.

Divers billes exhibited to the most reverend father in God, Thomas, Cardinall Legate *de latere*, Archbishop of Yorke and Chancellour of England, to grant processe for the defendants apparance to answere before his grace and others of the Kings honourable Counsell in the Whitehall: amongst the records of 10.H.8.

11.H.8.

A Bill exhibited to the sayd Cardinall to the sayd purpose, by Edmond Langley, plaintife, against the right
[fo. 161v (p. 162)]
honourable the Lord Cobham for 1000 acres of arable lands, 500 acres of pasture, 50 acres of medow, 100 acres of wood, and 10 libri rent. 6 July, amongst the records of this Court.

21.H.7.

A Commission to heare and determine etc. touching a messe and certaine landes and amercements in Arnall in the County of Nottingham, betweene Christopher Hides and Margaret, his wife, plaintiff, and Robert Jakes, defendant, signed by the king himselfe and subscribed by G. Simeon, the direction on the backe of the bill, being signed by the sayd Simeon, one of the Kings counsell of this Court. 5 February.

21.H.7.

A Commission to heare and determine etc. touching certaine messes and landes betweene John Dingell of Devon, plaintife, and Robert Mede, defendant, signed by the King himselfe, and subscribed by G. Simeon aforesayd. 10 February.

23.H.7.

A Commission to heare and determine etc. touching certaine landes and tenements betweene William Seller of Bedford, plaintife, and Robert Heth, defendant, signed by the King himselfe, and subscribed by John Ednam. 1 July.

4

STATUTORY AND COMMON-LAW
PRECEDENTS CONCERNING THE
COURT OF REQUESTS

[fo. 174v] Bookes of the Common
lawe and the Statutes to prove the
aucthoritie of the kinges Counsell.

37.E.3, cap. 18.[1] It is ordained, that wheras divers persons made
suggestions to the king for matters of freehold, and other thinges:
such suggestions shall be sente before the Chauncellor, Treasurer,
and Counsell. And that processe of lawe be made against the other
parties after that the plaintif have founde sureties to pursue the
same.

13.Rich.2, [Stat. 1] cap. 2°.[2] It is ordained that if the Court of
the Constable and Marshall shall hold plea of any matter that is
pretended to appertaine to the common lawe. A privie Seale shall
be graunted to the Constable and Marshall to surcease untill it be
discussed by the kinges Counsell: whether the matter doth
rightlie appertaine to that Court or not.

16.Rich.2 [cap. 5].[3] It is ordained, that if any pursue in the Court
of Rome or elsewhere any matter against the Crowne and Regaltie
of the king, he shall incurre the daunger of *Praemunire* and that
such persons shall be attached and brought before the king and his
Counsell to answere to the matters aforesaid.

17.Rich.2, cap. 6.[4] It appeareth by that statute that the kinges
Counsell did use to heare causes
[fo. 175r]
betwene partie and partie, as the Chauncerie did, for the kinges
Counsell, and Chauncellor and there joyned together in degree.

---

[1] See *supra*, fo. 10v.   [2] See *supra*, fo. 10r.
[3] See *supra*, fo. 10r.   [4] See *supra*, fo. 10r.

Assisarum librarum 20, *Assissa* 14.[1] An Abbot released his right in certaine lande to the Kinges Purveyor by duresse done to the Abbot by taking of his Cattle. And an Assise was brought for this lande at the common lawe, and a verdict geven therin. Yet afterwardes this matter was brought before the Kinges Counsell, and there the Release adjudged voyd, being for title of lande.

     *And 20.E.3, Fitzherbert, *titulus*: Verdict 32.

Assisarum librarum 43. *Assisa* 38.[2] Certaine persons went into the Countrie of Coteswould, and there in deceipt of the kinges people, gave forth in speaches that noe woolls that yeare should passe beyonde sea, for that there were such great warres beyonde sea wherby the prices of woolls did fall. And for this their offence they were called before the kinges Counsell and there fined and ransomed.

13.E.4, fol. 9.[3] A marchaunt stranger that
[fo. 175v]
came into the Realme by safe conduct, delivered a packe of goodes to be carried to an other place. The carrier breaketh upp the pack and taketh awaie divers of the goodes for which the merchaunt sued before the Counsell who called the Judges of the lande unto them for their advise in the matter. In that booke it is excepted unto that this matter was determinable at the common lawe and not before the Counsell. And yet notwithstanding the Lord Chauncellor and others than [*sic*] over ruled it, that the matter was determinable before them.

     Fitzherbert, *Natura Brevium*, 233.A. In brief *de Ideota inquirendo*.[4] If a man be founde Ideot by office, before the Sherif or Escheator he that is so founde Ideot may come before the Chauncellor and Counsell of the King and praie to be examined before them whether he be an ideot or not. And if he be founde by examinacion before them to be noe Ideot then is the office taken before the Sherif of none effect.

     46.E.3, forfeiture 18 in Fitzherberts abridgment.[5] It was founde by office that the Bishop
[fo. 176r]
of Chichester had made a lease for lief without licence to a man of the Mannor of S. parcell of the Bishoprick which was of the guift of the Kinges progenitors and that he had reserved to him and his

---

[1] See *supra*, fo. 8v.   [2] See *supra*, fo. 8r.   [3] See *supra*, fo. 10v.
[4] See *supra*, fo. 8v.   [5] See *supra*, fo. 8v.

successors 60 libri *per annum*. And after released 30 libri therof by assent of the Deane and Chapiter. And this office being returned to the Chauncerie the manner was seased into the kinges handes. And thereupon the partie grieved sued before the Counsell who held that the mannor was forfeited to the king and yet did agree with the Bishop for a fine.

40.E.3, 34 D Amendment 15 *Termino Trinitatis*.[1] A doubt falling out amongst the Judges whether a worde wanting in a Recorde, might be amended or not by the Statute of 14.E.3, cap. 6. The Judges wente to the Kinges Counsell consisting then of 24 Bishopps and Erles and demaunded of them whether the Record might be amended or not for that they were at the making of the statute who gave a resolucion to the Justices therin.

5.E.3, cap. 10.[2] Jurors which toke money being attainted, shall not afterwardes be putt in

[fo. 176v]

any Juries or enquestes: but shall be imprisoned and ransomed at the kinges will: which ransome (as it seemeth) was to be assessed by the Counsell.

22.E.3, *liber 22. Assisa Placitum*[3] 75. The king graunted certaine tithes out of the forrest of Kockingham unto the Provost of C. etc. who for the same sued divers spirituall persons in the Kinges Bench where the plaintif prayed judgment; whereupon Thorp, Justice, said, we doubt whether we may geve judgment or noe for though the lawe hath bene used that the king might have and graunte at his pleasure the tithes of such places as are out of any parish and not the Bishop of that place yet hath the Archbishop of Canterbury this yeare commenced a suite before the Kinges Counsell for such tithes, which suite nowe dependeth in Counsell undetermined. And therefore you shall have none execucion untill the said suite shall receave ende.

27.E.3, cap. 13.[4] If goodes robbed upon the seas come into this Realme. The partie robbed shall be receaved to prove the same to be his owne. And upon good prouf the same shall be

[fo. 177r]

delivered unto him without making suite at the common lawe. The said prouf to be made before the Counsell. As appeareth by 2.Rich.3, fol. 1, *quem vide*.

---

[1] See *supra*, fo. 8r.
[2] See *supra*, fo. 8r.
[3] See *supra*, fo. 8v.
[4] See *supra*, fo. 8v.

39.Edw.3, fol. 14.[1] In an assise upon bastardy alleadged in the Tenant, the Bishop certified that the Tenantes mother after mariage with his reputed father, leaft him and contynued in adultrie with one Francis Sulyard, who during that tyme begatte the tenant and so he is a bastard. Hereupon the tenant suggested to the Parliament that this certificat was contrary to the lawe of England and so procured a writt to the Justices of Assise to forbeare any furder proceeding therin. Which notwithstanding they did proceede and tooke the Assise in right of damages and adjourned the parties into the Common Plees. Afterwardes a writte came to them to cause the Record to come to the Counsell before the Bishops of London, Bath and Ely who adjudged the said certificat good for the cause aforesaid. And for that the Justices tooke the Assise contrarie to the writt aforesaid. Therefore the Chauncellor reversed the

[fo. 177v]

judgment before the Counsell (where it was adjudged as the Bishop had certified) and sente backe the Record into the comen plees. Where the Judges gave judgment for the plaintiff without having regard to the Reversall, for that it was noe place where a judgment might be reversed. But it seemeth by the removing of the Record before the Counsell, that they used a supereminent aucthoritie aswell over the Bishops in causes ecclesiastical as over the judges in causes temporall.

42 *Liber Assisarum, placitum* 5.[2] Where a commission was pleaded to be awarded out of the Chauncery to apprehend a man and to take his goodes and chattels. The Justices of Oyer and Terminer toke the Commission affirming it to be unlawfull and injurious for that such ought onlie to be awarded upon indictment or other due processe of lawe. And therefore said that they would shewe the same to the kinges Counsell. Whereby it appeareth that the Counsell then had a supereminent aucthority over the Chauncellor.

12.Rich.2, cap. 11.[3] Reportes of false newes and false messages shall be punished by the advice of the Counsell.

[fo. 178r]

13.H.4, cap. 7.[4] If the ryott cannot be founde before the Justices of Peace upon inquisicion: then the Justices of peace and Sherif shall certifie before the king and his Counsell the circumstances

---

[1] See *supra*, fo. 8v.
[3] See *supra*, fo. 8r.
[2] See *supra*, fo. 11r.
[4] See *supra*, fo. 10r.

therof. Which cerificat shall be of like force as a presentment by xii men and the parties convicted shall be punished by the discrecion of the king and his Counsell.

3.H.7, cap. 1.[1] The Chauncellor, Treasurer and Lord Privie Seale, or two of them calling to them a Bishop and a temporall Lord of the Kinges most Honorable Counsell, shall have aucthoritie to examine, heare and determine all unlawfull maintenaunce, giving of lyveries, signes and tokens, reteinders by indentures or otherwise, imbraceries, untrue demeaning of Sheriffes in pannells and false returnes, taking of money by Jurors, great ryottes, and unlawfull assemblies, calling the parties offendors before them by writt of Privie Seale. And the parties founde therin defective shall receave punishment according to the Statutes therof formerlie made as they should if they had bene convicted after the due course of the lawe.

[fo. 178v]

21.H.8, cap. 20.[2] Addeth the President of the kinges most honorable Counsell attending upon his person. *who or any 2 of the 4, etc.

O[ld] *Natura Brevium*, fol. 17. Erronious judgmentes geven in the kinges Bench must be reversed in the Parliament or before the great Counsell of our Lord the king by peticion brought before them. 7.&8. Elizabeth, in divers [i.e. Dyers] repourtes, fol. 245.[3]

A Record is cited 34 *liber*, *rotulus* 37. Howe that one Verney, prisoner in the Fleete for divers great sommes due unto the king and others procured himself to be indited of felonye, and so removed to the Marshall sea, to the ende he might be founde guiltie, and by his Clergie be delivered, and so sett free. Wherof the king understanding, sent a privy Seale to the Judges, commaunding them to surcease, till they heard furder from the king and his Counsell, wherby the aucthoritie of the Counsell appeareth to be supereminent over the Judges.

4.Hen.4. Among the records at the Tower of London:

[fo. 179r]

The King to the sheriffs of London, greeting. For the greater peace and tranquility of our royal person and of one and all of our subjects who wish by their petitions to proceed in future before our presence for the execution of any business whatever; on the advice of our council we have resolved and decided that one and all

---

[1] See *supra*, fo. 10v.　　　[2] See *supra*, fo. 10v.　　　[3] See *supra*, fo. 8v.

such subjects of ours from now on should come before our presence, or that of others whom we have delegated for this purpose in our name and place, to proceed with such business of theirs every week on two days, namely Wednesday and Friday, only in certain places and at certain times on those same days which are to be appointed on our behalf; in order to present their petitions in this matter under seal to us or to others so delegated for this purpose; and there we wish without doubt to have done and have shown to them and each of them from time to time full and speedy execution of their aforesaid business or a satisfactory reply according to the requirements of

[fo. 179v]

their situation and of reason. And therefore we command and strictly instruct you that, as soon as you have seen this present document, you have these premisses publicy proclaimed and made known on our behalf in every place in the aforesaid city and suburbs thereof where more expedient and necessary; to the end that we shall be able to concentrate with less interruption on, and have time to spare for, our other fitting affairs on fixed remaining days. And you are not to neglect this in any respect. Witness the king at Westminster, on the 9th day of November, in the 4th year of his reign.

By the king in person and his council. Divers articles agreed and declared by the Lords of the Parliament of the 8th year of Henry 4. Item, on the same day the said Master John Tybetot but forward in Parliament a roll containing many articles made by advice and assent of the King and of the Lords

[fo. 180r]

and Commons aforesaid, and prayed that the same articles could be enacted and entered of record in the parliamentary rolls. To this prayer was answered 'Le Roy le veut' saving to him, however, his estate and the prerogatives of his crown.

Item, because it is most proper and necessary that those subjects of the king our sovereign who wish to complain to him should be heard in their petitions: that it pleases our same sovereign the king to consider the wise governance of other Christian princes who govern well and in order to adapt to such goverance he is pleased to assign two days in the week for the reception of such petitions, that is to establish Wednesday and Friday, and to give this notice to all the estates of the kingdom in his present parlia-

ment to the end that the other days of the week it is possible for our said lord the king to better desport himself without being disturbed by such petitions, and that on the days of the reception [fo. 180v]
of such petitions there being around our said lord the king those of the said council, assigned to be around his person, or two of them at least, for receiving the said petitions, and after examining and disposing [of] them; and [also] those petitions by those demanding offices, vacant benefices or other things or profit, that our said Lord the king cannot keep to his own use, our lord the king can grant the same at his pleasure. Providing always that the customers, controllers of customs of the king, searchers, finders, weighers, packers of cloth and other ministers near to the office of Treasurer of England shall be named and made by the Treasurer of England who for the time will be. Parliament in the 8th year of Henry 6th, among other matters.

It is to be noted that certain clauses, which wee settled and advised by the lords of the King's Council for the future maintenance and observance of the sound and salutary government of the same council, and which are contained in a certain document signed by the same Lords and presented in the present parliament by the Lords [fo. 181r]
Secular and Temporal present at the same parliament, and were unanimously agreed; were read through in the presence of the lord king in the same parliament before the three estates of the realm. The contents of these clauses follow here:

1. First, that neither my Lord of Bedford nor of Glocester nor any other man of the said Counsell in any suite that shall be made unto him shall behote any favor, neither in bills of right, of office, or benefice, nor of other thing that belongeth to the Counsell, but onlie answere that the bill shall be seene by all the Counsell, and the partie sueing, so to have reasonable answere.

2. Item, that in the plaine terme tyme, the said Counsell shall two dayes in the weeke intende to the reading of the bills put to the said counsell, and to answering of them. And their answers shall be endorsed on the billes respectivelie by the clerk of the same counsell, and on the Fridaie declared to the partie sueing, unlesse great and notable causes touching the kinges realmes and his Lordships lett it.

3. Item, that all bills that comprehend matters
[fo. 181v]
> terminable at the common lawe shall be remitted there to be
> determined, unles that the discrecion of the Counsell feele
> too great might on the one side and unmight on the other, or
> els other cause reasonable that shall move them.
>
> *Item, that the Clerk of the Counsell [shall be that] everie daie
> that the Counsell sitteth on any bills betweixt partie and partie,
> [that he] shall, as farre as he can, looke which is the poorest
> suiters bill and that first to be read and answered. And the
> Kinges Sergeantes to be sworne truelie and plainelie to geve
> to the poore man (that for such is accept to the Counsell)
> assistaunce and true Counsell in his matter so to be sued,
> without any good taking of him [or peny] *under paine* of
> dischardging of their offices.   *

In the 22nd. year of Edward 3rd. Close[1]

The king to the sheriffs of London, greeting. Because we are daily
increasingly occupied in many ways with various matters concerning us and the situation of our kingdom of England, we wish that
anyone having business with us ourselves concerning the common
law of our kingdom of England and our special favour,
[fo. 182r]
and should from now on proceed with the same business, namely
business at common law, before the venerable gentleman, the
elect of Canterbury, confirmed, our Chancellor, for it to be executed by him; and should proceed with other business concerning
the granting of favour before the same Chancellor or our beloved
clerk the Keeper of our Privy Seal; so that they send to us their
petitions concerning business which cannot be executed by them
without consulting us, together with their advice thereon, or he
send the petitions before us without any proceedings being conduc-
ted thereon, in order that when these have been perused we may
further indicate our wishes thereon to the aforesaid Chancellor
or Keeper, and so that no one else proceed in future with such
business. We command that, as soon as you have seen this present
document, you have publicly proclaimed in the aforesaid city in
the places where you consider it expedient. And you are not to
neglect this in any respect.

[1] *Cal. Cl. Rolls. Edw. 3. 1346–1349*, p. 615.

Witness the king at Langley on the 23rd day of January in the 22nd year of his reign.

By the king in person.

[fo. 182v]

Endorsement of Close Roll of 16th Year of Edward 2nd, membrane 5. Henry of Belmont, sworn member of the great and privy council of the king.

See 10 November 1551 in the Privy Council booke of Edward 6[1] that noe billes were presented to the king to be signed unlesse first the same were subscribed by 6 of his Counsell and howe that course was altered and the cause.

18 Aprill 1552 in the said Privy Council Booke of Edward 6[2] order geven to the Lord Chaunccellor to distribute 500 libri sterling of the kinges gifte upon the Lord Chief Justice and other Justices and officers and Clerkes for their paines in the Parliament.

*Master William Cecill sworne Secretarie to the King, 5 September 1550 at Otelandes, in the Privy Council Booke of 4.E.6.[3]

*A commission graunted from the king to the Erle of Bedford,

---

[1] 'Where it hath byn used to all suche bylls as sholde cume to the Kinges Majesties signature syx, at the least, of his Highnes Counsell sholld set theyr handes as a testemonie that the same came to his Majestie to be signed by theyr counsell and advise, which ordre hath nowe a long season contynewed, for as muche as the same setting of the same Counselles handes to those thinges that his Majestie signeth as hath byn hitherto used semeth summe derogacion to his Majesties honnour and royall authoritie; namely, for that sundrie thinges so passed by his Highness and signed by his sayd Counsell have either for hast or negligence passed in to forraine realmes; in avoyding whereof, and that his Majesties doinges may appere to the worlde to be, as they ar indede, of such force as nedeth not to be either authorised or directed by any other, his Majestie, by the advise of his Highness sayd Counsell, hath nowe resolved that from hence forth all such thinges as shall passe his Majesties signet shall not any more be signed by his sayd Counsell; albeit, for the discharge of them which shall preferre any manner of bill to the signature, it is ordered that a brief summe of those bills that shall cumme to his Majesties signature shalbe put in a docquet or codicill, which shalbe signed by the Counselles handes, witnessing that the same commeth to his Majestie by theyr advise, and the same docquet to remayne as a warraunt with those that doe preferre the sayd billes to his highnes signature.' *A.P.C., 1550–1552*, p. 411 (10 November 1551).

[2] Unless this is meant to demonstrate the dependence of these officials upon the Crown there seems to be no point in Caesar's including this entry. The payment was not only for Parliament, it was 'for theyre paynes taken in the Kinges Majesties service and affayres in Michaellmass Terme and at the last Cession of Parliament'. *A.P.C., 1552–1554*, p. 21.

[3] *A.P.C., 1550–1552*, p. 118.

Lord Privy Seal, Lord Darcey, Lord Chamberlaine of the Howse, Lord Cogham, the Bishop of London, Sir John Mason and Sir Philip Hoby, knightes, John Cocks, and
[fo. 183r]
John Lucas, Esquiers, to heare examine and order all sutes presented to the king, his Privy Council or to any foure of them. Dated 9th day of March, 6.E.6.[1]

Dr. Leyson, Judge of the Admiraltie in the year 1551 as appeareth by the Counsell booke 10 July 1551 in the Counsell booke: no newe pensions to be graunted nor olde to be renewed.[2]

28[3] September 1551 in the Counsell booke. Noe bill to be signed by the king, unlesse first subscribed by a Clerk of the Signet.[4]

18 October 1551 in the Counsell booke.[5] A letter to the Masters of Requestes to heare and determine a cause betwene the Townesmen of Bedford and Master Standen.

9 March 1552 in the Counsell booke.[6] No letter nor other writing to be signed by the Lords unles the same were first subscribed by one of the 2 principall Secretaries or one of the Clerkes of the Privy Counsell.
[fo. 183v]
4.H.4, cap. 23. That neither by the king himselfe, nor the kinges counsell, nor the Parliament any iudgement given in the kinges Court shalbee reversed but by attaint or errour.
[fo. 184r]
ROSSE.[7] All courtes in England have their beginning by one of theise three wayes 1. by graunte from the king, 2. by Parliament, 3. by use and custome.

1. By graunt from the king and that three waies: *1.* by commission, as Justices of Eire, Justices of Assise, Justices of Oyer and Ter-

---

[1] See *infra*, fos. 163r–167r.
[2] *A.P.C. 1550–1552*, p. 315. The entry is as Caesar has entered it except there is no mention of a Dr Leyson.
[3] 28 September should read 27 September.
[4] 'This day fault was founde with bringing in of certayne bookes to be signed by the Kinges Majestie which were neither examined nor subscribed by any man, and bycause of late dayes there hath byn a great disordre and many thinges escaped out of course by reason sundrie persones have brought bookes of theyre awne (*sic*) making for theyre awne causes, therfor it was this day resolved that no byll or booke made to be signed by the Kinges Majestie shall passe to be offred unto his Highness signing without the subscription of one of 'the Clerkes of the Signet.' *A.P.C., 1550–1552*, p. 366.
[5] *A.P.C , 1550–1552*, p. 392.   [6] *A.P.C., 1550–1552*, p. 500.
[7] It is not possible to identify 'Rosse' as a source to which J.C. referred.

miner, Justices of *nisi prius*, Justices of Forest and High Commissioners, 2. by particular letters patentes, as the Court of High Constable, the Court Marshall, the Courtes of Marketes newyl erected, Courtes of faires and Courtes Leetes, 3. by generall constitucion and ordinance. So Edward the 1 King of England erected the kinges Bench, the Exchequer and other Courtes as appeareth by Britton.

2. By Parliament as the Court of common plees by the statute of Magna Charta, 9.H.3, cap. 11 *comunia placita non sequatur Curiam nostram*. The Court of Augmentacions by 27.H.8, cap. 27. The Court of Wardes by 32.H.8, cap. 46. The Court of First Fruites and Tenthes, the same, cap. 45 and the Court of Surveyors by 33.H.8, cap. 39.

3. By use and custome, as the Courtes of Counties Palatine, of Chester, Durham and Lancaster; the Court of Stanneries in Cornewall; the Mayors Court in London. So divers men have letes by prescription. So the High Court of Parliament. So the Chauncerie, as it appeareth by 28.E.1, cap. 5. So that Court of Starrechamber by 3.H.7 albeit

[fo. 184v]

it was not then first instituted nor established for before that time, *vide licet*: 2.Ric.3, fol. 9 it is said that the king called into his inward Star chamber divers Justices, and demaunded divers questions of them. So by custome and use the Court of Requestes is established, in the which causes brought before the kinges Counsell were discussed. And as the kinges Counsell hath power in the Starrechamber to examine criminall causes so in this Court, the said Counsell examineth privat causes betwene partie and partie. Which court being first established for the ease of suitors and having nowe contynued ever since 8.H.7 is by contynuance of tyme fullie ratified and confirmed without assistance of the kinges graunt or parliament.

The Saxon lawes of king Edgar of England and of Canutus, likewise king here, have thus let noe man in suite appeale to the king, unlesse he may not have right at home and if that right be too heavie for him, let him sue to the king to have it lightned. In which wordes there is plaine shewe of both right or lawe and lightening or ease therof which is equitie. Which equitie also was to be had at the handes of the kinge. *Leges Edgardi Regis*, cap. 2, fol. 79 *et leges Canuti Regis*, cap. 16, fol. 108, which laws are found in ARCHAIONOMIA and a book of old English laws by William Lambert; printed by John Dayn, London, 1568.[1]

Master Bracton saieth in *tractatus de actionibus*, cap. 9 [fo. 185r] et 10: The king and no other should be judge, if he is able to cope with that by himself, since he is held bound to this obligation by virtue of his [coronation] oath. The king should, therefore, exercise this legal authority as vicar and servant of God on earth. But if the lord king be unable to cope with the settling of each individual case, in order that his work be lighter, he should share the burden among several people and choose justices.

King Edw. 1 in his booke of lawes (commonlie called Britton) fol. 1, having set forth the distribution of his chardge saieth: we wish that our jurisdiction will be over all [other] jurisdictions in our kingdom, issues that in all matters we have been able to give judgements, such as appertain, without other process.

That the king judgeth by his Counsell in his Chamber, see 28 *liber assisarum*, plea 52; and 13.E.4, Easter Term, fol. 10; and 2.Rich.3, fol. 2; and 13.H.4, cap. 7; and 31.H.6, cap. 2; and 19.H.7, cap. 13; and 37.E.3, cap. 15; and 38.E.3, cap. 9; and 17.Rich.2, cap. 6.

In the Parliamentes of Glocester, 2.Rich.2, 13.Rich.2, 4.H.4 and 3.H.5 the kinges answered the motions against the jurisdictions of themselves and of their Counsell thus, the king will save his regalitie as his progenitors have done, let it be used as it hath bene heretofore the king will be advised of these thinges, etc.

Of Referendaries, see Peter Andrew Cambarus[2] [fo. 185v] of the authority of the legate *de latere* with regard to dues paid for entry into possession [illegible] 153, membrane 30 and the following discussion, tome 13, part 2, extensively discussed.

The Book of Universal Law, by Peter Gegory,[3] book 47, cap. 29, membrane 18, of referendaries; and book 15, cap. 42, membrane 18, *quem vide*.

---

[1] William Lambarde, Αρχαιονομια *sive de priscis Anglorum legibus libri, sermone Anglico, vetustate antiquissimo, aliquot abhinc seculis, conscripti, nunc demum e tenebris in lucem vocati*, (1568). This was printed by Day rather than Dayn.

[2] Gammarus, Petrus Andreas, *De officio et auctoritate legati de latere* in *Tractatus universi juris* (Venice, 1584).

[3] Gregoire, Pierre, *Syntagma juris universi, atque legum pene omnium gentium* (Frankfurt-on-Main, 1591).

The notary, Troisieme du Papon, cap. of Privy Council and cap. of the Masters of Requests.

The lawe of the Forestes, the lawe of the Marshall and the law of the Admirall are the common lawe of the lande, as saieth Vavisour, 10.H.7, Mich. Term, plea 12, fol. 7.

See of referendaries, Octavia, *Vestrium in Romanae Aulae actionem*,[1] book 1, cap. 3, with annotations, membranes 2, 10, and 11.

See Louis Gomez[2] in rules of the chancery discussing all of the appurtenances of the seals, where the referendaries and their office is extensively discussed.

---

[1] This reference utterly baffles. It has not been possible to identify this source.
[2] Gomesius, Ludovicus [Bishop of Sarno], *et alia, Elenchus omnium auctorum sive scriptorum, qui in jure tam civili quam canonico vel commentando, vel quibuscunque modis explicando et illustrando ad nostram aetatem usque clarverunt, nomina et monumenta . . . complectens*, (Frankfurt-on-Main, 1579).

5

THE FOLLOWING ARE ORDERS NOTES AND
COMMISSIONS FROM 4. HENRY VI UNTIL
1630 ALL OF WHICH DEAL WITH THE COURT,
COUNCIL OR THE COURT OF REQUESTS
AND MEANS FOR BETTER ORGANISING AND
REGULATING THEIR AFFAIRS. CAESAR
HAD THEM SPREAD THROUGHOUT BM
LANSD. MS 125 BUT THEY MAKE BETTER
SENSE PLACED TOGETHER IN
CHRONOLOGICAL ORDER.[1]

[fo. 35r]

[I]

1 Orders for the Kinges Counsell. 4 Henry VI. Tower of London
First that neyther my Lord of Bedford, of Glocester or any other
man of the said Counsell in any sute that shalbe made unto him
shall shew favour, neyther in bill of right, of office, of benefice,
nor of other thinges that belonge to the said Counsell, but onely
answere that the bill shalbe seene by all the Counsell, and the
parties sueinge soe to have reasonable answeares.
2. Item, that in the plaine tearme the Counsell shall one day in the
weeke intend to the readinge of the bill
[fo. 35v]
put to the said Counsell, and to the answeareinge of him. And their
answeares should be indorsed in the bill by the clerke of the same
Counsell and on the Fryday declared to the party sueinge unlesse

---

[1] None of these documents are in J.C's holograph. Judging from the range of
dates, up to 1630, we may assume that he collected the material throughout his
career and only bound them towards the end of his life.

greate and notable causes touchinge the Kinges realmes and Lordshippes lett it.

3. Item, that all bills that comprehend matters determinable at the common lawe should be remitted there to be determined. But if soe be the discreation of the Counsell feele too greate might on the one party and unmight on the other, or other causes reasonable that should move them.

4. Item, that noe man of the said Counsell shall take upon him to be party in any matters to be specified in the Counsell unlesse it touch himselfe. In the which case he whom the matter toucheth shall not be present

[fo. 36r]

whiles the matter is in comoniunge[*sic*].

5. Item, that every man of the Counsell shall have full freedome to saye what he thinketh to the matters that shalbe demeaned or treated in the said Counsell and noe person of the said Counsell shall conceive indignacion, displeasure or wrath against any of the said Counsell for sayeinge his advise or intent to any request or matter that shalbe spoken or purposed in the said Counsell, whomsoever the matter touch allwayes due reverence kept to every estate and person.

6. Item, that forasmuch as it hath oftentymes bene knowne that such matters as have bene spoken and treated in the said Counsell have bene before tymes often published and discovered, which thing hath caused persons of the said Counsell to ymagine strangly, one of an other, and diverese persons of the said Counsell to runne in maugre and indignacion of persons out of the Counsell and other greate inconvenience.

[fo. 36v]

That therefore from this tyme forward noe person of what degree or condicion soever that he be of shalbe for ever suffered to abide in the said Counsell, while matters of Counsell are treated therein, save onely the persons that are sworne unto the said Counsell unlesse they be specially called therunto by authority of the said Counsell.

7. Item, that in all thinges that ought to passe, and be agreed by the said Counsell, there be sixe or fewer present at the least of the sayd Counsell without the officer assembled in forme of Counsell and in place appointed therfore, and if they be such thinges that the Kinge hath bene accustomed to be counselled of, that then the

sayd Lords proceede not therin without the advise of Lord Bedford, he beinge in the land, or by my Lord of Glocester in his absence, or else

[fo. 37r]

by his assente; soe allwayes that noe matters be taken as assented unlesse at the least fewer Counsellors and one officer assente thereto, whose assent nevertheless shall not suffice but if they make the more partie of the number that is then present in Counsell.

8. Item, that noe bill be sped but in place ordained for Counsell, the Counsell beinge there assembled in forme of Counsell, and the bill to be read there first before them all, and that every man particularly shall saye his advise therunto, and after that it shalbe subscribed by the Lords, be it the sameplace or in other where the sayd clerke of the Counsell shall bringe it himselfe unto him.

9. Item, that coreccion, punishinge or removeinge of any Counsellor greate officer of the kinge shall proceede of the advise and assente of the more party of all those that are appointed of the kinges Counsell.

[fo. 37v]

10. Item, that all matters that touch the King should be proferred before all other as well in Parliament as in Counsell.

11. Item, that in benefices and offices belonginge to the Kinges disposicion when they are voyde those that have bene servantes to the kinges father or grandsire or to the kinge that now is, should be hereto preferred, if there be found amonge them persons able therto.

12. Item, that out of the tearme tyme nothinge shalbe spedd in the Counsell, but such things that for the good of the kinge, or of his landes asketh necessary and hastie speede and may not well abide till the Tearme tyme.

13. Item, if soe be that a thinge sued in the Counsell fall into divers opinions, if my Lord of Bedford or of Glocester houldinge houldinge [sic] the one party, though it be the lesse

[fo. 38r]

will stirr the other party by reason to fall unto him, their reasons beinge heard, unlesse the reasons of the other party cause him to condiscend forthwith unto him, the matter shall dwell in deliberacion till the next day of the Counsell, at the which day every man shall shewe his reason. After communicacion soe had finally shall stand the opinion of the party in number and if the number be equall at any tyme that party in the which my Lord of Bedford or of Glocester is come shall hould the most party.

14. Item, for as much as it is likely that many matters should be treated before the Counsell, the which touch the kinges prerogative, and freehold on that one party and other of his subjects on that other, in the which matters the Counsell is not learned both in his prerogative and in his common lawe, that in all such the Kinges judges should be called therto and their advise with their

[fo. 38v]

names allsoe to be entered therto of Recorde, what and howe they determyne and advise therin.

15. Item, that the clerke of the Counsell shalbe sworne that every day that the Counsell sitteth betwene party and party on bill that he shall, as farr as he can, looke which is the poorest suetors bill, that it may first be read and answeared and the kinges serjeants to be sworne playnely and truly to give the poore man that (for such is accept in the Counsell) assistance and true counsell in his matters soe to be sued, without any good takeinge of him, on paine of dischardginge of their offices.

16. Item, the eschewinge of Ryottes, excesses, misgoverances and disobeisance against the kinges estate and his lawes and examples giveinge of restfull rule and good goverance

[fo. 39r]

after to all his subiects, it is advised, appointed, and agreed that noe Lord of the said Counsell of what estate, degree or condicion that he be of, shall wittingly receyve, cherish, hould in household, ne maynetaine pillors, robbers, opressors of the people, manslayers, fellons, outlawes, ravishers of women against the lawe unlawfully, hunters of forests, parkes and warrens, or any other open misdoers or any openly named or framed for such, till his inocencie be declared. And that neyther by or occasion, or feoffent or guifts or goodes moveable passed by deede, nor otherwise any of the sayd Lords shall take any other mans cause or quarrell in favor or supportacion or maintenance, as by word by deede or by message of any person, ne by writinge to Judge, Jurie or party or by guift of his cloathinge or lyverye of takeinge into his service

[fo. 39v]

the party. Ne conceyve against any Judge or officer indignacion or displeasure, for doeinge of his office in forme of lawe, and that they shall keepe not onely in their owne person but that they see all other in their countreyes in as much as in them is and their servantes and all other such as buine [*sic.* bene?] under them doe the same and if they doe the contrary make them without any delay leave it or ells put them away from him.

17. Item, that neyther by collor or occasion of guift or purchase any of the said Lords shall by them or by any other person to their use or behoofe, receive or take any estate, feoffment or possession in landes, possessions or other good that standeth or shall stand in debate of demand without that it be first spoken therof and commended to the kinges
[fo. 40r]
Counsell and the more party therof consideringe the circumstances and the truth of the matter lefull and lawfull soe to doe.

18. Item, that none of the sayd Lords of the Kinges Counsell shal receyve or take by him, ne suffer to be receyved by any other person to his profitt and behoofe any guift of good bond or promise of good, for to favor or further any matter to be demeaned in the sayd Counsell, ne for promocion or furtheringe of any person to office or benefice to be disposed by them of the sayd Counsell, or any officer of the Kinges to doe anythinge that longeth to his office. And who soe doeth the contrary (if it be knowne) shall restore to the party the double and to the Kinge six tymes as much as he receyved and not be suffered to be further or sitt in the sayd Counsell till the Kinge be otherwise advised.
[fo. 169r]
[II] Hereafter followe such orders and rules as are appointed by the Kings Honorable Counsell to be observed and kept in all manner of causes and suites afore them to be heard in the Court of Requests, which hereafter consequentlie ensue founde written in an old paper book, written by Robert Dacres, esquire, Privy Councillor to the King Henry 8, and Master of Requests. *Anno Regni Domino Regis* 35.[1]

1. First, that all makers of Bills brought into the same Court subscribe their names, both to answers, replicacions and rejoynders. And every person omytting the same to repaie the fee by him receaved to the parties thereby hurte and damnified. And in case the same maker for lack of learning or knowledg shall otherwise penne or settforth any poor mens causes contrarie to the truth

---

[1] I have searched for this 'old paper book' with no success. If it could be found it would be the earliest conspectus of Requests' practice.

or matter afore him shewed in writing, or other good or sufficient informacion to him evidentlie geven, whereby the parties so greeved shall be compelled of

[fo. 169v]

reason to reforme and make newe matter by that occasion onlie: then the maker to repaie his fee receaved with such other chardges as shall be thought requisite for his negligence or remisse doeing in that behalf.

2. Item, that everie person upon his appearaunce by the Kings Privie Seale, or otherwise, bring their answere at the daie to them assigned by the Court: and in like case the replicacion and rejoynder. And everie partie, that not performeing, to paie the partie thereby offended viii d. by the daie, to be satisfied and delivered immediatlie into the Court, and so consequentlie for every daie so assigned as aforesaid. The Court dayes therefore appointed of common course to be Mondaie and Wensdaie and Fridaie, those dayes to be peremptorie to all parties for bringing their said answers, replicacions and rejoynders; the same to be brought in their proper persons and not by their Counsell learned, considering that thereby arise chardges without neede.

[fo. 170r]

3. Item, that all gentlemen which bringe complaintes to the Kings Grace or his Counsell, not being his Graces howshold servants attendant upon his person, having landes to the yearelie value of [1] or all such other persons that have goodes and chattells to the somme of [2] be remytted to the common lawe. And in default of remedies there, [to be remitted] to the Kings high Court of Chauncerie; considering their suites to be greatlie to the hinderaunce of poore mens causes admitted to sue to the kings Grace, and that all such persons be tried by their oathes, touching their landes and goodes.

4. Item, that all persons contemming the Kings Privie Seale to them delivered be from henceforth chardged and chardgable with the payment of the second processe against them sued out in defaulte of their apperaunce

[fo. 170v]

if due prouf doe appeare of the first deliverie made accordinglie. And if not, then the plaintiff to stande to his owne chardges.

---

[1] This is blank in the MS.   [2] This is blank in the MS.

5. Item, that all gentlemen being learned in the Kinges lawes having any causes for their Clients to be heard and determined by the Kings Counsell keepe three dayes appointed afore them, sitting the Court, so that therby their clients may not be chardged with double fees in default of their Counsell learned or of themselves for lacke of solliciting of them, upon the danger that may therof followe and ensue, with the payment of such costs as shall be assessed to be paide by the offendors.

6. Item, that all persons presenting complaints to the Kings Grace or his Counsell, which prosecute not the same during the space of one whole terme, neither by himself, neither his Couhsell learned, nor sheweing cause sufficient to the contrarie, be compelled to paie the defendants costs and

[fo. 171r]

the matter remitted to the common Lawe.

7. Item, yt is ordered that noe person after his appearaunce made before the Kings Counsell, departe before his answere made and to them presented, and license to them geven in the Courte where they shall in like case enter the name of his Atturney and Counsell learned to speake in his absence. So thereby noe delaie from hencefourth be made and used to the hurte and prejudice of any partie, whether he be plaintif or defendant, that so wilfullie departeth noe license had, which daylie is used to the great hinderaunce and delaie of poore mens causes. And everie offendor in this behalf to be chardged with such Costs as by the Kings Counsell shall be awarded.

8. Item, that all persons which refuse or wilfully disobaie any decrees made by the Kings Counsell

[fo. 171v]

supposing them to have matter or title sufficient to disprove the same: be, upon the said surmise so alleadged, chardged to paie all such costs as in the decree were awarded, and that done to be heard accordinglie. And in case the matter prove not sufficient in dischardge of the said decree, then the partie to be compelled to paie all such other costs, as by the Counsell shall be awarded, afore his departure out of the Court. Or such other punishments as may be thought convenient for his contempt in that behalf commytted and done. And over this, that the same partie so disobeying as aforesaid be examined who was his counsellor or provoker to doe the same. And that proved and founde, the Counsellor to be compelled to paie all such costs as shall be awarded and further to be punished as by the Counsell shall be devised.

[fo. 172r]

9. Item, that all bills presented and brought afore the Kings Counsell, wherby yt may be knowne or seene that the plaintif or his auncestors have not bene possessed of such landes as are in the same complaint specified by the space of   ,[1] the same parties and the matter by them brought to be remytted to the common lawe, and the Court thereof to be dischardged forever. The parties in such case are to be examined by their oathes.

10. Item, that all persons wittinglie of their owne knowledg, which doe of their wilfull mindes provoke and bring afore the Kings Counsell such causes as against them have been determined, either by the course of the Kings Common Lawes, the Courtes of Chauncerie, Starrechamber, or otherwise by their owne releases with warrantie, and such like matter being against them a sufficient barre in the lawe, as nowe

[fo. 172v]

is daylie practiced by wilfull persons, be dischardged of their suites and commaunded to paie the parties costs being so greeved, and wilfullie vexed without iust cause. Ne also that noe woman being under covert baron, their husbandes neither blinde ne lame, be suffered to sue afore the Kings Counsell, but such persons to be sequestred considering their importune and unreasonable requests daylie used to the hinderaunce of good matters.

11. Item, that all bills concerning copiehold landes (noe default alleadged against the Lord or his Steward) be alwayes remitted to the Lordes officers of the Mannor, whereof the landes are holden, there to be tried according to the custome of the same. And if default be supposed against the Lord or his Steward: then a Commission to be awarded to some indifferent gentlemen by the Counsell nominated to sitte with the Steward for knowledg of the

[fo. 173r]

truth in that behalf.

12. Item, that all persons which upon their requests, or suites made to Kings Counsell, doe obtaine and have processe to them graunted and made under the Privie Seale, doe fetch and sue to the Clerk of the Courte for the same at tyme convenient. And in default therof, if the partie sufficient made processe to remayne

[1] This is blank in the MS.

above the space of one terme: the suitor thereof to be chardged with the payment of the fees due to the Clerk.

13. Item, yt is finally ordered by the Kings Counsell, to the intente that all manner of causes afore them depending, may be well and indifferentlie heard without any exclamacion, or interuptions of any persons standing, or being present at the hearing of the same. That they and everie of them not being Counsellors in the same cause, doe keepe silence without interupting thereof untill such tyme, as order in that behalf be had

[fo. 173v]

or taken, upon the daunger and perill that by the said Kings Counsell againste the offendors from tyme to tyme, shall be by their discretions ordered and devised for their condigne punishments in that behalf.

[fo. 163r]

[III] 9 Martii, 6° Edward 6

A Commission to certaine Counsellors to heare and determine the suites preferred either to the King or to his Privie Counsell.

Edward the VIth, etc. To our trustie and right welbeloved Cosen & Counsellor John, Earle of Bedford, Keeper of our Privie Seale; our right trustie and right welbeloved Counsellor Sir Thomas Darcy, Knight of our order; Lord Darcy Chichey, Lord Chaimberlaine of our howse; Sir George Brooke, Knight of our order; Lord Cobham; the right reverend father in God, Nicholas, Bishop of London; our trustie and right welbeloved Counsellors Sir John Mason and Sir Phillipp Hobye, Knights; and our trustie and welbeloved John Cocke and John Lucas, Esquires, Masters of our Requests ordinarie, greeting. Whereas through the great nomber of suites and requests which be daylie exhibited unto us, and the importune calling on of the suitors of all sortes, the

[fo. 163v]

Counsellors of our Privie Counsell have heretofore and yet be often tymes so encombred and overchardged as they cannot so well attend the great and waightie causes of our estate Royall as were requisite. We minding the redresse thereof, and being also desirous that suiters of all sortes aswell our owne subjects as strangers, making their suites unto us or our Councell of estate may have speedie answers, and be reasonablie dispatched without longe delaie trusting in your approved wisdomes discretions and uprightnes have appointed you our speciall Commissioners for the heareing, examineing and ordering of all the suites and requests aforesaid, and such other suites as to you altogether eight, seaven, sixe, five or fower of you shall be exhibited. And because the suites and requests commonlie exhibited be of such severall natures as doth require severall orders and directions, we have caused certaine speciall instructions signed with our owne hande to be made for the manner of your proceedings and ordering of all sortes of matters according to their severall natures. Wherefore our pleasure

[fo. 164r]

and expresse commaundement is, that following the order which we have by our said instructions appointed you eight, seven, sixe, five or fower of you shall from henceforth diligentlie applie the order and speedie dispatch aswell of all such suites and requests as remayne not yet ordered, as also of all others that from henceforth shall in forme aforesaid be made and presented, straightlie chardging and commaunding all Justices, Mayors, Bayliffs, Sheriffs and other our officers, ministers and subjects that they and everie of them be to you ayding and assisting in the execution of this our Commission, as they tender our pleasure and will answere to the contrarie. In witnes, etc. *T.R. apud Westminster 9° die martii Anno Regni Regis Edwardi sexti sexto.* [At Westminster, 9 March 6.Edward VI.]

per ipsum Regem

[fo. 164v]

[IV] Articles for the manner of the commission directed to certaine of the privie Counsell and others associat unto them for the hearing and determyning of certaine requests made as hereafter followeth.[1]

The Lord Privey Seale.
The Lord Chamberlaine.
The Lord Dobham.
The Biship of London.
Sir John Mason.
Sir Phillipp Hobie.
Mr. Cocke.
Mr. Lucas.

The said Commissioners shall heare all such suites as shall come

[1] These articles refer to the commission of 9 March 6 Edward VI which come before.

to the Masters of Requests handes from the Kings Majestie, or by the order of the privie Counsell for the state, or such as shall be presented and delivered by any suitors to the same Commissioners being assembled to sitte.

The Masters of Requests or one of them shall make declaracion of the suites to the rest of the Commissioners when they be assembled beginning

[fo. 165r]

in order with such suits as be delivered to them in order first (except there be any that seeme to concerne the state of the Kings Majestie) or that is or ought to be kept secreat: and those suits shall be first considered and delivered to one of the two principall Secretaries to be declared to the privie Counsell assembled for the state. Item, upon the other suits heard and understod as many of the same as be determinable in any Courte of equitie, or may be by honest gentlemen and Justices of the Countrie convenientlie determined shall be distributed thether by indorsing upon the bills of the same suits wordes of direction for that purpose, with the handes of two of the Commissioners, and the Masters of the Requests or one of them, and the daie and place of the expedicion therof, orells in cases to them thought requisite, the said Commissioners or sixe of them may write their letters to the same Courte or gentlemen and Justices for the expedicion and good order of the same suits.

Item, such suits as be made for to have payment of any somes of money out of the Kings Majesties Coffers for any debt alleadged to be due to them shall as cause requireth be participated to the Commissioners for the order of the revenuewes, and

[fo. 165v]

for calling in of debtes, and upon answere or allowance had from them or by their order, or otherwise knowledg certainelie had of the due therof, the same reqisite shall be expedited and paid by Warrant signed with sixe of those Commissioners handes at the least being assembled; or otherwise the suite to be determined yf noe cause be of the payment therefore and such other suites as be made of peticion for rewarde of service shall be so considered, that there be just reportes made of the parties worthines from them, under whom they doe or have served, by reason of which service the peticion is made.

And in those and all other they shall consider by their wisdomes that the parties may be relieved and helped as reason is observing comon orders, and as nigh as convenientlie may be the avoyding of the Kings Majesties chardge.

Item, they shall particpat to the Commissioners appointed for the furtherance of penall lawes all such complaintes as be made against any manner of person for the breaking of the same penall lawes or proclamacions for seeing that the same suits have likelihood of truth for the avoyding of causeles vexacions or troubles.

[fo. 166r]

Item, they shall provide that noe manner of booke of any graunt shall be preferred or allowed by them to be had to the Kings Majesties Signature, but that the same bill or booke shall be subscribed with the hande or handes of some ordinarie officers of the place or Court to the wich the same booke shall be directed from the Signature, and remaine of recorde, or be otherwise expedited to the intente that the laudable order of writing of the same be not abused to the damage or deceipt of the King; and if the same cannot convenientlie be so subscribed for lacke of such officers in progresse tyme, then two of the Commissioners wherof one to be Master of Requests shall subscribe the same.

And if any letter or booke be thought meete to the said Commissioners to passe to the Kings Majesties Signature, the said Commissioners or sixe of them shall signe a brief or docquet in paper contayning the effect of the same booke or letter, which docquet with the booke shall be ioyntlie presented to the Kings Majestie.

Item, the Master of the Requests shall keep

[fo. 166v]

an ordinarie booke of the expedicions of their sittings, and speciallie observe the names of all such as shall receave any benefit of the Kings Majestie with the brief cause of his suite graunted, that his Majestie may therby with the more equalitie distribute his benefits upon knowledg had who hath receaved the same benefits.

Item, the same Commissioners shall diligentlie cause all false clamors to be punished, and the obstinat and shameles haunters of the Court to be bannished.

Item, in suites for Almes-mens roomes in the Kings Majesties colledg and Cathedrall churches, it shall be a sufficient warrant for the graunting of the same being voyd to have a bill therof subscribed by three of the said Commissioners, wherof one to be of the Masters of the Requests; and those bills to be assigned at the tyme of the assemblies, and the graunts to be made onlie to poore men and speciallie to men hurte and lamed in the Kings Majesties service.

[fo. 167r]

Item, the said Commissioners shall also cause certicat to be made to them of the state and nomber of the same roomes from tyme to tyme as they shall see occacion.

Item, they shall sitte nowe in the beginning as often as they shall see yt to be needfull, but afterwardes they shall sitt but once in the weeke, if the quantitie of the causes requireth not necessariely otherwise.

Provided alwaies that the said Commissioners shall not by any parte of their Commission, or by theis instructions prejudice the aucthority of the Lord Chauncellor, or any other Courte or places ordinary for Justice.

[fo. 28r]

[V]   9.[1] Notes tuching suits made and to
                  the Kings most excellent Majestie.
                       29 July 1604

All suites made to the King are either for 1. Justice or for 2. Grace.

1. Justice, either against
   1. The King himself, or
   2. Against other.
      1. Justice against himself is either for
         1. Deptes owing by him to the complainant, or
         2. Wrongfully withoulding the landes or goodes of the complainant.

All which are to be referred to the Court of Exchequer or to the Lord Thresorer, or some subordinate officer of the Revenue.

      2. Justice against others, is to redresse oppressions and wronges offered either by
         1. Magistrates, or
         2. Private men.
            1. Tuching wronges offered by Magistrates, they are either for,

[1] There is no indication of the meaning or significance of the number '9'. These were probably taken from a collection in several parts and the number was transcribed along with the notes.

1. Doing meere injustice, or
2. Extreame delying of justice without cause, or
3. Stopping the course of justice in other Courtes.
    1. Where injustice is done by wrong sentences, judgementes, etc. there lyeth an appeale, witte of error, attaint, or some other remedie, unto which the partie is to be referred.

    And where all the ordinarye remedies are past, there the partie is not to be releeved without

[fo. 28v]

    shewing very manifest notes of the former injustice, or his just greevances: which suites for such extraordinary relief are fitt to be referred to the Lord Chancellor of England to advise the King what is fitt to be done in the same.
    2. Tuching delaye of justice, the judges are to be required in the Kinges name, either to give expedicion, or to returne the causes of their delay to the King.
    3. Concerning stopping of justice in other courts by prohibicions, injunctions, Habeas Corpus, certiorari or the like, the judges who grant such processes, should be required will all convenient expedicion to revoke the same uppon the hearing of both parties if there appeare just cause; or els to certifie the causes to the contrarye, which are to be examined by such of the Privie Counsell, as his Majestie shall depute for that purpose.

In all which causes, if the peticioners to the King can certifie their complaintes; they are then to receive present and speedie relief: but if their sayd complaintes shalbe found frivolous and unjust, then they are to paye all the costes of the adverse partie spent in the answering of that complainte; or (if they be poore) to

[fo. 29r]

receive corporall punishment by whipping from the Court, according to the statute of 23.H.8, cap. 15.

  2. Wronges offered by private men, are either,
    1. Against lawe, or
    2. Against conscience.
      1. Wronges against lawe are to be redressed in Courtes of Lawe, whereunto they are to be referred.
      2. Wronges in conscience are to be redressed, wherein there must be speciall regard had, that the complaining subjectes for wronges maye be referred to the places, where they maye with the least charge and most convenience (in respect of the habiticion of both parties and especially of the defendant) have such speedie dispatch, as to justice appertaineth: and if the parties be poore, such speciall regard maye be had without charge of suite, according to the statute of 11.H.7, cap. 12.

2. For matters of grace, they are either for,
  1. Guiftes,
  2. Commissions of favor,
  3. Letters of favor,
  4. Protections,
  5. Pardons
    1. Guiftes; as either of landes, leases, pensions, presentacions to, or advousons of some spirituall

[fo. 29v]

livinges, concealementes, almeshowses, offices, guiftes of forfeitures, or summes of moneye, licences to dispence with statutes, and licences to begge, mortmaines, charters or confirmacions of liberties, priviledges, fayres, markettes, free denizonshippes, manumissions, allowances of tonnage for newe shippes buylte, grantes of free warren, either for deere or connies, etc.

    1. Guiftes of landes, leases, pensions and whatsoever els issuing out of the kinges revenue present or future, in possession or reversion, within the survey

of the Exchequer, are fitt to be referred to the Lord Thresorer and Chancellor of the Exchequer for their advise. Those within the surveye of the Dutchye to the chancellor there.

2. Presentacions to, or advousons of spirituall livinges, under Bishoprickes and Deaneries (which are places specially reserved to the Kinges knowledge of the persons worth and fittnes for the place voyd), to be referred to the Lord Arch-Bishop of the Province and the Lord Bishop of the Dioces, or either of them, to take care that the persons to be preferred be of sufficient learning and honest conversacion.

3. Almesromes to be bestowed either uppon maymed souldiors not sufficiently provided for

[fo. 30r]

by the statutes or uppon old servantes in his Majesties howshould.

4. Offices vacante, jointpatentees, or revercions (excepte the principall offices, of which and of men worthy therof the king himself taketh speciall knowledge) are to be referred to the chief officer under whom the partie to be preferred must serve; *viz.*, the Lord Chancellor for the Chancery, the Lord Treasurer, for the Exchequer, the Lord Admirall for the Admiraltie, the Master of the Wardes for the Court of Wardes and soe forth in the rest, to examine and certifie the sufficiency of the sutors for the places sued for, that unfitt men not preferred to places of service.

5. Guiftes of forfeytures or summes of money being rewardes of service, either forraine or domesticall (excepte such as to whom the king himself out of his particular knowledge of their desertes will secretly allotte certain summes) are to be referred to the reporte of the chief Secretary of Estate, who commonly knoweth best how to proporcion rewardes given in this kind: provided allwayes that such of the kinges houshold as shalbe suitors for recompence of their services, are to be referred to the reporte

[fo. 30v]

of the Lord Chamberlaine or of the officers of the Greenecloth, who are best acquainted therwithall.

6. Licences to travell to be referred likewise to the principall Secretary of Estate.

7. Licences to dispence with statutes and licences to begge to be referred to the Lord Chancellor of England who should best knowe what is fitt in those kindes.

8. Mortmaines, for that their grantes may prejudice the king in his Court of Wardes, are to be referred to the Master of the Wardes, to avoyd the passing of landes held *in capite*, or knights service.

9. Grantes or confirmacions of liberties, priviledges, fayres or Markettes in the partes of Wales to the the Lord President of the Marches; in the North to the Lord President at Yorke; and elsewhere in England to the Lord Lieutenant of the same shire wherin the place is wherunto with a writt *ad quod damnum* directed to some principall men nere dwelling to the places respectively.

[fo. 31r]

10. Freedenizonshipes, for that they be not fitt to passe without a substantiall certificate returnable into the Chancery of the petitcioners religion, and manors are to be referred to the Lord Chancellor.

11. Manumissions, because they cary from the king an unrevokeable grant of the landes and goodes of the bondmen, who sue to be munmitted, are to be referred to the Lord High Treasurer of England.

12. Allowance towardes the bildings of new shippes according to their tonnage, to be referred to the Lord Admirall, to whom it appertayneth to see a true certificate returned into his office of the true tonnage of the ships that his Majestie be not therin deceived; who is also to take bond for everie such shippe, that the same shall not be sould out of the land without his highnes leave first obtayned.

13. Grantes of free warren for deere or connies on this side Trent to be referred to the Lord Chief Justice

of an Eyre of this side Trent; and those beyond
Trent to the Lord Chief Justice of an Eyre there.

[fo. 31v]

2. 14. Commissions of favor concerning either causes
ecclesiasticall or temporall; ultramarine or marine.

15. Commissions in causes ecclesiasticall, as commissions of revewe, after all appeales past or commissions originall to certaine delegates for private respectes in causes matrimoniall or concerning church livinges or controveries or reformacion of Church disorders or establishing of discipline or ceremonies in the Church or the like are fitt to be referred to the Lord Arch-Bishop of Canterburye, and to the Lord Chancellor.

16. Commissions in causes temporall or laye as commissions to heare causes betweene private parties concerning landes etc. to the Lord Chancellor and the Lord Chief Justice of England that the king may be assured to grant noe commission that maye be repugnant to the lawe and equity of the land.

17. Commissions in causes ultra-marine, to the Lord Admirall and the Chief Secretary of Estate to make reporte to the king of their opinion therin.

18. Commissions in causes marine, as reprisall for Justice denied, to any particular person, or commissions to apprehend and take pyrates; commissions to trade or to streighton trade, etc. to the Lord High

[fo. 32r]

Admirall of England and the Chief Secretary of Estate to make reporte as aforesayd.

3. Letters of favor are either foraine or domesticke

1. Letters of favor forraine are to be referred to the principall Secretary of Estate.

2. Letters of favor domesticall are either for,

1. the furtherance of justice in ordinarye Courtes, or

2. for referring of causes to private commissioners, under the Privie Seale, or in the Kinges name, or

3. to recommend schollers to some colledge, for fellowships, etc., or

    4. to recommend servantes [unto] or others for their sakes to colledges or corporacions for leases, offices, or the like.

      1. Letters of favor domesticall for furtherance of justice ordinary, left to the Masters of Requestes to certifie the kinges pleasure in his name.

      2. Letters of favor domesticall for referring of causes to private commissioners, under the Privie Seale, or in the kinges name, to be signed by his Majestie or otherwise, lefte likewise to the Masters of Requestes.

      3. Letters of favor domesticall for preferment of schollers to colledges or schooles not to passe from the king without a certificate, first returned of their povertie, honest caryage, and likelyhood to prove schollers.

[fo. 32v]

      4. Letters of favor domesticall to recommend servantes or others for their sakes to Colledges or Corporacions for leases, offices or the like, to be referred to the Chancellors of the Universities respectively, for the causes respecting the universitie; or to the Lord Arch-Bishop of the Province, for causes concerning the Church; that by meanes thereof neither Colledges nor Churches may be undone by overawing; nor be enforced to receive unworthy officers or tenantes.

  4. Protections from arrestes are to be referred to the Lord Chancellor and Chief Justice of England who knowe best both by lawe and precedentes to whom they maye be granted.

  5. Pardons are either

    1. of fines and amercementes, or

    2. of subsidies and fifteenthes, or

    3. of losse of landes and lief, or of either, or

    4. of forfeitures by reason of panall statutes, or

    5. of punishments inflicted by sentence in the Starre-Chamber, or elsewhere.

All which (saveing pardons of losse of lief and of corporall punishments) are to be referred to the Lord High Treasurer of England: but pardons of losse of lief or of corporall punishment are to be referred to the Judges respectively before whom the parties supplyantes were arraigned or indited, or who can in likelyhood judge best of the same, that the king maye not erre in bestowing his favors for wante of advise.

[fo. 33r]

[VI]   Orders sett downe by his Majesty for Civility in sittinges eyther in the Cappell or elsewhere in Court, primo Januarii 1622.[1]

Whereas wee have to our greate greife obeserved a genrall breach of the ancient and laudable orders of our court, wee are resolved to give redresse therunto. And first to begin our reformacion with that parte which hath most immediate reference to Godes service and therefore commanded these followinge orders to be straightly observed by all. That in our goeinge and comeinge from the Chapell all men keepe their ranckes orderly and distinctly, and not break them with pretence of speakinge one with an other or any other occasion whatsoever, but procede both for our honor and their reputacion, that beinge one of the most eminent and frequent occasions wherby mens ranckes in precedency are distinguished and discerned.

[fo. 33v]

That noe man whatsoever presume to wayte upon us to the Chappell in bootes and spurrs heere at London, nor presume to enter booted the presence or privie chamber upon Sundayes or festivall dayes. That noe man come into our Inner Closett under the degree of a Baron unlesse he be one of our privie counsell.

That in the lower chappell on the right hand of the enterance noe body presume to come into the seate of the Deane of the Chappell but leave both his seate and his cusshion free before him, whether he be present or absent.

That all the stalls beyond his seat to the first goeinge downe be kept onely for the Ladyes and that noe man whatsoever presume to come in there whether there be many or fewe women.

[fo. 34r]

That on the side of the Cappell none to presume to come into any of the stalls under the degree of a Baron unlesse he be a privie counsellor, the Captaine of the pencioners, and the Captaine of the Guarde in regard of their attendance on our person.

That when wee or the Prince are present, noe man presume to put on his hatt at the sermon, but those on the stalls on the left hand, which are noblemen or counsellors, and the Deane of the Chappell. That when wee or the Prince are absent as our expresse pleasure

---

[1] See *supra*, Introduction, p. xx.

is, that our Chappell be all the yeare throughly kept, both morne-
inge and eveninge (with solempe musicke like a collegiate Church)
unlesse it be at such tyme in the summer when wee are pleased to
spare it, soe wee will have all decent honor and order kept, and
therfore when ay of the Lords of our Councell be belowe, our
pleasure is, soe

[fo. 34v]

much respect to be given unto them (beinge our representative
body) as that noe man presume to be covered untill they shall
require them, and then onely as serve us and the Prince in eminent
places. That in all these places, both noblemen and others, use
greate distance and respect to our person, as allsoe civility one to an
other, and those that are younge offer not to fill up the seates from
those which are eyther elder or more or counsellors, though per-
happs belowe them in rancke.

These wee commaund to be in every pointe imitably observed,
and as wee shall take especiall notice of those which conforme
themselves with care and reverence to observe our commaunde,
soe wee straightly chardge and commaund all our officers and
servaunts to whom it shall belonge, to make

[fo. 35r]

severe example by punishment and open disgraces upon any such
as shall violate these our direcions without respect of persons.

[fo. 40v]

[VII]   Orders to be observed in assemblies of Counsell agreed on
7 November 1630 beinge Sonday in presence of the Kings Majesty
at the Courts at Whitehall[1]

1. The Lordes are to be warned to meete in counsell either by
order of the Lord President of the Counsell or one of the Principall
Secretaries of Estate.

2. When the Councell is warned, every Councellor is to keepe the
hower of meetinge, if urgent occasion suffer him not to come he is
then to sende his excuse by that hower, that soe the Lords may not
stay for him.

3. The Councellors of ordinarie course are to sitt on Wednesdays
and Frydays in the afternoone, for dispatch of sutors, if the greater
occasion of state doe not hinder.

4. When anie three of the Lords are assembled in the Councell
chambre, the Clerke of the Councell attendinge is to take order

_____
[1] See *supra*, Introduction, p. xx.

that all sutors, attendants, and others are to avoyde the roome, and the chambre to be kept private both for the digr.itie and that the Lordes may with privacie confer together and prepare busines before they sit as occasion shalbe.

[fo. 41r]

5. When the Lordes are set, if it be a day of ordinary busines, all peticioners are to be admitted and everie one to deliver his peticion at the upper ende of the table kneelinge and haveinge theire presented theire peticions they are without talkinge or troublinge the board to withdraw themselves and not to come in afterwardes, except they be called for. This belonges likewise to the Clerke of the Councell to see performed before the Lordes enter into busines.

6. When the Lordes are set, then the Lord President or one of the Principall Secretaries are to acquainte the Councell with the cause of that meetinge and if his Majestie sende anything to be considered of or that anythinge requires dispatch for the publique, that is to be preferred before any privat busines.

7. If any of the Principall Secretaries have any thinge to deliver from the Kinge or of ether intelligence this is to be done by the Principall Secretaries standinge at the upper ende of the boarde and when he hath put the busines in a way, then he is to goe back and take [h]is owne place, and if any other hath any thinge to move, he is to doe it in his owne place.

8. In debate uppon all busines ther is to

[fo. 41v]

be freedome and secrecie used, everie one is to speake with respect to the other, and no offence to be taken for any free and fittinge advice delivered, but as little discourse, or repiticion, to be used as may be for saveinge of tyme, and when any Lord speakes at the boarde to the councell he is to be uncovered, and good attention is to be given without interupcion by privat conference, and with regard, that not more then one speake at once.

9. When any causes are handled, and the parties hard speake on both sides, the Lordes may by questions and otherwyse informe themselves of the truth of the matter or fact, but not to discover any opinions tell all be fullie heard, and the parties removed, nor any debate to be herde or resolucion taken in their presence.

10. When any cause is fully heard the parties are then to retyre and the Lordes to debate alone, and if any varietie of opinions

continew which cannot be reconciled, then the Lordes are to vote it and the Lord President or one of the Principall Secretaries if the Lord President be absent, to take ther vote.

[fo. 42r]

11. In votinge of any case the lowest councellor in place is to begin and speake first and soe it is to be carried by most voyces because every Councellor hath equall vote ther. And when the busines is carried accordinge to the most voyces, no publicacion is afterwardes to be made by any man how the particular viyces and opinions went and the busines to stand as an order of the whole boarde.

12. Upon the peticions of sutors, the Clerke of the Councell who then waytes, shall set a note when the peticions was [sic] exhibited that the Lordes may therby see how the sutors stand in order, and accordinge to that and other necessitie of occasion they may be dispatched wherin respect is to be had to the poorest peticioners, that they be not wearied with longe attendance.

13. There is [sic] but twoe Clerkes of the Councell to be allowed in the Chamber when the Councell sitts, whose month it is to wayte allwayes to be one, and that Clerk that wayted the moneth before to attend with him the first week at the least, and the Clerk that is to waite the moneth followinge to come and give his attendance

[fo. 42v]

at the least a weake before his waiting moneth come in, that soe he may acquainte himselve with the busines dependinge against the tyme he comes to waite, and the Clerkes extraordinary not to come in but when they are called, nor the ordinary if it be a close Councell.

14. When the Kinge is present it is allwayes to be understood a close councell, and no Clerke of the Councell to be present except he be called, unlesse it be at the hearinge of a publique cause.

15. When any order is agreed upon, the Clerke of the Councell attendinge shall take notice therof in wrighting and presently reade openly how he hath conceived the sence of the board that if any thinge be mistaken it may then be reformed. And afterwardes when the said Clerke shall have drawne the saide order at large in any cause of importance, before he enter the same into the Councell Booke or deliver it to any partie, whom it may concerne, he is to shewe the draught to the Lord President or in his absence

to one of the Secretaries of State, to be allowed and signed under one of their handes before the entrie and deliverie therof. [fo. 167v]¹

16. Accordinge as any orders are agreed upon and commandments gone out from the board either in his Majesties name or otherwise as shalbe thought fit by the board for his service, special care is to be had of seinge from tyme [to time?] the saide order and commandments put in execusion by calling for an accompt of them.

17. All noblemen and noblemens children who are to passe the seas are to have their licence for travaile or pasport under his Majesties signature: others for persons of meaner qualitie granted by the Lordes are first to be signed by one of the Principal Secretaries, who is to speake with the partie who demandes it, and take particular informacion of his religion and condicion.

18. At every Councell before the Lordes arise from the board, the Lord President or on[e] of the Principal Secretaries in his absence is to signifie to the Lordes what business of the day doe remaine and to take theire resolucion with which to begin the next sitting if greater occasions intervene not. [fo. 168r]

19. All Councellors are to keepe their places at all tymes but speciallie when any parties are called in, and if at any time they arise out of theire places they are to stand uncovered.

20. When the body of the Counsell doth assemble, they are allwayes to passe through the presence chambre, and not to come the privat way, except upon speciall and secret committies.

21. If any cause be heard at the councell which doth concerne anie councellor ther present, he is to retire when the Lordes come to determine the saide cause.

22. For execucion of these orders the Lord President, if he be there, or one of the Principall Secretaries in his absence, are [sic] to take charge.

¹ This was the only part of the collection found in Lansd. MS. 125 that J.C. did not bind in consecutive order. Thus we find part on fos. 40v–42v and the rest on fos. 167v–168r.

INDEX OF LITIGANTS

Duffeld, Richard v. Richard Hurting, 138n.2

Duffield, — — v. — — Webbe, 137n.1

Ex parte William Dulcoke v. Joan Mitton, 100n.2

Duncombe, Alice, widow v. William Skipworth, esq., 185n.1

Dungate, William v. Henry Nevill, Lord Abergavenny, 188

Dunning, John & Elizabeth, his wife v. Henry Coote, 71

Durden, Randolph, Alice Harris, & Katherine Durden v. Thomas Moddy, 147n.1

Durrant, William, 47

Durueford, Edward & his son, Nicholas v. Elys Churchill, 176n.2

East, William v. John, Abbot of the Monastery of Charlesley, 124

Eaton, Thomas v. John Tomlinson, 202

Edmonde, Thomas v. John Baker, & Stephen Terry, 73, 73n.5

Edmonde, Thomas v. John Harvy, 61f

Edmoundes, Robert v. Robert Sludham, now Abbot of the Monastery of Barmondsey, 104

Edwards, John and Agnes, his wife v. David Lewes and Alice, his wife, 108n.1

Eglenby, Anne, widow v. Sir John Nevill, Lord Latimer, 169, 169n.2

Eglestone, William v. William Farewell, 153n.2

Egliston, the Abbot of v. Bartholomew Harwood, 83

Eire, Izabell, widow v. Sir Thomas Buckley, 94

Elkins, William v. Sir William Kingston, 173

Elliot, Peter v. John Cheston, 199

Ellis, John & Elizabeth, his wife v. Richard Bowes & Joan, his wife, 117

Ellis, Richard, 80

English, John v. Thomas Fitzwilliams, lord of the manor of Kempton, 166n.1

Erudley, Sir John, C.J.C.P., 100

Essex, Earl of, 34, 75

Estcourte, Thomas v. William, Lord Storton, 77

Everarde, Thomas, gent., 103

Everarde, William v. Lady Margaret Marrin, widow, 116

Everyngham, Mary v. John Leyke, esq., 139n.5

Ex parte John Evyn v. William Warren & John Susan, 77n.1

Exeter, Mayor and inhabitants of v. John Bonefante, 57

Fanne, John v. Thomas Haloway & others, 153n.1

Farmingham, James v. John Garnish, 62

Fawley, John, 63, 64

Fields, Richard v. Edmond Brudenell, 164

Fiennes, Gregory, Lord Dacres of the South, 33

Filtmersh, Edward and his wife, Frideswith v. Henry Nevill, Lord Abergavenny, 186, 187

Fisher, John v. Gowen Ratcliff, 93

Fisher, Richard, gent. & his wife, Anne v. Nicholas Adams, 157n.4

Fisher, Robert, clerk v. Abbot of the Monastery of the Blessed Virgin Mary of the Fountains, 79, 81

Fisher, Robert & Margaret, his wife v. John Grendon, gent., 113

Fitzherbert, Humphrey v. Nicholas Lowe, 147, 147n.4

Ford, Erasmus v. John Lewes, clerk, Parson of Elsted, 160n.1

Foster, — — , esq., 174

Fountain, John and Thomas, John More and William Jackman v. Lawrence Fountain, 64

Fox, Robert v. Thomas Portington, late Sheriff of Lincoln, 123

Fox, Thomas v. John Plantree, 167n.1

Ex parte James Framlingham v. Elizabeth Bardwell, widow, 74n.2

Francklin, Richard v. Lord Cromwell, 201

Franke, John, 115

Freeman, John v. Thomas, Lord Howard, 154

GENERAL INDEX

It has been necessary to use the following abbreviations in the index to identify various individuals and their rôles in the Court of Requests: (a) attorney in the Court of Requests; (c) counsel in the Court of Requests; (p) proxy appearing in the Court of Requests; (comm) one commissioned to undertake some function of the Court of Requests on its behalf; (comm C.R.) councillors and others commissioned to sit as judges in the Court; (a KB) being attorney in King's Bench and (a CL) being a common law attorney (distinctions peculiar to Caesar's use and thus retained) are used to distinguish attorneys at law whose actions in their clients behalf were interrupted by the Court; J.K.B. and C.J.K.B. being Justice and Chief Justice of the King's Bench and likewise, in the instance of Common Pleas, J.C.P. and C.J.C.P.; (IT) Inner Temple; (MT) Middle Temple.